MOLIÈRE
A THEATRICAL LIFE

Jean-Baptiste Poquelin, known as Molière, is an important figure in European literature and drama, whose plays are still frequently taught and performed throughout the world. Locating his life and work in the social, literary, and theatrical contexts of the period, Virginia Scott offers a narrative account of Molière's life and an overview of the place of his plays in the wider setting of the development of seventeenth-century French theatre. Her research extends from Molière's boyhood and his Jesuit education at the Collège de Clermont, through the beginning of his theatrical career in Paris and as a vagabond actor in the provinces, to his days as a court dramatist under Louis XIV. He was a controversial playwright, striking out against hypocrisy in religion and medicine, and finally a cynical survivor of literary, cultural, and marital wars. His relationships, public and private, with patrons, lovers, friends, and enemies inform his work and make for a fascinating life. This full-length biography, the first to be written in English about Molière since 1930, will appeal to the general reader as well as specialists in French and theatre studies.

VIRGINIA SCOTT is Professor of Theater at the University of Massachusetts at Amherst. She is the author of *The Commedia dell'Arte in Paris* (1990), winner of the George Freedley Award for best book in theatre studies, 1991.

MOLIÈRE

A Theatrical Life

VIRGINIA SCOTT

CAMBRIDGE
UNIVERSITY PRESS

PUBLISHED BY THE PRESS SYNDICATE OF THE UNIVERSITY OF CAMBRIDGE
The Pitt Building, Trumpington Street, Cambridge, United Kingdom

CAMBRIDGE UNIVERSITY PRESS
The Edinburgh Building, Cambridge CB2 2RU, UK
40 West 20th Street, New York, NY 10011–4211, USA
10 Stamford Road, Oakleigh, VIC 3166, Australia
Ruiz de Alarcón 13, 28014 Madrid, Spain
Dock House, The Waterfront, Cape Town 8001, South Africa

http://www.cambridge.org

First published 2000
Reprinted 2001

Printed in the United Kingdom at the University Press, Cambridge

Typeface Monotype Baskerville 11/12.5 pt.   *System* QuarkXPress™   [SE]

A catalogue record for this book is available from the British Library

ISBN 0 521 78281 3 hardback

In loving memory of my teacher
David Knauf
and my student
Michael Quinn

Contents

Illustrations

Acknowledgments

My deepest appreciation to the Camargo Foundation for its gift of a resident fellowship that enabled me to write the first four chapters of this book in France, in a splendid apartment overlooking the Mediterranean. My thanks, too, to the director of the Foundation in Cassis, Michael Pretina, and his staff, and to my "fellow fellows."

I am also grateful to the National Endowment for the Humanities for a summer in Paris at a seminar on Paris history and for a University Fellowship.

Much of what I know or think I know about Molière's plays comes from my work with directors, designers, and actors producing those plays at the University of Massachusetts and elsewhere. I should especially like to mention my colleagues Ed Golden and June Gaeke and my friend Bob Healey, who first commissioned from me a Molière translation. I am also indebted to my former student John Dias, now the dramaturg at the New York Public Theater, who wanted to know why there was no recent biography of Molière in English and thought I would be the person to write one.

As always, my children – Peter, Garet, and Sarah Scott – have been interested and supportive, as have been my wonderful daughter- and sons-in-law, Suzan Phillips Scott, Kevin Thomsen, and Peter Arensburger.

All translations from the French are my own, unless otherwise indicated.

Introduction

Jean-Baptiste Poquelin, sieur de Molière, would be astonished to learn, if he were to return to us, that he has become one of the most popular playwrights in a vast nation that did not even exist when he died in 1673. His plays, usually in the brilliant translations of Richard Wilbur, appear on the stages of resident theatres and colleges from Portland, Maine, to Portland, Oregon. Second only to Shakespeare, Molière represents classical theatre to American audiences.

Although many books on Molière's works are available in English, those who want to learn about the playwright's life – if they read only English – are essentially limited to a biography published in 1930, but still widely available in libraries. Palmer's *Molière* is by no means of no value; indeed, it is an elegantly written book. But it is seventy years old, and times have changed and so has biography.

The idea of telling Molière's story anew for a new century began while I was writing a book on the Italian troupe that shared his theatres. A biography became inevitable when I found myself looking for Molière all over Paris. Paris is a well-preserved city, and it seemed likely I would come across some material remains related to one of her most-applauded sons, some seventeenth-century pavement Molière walked across, some seventeenth-century wall Molière leaned against. But I began to pursue this elusive ideal in 1984 and have little to show for it but photographs of plaques: "on this site in 1622 Molière was born"; "on this site in 1673, Molière died." No stone remains of his place of birth or place of death, or of any of the many houses where he lived, or of any of the theatres where he performed – except, I finally realized, one. On the night of October 24, 1658, Molière and his troupe entertained Louis XIV for the first time in the Salle des Gardes, the present Salle des Caryatides, a space in the Louvre that still exists and now exhibits Roman antiquities. I went there excited and full of hope, but the room – where Mary Stuart was married, where the effigy of the assassinated

Henri IV was displayed, and where Louis XIV's brother, Monsieur, first presented his new acting troupe to the court – is perfect, characterless, and uncontaminated by history. Nothing speaks of Molière, except, of course, the plaque.

Almost all biographers experience this strange passion to share a subject's geography. What we are searching for, I think, is the sort of moment Julian Barnes's fictional biographer, Dr. Braithwaite, experiences when he visits the Hôtel-Dieu in Rouen, looking for material evidence of Flaubert. Braithwaite, an Englishman, has been tracking Flaubert throughout Rouen, waiting to feel some connection with his subject. He goes to the hospital because Flaubert's father had been head surgeon there and the writer had actually lived there during his childhood. Amidst a confusion of relics bundled into a sort of museum Braithwaite encounters a stuffed parrot with an inscription: "Parrot borrowed by Flaubert from the Museum of Rouen and placed on his worktable during the writing of *Un Coeur simple.*" Writes Braithwaite: "I gazed at the bird, and to my surprise felt ardently in touch with the writer . . . His statue was a retread; his house had been knocked down; his books had their own life – responses to them weren't responses to him. But here, in this unexceptional green parrot, was something which made me feel I had known the writer. I was both moved and cheered."

Once committed to writing a life of Molière, I had the good fortune to spend a semester at the Camargo Foundation in Cassis in the south of France, where I continued to track my quarry through Languedoc, from Montpellier to Béziers to Pézenas, all places where Molière had certainly performed during his years of exile in the provinces. In the Maison Consulaire in Pézenas (not open to the public) he entertained the États de Languedoc; in the Grange des Près (not open to the public) he performed for his patron, the prince de Conti. Peering through a gate in the high wall, I saw the remnants of Conti's celebrated garden, but nothing of Molière was visible – except the plaque. Gély's barber shop, where Molière is rumored to have sat and observed the comic behavior of the provincials, remains open, but Gély's barber shop is now the Pézenas tourist office and lacks magic – and parrots.

One night in late October I was in Cassis reading a biography of Esprit de Rémond, comte de Modène, the first lover of Madeleine Béjart, who was also the lover and valued colleague of Molière. The count became embroiled in an anti-Richelieu conspiracy in the late 1630s and escaped back to his seigneury of Modène in the Comtat Venaissin near Avignon, papal territory and out of the reach of the cardinal. With him went Madeleine's aunt, Marie Courtin, the wife of Jean-Baptiste L'Hermite, another conspirator then in prison in Paris. When L'Hermite arrived to reclaim his imperfectly faithful wife, Modène assuaged his jealousy by giving the L'Hermite couple a property adjoining his own: the mill of La Souquette. In 1661, the L'Hermites sold the mill to Madeleine.

I found myself wondering about Modène and La Souquette. Might they still be there, north of Carpentras and east of Avignon. The next nice weekend I drove to the Comtat. La Souquette was a disappointment; nothing there but a car dealer on the highway, and no sign of Madeleine's mill. I turned down a narrow road to Modène and found first the millstream and then the village, a circle with the backs of the houses joined. An archway next to the church leads to a path through the interior of the village to the rear where, on the highest ground commanding a view of the valley, I found the ruins of the Château de Modène. I spent an hour or so taking pictures and sitting in the November sunshine thinking about Madeleine and wondering why she had bought the mill in 1661. By then she was, after all, back in Paris, where she – a born Parisian – had long wanted to be. Did she buy the mill because she hoped to rekindle the affair with Esprit de Rémond? Or did she just want a country place? Or was the mill productive and a good investment? Madeleine was a sharp business woman. Or was she looking for somewhere isolated to escape to? But escape from what? A good place to think, Modène, but no parrot flew by.

I was just starting back to my car when a gentlemen parked an old 2CV, got out, and asked very politely if he could be of service. I explained that I was writing about Molière and Madeleine and wanted to see Modène. He knew about Madeleine and the count, said not to bother trying to find the mill, told me the château was for sale, and asked if I knew any rich Americans who would like to restore it. But then he said, rather seriously, that he still didn't exactly understand why I was there. Nobody ever comes to Modène. I tried to find a way, in my awkward French, to explain that I had thought perhaps that being there would bring me closer to Madeleine and, through her, to Molière, that I was hoping to feel their presence by experiencing a material reality they had experienced. And then his face lit up and he said: "Ah, oui, madame, bien sûr, madame. Ces pierres ont des âmes." These stones have souls. And that was when the ghosts walked for me.

Ah, but to what purpose? What was this but a sentimental interlude? The sort of thing we all believe should happen to us in France, but which rarely does? What is there in this anecdote that is serious, useful to the real work of the biographer? After all, I have no proof that Molière, or for that matter, Madeleine, ever set foot in the Château de Modène. Yet thinking about that moment and my reaction to it led me to a small illumination. I did not find Molière in the ruins of Modène. What I found was that I was on a quest, not for information, not for a new fact or a new document, but for whatever would awaken my imagination to the people and the world I was trying to write about, a world that is so distant and so strange and yet so attractive to me. I began to discover that my agenda is to express those intersections between myself and the past that I experience imaginatively. What that means is that I order what I know or believe I know so as to create characters – whom I choose to call Molière and Madeleine – who could have made with some degree of probability the choices I believe the real Molière and the real Madeleine to have made. I am not in pursuit of "truth," so much as what Elizabeth Hardwick calls a "consistent fiction."

This is not meant to suggest that a biography is purely a work of fiction. Like Virginia Woolf, I have often been forced to ask: "How can one cut loose from facts, when there they are, contradicting my theories." The biographer of Molière is not, however, overwhelmed with facts or even with information. There are no original manuscripts, no letters, journals, or written documents from the hand of Molière, nothing of what biographers usually require for reasonably reliable evidence of a subject's life and inner life. On the other hand, Molière was a very well-known public figure, both celebrated and notorious. He was praised and denounced in his lifetime. A brief biography appeared as a preface to his collected works nine years after his death, a longer though perhaps less credible biography twenty years after the first. Furthermore, France is a country with a passion for preserving documents. It is possible to construct a reasonably complete bibliography of Molière's works, a chronology of Molière's life – with rather a lot of documentary support – and a fairly reliable geography. Along side those foundation stones, however, is a builder's yard stocked with materièl which can be used to create a variety of structures. How one uses it is very much a question of one's agenda, of the structure which one designs in the imagination.

Beginning with that 1682 biographical *Préface* by La Grange and Vivot much of Molière biography is hagiography, and most biographers have been in the business of creating a "great man of France," an iconic figure whose neoclassical genius is matched only by his bourgeois rectitude. By the nineteenth century, when a small group of French literary and theatrical historians christened themselves the "Moliéristes," and began to publish a monthly journal and eat an annual dinner, the limits of positivist historicism and the limitations caused by French cultural chauvinism combined to make it difficult or impossible to consider most of the nondocumentary evidence pertaining to Molière. Documents were, of course, irrefutable; everything else was just so much gossip and libel, usually repeated, of course, but only to be discredited.

Most Molière biographers have agreed, I think, with Molière's friend Boileau, who did not want to recognize the author of *The Misanthrope* in the clowning of Scapin, who may have suggested (though this is only gossip) that Molière should leave off acting so that he would be acceptable to the immortals of the Académie Française. La Grange, though an actor himself, stresses Molière's intellectual and literary accomplishments, and most of his descendants – up to Roger Duchêne whose *Molière* was published in 1998 – have done the same.

But not only was Molière an actor, a wonderful actor, he was also a libertine – in thought (to which no one objects) and in deed. He lived for years with a woman he did not marry and then very probably married her daughter instead. He spent a certain amount of time in some rather disreputable places with some rather unsuitable friends, unsuitable, that is, if one wants to think of him as a "great man." He died infamous and excommunicated, because he was an actor, and it was only with the greatest misgivings that the Church permitted him to be buried in Holy Ground.

Our understanding of the Moliériste agenda that has so dominated Molière biography can be enhanced by looking at their treatment of one of the great mysteries of Molière's life: who was his wife Armande? Was she the sister or the daughter of Madeleine? All biographers of Molière find this question infinitely seductive, although on the surface it appears to be a relatively minor issue with prurient appeal. In the seventeenth century it was universally believed that Armande was the daughter of Madeleine Béjart. Not only did Molière's various enemies accuse him in pamphlets and plays of having married the daughter of his former mistress, some of the boldest accused him of having married his own daughter. A rival actor Montfleury actually submitted a petition to the king alleging that Molière had married the daughter after having slept with the mother, implying if not actually stating that he had wed his own child.

Molière's enemies may have stressed the possibility of incest, but even his friends believed that Armande was Madeleine's daughter. Boileau, one of Molière's closest friends, told his amanuensis Brossette that "Molière had been first in love with the actress Béjart, whose daughter he had married," while Grimarest, whose biography of Molière appeared in 1705 and who had interviewed Molière's protégé Baron, his daughter Esprit-Madeleine, and several of his surviving friends, refers to Armande as "the daughter of La Béjart."

Biographers throughout the eighteenth century accepted as fact that Madeleine was Armande's mother. Then in 1821 Commissaire de Police Beffera, an ardent amateur historian, found an act of marriage that clearly states that the bride Armande was the daughter of the late Joseph Béjart and his widow Marie Hervé. Some years later a marriage contract, which has the same information, came to light. These documents, drawn up by notaries, sworn to and witnessed, were accepted as incontrovertible fact by the Moliéristes, delighted to have confirmation of the bad faith and ill-will of the seventeenth century. Given this documentary evidence, this proof that Armande's birth was legitimate, the biographer no longer had to contend with the possibility that Molière had made an incestuous marriage.

The lengths to which a biographer will go in defense of his agenda is demonstrated in the work of Gustave Michaut, a French man of letters who wrote three volumes on Molière in the 1920s. John Palmer, the last American to write a life of Molière, was his disciple. Both Michaut and Palmer are certain that the official documents resolve the controversy; Armande was the daughter of Marie Hervé. Palmer cannot understand why anyone would think differently; such a perversion of the truth can only result from "an unconscious human bias in favor of scandal," and Michaut – after an exhaustive analysis of the arguments – concludes that any other hypothesis is vain since "the official documents are there."

Michaut's agenda is both to construct an uncorrupted Molière and to defend the idea that truth can be determined from documentary evidence and only from documentary evidence. Testimony he can usually dismiss with a sentence or two, but occasionally he comes up against something that is harder to overlook. Boileau's statement that Molière married Madeleine's daughter is an example.

The testimony of Boileau, at first reading, is impressive and seems decisive. Here is a contemporary who is not suspected of hostility toward Molière; here is a man intimately linked to him and more likely than anyone to have heard the truth from him; and this friend takes Armande to be the daughter of Madeleine. But, even if it were proven that Boileau really said "dont il avait épousé la fille" [whose daughter he married], the question would still not be settled. What if these words express what he believed; we cannot then conclude that he knew it . . . But it is not even established that Boileau ever really said "whose daughter he married." He could have said "sister," without Brossette noticing, preoccupied as he was with the contrary idea . . . Or it could very well be that Boileau said "sister," that Brossette heard it perfectly, and that he corrected what he took to be a simple lapse. What if Boileau had said one day to Brossette: "Corneille and before him Racine . . .," and Brossette, in writing it down, corrected it: "Corneille and after him Racine . . .," without taking the trouble to warn the reader. I do not see anything impossible in that."

Of course, in one sense Michaut is perfectly right. Boileau's remark to Brossette is not a fact on the path to truth. It is only one stone in that pile of materièl waiting for someone to design and construct yet another "life." But so is the marriage contract one stone, and so is the act of marriage. They, too, can be explained and even explained away by someone who thinks that Molière did marry the daughter of his former mistress. Someone like me.

I believe Armande was the daughter of Madeleine and the comte de Modène, partly because certain other information intersects coherently with that conjecture and creates credible character choices, and partly – I confess – because it stirs my imagination and produces a more interesting narrative. Thus, I reveal that I, too, am of my time and place.

Another problem with the positivist view is its refusal to consider the plays themselves, not as evidence of Molière's actual life so much as suggestive signs of his emotional and inner life. He left us no journals or letters, but his great plays – unlike, for instance, Shakespeare's, that are always distanced in time and place – are set in his immediate world, the bourgeois *salles* and aristocratic *salons* of seventeenth-century France. Some of them are *pièces à clef*, plays with characters based on models known to all. Many of them engage the issues of Molière's own life, especially his feelings about love, marriage, and medicine. Palmer writes in 1930 that "we may at once dismiss the grotesque notion that Molière was deliberately taking himself for a subject or writing in any sense an autobiography. His genius was peculiarly a genius of detachment." But Palmer is simply wrong. Molière is passionate, not detached, and he mines his own life, his own values and ideas, and his own feelings for every play he writes. This is not to argue that he was writing autobiography; the works of Molière are not a seventeenth-century version of the tell-all personal memoir. But just as we are no longer limited by the positivist view of evidence, so we are also free of the new critical assumption that an artistic work is somehow independent of the artist that produced it.

Without Molière's plays, without the *libelles*, the pamphlets that were the ammunition of the literary and theatrical wars, without the gossip, without the error-ridden early biographies reflecting the dim memories of old men, a life of Molière would be nothing more than a banal chronology, an expanded version of what can be found in every French school text of *Tartuffe*. With them, a story of his life can be told. It may not be a true story, but no biography is that. It may be more than one story, a set of possibilities, each potentially to be considered, kept, discarded. It definitely is an arrangement of facts, opinions, conjectures, rumors, and lies. I hope it will be useful to the actors, the directors, and the dramaturgs who produce Molière's plays and to the public that sees them and to all those who love the theatre and France.

CHAPTER ONE

Jean-Baptiste Poquelin

The young man was only twenty-five. He had just reached his majority in the year of our Lord 1620 and was already a master of his trade: Jean Poquelin the younger, master merchant *tapissier*.[1] It was time for him to leave his parents' establishment on the rue de la Lingerie, under the pillars of the market, and set up his own business in a more elegant quarter of Paris, closer to the Louvre. The old house he leased on July 20 from a family connection had stood for four centuries on the corner of the rue St-Honoré and the rue des Vieilles-Étuves and was known to all as the Pavillon des Singes, the Monkey House. The rent was 850 *livres* a year, a very substantial sum, and the lease was for four years. Jean Poquelin had no small ambitions. He also had a father and mother willing to provide security for the lease.

Along with a shop, workrooms, and handsome living quarters, Jean Poquelin acquired, for the sum of 1,516 *livres*, the merchandise of his deceased predecessor, Jean Coustart, a *tapissier* who had rented the Pavillon des Singes after the death of its longtime owner, another *tapissier* Martin Morot. Tradition was a matter of importance in early seventeenth-century France, and by tradition the house on the corner was a place where one went to buy tapestries and furnishings and magnificent matrimonial beds.

The matrimonial bed to which Jean Poquelin would soon bring his young wife, Marie Cressé, was made of walnut, furnished with its straw foundation, its feather bed and bolster, its blankets, and its handsome spread. The curtains that could be pulled around it were of good warm wool, olive green, but decorated with silk fringe and lace.[2] This was the bed in which Marie Cressé gave birth to her first son, Jean-Baptiste, later the self-styled sieur de Molière, and five more children.

Both Jean Poquelin the younger and Marie Cressé came from families of *tapissiers*. The Poquelins were from Beauvais. Jean the elder was born there around 1555. His father was a weaver, but Jean was orphaned

9

at the age of sixteen and adopted by his mother's half-brother, Nicolas Payen, who was a *tapissier* in Paris. Payen brought his nephew to the capital, taught him the trade, and saw to it that he was received as a master.[3]

The Poquelins (more frequently spelled Pocquelin)[4] were an old bourgeois family of Beauvais, and perhaps originally of Scottish origin. Supposedly 4,000 Scots soldiers had – out of hatred of the English – helped Charles VII liberate France. And supposedly the survivors of this band included a Pocquelin who settled in Beauvais. In any case, a tombstone of the fifteenth-century memorializes one Martin Pocquelin, "an honest merchant and good bourgeois, loved, valued and esteemed by all."[5]

His descendent, Jean Poquelin the elder, was a master *tapissier* who seems not to have initially practiced his trade. Allied in 1586 with his first father-in-law, Guillaume Tournemine, a furrier who supplied the court, Poquelin married – after the death of his first wife – Agnès Mazuel, who was herself a *maîtresse toilière-lingère*, a dealer in linens. And a good thing, too. For when Jean Poquelin ended his association with his former father-in-law, he found himself without merchandise and without clients. Agnès's dowry went to reestablish her husband in his trade, and between them, Agnès and Jean eventually became prosperous enough to buy a building lot on the rue de la Lingerie in Les Halles, near the entrance to the leather market. The lot was not large, but large enough for the four-story house at the Image Sainte-Véronique "where Agnès Mazuel was to reign for forty-two years."[6]

Although Agnès herself was a tradeswoman with her own shop in the market, her family was an odd mixture of artisans and musicians. Her paternal grandfather was a cook, but both of his sons were instrumentalists. Ten of the cook's grandchildren and great-grandchildren were court musicians, although in Agnès's immediate family only one half-brother followed his father's profession. By the time of her marriage to the orphaned Jean Poquelin, Agnès Mazuel was also an orphan, her mother dead for many years, her father a victim of the siege of Paris in 1590. She had taken the oath of her corps or guild at Châtelet on December 13, 1591, two and a half years before her marriage, and she continued to practice her trade for many years after it.

Jean Poquelin and Agnès Mazuel raised eight children in the house on the rue de la Lingerie; Jean the younger was the eldest son and heir to the paternal profession. He was apprenticed for three years at the age of thirteen to a *tapissier* married to one of his mother's cousins. Of his brothers, Nicolas also became a *tapissier* while Guillaume learned the mercer's trade and Martin was apprenticed to an iron merchant. Three daughters, well dowered, married masters of various guilds; the fourth daughter became a nun. This was a successful and well-to-do bourgeois family, if not perhaps exactly exemplary, since Agnès was clearly its mainstay.

Marie Cressé, who was twenty when she married Jean Poquelin in 1621, was a more docile daughter of the bourgeoisie than her prospective mother-in-law, and perhaps the issue of a family slightly higher in the social order. Although her father Louis, like her betrothed's father, was a *marchand tapissier*, the family – long qualified as "*bourgeois de Paris*" – included goldsmiths as well as *tapissiers*, and goldsmiths were part of Les Six-Corps, the six guilds that by statute and custom took precedence over all the others. Louis, who as time went on increasingly signed himself Louis *de* Cressé (the particule implying that he was a gentleman), married well. His wife was Marie Asselin, the young widow of *tapissier* Guillaume de Launay, and she brought to her second marriage, along with a young son, nearly 3,000 *livres* in furniture, clothes, jewels, and her first husband's merchandise. The couple lived in the Asselin family house, a vast dwelling of eight rooms, at the Image Sainte-Catherine in the Marché aux Poirées, and raised their five children there. Marie was the oldest.

A contract of marriage was signed on February 22, 1621, uniting the son and daughter of the families Poquelin and Cressé in a community of marriage, according to the customary law of Paris. The bride's prosperous father and mother, seconded by a bevy of uncles and aunts, donated 2,200 *livres* to the new Poquelin-Cressé community, 1,800 in cash, 400 in furnishings, clothes, and linen for the use of their daughter. The groom's parents, backed by their own flock of relations, countered with another 2,200 *livres*, though not in cash. In this case, the groom's family offered to the new community the merchandise they had purchased from Jean Coustart's estate to set their son up in business.[7] In both instances only half of the value of the parental gift was to become community property; the other half was to remain the personal property of the son or daughter and pass by inheritance to his or her children.[8]

There is no way to know if this was a marriage of commerce or of affection. The young spouses were from the same milieu and lived in the same neighborhood. Their fathers practiced the same trade. Possibly they met and fell in love, possibly their fathers and mothers thought the match was a suitable one. Possibly both things were true. In any case, this

new household began under a benevolent star, well-endowed with meas-
ured good wishes and the necessaries of daily life.

Whether they loved each other or not, their community prospered.
When their property was inventoried after Marie Cressé's death in 1632,
they had accumulated assets of 13,333 *livres* and owed less than 1,000
livres.[9] Jean Poquelin, who at the time of his marriage had identified
himself simply as "*marchand tapissier*," now claimed in addition the qualities of "*honorable homme*", "*bourgeois de Paris*," and "*tapissier ordinaire de la
maison du roi*," thus an honorable man, a citizen of Paris, and the holder
of a royal office.

The qualification "*bourgeois de Paris*" was a legal one, conferred by the
Bureau de Ville on someone who could give evidence of having achieved
a certain economic and social stability. The candidate had to have lived
in the capital for a number of years and be established as the owner or
principal lessee of his dwelling. Most of his property, real or personal,
had to be physically in Paris. He had to produce, from the *curé* of his
parish, a letter confirming that he practiced the Catholic religion. And
he had to have paid his city taxes and to have armed himself, at his own
expense, so that he could be called on to defend the city in time of need.
Once approved, the candidate received his *lettres de bourgeoisie*. Only
about one-sixth of the artisans and merchants of seventeenth-century
Paris achieved this status.[10]

As to the qualification "*honorable homme*," the term was used primarily
by men who can be described as entrepreneurs and heads of businesses.
Roland Mousnier, who has used data derived from the legal documents
of the Minutier Central to define nine levels of Parisian society, places
the *honorable homme* in Level V, below advocates and notaries, above ordinary merchants. Mousnier reconstructs the style of life of the honorable
men of Level V, based on inventories after death. They possessed little
land. Their estates consisted largely of personal property, interest-
bearing investments, and debts owed to them. About half of them lived
in houses, a third in rooms, the rest in apartments. The houses and apartments averaged two to three rooms, but only a third had kitchens. Most
of the families owned silver utensils and some jewels, up to 600 *livres*
worth. More than half had a servant, but none had carriages and
horses.[11]

Jean Poquelin was clearly a member of this class, not a high official or
a *rentier*, living off his income, passing for noble, but not an average bourgeois either. The bulk of his assets were personal and professional property and debts owed to him. He and his family lived in a house; the

family occupied four rooms, including a kitchen. They had a servant. They had silver utensils worth 864 *livres* and jewelry worth 1,516 *livres*, substantially more than the average. Furthermore, unlike all but six percent of his peers, Jean Poquelin owned a royal office. At the beginning of April 1631 this Paris *tapissier* commenced his first quarter's service as *tapissier ordinaire du roi*.

The number of royal offices multiplied exponentially during the reign of Richelieu, avid for *livres* for the royal and the ministerial purses. Poquelin's office had been originally purchased for his brother Nicolas for 1,200 *livres* in 1629. In April 1631 Nicolas resigned the office in favor of his older brother, who immediately embarked on his first quarter *en exercice*. Like all offices of the royal household, this one was divided among several men who served for three months each. According to *L'État de France,* a sort of yearly almanac of the state bureaucracy, the job of a *tapissier ordinaire du roi* was to take care of the king's furniture and make the royal bed at the foot while the *valet de chambre ordinaire* made it at the head. Every day, then, during his quarter of service, Jean Poquelin would leave his family and business and, accompanied by two royal valets, make his way to the Louvre to perform his important duties. In recompense, he received 300 *livres* a year – a more than reasonable return on an investment of 1,200 – and the opportunity to profit from state contracts.

Jean Poquelin's specialty seems to have been selling bedding. During his first term as an officer of the court, he received a lucrative contract from the minister of war to provide the furnishings for 300 beds, presumably camp beds: that is, 300 straw foundations, 300 mattresses, 300 bolsters, 300 blankets, and 600 pairs of sheets.[12] What is more, the inventory of 1,633 includes pounds of feathers, wool, and horsehair, all used for stuffing mattresses and bolsters, while on display in the shop were bed furnishings of all kinds, a large inventory of fabrics, and a number of beds. The only other furniture noted are two benches, a dozen wooden chairs, and three *chaises percées*, that is, chairs with open seats into which one could slide a chamber pot.

The building that sheltered both professional activity and family, the celebrated Pavillon des Singes, occupied the eastern corner of the rue St-Honoré and the rue des Vieilles-Étuves. The corner of the building itself was occupied by a vertical beam carved in the likeness of an orange tree. Perched in the tree, six monkeys each handed an orange to the monkey below, while a seventh monkey waited on the ground to collect the fruit.[13] As to the house itself, it had a ground floor with a shop and a room behind the shop used as the family kitchen. Below were cellars, above were three floors, each with a main room and a smaller room or *garde-robe* with a fireplace.[14] The Poquelin family lived for the most part on the first floor in the room above the shop. The kitchen was the domain of the servant, Marie la Roche, who probably occupied the *sou-pente*, a little room tucked between the floors, just large enough for a bed, a table and a trunk with a lock where she could keep her clothes and other property. In the kitchen itself, besides the armoires full of pots and plates and copper cauldrons, were a bench and six little armchairs meant for having a chat, perhaps also providing a place near the fire for some tired, muddy little boys with a mother resting upstairs. What were not in the kitchen were the table and chairs for family meals; those shared the first-floor chamber with the great bed and two more of those invaluable armchairs, these somewhat worn and valued by the appraiser at fifty *sous* the pair. The room was hung with tapestries, appropriate for a *tapissier*, but not of especially high quality. These were only tapestries of Rouen, tapestries for the poor according to Furetière's *Dictionnaire universal*, and valued at a mere thirty-two *livres*. The impression given by the inventory is that with the exception of the family table, the great bed, and a set of tapestry-covered coffers, the Poquelins did not own very much valuable furniture. Their assets were rather in silver and jewelry.

The parents, of course, occupied the matrimonial bed; the children seem to have slept in the *garde-robe* next door, near the fire. Two beds were there, one with high posts, one with low, neither furnished with curtains since the fire provided warmth and children had no need of privacy.

There were six children in all. The oldest, baptized on January 15, 1622, simply as Jean, was known as Jean-Baptiste. He was followed in less than a year by Louis and in less than two years after that by a second Jean. A first daughter, Marie, arrived barely ten months later, in early August of 1625. The Poquelins now had four children; the oldest was barely three-and-a-half. Two more years passed before the birth of Nicolas, followed by Madeleine eleven months later in June 1628. And then there were no more babies. This rather astonishing rate of procreation – six children in six and one half years – suggests that the Poquelins were following the custom of their class and putting their babies out to nurse, probably in the Paris suburbs. The result, of course, was that Marie Cressé, though relieved of the burden of nourishing her infants, also denied herself the contraceptive effect which nursing often has. Still, the children were well cared for, whoever cared for them, since at least five survived infancy, a most unusual achievement in seventeenth-century Paris where half of all children died, most of them before the age of five.[15]

In the 1630s the family's luck changed. Little Marie died in 1630 and Marie Cressé, her mother, in 1632. Nor were the fates finished with the Poquelins. Jean Poquelin's second wife Catherine Fleurette and their daughter Marguerite died in November 1636 and both of Marie Cressé's parents in 1638.

The death of a child was not surprising, nor were the deaths of the grandparents, who were in their sixties at least. But the death of Marie Cressé is somewhat puzzling. Her last child was born in 1628, and although she may have died in childbirth, the usual cause of death of young women in the 1630s, no record of a hurried baptism confirms a dead or dying infant, nor did another child survive her. Because her son Jean-Baptiste was to die many years later of tuberculosis, it has become part of the lore of the Moliéristes that his mother died of the same disease. The four childless years before her death do suggest a long-term illness. Whatever its cause, however, this death and the deaths of the others must have been very hard on the boy left behind.

To be ten years old in Paris in 1632 was to be half-way between infancy, which ended when the milk teeth began to fall out, and adolescence, marked by the signs of sexual maturity. Until a boy was five, he wore exactly the same clothes as his infant sister, bodice, skirt, and apron; from five to perhaps seven or eight, he continued to be dressed in a skirt, but with a doublet and without the apron. At eight he began to wear culottes and was ready for life outside his home and even for school.[16]

One of the few things known with reasonable certainty about the childhood and adolescence of Jean-Baptiste Poquelin, aside from his date of baptism, is that he attended the Collège de Clermont, a Jesuit secondary school located across the river in the Latin Quarter. The *Préface* to the first edition of his collected works, published in 1682 by his friend and long-time colleague La Grange, includes the following: "He did his humanities at the Collège de Clermont . . . The success of his studies was what would be expected of someone with a predisposition as happy as his. If he was a fine humanist he became a still greater philosopher."[17] Nothing here tells us when Jean-Baptiste began his humanities at Clermont, nor when he finished them.[18] Vast forests have died in vain as scholars have tried to prove that he entered the 5th class in 1637 or the 6th class in 1631. But, in fact, this is one of the hundreds of thousands of things about the life of Molière we cannot know. What matters, surely, is not when he went to Clermont but that he went to Clermont, since the experience of the school left deep and abiding marks.

The logical thing to assume is that Jean-Baptiste Poquelin received the education due the eldest son of an ambitious and successful *"bourgeois de Paris"* and *"honorable homme."* At his *petite école* he learned to read and write French and may have begun Latin. Some bourgeois children were taught to read at home by their mothers, and there were books in the Poquelin household – a Bible, Plutarch's *Lives* and several "little books" – but more probably the Poquelin children went to neighborhood petty schools.

An ordinance of 1560 backed up by an act of Henri IV in 1598 ordered parents to send their children, boys and girls, to school. Of course, these laws were not enforced, but Parisian children were well-supplied with petty schools, at least seventy (including twenty for girls) early in the century and 167 toward the end. Petty schools were a counter-reformation device meant to make sure that small children were not lured into private schools run by Protestants and contaminated by pernicious doctrines. In Paris the petty schools were under the jurisdiction of the Precentor of the Cathedral of Notre-Dame, who annually licensed the masters and mistresses and enjoined them to "take care that the children do not bring evil, heretical or immoral books to school." Even worse was the idea that children of the same sex might attend the same school. That was absolutely forbidden.

Once licensed, a petty school teacher put up a sign: "Here one keeps a petty school where Master (or Mistress) N. teaches young people the church service, how to read, write and form letters, grammar, arithmetic, and calculating, both by pen and by counters. Boarders welcome."[19] Parents were expected to pay the masters and mistresses who were, however, also supposed to teach the children of the poor for free.

Exactly how long children spent in these schools is not known, but it seems likely that by nine or ten a bright child would have learned to read and write French, to do basic arithmetic, and to parrot the rudiments of Latin grammar. He would be ready for a *collège*.

The Collège de Clermont was the most fashionable school in Paris in the 1630s; Jean Poquelin chose it for his son. He may have done so because Clermont was free, unlike the colleges that made up the Faculty of Arts of the University of Paris. On the other hand, attendance at Clermont could put a child in touch with young nobles and the sons of officers of the court and the Parlement. A father ambitious for his son might well believe that Clermont could pave the way to a career high in the state bureaucracy: Clermont, then the law, then an office, perhaps in the royal secretariat or in the Parlement.[20]

In fact, the Jesuits were well aware that their school, more than any other, met the objectives for secondary education laid down by Henri IV in new statutes for the University of Paris published in September 18, 1600. Before that time, the purpose of the colleges was to prepare students for careers in the Church; after, their mission was to prepare students for legal and administrative careers as well. The University paid lip service to the statute; the Jesuits acted on it.

What also distinguished the Collège de Clermont, and the other Jesuit schools in the kingdom, was good teaching by young and highly qualified teachers combined with an idea of how education should be conducted, a pedagogy "founded on realism, good sense, and tenacity."[21] Jesuit pupils, like their peers, attended school for up to eight hours a day, five days a week, and on Saturday mornings. The goal was "a perfect knowledge of Greek and Latin" followed by "intimate contact with the great writers of antiquity and the study in depth of their works."[22] The Jesuits had a bag of ingenious tricks to help their students achieve mastery. Besides translating and writing essays and epigrams and inscriptions, the boys engaged in oral discourse and disputes. They sustained theses. They acted in comedies and tragedies, in prose and verse, all in Latin. They spoke nothing but Latin to their masters and to their fellow students, although they were grudgingly permitted a little French right after lunch.

The Jesuits also specialized in the teaching of rhetoric. Père Richeome explains how this study, above all others, gave men power over others:

It is a thing humanly divine and divinely human to know how to treat a subject with the marriage of mind and tongue, to conceive it in the soul with beautiful and judicious thoughts, to arrange these thoughts wisely, to dress them in rich language and convey them to the ear of the listener by means of a firm memory, a lively voice that rings forth but penetrates softly, and such an action of the body that makes them effectively understood; to plant new opinions and new desires in men's hearts and snatch out the old ones; to get the rigid wills to fold, submit; to address and straighten the crooked and corrupt; and victoriously persuade and dissuade as one will.[23]

Clermont was a large school; in 1627, a few years before Jean-Baptiste Poquelin entered it, it had 1,829 students, 299 in the superior classes (theology and philosophy) and 1,530 in the inferior classes. Beginners learned the rudiments of Latin and Greek in the sixth, continued classical languages and literature in the fifth, fourth and third, advanced to

Humanities in the second and Rhetoric in the first. The offerings in philosophy and theology were not so well-attended. Many students aiming for the professions left Clermont to do their philosophy elsewhere and take the degree of Master of Arts that Clermont was not permitted to give. But so did many others leave because they had essentially completed their general education.

The scholars of Clermont were not only divided by classes, they were also divided into *internes* or *pensionnaires*, students who lived in the college, and *externes* who lived elsewhere. In general, the *pensionnaires* – usually numbering about 300 – were sons of the nobility, although some were poor boys serving as domestics to their noble classmates. Most of the *externes* were, like Jean-Baptiste Poquelin, sons of officers, merchants, and businessmen. *Externes* did not necessarily live at home. Many were not Parisians, but even the Parisians were often housed with *maîtres de pension* who oversaw homework and sometimes added courses in mathematics or handwriting.

Very likely Jean-Baptiste also lodged with a *maître de pension*.[24] We may even know his name. A certain Georges Pinel, who qualified himself as a writing master, borrowed money from Jean Poquelin in 1641 and again in 1643. This same Georges Pinel joined with Jean-Baptiste Poquelin and eight others to form the Illustre Théâtre in 1643. According to a tale passed on by Charles Perrault, Jean Poquelin, desperate to persuade his son to give up the foolish notion of becoming an actor, sent him to a former teacher who – the father believed – still had some authority over the boy. Instead of the master persuading the pupil, the opposite happened and the master became an actor, too. Georges Mongrédien thinks that Pinel may be the teacher referred to by Perrault, "the master in whose home [Molière] had lived during the first years of his studies."[25]

Maîtres de pension were often members of the corps of writing masters and empowered to teach children who had completed petty school arithmetic, spelling, and the seven varieties of handwriting known and used by literate Frenchmen.[26] If Jean-Baptiste did a stint with a writing master that would further suggest that he was being prepared for the law and an eventual place somewhere in the state bureaucracy.

Still, learning to write a correct and elegant hand was of middling importance. What mattered were the forty-four hours a week spent in class at Clermont. The secret of the Jesuits' success, what enabled them to overcome suspicion and angry opposition from the University, the Gallican clergy, and the Jansenists, was the effectiveness of their pedagogical system. A traveler wrote about Clermont in 1687: "One notices nothing special in the buildings of the college; however there are many things to be observed here that one will not find elsewhere." The most remarkable was that a great number of *pensionnaires*, most of the "quality," and "a multitude of *externes* sometimes two or three thousand, study all together in the most regular order and discipline in the world."[27]

How did the Jesuits manage this, with as many as 320 students in a class? The Jesuit system was based on what they called "emulation," what we would call cut-throat competition. Within each class, students were constantly compared on the basis of their work. "Son banc disait son rang": his bench proclaimed his rank.[28] This was a moral issue according to Jesuit theory. It was important to awaken in the boy the desire to surpass his comrades; this was the means to avoid laziness and to plant in his soul a passion for work. The masters were advised, however, to use the carrot rather than the stick, to avoid threats and blame. Discouragement was the great enemy of progress; confidence gave a boy the strength to overcome his defects.

In practice, what "emulation" meant was that school was a constant series of contests: boy against boy, class against class. The best home-work went into the notebook of honor or was displayed on the walls of the classroom or even in the courtyard for other classes to admire; the very best work was selected for an annual public exhibition held every year on July 22. The best students in each section – Philosophy, Humanities, or Grammar – were chosen for "academies" that formed an "aristocracy of talent."[29]

Finally, Clermont held its annual Public Exercises that attracted a large audience from the court and the town. Students in the superior classes defended their theses on such subjects as cosmography, astron-omy, and military architecture while the audience judged them on keen-ness of wit, speed of riposte, and elegance of delivery. The younger scholars explicated enigmas. The boys were presented with a painting or a word picture taken from history or myth; each boy then proposed and defended a key word or enigma that he thought best expressed the picture's essential moral meaning. The audience picked the winner. Near the end of the school year, in August, Clermont held its Prize Day. The prizes, provided by the king, were books, magnificently bound and gilded, with the royal arms and the seal of the college. On Prize Day the cream of the cream rose to the top; only thirty-three prizes were offered to nearly 2,000 boys. It was also on Prize Day that the boys of Clermont performed in Latin comedies and tragedies, some classical, some written by their Jesuit teachers. Unfortunately, there is no way of knowing if Jean-Baptiste ever acted at Clermont.

But let us take a leap of faith. Let us conclude that he did and was noticed and praised. Let us further proclaim that Jean-Baptiste Poquelin was victorious at Clermont, surely an "academician," possibly a prize winner.[30] To his natural talents for language and invention he joined habits of industry – a passion for work – that served him all his life. The Jansenists accused the Jesuits of cultivating pride, and the Jansenists were clearly on the mark. The Jesuits did encourage pride in one's self and one's work as necessary and moral, while lack of pride was considered dishonorable. The hierarchy of the school was not like the hierarchy of the greater society; birth counted in the *pension*, but not in the classroom. A boy from the rue St-Honoré could triumph here, and could carry the memory of that triumph into his adult life – along with the anxieties, the self-doubts, and even the vanity that can also be the consequences of intense competition.

The man Molière was, above all, a chronicler of obsessions, although he never wrote about his own principle obsession which was work. Actor, playwright, director, manager, orator, officer, courtier, his life was unimaginably busy. Convention would have it that the Molières of the world are dreamy backbenchers in their youth, but the image seems unconvincing here. What seems more likely is the triumphal march of young Jean-Baptiste across Paris every Saturday afternoon, bearing the week's trophies home to his father.

Giving up a scenario so dear to the hearts of so many is hard: the boy traverses Paris twice daily between his house on the western edge of Les Halles and his school half-way up the rue St-Jacques. He crosses the Pont-Neuf, stops to listen to a ballad, stops again to laugh at a flour-faced clown, stops a third time to take in the spiel of a quack. Dreams of Pantalone and Zanni fill his head. What does the boy who is going to be the greatest actor of his generation care about Pliny? That Jean-Baptiste would not have been a star student at Clermont. Hence our Jean-Baptiste who, like most of his fellows, lived in a pension near the school so he wasted no time in comings and goings. But on Saturday afternoons and Sundays and on feast days and their eves, and during the long vacation in early fall, he was free. The Pont-Neuf with all its attractions was a block away from his father's house, but it was only one of the many delights Paris had to offer.

After virtual stagnation in the sixteenth century, Paris began to grow and prosper. In the 1630s, when Jean-Baptiste was old enough to explore it, it was the largest city in Europe with a population of just over 400,000. Les Halles, where the Poquelins and their relations lived, was old; an open-air market had been established there first in the reign of Louis VI. The first two market buildings were constructed in 1183 and were rapidly encircled by small shops. A third building for the mercers was added in 1263, soon joined by a salt-fish market and a fresh-fish market, while Saint Louis permitted the linen sellers to set up along the wall of the Cemetery of the Innocents. Rebuilt in the sixteenth century, the vast market grew, and the district around it, with its huge somber parish church of St-Eustache, its pillory and its killing grounds, its cemetery and charnel-houses, and, especially on its west side where Jean Poquelin had set up shop, its great aristocratic mansions.

St-Eustache, the last of many chapels and churches on its site, the church where Jean Poquelin, son of Jean Poquelin, was baptized without the Baptiste, was begun in 1532 and was not yet finished when the master *tapissier* brought his first son to the font. Fifty-one years later, when Molière was residing once again in the parish of his birth and the magnificent church was more or less complete, its priests would refuse to attend his deathbed and its *curé* would try to deny him burial in conse-crated ground. During much of his childhood the church – one short block to the east and one long block to the north – was under construc-tion and when the building was finally consecrated on April 26, 1637, surely Jean-Baptiste sat with his family in the superb nave admiring the new painting, *The Martyrdom of Saint Eustache*, commissioned by Cardinal Richelieu himself in honor of the occasion and executed by Simon Vouet.[31]

The market to the south and east of the church was a vast bazaar. Foodstuffs of all sorts were sold there, of course, but so were shoes and hats and combs and mirrors, pots and pans, furs and jewels. Beyond the market buildings rose the merchants' dwellings, high narrow houses, each with its shop facing the street. Around the main market buildings, the ground floors were recessed, the upper stories supported by pillars. These formed galleries where shoppers could walk, safe from rain and muddy streets. "Under the pillars of the market" was an address every-one in Paris knew how to find. The Poquelin children certainly knew the area "*sous les pilliers*"; their Cressé grandparents lived there, at the Marché aux Poirées, the vegetable market, as did their grandmother Agnès Mazuel on the rue de la Lingerie.

This street, the name of which memorializes the rights granted the linen dealers by Saint Louis, separated the market from the Cemetery of the Innocents, the largest in Paris. It had been there long before the market, perhaps since the time of Roman Lutece. Buried there were those whose parish churches had no cemeteries, along with paupers from the hospital and unknown persons found dead in the public streets. Although the Innocents had a few private tombs, most corpses, sewn into their shrouds, were placed in common graves. Two or three of these graves were always in use, covered with planks until they were full. Some years later, when the space was needed again, these same graves would be reopened, the bones removed and placed in the charnel house along the wall of the cemetery. This was where the Poquelins brought their wife and mother Marie in 1632.

All Paris knew the famous fresco of the *danse macabre* on view behind the charnel house. It had been there since 1424, each of its thirty panels portraying a living man and his dead twin representing one of the various states and conditions of life: pope, emperor, cardinal, king, squire, knight, soldier, abbot. Perhaps because the *danse macabre* displayed a social order not representative of seventeenth-century Paris, or perhaps simply from a desire to cock a snook at death, the Innocents was not a lugubrious spot shunned by all. In spite of the famous fresco, in spite of the smell from the open graves, in spite of the skulls and bones displayed in the charnal house, Parisians used their cemetery as an adjunct to the market, and as a meeting place and promenade.

The Poquelin children visiting their grandmother Agnès might well have avoided the cemetery with its sad memories, but around the corner where the Cressé grandparents lived, there was often a lively opportunity for amusement. At the crossroads of Les Halles, between St-Eustache and the Marché aux Poirées and during the Wednesday and Saturday street markets, was meted out the punishment of the pillory. The pillory was a raised structure with a revolving platform upon which several minor malefactors could stand with their heads and hands clamped into a wheel above. Periodically, the platform and wheel revolved, displaying the delinquents to the contempt of all. The crime most likely to deserve the pillory was fraud of one sort or another, including the use of bad weights, never popular with market-goers. Onlookers were encouraged to augment the punishment by throwing mud – the famous Paris *crotte* – or the leavings of the market, but rock throwing was frowned on. An engraving from a somewhat later period shows a gang of fraudulent bankrupts undergoing the pillory watched by a band of children, boys and girls, armed and ready to do their duty.[32]

More important punishments – executions even – took place closer to home at the Croix de Trahoir, a great cross that surmounted a fountain just opposite the Poquelin house on the rue St-Honoré. Down that main street of the Right Bank passed "justices, triumphs and funeral processions," or so said the aged owner of the Pavillon des Singes, Gillette Danès, who was living with her daughter but who reserved in the lease the right to the windows of the first-floor chamber whenever anything magnificent was happening.[33]

Magnificence was an everyday matter only a few blocks away to the west. After all, Louis XIV took his first communion in the Poquelins' parish church. The Louvre was, as it had been for more than a century, under construction. So was its near neighbor, Richelieu's Palais-Cardinal with its superb garden. Even closer to home, one short block north along the rue des Vieilles-Étuves, rose the enormous Hôtel de Soissons, the former Palais de la Reine, built fifty years earlier for Catherine de Médicis. Everyone knew the story of the dowager queen's Italian astrologer who had warned her that she would die under the sign of Saint Germain. Since St-Germain L'Auxerrois was the parish church of both the Louvre and the Tuileries, Catherine refused to live in either and moved east to Les Halles. There she forcibly disestablished an order of nuns, had several blocks of houses demolished, and erected a sumptuous mansion on the model of the Pitti Palace in the midst of vast gardens. By the time Jean-Baptiste Poquelin was old enough to explore his neighborhood, Catherine was long gone, dead at Blois in the arms of a priest named Saint Germain. Her mansion had been sold to pay her debts and eventually acquired by a son of the prince de Condé, the comte de Soissons. He got rid of this white elephant by making it part of the dowry of his daughter when she married a prince of Savoy. The Savoys lived in a bit of it and rented out the rest. The queen's elegant townhouse became an elegant rooming house where Madeleine de Scudéry wrote novels to be published in her brother's name and – maybe – neighborhood children played in the garden and developed a taste for grandeur.

Finally, to the south there was the bridge. The Pont-Neuf was begun in 1578. Work on it was abandoned during the wars of religion and begun again in 1598. It was opened to the public in 1607. The Pont-Neuf was, of course, the first bridge in Paris built without houses. It was wide, made wider still by its half-moons or bays. One could stand on it and admire the view or watch the construction of the Grand Galerie linking the Louvre and the Tuileries; one could promenade across it, on pavement, safe from the Paris mud. Another attraction, at the north end of the bridge, was La Samaritaine, a great pump that brought water up from the river for the royal domaines. The pump was housed in an elaborate little castle topped by a campanile and an "industrious clock" that marked the hours, the courses of the sun and moon, and the signs of the zodiac. When it was time for the clock to sound, the bells of the campanile rang out with one of several tunes, a concert that was "long and very recreational."[34] In the center of the bridge was the equestrian statue of Paris's favorite king, Henri IV, opposite the brick-trimmed houses of the new Place Dauphine. The Pont-Neuf represented growth and hope to the war-weary Parisians of the early seventeenth century. It was the first of the great public works projects of the Bourbons to be completed and a symbol of what was promised: a capital reborn, its streets clean and well-lit at night, its beggars and thieves and whores rousted from their courts of miracles and housed in hospitals and almshouses, its river lined with magnificent public buildings.

What drew Jean-Baptiste Poquelin to the bridge was probably not the view, but the street life that grew up there. The Samaritaine end was the precinct of the song peddlers who offered ballads describing the latest scandals of the court and the town. Along the parapets of the bridge were the *bouquinistes*, then as now specialists in old books, but also a source for the subversive pamphlets that reached their peak during the anti-Mazarin campaign of the 1640s. Temporary stages in the Place Dauphine exhibited the charlatans and their troupes of entertainers who sold cures for "everything from baldness to warts."[35] An engraving of the 1630s shows the trestle stage of Christophe Contugi, from Orvieto. He was known as l'Orviétan, as was his remedy (which was actually made on the rue Dauphine). The legend next to the engraving reads:

> Orviétan is the best
> Against all sorts of pest.
> Against the venom of asp.
> Against the poison of wasp.
> Against the plagues that defeat us.
> Against the worms that eat us.
> Against the mad dog that bites us
> Against the smallpox that frights us.[36]

The most successful, at least theatrically, of the early charlatans on the bridge was Antoine Girard, known as Tabarin, head of a little troupe of *farceurs* including his brother who played Mondor, a *vecchio* or Pantalone, and a Rodomont, or *capitain*. Tabarin had a wife who played the *servante*. Although Rodomont died in 1626, before Jean-Baptiste was out of leading strings, the little troupe continued until the deaths of Tabarin and several others in 1633, and even then Mondor continued to perform on the bridge. The material attributed to Tabarin was so popular that it was collected and published, beginning in 1622. According to Charles Sorel in *L'Histoire comique de Francion*, the "works of Tabarin" sold more than 20,000 copies in the 1620s.[37] Even if Jean-Baptiste saw the troupe only in its late years when it was no longer as popular, he might well have gotten his hands on a copy of a collection of Tabarinesque materials made up of dialogues, salacious sayings, and prophecies of all sorts. The troupe of Tabarin also played farces, though apparently only on Friday.

Boileau later accused Molière of shamelessly linking Tabarin and Terence, not wanting to recognize the author of *Le Misanthrope* in the ridiculous Scapin and his sack. Tabarin was best known for his lazzi of the sack based on the "tabar" or cloak he wore that could be converted into a sack at first sight of a pigeon. Although there is no proof that Jean-Baptiste watched enchanted as the old clown lured his even older master into the enveloping folds of the tabar, there is at least a more than reasonable likelihood he did. But not on Fridays during the school year.

Farce was also still being played at the Hôtel de Bourgogne during the early adolescence of Jean-Baptiste Poquelin. According to Molière's first biographer Grimarest – who has been believed on this point by many who disbelieve him in general, because it seemed to them necessary to explain why this nice bourgeois boy should have become enamored of the stage – it was Grandfather Cressé who had a passion for the theatre and took his young grandson with him to share the free box provided by a brother *tapissier* who was Dean of the Masters of the Confrérie de la Passion, owners of the Hôtel de Bourgogne, Paris's oldest theatre.[38]

What might the two of them have seen, from the box or standing with the other bourgeois in the parterre? Until 1633 they would have seen the three great *farceurs* of the Hôtel de Bourgogne: Gaultier-Garguille, the old man, Gros-Guillaume, the flour-faced fat man, and Turlupin, the braggart. All three appeared together, probably for the last time, in Gougenot's *Comédie des Comédiens* in 1633. Gaultier-Garguille died that same year, Gros-Guillaume a year later, and Turlupin in 1637. They represented a tradition that almost died with them, until first Scarron writing for Jodelet and later Molière himself brought it back to life. Farce in the theatre was no more refined than farce on the trestle stages of the Pont-Neuf. Its subject matter was betrayed husbands and old men in love with young girls; its language was not the language of the salon. What had seemed wonderfully funny in the time of Henri IV, himself no model of polished manners, was now deemed gross, unsuitable, and unlikely to attract society women to the theatre.

The theatre changed radically in the decade of the 1630s. Paris, unlike the capitals of England and Spain, had no established theatre companies until 1630. Its only theatre, the Hôtel de Bourgogne, designed for the amateur production of religious plays, had been a road-house for eighty years, and was totally unsuited to the Italianate style of theatre production coming into vogue. Although both supported theatre to some extent, Henri IV and Louis XIII preferred the Italian *commedia dell'arte* troupes to the itinerant French ones, and were more likely to support them. Only after the ascension to power of Richelieu, with his passion for all things French, did the Paris theatre begin to develop both established companies and a repertory.

After a certain amount of prompting from the king, the Confrérie de la Passion accepted the act of the king's council of December 29, 1629, installing the Comédiens du Roi for three years in the Hôtel de Bourgogne. The troupe was led by Robert Guérin, already met in his *farceur* guise of Gros-Guillaume. In the same year a troupe led by Montdory took the first of several leases on one or another of the Marais tennis courts; in 1634 the troupe settled into its final tennis court on the rue Vieille-du-Temple. Paris now had two established theatres, and Jean-Baptiste Poquelin was thirteen years old.

The repertory was changing as well. Throughout the 1620s and until 1635, most troupes played – in addition to farces – pastorals and tragicomedies in the Italian mode. Suddenly there was a whole troop of young French writers: Rotrou, Mairet, Scudéry, Tristan, the elder Corneille. New kinds of plays were being written and new audiences filled the theatres. More women attended the plays and more men and women from the well-to-do classes. The various literary circles and salons began to take plays seriously and promote them. Another sign of the times: a group of plays about the theatre – Corneille's *L'Illusion comique* is the best known – that shows the life of the actor in a positive light.

The cardinal transformed a room in his palace into a small theatre seating 600, then set his architect, Mercier, to planning a large, splendid theatre that would open in 1641 and would eventually become Molière's theatre at the Palais-Royal. In that same year the king issued a formal statement declaring that the theatre was good and proper recreation for his people and that actors ran no risk of blame or infamy so long as they led decent lives and performed decent plays.

To a youngster just discovering the power of the enacted word, the Parisian theatre of the 1630s was a wonderland of action and character. Too young perhaps for the first group of Corneille's comedies, he could have been there wide-eyed at the rebirth of French tragedy, Mairet's *Sophonisbe* in December 1634, and at Corneille's *Illusion comique* the next year. Surely he saw Montdory play the Cid in January 1637; perhaps he was even in the house the day later that year when that same actor, determined to "out-Herod Herod" in Tristan's new play, suffered the paralytic stroke that ended his career. The Hôtel de Bourgogne was only a five-minute walk from the Pavillon des Singes, the Théâtre du Marais fifteen. According to Grimarest, Grandfather Cressé had one wish for his grandson: that he be as good an actor as Bellerose. Had the thought occurred to the boy? Possibly. But in the meantime, there were those humanities and maybe the law and the looming prospect of adulthood.

When Jean-Baptiste left Clermont, it would appear that one decision about his future had already been taken. The office of *tapissier du roi* that Jean Poquelin had assumed in 1631 enjoyed the right of *survivance*, that is, Jean Poquelin could assign it to one of his heirs. On December 14, 1637, that is exactly what he did. The office was transferred to his eldest son, who took the oath on December 18. The *État général* of the royal household for 1637 reads: "Jean Poquelin succeeded Jean Poquelin his father."[39]

The boy was not quite sixteen but – so it has been assumed – already trained in the skills of his father's craft, ready to practice the trade of master *tapissier*. The problem is to discover how he could have been. There is no record of any kind suggesting that he was ever apprenticed to his father or to any one else. As the son of a master, his term of apprenticeship could have been reduced from six to three years, but in order to complete his training by the age of fifteen, he would have had to have begun it at twelve, when we assume he was learning to parse Latin. In any case, even if he had been apprenticed, no boy of fifteen was ever received as a master, in the *tapissiers* or in any other *corps de métier*. The minimum age for the mastership was twenty-one.[40] So, the question is how could Jean-Baptiste Poquelin at fifteen be prepared to follow in the footsteps of his father?

The answer is that the transfer of the *survivance* to Jean-Baptiste had nothing to do with being a *tapissier* and everything to do with being an officer of the royal household. Special training was no longer a

qualification for an office such as *tapissier du roi*. The sale of royal offices
to anyone with the cash to buy one became a matter of such great
concern to the masters of the Paris *corps de métier* after 1635 – when the
French declared open war on the Hapsburgs and the gaping maw of the
royal purse became insatiable – that the masters found it necessary to
accumulate funds to purchase certain offices when they came on the
market and prevent their sale to unqualified buyers.[41] It was thus of no
importance to the keepers of the purse that a *tapissier du roi* be a *tapissier*.
Anyway, one could always assume that the fifteen-year-old son of a
tapissier would, in the normal course of events, become one himself. And
if not, well, the functions of a *tapissier du roi* were largely ceremonial and
administrative. He was not expected to whip out a needle and thread
and sew up a rip in the king's featherbed.

Still, none of this really explains why Jean-Baptiste Poquelin, a schoolboy, took the oath of his office in December 1637 and apparently began
to exercise its functions the following spring.[42] A possible reason might
be the war with the Hapsburgs that was declared officially in 1635. With
the country at war, the king – although never in robust health – felt it
was his duty to go on campaign, to stimulate the patriotism of the troops
and assure the loyalty of the generals.[43] One of the duties of a *tapissier
du roi* was to accompany the king when he went on a military campaign
and oversee his accommodations. The king had two identical tents and
sets of furnishings, each in the care of a *tapissier*. While the king was
using one, the other was taken ahead to the next stopping place and
arranged. Much more demanding than merely making the foot of the
king's bed, this service meant being away from Paris for long periods of
time, not something a busy man like Jean Poquelin would have found
worth his while. According to Grimarest, Jean-Baptiste was definitely
with the king in the summer of 1642 at Narbonne; perhaps he spent
earlier summers the same way, fulfilling the functions of his office and
learning the ways of the court as well. When not *en exercise*, he could have
served his three years of apprenticeship or – like many other young men
– he could have read philosophy with a private tutor and begun his study
of the law. If Jean Poquelin had great ambitions for his son, Jean-
Baptiste's assuming the office of *tapissier du roi* would not have interfered
with them and might even have forwarded them.

Some think that after Clermont Jean-Baptiste Poquelin studied with
the philosopher Gassendi. The connection was Chapelle, a close friend
in later years, who had also attended the Jesuit college. Chapelle, whose
real name was Claude-Emmanuel Luillier, was the legitimized son of

François Luillier, a high officer of the royal administration. The father arranged for Gassendi to come to Paris and tutor the son in 1641. One would like to think that perhaps young Poquelin joined the circle around the distinguished libertine philosopher, but the date does not make that especially plausible. Chapelle was four years younger than Jean-Baptiste, and finished Clermont only in 1641, by which time the older boy should have begun his study of the law.

The hagiographers of Molière have found it useful to assume that his mind was formed in part by the thought and teaching of Gassendi. A theologian, scholar of Greek and Hebrew, canon at Digne, and former member of the faculty of theology at Aix, Pierre Gassendi grew weary of Aristotle and devoted himself to study and writing instead of teaching. He became one of the new scientific philosophers, corresponding with Galileo, refuting Tycho Brahe, rejecting dogmatism and authority in all scientific matters. He was a declared Epicurean and his major works, published in 1647 and 1649, are studies of the life and moral teaching of Epicurus. That a priest should adhere to a materialist and sensualist philosophy is not as paradoxical as it might seem, according to Gérard Escat.[44] In fact, Gassendi's ideas are consistent with the ideas of Bacon, Galileo, and Kepler. Not at all a proponent of an Epicurean style of life, Gassendi was essentially a mechanist who believed that nature and its laws would eventually yield to mathematics. He tried to reconcile faith and science at a time when this task did not seem insurmountable if only one were permitted liberty of thought.

His libertine disciples like Luillier and his son Chapelle were, unlike their master, devoted to free-living as well as free-thinking. Luillier was "exceptionally cultivated" and "notoriously debauched."[45] To a taste for scientific research and philosophical reflections he added a penchant for obscenity and even schoolboy scatology. His treatise *Le Pissographie* gives instructions for urinating in the streets of Paris without being seen. His son was the result of a liaison with the fifteen-year-old wife of another high official. Chapelle also led a scandalous life. Nothing convinces us that Jean-Baptiste Poquelin was part of that life as early as 1641, but we can enjoy the vision of a young man with intelligence and curiosity, newly freed from the exhausting pedagogy of the Jesuits, discovering the world of scientific thought that, at mid-century, was challenging the immutable union of Aquinas and Aristotle.[46]

Most seventeenth-century sources agree that after Clermont and possibly a course in philosophy Jean-Baptiste Poquelin studied the law. La Grange speaks of his "exit from law school," Le Boulanger de Chalussay goes farther and indicates that he took a license at Orléans, became an *avocat*, and practiced law for five or six months, while Grimarest, who at first did not think Molière had been a lawyer, was later "positively assured" by the family that his subject had studied law and had "left the bar to mount the stage."[47]

The study of the law would not have provided young Poquelin with any great intellectual stimulation, yet a degree in law – a *license* – was definitely necessary for practice at the bar or for any high administrative or judicial office. The problem was that the study of civil law was entirely the study of Roman law; French law was not introduced until 1679. Another problem was that civil law was not taught in Paris. The University of Paris, which in any case Jean-Baptiste Poquelin as a graduate of Clermont was not eligible to attend, taught only canon law. For civil law one had to go either to Poitiers or Orléans, and most Parisians chose Orléans. Few of them, however, spent any significant amount of time in that city, since the University of Orléans had fallen upon hard times.

Founded in 1219 by the faculty of civil law of the University of Paris exiled when that university decided to teach only canon law, the University of Orléans was not a full university but only a law faculty. By the mid seventeenth century, this faculty had dwindled to four professors who resisted additional colleagues, since that would have meant more to share in the profits. Very little teaching was done; an edict of 1625 permitted the license to be awarded after one year in residence and one-semester's class attendance. Few of the 400 students who received their *licenses* each year bothered with even that much.

Pierre Helluin, living in Orléans during the reign of Louis XIII, describes the university building, the Grand-École, as a "vast barn with five rows of benches and a chair in the middle" that did not correspond to its pretentious name. No one was refused a degree who could pay for it. Exams consisted of two or three feeble arguments, after which the candidate was declared worthy.[48] Apparently many students found even this abbreviated study of Roman law pointless and unsuited to their needs. A usual course of action was to sign up in Paris with a tutor who gave lectures and taught what little Roman law a candidate at Orléans needed to know. Some students managed to avoid even an overnight stay in Orléans since, according to a report submitted to the Parlement de Paris, blank diplomas with the seals already applied were sold to the tutors who awarded them directly to their students.[49] These tutors were not necessarily negligible people; Jean Ron studied for a year with Le Coq, an officer of the Parlement de Paris.[50]

A reasonable assumption is that young Poquelin did something of the sort: a course of lectures, a bit of reading in the Institutes, and a quick trip to Orléans. The real learning could be done "on the job" whenever a "job," or office, should be his. Exactly when all this took place is impossible to determine, nor can we document the young man's growing distaste for his father's master plan. All we know for certain is that Jean-Baptiste's decision to make a life in the theatre had been taken by January 1643 when he received 630 *livres* from his father in return for agreeing to give up his office as king's *tapissier*. Six months later he signed a Contract of Association with nine others and the Illustre Théâtre was formed.

Jean-Baptiste Poquelin, barely ten years after the establishment of professional theatre in Paris, may have been one of the first (though certainly not the last) bright and promising middle-class children to deeply disappoint a parent dreaming of a secure and well-paid future for the young luminary, one of the first to speak those dreaded words: "I want to be an actor." How to account for it? How to comprehend the incomprehensible? Was it because of Clermont? All the fault of those Jesuits who kept putting on plays? Or perhaps it was Grandfather Cressé's doing, dragging the boy off to the theatre every time he had a day free of school? Or maybe it was those rascals on the bridge? Or . . . ?

No, in fact, the truth was simpler and La Grange, also an actor, was the one who knew it. Molière "chose the profession of actor from the invincible inclination he had for the theatre."[51] Jean-Baptiste Poquelin, like some before and many after, went on the stage because he wanted to, had to, because nothing else he could have done would have been as satisfying or would have brought him as close to happiness. And then, of course, there was Madeleine.

CHAPTER TWO

Madeleine

She was beautiful, she was elegant,[1] she was very witty, she sang well, she danced well, she played all sorts of instruments, she wrote very prettily in verse and in prose and her conversation was very diverting. She was one of the best actresses of her century and her acting had the power to inspire in reality all the feigned passions that one sees represented on the stage. This agreeable actress was called Jebar and, as Abindarrays sought to divert himself and efface the memory of past adventures, he went to the theatre where he saw her play the role of Sophonisbe in a manner so touching and so passionate that first he admired her and then he loved her, first his heart was tender with pity, then she stole it from him.[2]

Her name was Madeleine Béjart. She had glorious Venetian-red hair like Titian's saint, for whom she was named. She was four years older than Jean-Baptiste Poquelin and her family, while bourgeois, was neither as prosperous nor as respectable. She grew up in the Marais, a garden district to the east of Les Halles, foreign territory to Jean-Baptiste except on his forays to the Théâtre du Marais. She was part of the fashionable world of politics, literature, and sexual intrigue while Jean-Baptiste was still a schoolboy. It seems almost unimaginable that they met, but they did meet, and from that meeting followed all the rest.

The Béjart family descended from a royal notary of Troyes whose younger children deserted the place of their birth for Paris. The stay-at-home oldest son became a notary; the next son became a sergeant of the Châtelet, the daughter married another sergeant of the Châtelet, and the youngest, Joseph, father of Madeleine, apparently studied law, but was indecisive. He was ambitious for high office; at the time of his marriage he qualified himself as "maître," "procureur de For L'Évêque," the prison belonging to the Bishop of Paris, and "temporalité" of the see. He was also well connected. His uncle Pierre was a procureur at the Châtelet and his cousin Samuel Dacolle, who was also his godfather, was a procureur in Parlement. Joseph did not measure up to Béjart standards.

In the first place, there was his marriage. Unlike his cousins who married into legal families, Joseph married in 1615 a young *toilière-lingère* named Marie Hervé. She was twenty-two, the daughter of a deceased mercer of Château-Thierry and a woman named Madeleine Nollé, who had moved her children to Paris after her husband's death and taken another mercer, Simon Courtin, as her second husband. Marie had completed her apprenticeship and taken the oath of her guild on March 8, 1614, and had practiced her profession until her marriage eighteen months later. She brought to the marriage 1,800 *livres* in cash "from her trade in linen goods," and 600 in clothing and furnishings. The groom brought nothing, a sign of things to come.

Then there was Joseph's lack of perseverance. He changed his profession almost as frequently as he changed his place of residence. Shortly after his marriage, he became, probably on the recommendation of his uncle Pierre, the administrative secretary of a military academy. He worked for one of the three partners in the enterprise, a secretary in the Chambre du Roi named Pierre Lenormant who became a lifelong friend of the Béjarts and played an interesting minor role in the life of Madeleine. Shortly after taking on the task of inscribing the names of the young gentlemen who came to learn the use of the musket and pike (and the more onerous task of getting their parents to pay for it) Joseph Béjart – undoubtedly with his wife's money – bought another office, that of *huissier-audiencier* in the court of Waters and Forests of France, situated at the Palais, the center of administration and justice. A *huissier-audiencier* is a bailiff who oversees decorum in the court and serves as the court-crier.

The Béjarts moved almost yearly. At first dwelling on the rue St-Antoine, with or near Marie's family, they were later to be found on the rues Couture-Ste-Catherine, des Écouffes, de Jouy, Neuve-St-Paul, des Blancs-Manteaux, des Jardins St-Paul, and de Thorigny, always in the Marais, nearly always in the parish of St-Paul. By the time Joseph Béjart died in 1641, he had lived in eighteen different dwellings.[3] A greater contrast to the stable and settled life of Jean Poquelin's family is hard to imagine.

The Marais was one of the most fashionable districts of Paris. It stretched from the river to the Temple and from the rue du Temple to the Porte St-Antoine. Its main street, variously the rue François Miron and the rue St-Antoine, ran from near the Hôtel de Ville to the Bastille and separated the old riverside Marais with its half-timbered buildings and narrow, twisting streets from the new Marais, a district of

MADELEINE BÉJARD

1. *Madeleine Béjart*

magnificent private mansions built in the sixteenth and seventeenth centuries. Unlike Les Halles, the Marais was not a commercial district; very few buildings had shops on the ground floor. Most had courts and gardens. Many of the inhabitants were "persons of consideration," the old nobility "of the sword," the new nobility "of the robe," bankers, financiers, and tax farmers. It was convenient for the Palais, where Parlement met, on the Île de la Cité. The streets were reasonably wide, carriages could come and go, and the ladies and fashionable gentlemen of the district could pay their visits, attend their theatre, and take the air at the Porte St-Antoine. Living in the Marais, even one step ahead of the bailiff, gave the Béjarts a certain distinction.

Nine children were born to the family, five of whom died in infancy. The survivors were Joseph, born in 1616, Madeleine, born in 1618, Geneviève born in 1624, and Louis born in 1630. All became actors and were allied with Molière. A tenth child, Armande, who may have been Madeleine's youngest sister or Madeleine's own daughter, was to become Molière's wife.

A few scattered legal documents suggest how disquieting it must have been to be the wife or child of Joseph Béjart, always looking for the pot of gold, always in debt, always robbing Peter to pay Paul.

Marie did her best. She devised a beauty lotion of river water, cucumber, and verjuice that she sold to the elegant women of the district.[4] But in 1632, with all those children to look after, Marie Hervé took the difficult step of applying for separation of property. This was not a "legal separation" in the modern sense; there was to be no separation of persons. The marriage would continue but the "community" would be dissolved, and Marie would receive back what she had contributed. The process took two years, but finally on April 12, 1634, a sentence of separation was pronounced that required Joseph to return the 2,400 *livres* he had received at the time of the marriage and to pay his wife 60 *livres* a year for his shelter and nourishment. His property was ordered seized and sold so that these obligations could be met.

The Béjarts were living at this time on the rue de Thorigny, sharing a house with their old family friend Pierre Lenormant. Lenormant, who had hired Joseph Béjart to help him administer the military academy near the Place Royale, was a man of standing. He had been secretary to Catherine de Bourbon, the sister of Henri IV, and involved in the affairs of Marguerite de Valois, Henri's discarded first wife. After her death in 1615, he became secretary of the Chambre du Roi and later *porte-manteau ordinaire* of the prince de Condé. He was apparently as improvident as his friend Joseph. In 1620, for instance, he pawned for 5,000 *livres* jewels given him by Marguerite de Valois and the following year abandoned them to his creditors.

For reasons barely conceivable, on February 23, 1633, a contract of marriage was drawn up between Pierre Lenormant, a man at least in his fifties, and the fifteen-year-old Madeleine Béjart. Such a disparity of age between spouses was hardly unknown in the seventeenth century, but usually indicates a social or financial benefit. Typically, a rich bourgeois family might marry a daughter to an aging nobleman in order to create an aristocratic connection, or a poor noble family with a pretty daughter might sacrifice her to a rich financier. But in this case, neither family had the proverbial pot. Joseph styled himself in the marriage contract "formerly *procureur* of the Châtelet," which was simply a lie. The contract did not establish a financial community but ordained "separation of goods" from the beginning, which sounds like Marie Hervé trying to save her daughter from the financial nightmare she herself had lived. The Béjarts promised a dowry of 2,000 *livres* to be spent on furnishings. Lenormant was seconded by three friends with titles and offices; Madeleine's witnesses were her father's uncle Pierre and her step-grand-father. The contract was signed, but not by the notaries who drew it up. They filed it and it remained in the files. The marriage never took place.[5]

In play after play, Molière will use the theme of a father trying to arrange an unsuitable marriage for a daughter with other inclinations. Orgon will want to marry Mariane to the hypocrite Tartuffe, Argan will try to arrange a marriage between Angélique and the idiot Thomas Diafoirus, Harpagon will insist that Élise marry old M. Anselme. In each case the father's need for security overpowers his affection for his daughter.

Madeleine Béjart would play Dorine in *Tartuffe* many years later. Maybe she speaks in her own voice when she says to Mariane: "Tell [your father] that a heart never loves under orders, that you will marry for yourself and not for him, that it's your business, after all, and it's you the husband must please, and that if his Tartuffe is so charming, no one's stopping him from marrying Tartuffe himself."[6]

Madeleine, in fact, never married. Possibly her parents' marriage made her apprehensive, perhaps her own brush with an arranged marriage did. In any case, Madeleine became an independent woman. In the seventeenth century all unmarried people – male or female – remained minors until the age of twenty-five and could not sign any sort of contract or carry on any kind of business. Madeleine had herself "emancipated," that is, declared legally free of the tutelage of her parents sometime before April 1635. In January 1636, though only eighteen, she wanted to buy a little house on the cul-de-sac Thorigny in the Marais. The house cost 4,000 *livres*; she claimed to have 2,000 and wanted to borrow the other 2,000. With the support of her step-grandfather, Simon Courtin, and her parents, she was granted the right to take out a loan. Unfortunately, something went wrong; she was unable to pay what she had promised, and another buyer was preferred.[7]

The other buyer was also a single woman, Nicole des Rideaux. The little house was apparently just the thing for a *"mademoiselle du Marais,"* a young woman embarked on a life in the world of *galanterie*. The great courtesans of Paris, Ninon de Lenclos and Marion de Lorme, lived in the Marais, and so did many other beautiful and talented young women who were making their own way. Marion was five years older than Madeleine Béjart, Ninon was two years younger. They were both from noble families. Madeleine was not. Still, she had an entrée into the great world and clearly she took it.

In 1636 her mother's half-sister, Marie Courtin, married a writer and actor named Jean-Baptiste L'Hermite, the brother of the playwright Tristan L'Hermite. Tristan was in the entourage of the king's brother, Gaston d'Orléans, and returned to France with him from exile in 1634. Also attached to Gaston's household was Esprit de Rémond, the comte de Modène.

Modène was twenty-eight years old in 1636. His father François de Rémond, baron de Modène, who was a cousin of Louis XIII's favorite, the duc de Luynes, was appointed to the Council of Finance and named ambassador to Madrid and Grand Provost of France. Under Richelieu he was deprived of office and sent back to his estate near Avignon. Esprit de Rémond joined the household of Gaston d'Orléans as a page in 1620 and was by the 1630s acting as his chamberlain. He was married to a much older woman, Marguerite de La Baume de la Suze, and was the father of one son. In April 1637 Marguerite "retired" to her château on the banks of the Sarthe, selling her house on the Place Royale to none other than Marion de Lorme, and her husband was free to amuse himself in Paris. He was one of a circle of young men, *gens de plaisir*, that included not only Tristan L'Hermite but sons and relations of great noble families: the comte de Nançay, who was related to the Guise and Condé families, Roger de Rabutin, grandson of the duc de Bellegarde, and the Archbishop of Reims, Henri de Lorraine, son of the duc de Guise and soon to be the duc de Guise himself. They were "elegant and gallant young men, beautiful dancers, mad for gambling, patrons of letters, the theatre and actresses."[8] The archbishop took as his mistress Mlle de Villiers of the Théâtre du Marais and for love of her wore yellow stockings;[9] the comte de Modène took Madeleine Béjart as his.

In April 1638 Modène rented a little country house at La Folie Regnault, east of the Bastille, and opposite the present site of Père-Lachaise cemetery.[10] Madeleine was pregnant. The child, a daughter named Françoise for Modène's father, was baptized on July 11, 1638, at St-Eustache. Modène accepted his illegitimate daughter and selected as her godfather his seven-year-old legitimate son, Gaston-Jean-Baptiste; the godmother was Marie Hervé. Since the seven-year-old was not present at this strange event, he was represented by Jean-Baptiste L'Hermite.[11]

There are some mysteries here. Françoise was a week old when she was baptized, and, although her mother claimed to be living on the nearby rue St-Honoré, the birth actually took place on July 3 in La Folie Regnault. Nothing more is known of the baby who was probably put out to nurse and died as so many babies did in infancy. The mother returned with her lover to the little house in the country.

In December of 1638 Modène bought – made a down payment on – another little house in Bagnolet.[12] Bagnolet, just to the east of twentieth-century Paris, outside the Périphérique highway that constitutes its modern walls, was even farther from the delights of the Marais than La Folie Regnault. The impression given by these pastoral retreats is that Modène was a jealous lover who wanted to keep his glorious young mistress to himself. Of course, Madeleine may have been trying to preserve her reputation and keep the liaison secret, but a public baptism at St-Eustache, a fashionable Parisian church, seems to militate against that.

In any case, Madeleine was not destined for a long stay in the country. Modène became embroiled in the affairs of his friend the archbishop who wanted to resign his various sacred offices in order to reveal his secret marriage to the princess Anne of Gonzaga. When Richelieu refused his request, he joined with the comte de Soissons and the duc de Bouillon in a conspiracy against the cardinal. Modène, who was an active agent of the princes, left Paris in 1639 for Sedan, northeast of Paris on the frontier between France and the Holy Roman Empire. He stopped making the payments on the house in Bagnolet, and Madeleine was forced to rent it for forty *livres* a year and six cream cheeses.[13] She returned to her parents, now living on the rue St-Sauveur.

Beautiful and gifted though she was, Madeleine did not continue a life in the *galanterie*. Her relationship with Modène was apparently the only one she had, and it was far from the kind of fashionable intrigue enjoyed by Ninon and Marion and celebrated by Tallemant des Réaux, the Parisian king of gossip. Instead of holding sway in the drawing rooms of the Marais, Madeleine found herself pregnant and exiled in the suburbs. But she had another string to her bow. Unlike the noble Ninon and Marion, she was not too proud to have a profession of her own. Madeleine was an actress.

Probably Madeleine was already an actress at the time she met Modène. There was a suspicion of a theatrical connection in the Béjart family. Joseph, on at least one occasion, was referred to by his widow as the sieur de Belleville,[14] a *nom de théâtre* used by Henri LeGrand, the famous Turlupin, when he was not playing farce. Actors frequently, almost invariably, used names carefully selected to imply noble birth, names that employed the particule and a noun both geographical and nonspecific: sieur de Belleville, sieur de La Grange, sieur Du Parc, sieur de Montfleury. Joseph's choice was already taken, which suggests that he was an actor not in reality, but in fantasy.

A more substantial theatrical association was the Courtin-L'Hermite connection. Marie Courtin, the half-sister of Madeleine's mother, not only married an actor, she became an actor herself. She and her husband played as the sieur and Mlle de Vauselle. They were married on March 6, 1636, in Paris, a month after the birth of their daughter, another Madeleine. The groom's mother was so irritated by the loss of her son to a little Paris bourgeoise – and an actress to boot – that she wrote a new will leaving everything to her other son, the poet, everything being 80 *livres* worth of furniture and a country property valued at 200.[15]

At the time of the birth of their child, Jean-Baptiste L'Hermite and Marie Courtin were very probably part of an itinerant theatrical troupe; their presence in Paris a month later, during Lent, is consistent with that, since most provincial actors went to Paris during the annual closing to see their friends and negotiate new contracts. Madeleine Béjart was certainly among those who greeted them on their return to the capital and may well have benefited from her new uncle's connections, both theatrical and social.[16]

Madeleine was already emancipated and planning to buy a house of her own. She had a foot at least on the slopes of Le Parnasse, literary Paris, since her quatrain to Rotrou on the subject of his *Hercule mourant* was selected by him to be published with the play in May 1636. She wrote:

Your Dying Hercules will render you immortal;
He proclaims your glory to Heaven and to earth,
And leaving here below a temple to your Memory,
His funeral pyre will be your altar.[17]

This standard hyperbole of the day is, nonetheless, nicely turned; the conceit has a certain complexity. Rotrou's *Hercule mourant*, though published in 1636, had been produced for carnival two years earlier at the Hôtel de Bourgogne, and it is doubtful that Madeleine Béjart, then sixteen, had any part in that production. By 1636, however, she may have been a *gagiste*, or small part actor, possibly at the Hôtel de Bourgogne, more probably at the Théâtre du Marais that, in 1636, produced Tristan L'Hermite's model tragedy *Mariane*, perhaps with his new sister-in-law's pretty niece as a lady of the court. Nothing is certain since no surviving cast list of the period includes her name; still, Madeleine learned her trade somehow and developed a sufficient reputation that in 1643 the inexperienced actors of the Illustre Théâtre granted her the right to cast herself in whatever roles pleased her. She may have gained her experience entirely in provincial troupes, but if so that experience was limited since documents confirm her presence in Paris during every season but 1642–3.[18]

The Théâtre du Marais was very near the house on the rue Thorigny that Marie Hervé seems to have owned or claimed to own and that the Béjarts and Lenormants inhabited from time to time. The Marais was the second established theatre in Paris, the home of a troupe led by two actors, Lenoir and Montdory, who had arrived in late 1629 and set up shop in various of the unused tennis courts of the Marais – unused because the game, so popular in the time of Henri IV, was no longer fashionable. In 1634 the company rented the Jeu de Paume des "Maretz," on the rue Vieille-du-Temple opposite the Capuchins, where it remained until 1673.

The theatre audience in the early 1630s was small. A new theatre needed a drawing card, some kind of competitive edge, and the Marais had one; his name was Pierre Corneille. He was twenty-three years old in 1629, a lawyer living in Rouen, when he offered Lenoir and Montdory the chance to produce his first play, *Mélite*. Impressed, they chose it to open their Paris theatre, and it had a considerable success, possibly because it was one of those rare things at the time, a comedy. Corneille continued to write for the troupe, a whole series of comedies, a tragicomedy, a tragedy, and finally that strange play, his baroque masterpiece, *L'Illusion comique*, performed in the season of 1635–6.

The Marais not only had a popular and fashionable playwright, it had several excellent actors, including Montdory and the celebrated Mlle de Villiers, whose presence attracted other playwrights. Mairet gave the company his precious *Sophonisbe*, the play that brought tragedy back to life on the French stage. Tristan gave them his *Mariane*, Georges de Scudéry his *Mort de César*.

The popularity of the Théâtre du Marais aroused the jealousy of the "official troupe," the Comédiens du Roi at the Hôtel de Bourgogne. They persuaded the king to order four actors from the Marais – Lenoir, his wife, and the two *farceurs* Jodelet and L'Espy – to join the royal troupe in December 1634. Montdory was forced to close his doors for a time, but he found new actors and, according to Tallemant, "in a little while his troupe was once again better than the other one, because he alone was worth more than all the rest."[19]

The only evidence that connects Madeleine Béjart to the Théâtre du Marais is the description in *Almahide* of her remarkable portrayal of Sophonisbe. Perhaps she actually understudied Mlle de Villiers at the Marais and had the chance to play the role there. Or perhaps she played it when both she and Georges de Scudéry were in the south of France after 1645.

Tallemant writes (in the 1650s, before Madeleine and Molière returned to Paris from their long exile in the provinces) that he had "never seen her play, but it is said that she is the best actress of all. She is in a country troupe; she played in Paris, but this was in a third troupe that was there only for a while. Her masterpiece was the character of Epicharis."[20] Epicharis was the leading female role in Tristan's *La Mort de Sénèque*, created by Madeleine for the Illustre Théâtre in 1644.

Madeleine became an actress approximately thirty years after the first actress known by name played in Paris. She was Rachel Trépeau, a member of the troupe of Valleran Le Conte. The very first mention of an actress in France is in the mid-sixteenth century when a troupe of Florentines that included actresses entertained Catherine de Médicis and Henri II at Lyon. This troupe may not have been fully professional, however they were handsomely paid by both king and queen for the pleasure they gave.

All of the celebrated sixteenth-century actresses were Italian. Among their number were several who followed a pattern that the Italian scholar Taviani has recently identified.[21] They were either courtesans, chased from Rome by the reform popes following the Council of Trent, or women who followed the courtesan model and led independent and often libertine lives.[22] One of the earliest pieces of documentary evidence confirming the existence of professional actresses is a contract of association between Lucrezia Senese and five other actors signed in Rome in 1563. Taviani identifies Lucrezia as a courtesan because of her name that, in the fashion of courtesans, joins a Roman first name to a geographical surname and because the contract was signed in a house owned or leased by her at a time when few women other than courtesans held property in their own names. Courtesans were well-educated women, noted for their conversation and for their musical accomplishments. These were the very skills that the actress needed, and especially the actress of the *commedia dell'arte*, who was expected to improvise beautifully composed dialogues on amorous topics. Many of these women became stars of the Italian theatre, some the leaders of their troupes as well.

Not all of the Italian actresses followed the courtesan model, however. The most celebrated of them all, Isabella Andreini, devoted herself to creating an image of the actress as a respectable and devout wife and mother. She was married to Francesco Andreini, an actor, and the mother of six children, four of whom joined religious orders. Isabella also wrote poems and pastorals, in the fashion of her day, and was even elected a member of a learned academy. She was extremely popular in France as well as in Italy, and died in Lyon while traveling back to Italy from Paris. Her epitaph, devised by her husband, reads: "A woman preeminent for her virtue, the ornament of morality, faithful to her marital relations, religious, pious, a friend to the Muses, the chief of theatrical artists, who here awaits the resurrection."[23]

Most French actresses in the seventeenth-century followed, at least superficially, the model established by Isabella. They married, usually actors, and often produced large families of children, some of whom also became actors. Of course gossip and rumor had it that many of these women entered into liaisons outside of marriage; they were, after all, actresses and automatically open to accusations of illicit sexuality. The truth of the matter is that some probably took lovers and some probably did not. The Illustre Théâtre had no married couples, but the later troupe of Molière included only married women with one exception: Madeleine Béjart.

Documents show Madeleine in Paris in September 1640 and September 1641, living on the rue de Thorigny,[24] perhaps continuing to play small parts at the Théâtre du Marais. The comte de Modène was in the north with the prince-conspirators who hoped he could help persuade Gaston d'Orléans to join them. In early May Modène sent his friend Jean-Baptiste L'Hermite with letters from himself and from the duc de Guise to Gaston, but L'Hermite was intercepted in the forest of Vincennes by the cardinal's men and thrown into prison.[25] Apparently, however, L'Hermite was his own betrayer, the one who told secretary of state Chavigny in advance about his mission.[26] A trial of the absent conspirators began in late June, based in part on the testimony of L'Hermite, who told everything he knew without being asked. On July 6 the princes engaged the royal troops at the battle of Marfée and won. The victory was Pyrrhic, however; Soissons died after the battle, according to legend when he raised the visor of his helmet with his pistol and accidentally shot himself in the eye. The duc de Guise escaped to the nearby Netherlands and Modène, wounded, retired to his castle in the Comtat Venaissin, near Avignon, a territory belonging to the pope and thus out of reach of any possible retribution by Richelieu.

The duc de Guise was condemned to death *in absentia*, while Jean-Baptiste L'Hermite was released from prison – in thanks for which he offered the cardinal a sonnet. Now styling himself "knight of the order of the king" and "gentleman servant of His Majesty," he was still in Paris at the end of 1642. Richelieu died in December 1642; three months later the king followed him, and the conspirators, even the duc de Guise, felt free to return to Paris, but L'Hermite left Paris for – of all places – Modène, where he received from Esprit de Rémond a property adjoining the castle known variously as the grange or the mill of La Souquette.

The traitor was thus welcomed by the betrayed, which could mean that L'Hermite's behavior was not part of "a clever comedy imagined by the cardinal"[27] but of an even more clever one imagined by Modène. Or, Modène may have felt that he had received satisfaction by substituting one form of betrayal for another. When Jean-Baptiste L'Hermite arrived in Modène it was to rejoin his wife, Marie Courtin, who had passed her time of exile by replacing her niece, Madeleine Béjart, in the comte de Modène's affections.[28] The apparent "sale" of La Souquette was a gift to the mistress and the complaisant husband. Modène seems to have had the habit of giving property to the women he slept with.

No document shows Modène in Paris until 1646, when, no longer attached to Gaston d'Orléans, he was First Gentleman of the Chamber of the duc de Guise. By this time the Illustre Théâtre had failed and Madeleine Béjart was performing in the provincial troupe of the duc d'Épernon. No document confirms that Modène and Madeleine Béjart met in the years between 1639 and 1646. And yet, the possibility must be entertained, since Madeleine may have had a second daughter in early 1643 and the father may have been Esprit de Rémond.

Somebody had a baby. On March 10, 1643, Marie Hervé asked to be permitted to renounce all claims to the debt-ridden estate of her husband on behalf of her children Joseph, Madeleine, Geneviève, Louis, and "une petite non baptisée," a little unbaptized girl.[29] When the baby was born is unknown, as is her date of baptism, but almost everyone who has thought about it agrees that this is the first known reference to Armande Béjart whom Molière would marry nineteen or twenty years later.

Armande Grésinde Claire Elisabeth Béjart[30] was "in the neighborhood of twenty" on January 23, 1662 when her marriage contract was signed. She was, according to that contract, the daughter of Marie Hervé and the "late Joseph Béjart, living nobly, sieur de Belleville." The issue is whether this claim of paternity is as fallacious as the other information about the late Joseph. Unfortunately, the question of Armande Béjart's parentage has never been settled and probably never will be. In the seventeenth century it was thought by most that Armande was the daughter not of Marie Hervé but of Madeleine Béjart. Molière's close friend Boileau certainly thought so.[31] Some went further and suggested that she was the daughter of Madeleine and Molière himself, although that was not generally believed. The Moliéristes of the nineteenth century were unnerved by even the remote possibility that their idol had married his own daughter and devoted hundreds of pages to proving that Madeleine could not possibly have been Armande's mother. More recent scholarship has again entertained the probability that the elderly Marie Hervé, estranged from her husband and living separately from him, was not a likely candidate for motherhood.

Joseph Béjart died in September 1641. Had he engendered Armande on his deathbed, she would have been born in June 1642 and thus been a *"petite non-baptisée"* of nine months in March 1643. But in this period babies were baptized within a day or two of birth, and for a child to still be nameless at nine months would be unheard of. Much more likely is that someone gave birth to the little girl in early March 1643. Marie was five months short of her fiftieth birthday at the time and her husband had been dead for eighteen months. Of course, she might have become pregnant by someone not her husband, but the chances of that seem slim.

On the other hand, why lie if the child was Madeleine's? Her first child was publicly acknowledged by its father and baptized in a fashionable church. One author proposes that Madeleine had been unfaithful to the comte de Modène and wanted to keep the child's birth a secret because she still hoped eventually to marry him.[32] Although this hypothesis is certainly possible, so is it possible that this child, like the other, was fathered by Modène. Although there is no record that he acknowledged Armande at her baptism (indeed, the time and place of her baptism remain unknown), twenty-two years later Esprit de Modène and Madeleine Béjart stood at the baptismal font as godparents of Armande's daughter, Esprit-Madeleine.[33]

Marie Hervé's inclusion of the "*petite non baptisée*" among her children is not the only questionable claim in her request that the children be allowed to renounce the inheritance of their father's estate. She also refers to her older children, Joseph and Madeleine, as "minors," although both were over twenty-five. Had these "minors" been recognized as legal adults, perhaps they could have been held responsible for their father's debts, while she – possessed of a legal separation of property – could not. The purpose of this lie seems clear; that of the lie – if it was one – about the baby does not. But perhaps the answer is simpler than it seems: the notary was there to compose the request, and the baby had to be accounted for. Marie Hervé, as many legal documents show, had a convenient sort of memory and was not always devoted to the truth.[34]

Henri Chardon, whose carefully researched and clearly reasoned book on the comte de Modène is a model of nineteenth-century scholarship, believes that Modène was Armande's father and that the delay in her baptism was caused by Madeleine's waiting for him to return to Paris, assuming he would want to recognize this child as he had the other.[35] When Modène, who was otherwise occupied with Madeleine's aunt Marie, did not appear, the women decided that it would be better for the infant to appear to be legitimate. Her date of birth was carefully kept vague, in case anyone wanted to compare it to the date of her "father's" death. What seems most improbable is that no one in the family knew Armande's age at the time of her marriage.

There remains, however, the question of where Madeleine and Modène met in the early summer of 1642. Henri Chardon constructs an elegant argument in favor of a meeting near Avignon in June. From the journal of Henri Arnauld, June 29, 1642, he discovers that a troupe of actors was playing outside of Avignon in mid-June. The king had spent several months campaigning in the south and was returning to Paris. Arnauld writes: "The king was at Montfrin, where he took the waters . . . Mme de Rohan was there and every day at her house there were balls and plays.[36]

Chardon argues that the plays were provided by the troupe of Charles Dufresne, one of the few provincial companies circulating in 1642 and known to have performed in Lyon seven months later. Their presence is further established by the publication that year, in Avignon, of a play by a member of the troupe, Nicolas Desfontaines. Also a member of the troupe, according to Chardon, was Madeleine Béjart.

He could well be right. Our last record of Madeleine in Paris is March 31, 1642, when she accepted a payment of 189 *livres* of the 300 still owed her by Denis Vitry and his wife who had bought the house in Bagnolet. The Vitry couple had been slow to pay and Madeleine had pursued them with a court order issued on March 19. But nothing more is heard of the 111 *livres* still owing. So perhaps Madeleine joined a provincial troupe during the annual Easter break, when contracts for the following year were signed, and left Paris. And perhaps it was Dufresne's troupe she joined. At some point a connection was made between Madeleine, Molière, and Dufresne, since it was Dufresne who rescued them after the failure of the Illustre Théâtre. Another "coincidence" that suggests that Madeleine may have been in Dufresne's troupe before 1643 is that Nicolas Desfontaines, known to have been with Dufresne in 1642, joined Madeleine in the Illustre Théâtre in 1644.

The connections are tenuous at best, but maybe Madeleine did meet Modène in or around Avignon in June 1642. The date is right for a birth taking place in March 1643 and the geography is credible. A man could easily ride the twenty or so miles from Modène to Montfrin, or there would certainly have been an inn or other meeting place available in Avignon. Chardon's hypothesis is finally unnecessary, of course, since the documentary evidence is sparse and large amounts of time unaccounted for make it wholly possible for Modène to have been in Paris or Madeleine in the south at almost any point. Yet what makes Chardon's theory uniquely tempting is that, according to Grimarest, Jean-Baptiste Poquelin went campaigning with the king in his function as *tapissier du roi* in the spring of 1642 and would also have been in Montfrin on the way back to Paris in mid-June.[37] Here's a scenario! The beautiful actress is still in love with the faithless nobleman – who has betrayed her with her own aunt. She begs to meet him once again; he takes advantage of her, knowing full well that the relationship is over. Meanwhile, worshiping her from afar is the young *tapissier*, his head full of romance and dreams of theatrical glory. Mere fancy? Probably. But since we will never know all the truth of it, the "whens" and the "wheres" or even finally the "whos," perhaps we should be satisfied with the best and the most stage-worthy story.

CHAPTER THREE

The Illustre Théâtre

In January of 1643 Jean-Baptiste Poquelin was ready to commit himself to a life in the theatre. Jean Poquelin, whatever his feelings in the matter, had given up and given in and – in return for Jean-Baptiste's promise to vacate the office of *tapissier du roi* – given his son 630 *livres*, partly the inheritance owing from his mother and partly an advance on what he could eventually expect from his father. The gift was not especially generous, given the financial circumstances of the family, but perhaps Jean Poquelin had a premonition that 630 *livres* would not be the final cost of this theatrical adventure.

By January 1643, then, Jean-Baptiste Poquelin knew Madeleine Béjart and plans were underway to found a theatre. Perhaps their meeting had taken place in Montfrin six months earlier, but a more pedestrian conjecture is probably closer to the truth. Two associations link the Poquelin and the Béjart families. The first and most important is that Jean-Baptiste's grandmother Agnès Mazuel and Madeleine's mother Marie Hervé were both *maîtresses* of the guild of *toilières-lingères* and undoubtedly knew each other. The second is that Phillipe Lenormant, co-tenant of the Béjarts on the rue de la Perle and daughter of the gentleman who nearly married Madeleine, borrowed in November 1637 some small sums of money from Louis de Cressé, Jean-Baptiste Poquelin's maternal grandfather.[1] The Béjarts and the Poquelins were too unlike to be close friends, but even a casual connection offered Jean-Baptiste the chance to claim acquaintance with the dazzling Madeleine – with whom of course we want to believe he instantly fell in love. La Grange says nothing about it in his *Préface* but La Grange, even in the detailed *Registre*, that recounts all the important events of the troupe after 1658, has very little to say about Madeleine. Grimarest contents himself with saying that "Molière . . . formed a strong friendship with Mlle Béjart"[2] The *libellistes*, Le Boulanger de Chalussay and the unknown author of *La Fameuse Comédienne*, were entirely certain that the two had been lovers, and

Molière's close friend and defender Boileau also told his friend Brossette that Molière's first love had been the actress Béjart.[3] The town gossip Tallemant des Réaux, in a marginal note he added to his paragraph on Madeleine, says that "a boy named Molière left the benches of the Sorbonne to follow her; he was in love with her for a long time . . . and finally set to it and married her."[4] Only, of course, he didn't, but Tallemant, writing in the late 1650s, thought he had. They were, one assumes, living together then as they had been for years.

They were living if not together at least in the same neighborhood on June 30, 1643, when they signed the contract that founded the Illustre Théâtre. Jean Poquelin had moved out of the Maison des Singes and into a house he owned at the Image de St-Christophe, under the pillars of the market.[5] His son left Les Halles and joined the Béjarts in the Marais.

We can only speculate about what Jean-Baptiste was doing between January 6, when his father gave him 630 *livres*, and the end of June. A bizarre possibility is that he shilled for one of the charlatans on the Place Dauphine, playing a victim of snake-bite cured by the marvelous anti-dote of Orvieto. The possibility is worth mentioning because, even if untrue, it leavens our idea of the young Molière, so hard working, so serious, so philosophical; it lightens the mix.

According to Le Boulanger de Chalussay in *Élomire hypocondre*, the dra-matic *libelle* published in 1670, Jean-Baptiste Poquelin left the law office for the charlatan's stage. The scene is between Élomire (Molière) and Angélique (Madeleine) who begins by claiming that Élomire's father bought him a law degree.

ANGÉLIQUE
> But, if you please, here's ingratitude for you,
> Instead of devoting himself to the law office
> And filing suits, to please this good old father,
> He went only one time to the Palace of Justice.
> And then, do you know what the clown did?
> He took a job with the two big charlatans,
> With the originals, Orviétan and Bary,
> Whose favorite the fop thought he was.

ÉLOMIRE
> Orviétan, right, I agree, but not Bary. I deny
> Ever having schemed for a place in his company.

ANGÉLIQUE
> You schemed for the fourth business with Bary:
> And Bary wouldn't have you; you complained about it to me,

And I remember well that my brothers made fun of you,
Calling you the snake-eater, for you
Were so deprived of reason and good sense
And so sure of his antidote,
That you offered yourself to demonstrate it,
Even though in my neighborhood we knew the widows
Of six famous buffoons dead on the job.[6]

Earlier in the play, Élomire himself admits that he once had studied under the charlatans and insists that without them his great talent for comedy would have died before it was born.[7]

No doubt Jean Poquelin would have been beside himself at the sight of his carefully brought-up oldest son tricking widows out of their mites in the Place Dauphine. In contrast, the profession of actor may have seemed positively respectable. Twenty years earlier, in the days of Jean Poquelin's youth, acting was certainly not an honorable profession, and even in the 1640s most people had an ambivalent attitude toward actors. On the one hand, the king himself had declared, in 1641, that "in so far as the said actors exercise such control over their actions in the theatre that these remain wholly exempt from impurity, we desire that their occupation, which is capable of providing innocent diversion for our people from certain blameworthy activities, shall not be held to their discredit, nor prejudice their reputation in public discourse."[8] On the other hand, the Church in Paris still excommunicated actors and, as Molière's family and friends were to discover, could deny Christian burial to actors who had not renounced their professions.

Playwrights and actors in the newly established theatres of the 1630s were quick to demonstrate that their plays and their acting style had little in common with the obscene farces and *farceurs* of the past, and Jean-Baptiste may have reminded his father of the words of the magician Alcandre in Corneille's *L'Illusion comique* to the distressed father who has just discovered that his son is an actor:

Cease your complaint. At present the theatre
Is at such a high point that everyone idolizes it,
And what in your day was viewed with contempt
Is today cherished by all the best minds, . . .
Even our great king, our Jupiter, whose thunderbolt
Strikes fear to the ends of the earth,
Forehead encircled with laurels, deigns sometimes
To lend an eye or ear to the French theatre.

And besides, Alcandre notes, the theatre can be very profitable.[9]

No doubt it was in expectation of profit that on June 30, 1643, Madeleine Béjart, her brother Joseph, her sister Geneviève, Jean-Baptiste Poquelin, and six others – Denis Beys, Nicolas Bonnenfant, Germain Clérin, Madeleine Malingre, Georges Pinel, and Catherine des Urlis – "joined together for the exercise of the theatre in order to preserve their troupe under the title of the Illustre Théâtre."[10]

Not much is known of most of the actors who comprised the troupe. Joseph Béjart, approximately two years older than his sister Madeleine, had studied theology at the University of Paris and suffered from an affliction that usually makes acting impossible: he stuttered. Geneviève Béjart was Madeleine's little sister, a girl of nineteen. Nicolas Bonnenfant was a *procurer*'s clerk, Denis Beys was a bookseller and the brother of the poet Charles Beys, Georges Pinel was a writing master, and Catherine des Urlis was an actress who had appeared the year before at the Hôtel de Bourgogne. Germain Clérin, who may have been related to Mlle Clérin of the Théâtre du Marais, went on to have a substantial career as a provincial actor, and Madeleine Malingre remains a mystery.

The contract includes the following clauses: (1) that no one is to leave the troupe without giving four months' notice nor is the troupe to dismiss anyone without four months' notice; (2) that new plays will be cast by their authors and no one will complain about the role he or she is given; that published plays, if the author is not available to cast them, will be cast by a plurality of votes by the troupe itself, except for the heroes, to be played alternately by Clérin, Poquelin, and Joseph Béjart, and without prejudice for the prerogative accorded to Madeleine Béjart to choose any role she likes; (3) that all things concerning their theatre and its business, the troupe will decide by a plurality of votes; (4) that those who leave the troupe amicably after four months notice will take with them their shares of all the common property that has been accumulated from the day they entered until the day of their withdrawal; (5) that those who leave the troupe because they "want things the troupe does not want," or those whom the troupe is obliged to dismiss for irresponsibility, cannot claim any share of the common property; (6) that those who leave the troupe and "maliciously" refuse to abide by the present articles may be obliged to pay damages; and (7) that anyone who withdraws before the troupe begins to perform will have to pay the others the sum of 3,000 *livres*. All agreed that their property – not that most of them had any – was pledged as security.[11]

The signatures of the ten, several of them minors who had agreed to "oblige themselves as if they were majors," were witnessed by Marie

Hervé, mother of the Béjarts, Françoise Lesguillon, the mother of Catherine des Urlis, and André Mareschal, a playwright and librarian of the king's brother, Gaston d'Orléans. The troupe's connection with Gaston, who was to become its patron, was then in some measure in place from the beginning. Perhaps it was in anticipation of Gaston's patronage that the actors called themselves the Illustre Théâtre.

The troupe has been variously described. According to Grimarest, who devises a scenario that still sounds familiar to a modern American, a group of young people got together and began to act plays for their own amusement and that of their friends. But then these children of the bourgeoisie made the error of trying to profit from their performances.[12] La Grange and Vivot tell a similar tale, though promoting the band of bourgeois to *enfants de famille*, young people who had been, as the French say, "born."[13] Both biographers seem to be trying to expunge from the life of young Poquelin the dread stain of professionalism. In republican Rome only the gentleman amateurs who performed the Atellan farces could show themselves on a stage without risking the loss of their citizenship. In seventeenth-century France as well, professional actors still risked civil infamy.

Whatever the efforts of La Grange or Grimarest to disguise it, the truth is that the actors of the Illustre Théâtre were planning a thoroughly professional operation. The company members were mostly young and mostly inexperienced and more than a little presumptuous, but their intention was to found a theatre that could compete successfully with the Hôtel de Bourgogne and the Théâtre du Marais.

The first order of business was to find a performance space. This should have been simple, since tennis courts stood empty all over Paris, and all actors knew that a tennis court could be readily converted into a theatre. However, it was more than two months before a lease was signed, and then the location of the property was far from ideal. The theatre audience in the early 1640s lived near the Louvre and the Palais-Royal, close to the Hôtel de Bourgogne, or in the Marais, in easy reach of the theatre on the rue Vieille-du-Temple. The Illustre Théâtre was forced to settle for the Jeu de paume des Mestayers located in the suburb of St-Germain-des-près on the left bank near the present site of the Institut de France. Although easily reached by the Pont-Neuf, it was not in a district where fashionable Paris was accustomed to take its pleasures.

The terms of the lease were exacting. The actors rented the property for three years from Noel Galloys, a tennis master, and his co-owners. What they got was part of a house and a covered tennis court fronting on the *fossé*, or moat, and the city wall. The lease was to go into effect "on the day the lessees bring lumber into the tennis court to construct their stage, galleries and boxes."[14] During the span of the lease the actors could do as they pleased with the building, inside and out, as long as they did not inconvenience the neighbors, but at lease's end they were obliged to return it to its original state, ready for a game of tennis.

The proprietor, who would go on living on the third floor of the house, made sure he had access to the well and the conveniences, located "beyond the court" on property belonging to a neighboring wheel-wright. He reserved the rear cellar for his own use to store his wood and wine. It was part of the bargain that the actors would furnish the place with "*biens meubles exploictables*," that is, movable property that could be sold in case the rent was not paid. The actors were also required to make any necessary minor repairs and pay the poor tax and the taxes exacted for cleaning and lighting the streets. The rent was 1,900 *livres*, payable in advance at the rate of 158 *livres*, 6 *sous*, 8 *deniers* a month. The actors put up their personal property, present and future, as security, but since their combined worth would not have paid a year's rent, this was found insufficient. To the rescue came Marie Hervé, who pledged her house on the rue de la Perle and other property as further security.[15] The Illustre Théâtre got no bargain from M. Galloys.

A tennis court provided a shell inside which a stage, boxes, and galleries could be erected. The Théâtre du Marais was the prime example of a tennis court become a theatre, but actors with experience in the provinces had also played in tennis courts throughout the kingdom. The advantages were a high roof with openings between the walls and roof that let in light and air and a gallery already in place along one side. The disadvantage was the basic shape of the thing, a narrow rectangle. With the stage in place at one end, sightlines from the side boxes were wholly inadequate. This doubtless encouraged the inclination of some upper-class audience members to think of the theatre as a place to see each other rather than the play.

The use of tennis courts created an odd financial arrangement in France, unlike anything practiced elsewhere in Europe Although actors rarely owned the buildings in which they played, they often did own the interior fittings: the stage itself, its scenes and machines, the boxes and galleries, the chandeliers, and so forth. When a troupe moved house it took all this along with it, leaving behind only an exterior shell. Each actor who had contributed to the original construction had a share in the common property and was paid back when he or she left the troupe, provided the formalities had been observed. Actors who joined later and had not contributed to the original construction were required to buy in. Thus, a share in a theatrical troupe was a capital asset as well as a source of daily income, and in certain cases an asset that increased in value as the troupe prospered. The actors of the Illustre Théâtre could thus hope that their investments would eventually be profitable, but first they had to get their theatre open.

A week after signing the lease with Galloys, the actors hired Claude Michault, a carpenter, and Jean Duplessis, a cabinet maker, to build their stage and boxes for the sum of 2,400 livres, payment to begin when the theatre opened for business. The company then departed for Rouen to play at the October fair.

The news reached them there in late October that nothing had been done; there was no stage, no boxes, and the tennis balls were still thudding against the walls. A court order issued in Rouen on November 3 demanding that Galloys, Michault, and Duplessis live up to their contracts or face damages did not solve the problem that seems to have arisen because of the unwillingness of Michault and Duplessis to spend their own money buying the lumber needed for the construction. Work only began after the actors returned to Paris and agreed to be responsible for whatever Michault and Duplessis might owe the lumber dealer, François Amlard.

In the meantime, before its departure for Rouen the troupe added another actor, Catherine Bourgeois, the daughter of Robert Bourgeois, a bourgeois of Paris. This triply bourgeois young woman was as inexperienced as her new colleagues, but went on to have a long career as a provincial actress, ending by playing queen mothers in a troupe led by her former fellow of the Illustre Théâtre Germain Clérin.

The actors also hired four musicians, Claude Godart, Michel Tisse, Adrien Lefebvre, and Laurent Gaburet, for a *livre* each per day, whether there was a performance or not, a total charge on the troupe of 28 *livres* a week. The musicians were permitted to take other work, but only if the Illustre Théâtre had no need of them. They were to be available not only for performances in the theatre but for "visits," that is, command performances in the mansions of the high nobility, and for rehearsals of the ballets. Evidently, dance was to play an important role in the offerings of the Illustre Théâtre. The contract with the musicians was arranged – in the absence of the actors – by Méderic de Gibrat, sieur d'Aulmont, who lived on the rue Couture-Ste-Catherine in the Marais and who was generous enough to guarantee payment to the musicians "in his own and private name."[16] Unfortunately, nothing else is known of this altruistic gentleman.

A final problem arose before the Illustre Théâtre could open for business, a not uncommon problem in the Paris of its day: mud. The troupe might be responsible for paying the "mud tax," but this was no real defense against the terrible Paris *crotte*, a gummy mixture of dirt, trash, and animal dung that even gave rise to a minor profession, that of *crotteur*, who was available in certain public places to brush the dried mud off of fashionable Parisian shoes and skirts.

The Illustre Théâtre was within four days of opening when the actors hired Léonard Aubrey to pave an area twenty feet by seventy-five feet in front of the theatre so the carriages of their audience members could safely and easily draw up to the door. It was late December in a city that enjoys few winter days without rain, and the company had to face the fact that their theatre could be approached only through a sea of mud. The expense was unanticipated and unwelcome, although Aubrey assured them he would use as much of the old paving as he could. Unlike many of the tradesmen and merchants the actors dealt with, Aubrey was a good fellow. He agreed to work continuously, weather permitting, and get the job done by Thursday, December 31, in time for an opening on New Year's Day. He also deferred payment without asking for security. Possibly Aubrey was connected somehow to the Béjarts, a friend or even a distant relation. In any case, some years later his son Jean-Baptiste Aubrey would marry Geneviève Béjart.[17]

By the time they hired Aubrey to pave their entryway, the actors had moved into the house next to their theatre, all eleven of them with Marie Hervé, her son Louis Béjart, and the infant Armande crammed into two or three rooms. No doubt they were rehearsing furiously, barely stopping to eat or sleep. The play they had chosen for the debut was *Alcidiane*, a tragi-comedy by Nicolas Desfontaines, the actor-playwright last encountered in the troupe of Dufresne in Lyon a year earlier.

Alcidiane ou les quatre rivaux was based on a *"harangue"* written by an Italian author, Giovanni Batista Manzini. Its central character, the princess Alcidiane, was undoubtedly played by Madeleine, while her three lovers, Périmène, Hermodante, and Philiste provided roles for Clérin, Béjart, and Poquelin. None of the three "heroes" would have wanted to play Thersandre, the foreign prince, whose men, disguised as moors, "pretend to want to kidnap the princess" so that Thersandre can appear and chase the kidnappers away. Thersandre is revealed to be a thorough villain later in the play when, in disguise himself, he tries to stab

Alcidiane. At this, Périmène faints, Hermodante turns away the blow, and Philiste pursues Thersandre and kills him. Oddly enough, after the three lovers plead their cases before the king, it is Périmène who receives the hand of the princess. According to the first historians of the French theatre, Claude and François Parfaict, "Everyone was happy" at this ending "except the spectators, who must have been furiously bored by the long speeches of Alcidiane's lovers."[18] No documents survive that describe the setting or costumes on view opening night, but no doubt they were as grand as the troupe's rapidly disappearing capital would allow.

According to Le Boulanger de Chalussay, the Illustre Théâtre was a failure from the start, a troupe of stuttering, one-eyed cripples starring a red-head with body odor. At its opening the actors aroused nothing but inappropriate laughter; in the days following no one came but their relatives who got in free.[19] La Grange and Vivot, more generously, agree that the theatre did not succeed, but point out that such is the fate of many new enterprises. Grimarest, the snob, assures his readers that the company's failure was caused by the other actors not wanting to follow the lead of "Molière . . . who had discernment and saw things more clearly than those who had been brought up with less cultivation than he."[20]

In fact, although the Illustre Théâtre finally failed, it was not necessarily a disaster from the beginning. It did survive for nearly eighteen months and it introduced to Paris works by several well-known playwrights. No doubt the "official" actors of the Hôtel de Bourgogne and the Théâtre du Marais sneered at the left-bank amateurs, but Tallemant's report that, although he had not seen her play it himself, he had heard that the role of Epicharis in Tristan's *La Mort de Sénèque* was Madeleine's masterpiece indicates a positive response to some of the Illustre Théâtre's work.

The troupe even had a piece of good luck two weeks after its debut. The Théâtre du Marais burned to the ground and did not reopen until September. During that time the Illustre Théâtre, while hardly living up to its name and increasingly behind in meeting its obligations, showed no signs of extreme distress. Only in September of 1644 did the actors begin the series of borrowings that would lead to their downfall.

In the meantime, the work went on. From the little known of the company's repertory, it seems as if the actors had no interest in comedy. Tragedy dominated the French theatre, so they introduced Magnon's

Artaxerxès, Du Ryer's *Scévole,* and Tristan L'Hermite's *La Mort de Crispe* and *La Mort de Sénèque,* all with subjects drawn from classical history. The troupe was doing its best to appeal to what it assumed the audience wanted; between 1643 and 1648, seventeen of the thirty-two tragedies written in Paris were based on Roman history.[21] These plays were, however, according to French literary historian Antoine Adam, too faithful to the old tragic tradition. Their heroes were victims, their dialogue was full of maxims and sententious reflections. Audiences were getting tired of the long monologues and the asides and all the other conventional elements of traditional tragedy.[22]

Beyond this, however, part of the problem for the Illustre Théâtre may have been that the company, whatever its basic talents, had chosen material outside of its range. Madeleine was a fine actress in tragedy, but her brother Joseph, now calling himself the sieur de la Broderie, was learning that a stutter was an obstacle to a career playing tragic heroes. In April 1644 his mother found a doctor Alexandre Sorin of the medical faculty of Angers who promised to cure him in twenty to twenty-four days for 200 *livres,* to be paid, thank heavens, only after the cure took effect.[23] Apparently it did not since Joseph, although he acted again with his sister and Molière in later years, seems to have left the Illustre Théâtre before June 1644.

Nothing is known of the heroic potential of Germain Clérin, the second of the three actors with a lock on the leading roles, but contemporary critics and apologists all agree that Jean-Baptiste Poquelin was not a good tragic actor. Tallemant says of him, probably in the late 1650s: "not a marvelous actor, except in ridiculous roles."[24] Grimarest has a long discussion of his early struggles: "in the beginning . . . he appeared to many to be a bad actor; perhaps because of the little hiccup or vocal tic he had, that at first made his acting seem disagreeable . . . When he first went on the stage he recognized that he spoke too quickly and that this made his acting disagreeable. And the efforts that he made to slow down his speech caused the vocal tic that stayed with him all his life . . . It is true that Molière was only good in comedy; he could not play serious roles, and several people have assured me that he failed so badly the first time he appeared on the stage that he was not allowed to finish his scene."[25]

He was also not well-suited physically to heroic roles. Of medium height, he apparently had rather bowed legs, hunched shoulders, and a short neck. Montfleury the younger described him as looking exactly like a hero of romance fiction stiffly depicted on a tapestry:

He enters . . . nose in the air,
Feet in parentheses, shoulder in the lead,
His wig, that swings from side to side as he walks,
Is more covered with laurel leaves than a spiced ham.
Hands at his sides, with a negligent air,
His head down like an overloaded mule,
His eyes rolling, he speaks his lines.
With that eternal little "uh" separating his words.[26]

The best-known physical description of Molière is attributed to an actress, Mlle Poisson, Angélique Du Croisy, who had performed in *Psyché*, was fifteen when Molière died, and seventy-six when the description was published in the *Memoirs* of La Serre: "Molière was neither too fat nor too thin; he was more tall than short, he had a noble bearing and a handsome leg; he walked slowly, gravely, with a very serious air. His nose was large, as was his mouth; he had thick lips, a dark complexion, heavy black brows, the various movements of which made his expression very comical . . . Nature . . . had refused him those external gifts so necessary to the stage, especially for tragic roles."[27]

Portraits of Molière, of which there are many, show a dark man with full lips and rather bulging eyes. He is by no means unattractive and in several of the portraits by Mignard done in the 1650s, he is positively good looking. Georges Mongrédien believes that his failure in tragedy was partly the result of his refusal to act it in the classical style, preferring a more natural delivery. This may be worth considering when we think of the mature actor and author of *L'Impromptu de Versailles*, but young Jean-Baptiste, struggling with the twelve-syllable Alexandrine couplet, was probably not concerned to develop a theoretical point of view about acting tragedy.

Sometime during its first six months (the logical time would be after the Easter recess) the Illustre Théâtre accepted a new actor – and playwright – into the troupe. He was Nicolas Desfontaines who wrote for them, in addition to *Alcidiane, Perside ou la suite de Ibrahim Bassa, Saint Alexis ou l'Illustre Olympie*, and *L'Illustre Comédien ou le Martyre de Saint Genest. Perside* and *Saint Alexis* were produced in the spring of 1644, *Saint Genest* in the spring of 1645.

At the end of June 1644 the troupe signed a contract with Daniel Mallet, a dancer from Rouen, to perform in plays and ballets. He was to receive thirty-five *sous* a day whether the troupe performed or not and five *sous* more on performance days. The actors of the Illustre Théâtre were always extraordinarily generous to their hirelings.[28]

The contract is of interest because for the first time Jean-Baptiste Poquelin adds to his signature the name "Molière." Several generations of biographers and critics have carefully explained to their readers that young Poquelin took an alias in order to spare his father the shame of seeing the family name in lights, as it were. In fact, with very few exceptions (and the Béjarts were an exception) all seventeenth-century French actors took stage names, as have many actors since. With actors it always pays to be suspicious of both names and dates of birth. "Molière" is, like most stage names of the day, geographical; several French villages employ the name. Because it is geographical it goes naturally with the particule "de," meant to suggest nobility and ownership of property, as in "sieur de Molière." It is euphonious, as Poquelin is not, and it is distinctive. Other members of the company were also adopting new names. Bonnenfant was calling himself sieur de Croisac, Germain Clérin sieur de Vallabé, and Georges Pinel sieur de La Couture.

The troupe may soon have regretted its generosity to its new dancer. On September 9, 1644, the Illustre Théâtre had to borrow 1,100 *livres* from a money lender for the rent due before September 15, and in order to pay Du Ryer, Tristan L'Hermite, and others for their plays. Marie Hervé once again put up her already heavily mortgaged property as security.

The only bright spot was that the troupe now referred to itself as under the protection of His Royal Highness Gaston d'Orléans, brother of the late king,[29] the result of intervention perhaps by Tristan L'Hermite, perhaps by the comte de Modène. Gaston was more than usually embarrassed financially in 1644, largely because he was an addicted gambler. His household accounts for that year show that he was able to pay only 228,612 *livres* of the 308,820 he owed. Tristan, supposedly pensioned by him, wrote pointedly that he – and all of France – was astonished that this "great and well-born soul" did not meet his obligation as a patron.[30] Small wonder that the actors of the foundering Illustre Théâtre also received nothing.

The troupe had problems other than financial ones. The *curé* of their parish church of St-Sulpice, M. Olier, was a leading member of the Compagnie du Saint-Sacrement, that organization of the rabidly devout that was to torment Molière for years. Olier attacked the young company relentlessly, finally forbidding his parishioners to attend their theatre on pain of excommunication and damnation. The actors gave up on the Left Bank. Flinging what few shreds of caution remained to the winds, the Illustre Théâtre rented a new performance space on the Right Bank in the old Marais. Noel Galloys agreed to their abandoning their lease of the Jeu de paume des Mestayers provided the rent was paid to date and the place left in perfect condition and ready for playing tennis. Until Galloys was satisfied, however, the furnishings of the theatre were to be held as security. Without cash, the troupe was power-less to carry out its plans.

The cash came from an unlikely source. On December 17 the actors borrowed 2,000 *livres* from François Pommier, their porter. He was per-fectly situated to make sure that the terms of the loan were carried out, namely, that all the revenues of the theatre, once expenses were paid, would pass into the hands of M. Pommier, among whose responsibilities was keeping the box office. The actors were required to enter into yet another *"accord."* Jean-Baptiste Poquelin, Germain Clérin, Nicolas Desfontaines, Denis Beys, Georges Pinel, Madeleine Béjart, Madeleine Malingre, Catherine Bourgeois, and Geneviève Béjart agreed in the presence of their notary that all the income they received from acting would be used to pay the troupe's debts. They would live on dreams and air, as actors are meant to do.

The actors had put up all their possessions, personal and professional, as security, but M. Pommier knew how much that was worth, so he required each actor to have a guarantor, someone who would give him 120 *livres* if the loan had not been paid back by *"mi-caresme,"* i.e., midway through Lent. Marie Hervé guaranteed the loan for her two daughters and Jean-Baptiste Poquelin with a contract for 500 *livres* for the sale of her husband's office.

Pommier did not risk his own money. Using as security his contract with the troupe, he borrowed 1,800 *livres* from moneylender Louis Baulot, the same man who had loaned the actors their rent money in September. They still owed Baulot 600 *livres* which were, according to the new loan agreement, to be paid back with money received from private performances. The regular box-office was Pommier's.[31]

The desperation is only too clear, but these actors – backed by the indomitable Marie Hervé, the most supportive stage mother in history – were determined to continue. Unfortunately, their tenacity was matched only by their naiveté.

A space for the new theatre was rented on December 19, 1644: the Jeu de paume de la Croix Noire, running between the quai des Ormes and the rue des Barrés directly south of St-Paul and much closer to the potential theatre audience living in the Marais. The terms of the lease were similar to the terms of the lease they had abandoned, although even less favorable since the living quarters consisted only of a kitchen and room above, and the tennis master, François Cocuel, reserved the right of entry into the kitchen at any time in order to use the basement stairs. Cocuel was not the owner of the premises, but merely the lessee. He paid an annual rent of 1,500 *livres*, but he was charging his subtenants 2,400, 200 a month, payable in advance. If the rent was not paid, Cocuel could put them out "without any formality of justice." The actors once again pledged all their property, including their stage, their boxes, and their theatrical paraphernalia and once again Marie Hervé pledged hers. Finally, Cocuel claimed a free box of eight or ten seats whenever he wanted to see a play, while another – the grilled box next to the stage – was to be available for the owner of the property, M. Parade.

André Girault, a carpenter, was hired to demolish the stage, boxes and other fittings in the old theatre, move them to the Right Bank, and reconstruct them in the new space. He was instructed to remount the stage and make thereon the same number of boxes as in the Mestayers, divided and with seats "as they are at present." In the house, however, the actors called for a new arrangement: two rows of boxes like those in the new Théâtre du Marais. The Marais had been rebuilt with facilities more in keeping with the audience it wanted to attract, and the other Paris theatres followed. For the Illustre Théâtre this meant the expense of six new boxes, not only for the wood for their frames but for the blue tapestry with a pattern of yellow *fleurs de lis*, suitable for the troupe of "His Royal Highness," that decorated the boxes and the seats within them. Carpenter Girault and upholsterer Michel Le Normant charged the actors, between them, 720 *livres*.

The theatre was meant to open on January 8; it didn't. But at this point a few more weeks without playing probably made no difference. By the end of March, the wolves were at the door, and the actors had been to the pawnshops. Using his full name and titles, Jean-Baptiste Poquelin, "sieur de Molière, *tapissier* and *valet de chambre du roi*," had borrowed 291 *livres* from Jeanne Levé, a "public merchant," and given in pawn two ribbons, one satin, one not, embroidered in gold.[32] Madeleine had been as well, bearing an armload of costumes and other treasures to Antoinette Simony, a woman with an almost unbearably ironic name. Madeleine got 500 *livres* in return for, among other things, a velvet dress the color of flame, another of cloth of silver with scarlet flowers, a man's suit in black velvet embroidered in blue and red silk, a silk cloak covered with flowers, a bouquet of plumes, and – saddest of all – an oil painting in a black frame of the Magdalen.

Then at the beginning of April 1645 Pommier and Baulot, the creditors, demanded their money. Far from having been paid back by "*mi-caresme*," the two claimed to be still short 2,200 *livres* of the 2,600 owed. In nearly three months the actors had apparently made only 400 *livres* above expenses, less than Molière's Palais-Royal troupe would make in an average day.[33]

Pommier lives on in Harpagon and Tartuffe, the miser and the hypocrite. The most telling document in a long, long series of sentences and acts and evocations is an affidavit of April 5, 1645, sworn before two notaries of Châtelet. In his deposition Pommier insists that the actors had paid him nothing of the 2,000 *livres* they had borrowed, that "on the days they played at the Jeu de paume de la Croix Noire, they made so little they could not even pay their expenses." And furthermore, he deposes, when they gave a private performance, they kept the money for themselves. And then, they fired him from the door, in clear violation of the loan contract, so they could keep the money themselves. And, finally, they owed him his wages of thirty *sous* a day from November 6 to January 26 and for seven other days since. In a previous request he had asked for forty *sous* a day from October 1 and for the thirty *livres* he claimed he had spent on the food and drink he had served to the actors while they were "attending to their common business." Before the notaries, however, he backed off slightly.

The actors had a different tale to tell. The judges did not believe them, but perhaps we should at least try to in order to see what inferences can be drawn. Speaking for the company were Madeleine Béjart, Jean-Baptiste Poquelin, and Germain Clérin. They had borrowed the money from Pommier and only Pommier.[34] They had further arranged with their good friend Pommier – no doubt while their heads were swimming with wine and good fellowship – that he should remain in charge of the money he was lending them and should pay whatever obligations had been or would be incurred. They asked now, reasonably, for an accounting from Pommier. How much of the 2,000 livres had ever actually been paid out? Did Pommier have the receipts? Pommier, of course, testified that he knew nothing of this, that he had not retained the money.

The actors were sentenced to pay back the entire 2,000 *livres*. Then the other creditors emerged. Antoine Girault, the carpenter who had set up the new theatre at the Jeu de paume de la Croix Noire, had not been paid, nor had Antoine Fausser, the candle maker, nor had one Dubourg, who sold linen goods. Mme Levé wasn't satisfied with ownership of those gold-embroidered ribbons; she wanted her 291 *livres* back in cash. But there was no money to pay anybody.

Then the wife of Pommier, one Catherine Gauvin, filed a complaint at Châtelet on July 20, 1645. The lady, seeking only what was owed her husband and herself, had paid a visit to the Jeu de paume de la Croix Noire, where – she deposed – she had been severely mistreated. She accused the actors of "outrages, theft and assault against her person," identifying herself – the porter's wife – as the wife of an officer of the *Menus Plaisirs* of the king.[35] A warrant for the arrest of Molière was issued. The other actors appealed for his release and asked that no action be taken against the person and property of Madeleine. On August 2 sentence was passed, freeing Molière on the condition that he pay Pommier 40 *livres* a week for two months. A guarantee was required.

Why Molière rather than the others? The debts had been contracted by the troupe, all for one and one for all. The usual answer is that by this point Molière had become the unchallenged leader of the troupe, although little in the documentary evidence supports this assertion. A more likely possibility is that Jean-Baptiste, who had had some legal training, had led the troupe in its battle with courts and creditors and thus had become the point man, first to fall to the enemy guns. Besides, most of the creditors undoubtedly knew, must have always known, that the Poquelins had money. Or, of course, perhaps it was Molière, pushed beyond endurance, who had "offered an outrage to the person" of the porter's wife.

Jean Poquelin did not come to the rescue with the guarantee of payment necessary to get his son out of prison. The unlikely savior was Léonard Aubrey, the future father-in-law of Geneviève Béjart and the paving contractor who had worked day and night for the troupe just before the opening of the Jeu de paume des Mestayers. It was Aubrey who stepped forward with the 320 *livres*.

Gradually some of the debts were paid off. Pommier called in the 120 *livres* from the various guarantors. Cocuel took possession of the stage, the boxes, and all those new blue tapestry covered seats, since the rent on the Jeu de paume de la Croix Noire had, of course, never been paid. Jean Poquelin relented and repaid Léonard Aubrey the 320 *livres* that had saved his son from prison, then added the amount to the running account he kept: "Memoir of what I have disbursed and paid for my eldest son."[36]

No one appears to have profited from the sale of Marie Hervé's house.

It had been mortgaged to its full value before she put it up as security for any of the borrowings of the Illustre Théâtre and was seized to satisfy a judgment against her. The last extant record that reminds us of the rout of the troupe is a receipt dated May 13, 1659, nearly fifteen years later, and signed by Jeanne Levé. Molière finally paid back the pawnbroker.

These were dogged but honorable people, these not so illustrious actors of the Illustre Théâtre. They were talented; most of them continued to make their living in the theatre and some of them became celebrated. They were determined to be competitive. Their plays came from successful playwrights of the second rank. Corneille did not give them a new play, but they could hardly have expected him to do so. Their theatres were as well equipped and as luxurious as they could manage. At least some of their costumes were magnificent and so, we must assume, were some of their settings. What went wrong?

Professional inexperience and financial gullibility certainly account for part of the shipwreck, but one other shoal is worth considering. The Illustre Théâtre had a star, Madeleine Béjart, who was best in tragedy and maybe even a great tragic actress. But tragedies in the early 1640s were not written to feature women.[37] Following the lead of Corneille, and hoping to match the success of his *Horace, Cinna*, and *Polyeucte*, playwrights turned to Roman history, sacred and secular. The known repertory of the Illustre Théâtre tells the story; almost every play has a male title character: Artaxerxès, Scévole, Chrispe, Sénèque, Saint Alexis, Saint Genest. But the company had no male star, no one to compete with Montfleury or Floridor. What it had was a man who stuttered and a man who was comic to his very soul.

There is something faintly uninformed and self-righteous about our myth of the Illustre Théâtre, that bunch of amateur bumblers, the laughing stock of Paris, and its survivors who quite rightly betook themselves to the provinces for thirteen years and learned their trade – as they should have done in the first place. Talent, however, is not the result of learning one's trade but the reason to learn it. Jean-Baptiste's talent may have been buried beneath the breastplates and plumes of the tragic heroes he was unsuited to play, but it was there. He knew it was there, and perhaps even then he knew it was a comic talent. He just did not want it to be. The only theatre that mattered in 1645, to Jean-Baptiste Poquelin and to everyone else, was the theatre of tragedy. Comedy at its best was an inferior genre, and in the early 1640s it was not at its best. The few comedies written were imitations of Italian neo-Plautine learned comedies with romanesque flourishes or of the Spanish comedies of Lope, Calderon, Rojas Zorilla, and others. In the second half of the decade, Scarron successfully mined this latter source, creating a number of vehicles for the actor Jodelet. By that time, however, Madeleine and Jean-Baptiste had left Paris.

CHAPTER FOUR

Exile

The actors' road out of Paris ran south and west, first to Brittany, then to Bordeaux. When the new season began after Easter of 1646, the two fugitives from justice – Madeleine Béjart, in default of a judgment, and her young lover Jean-Baptiste Poquelin, sieur de Molière, evading rearrest – had joined the troupe of the duc d'Épernon led by Charles Dufresne.[1] André Mareschal, a lawyer, playwright, and witness to the original contract of the Illustre Théâtre, dedicated his *Dictateur romain*, published April 28, 1646, to Épernon. He hopes the duke will accept his offering and that the play will be performed by the duke's company, recently enhanced by the addition of some "illustrious" actors."[2]

Bernard de Nogaret de la Valette et de Fois, duc d'Épernon, was the governor of Guyenne and Gascogne, a vast area that had its capital at Bordeaux. His father was a parvenu who began his climb as a favorite of Henri III. The son married, first, a bastard daughter of Henri IV and, second, a niece of Richelieu. This familial tie did not, however, prevent his participating in one of the many plots against the cardinal, the result of which was exile in England and execution "in effigy." Épernon was rehabilitated after the deaths of Richelieu and Louis XIII and made governor of his native province.

Charles Dufresne, who led the troupe patronized by the duke, was born around 1611, the son of a painter with a royal appointment. As early as 1632, the duc d'Épernon recommended to the city fathers of Bordeaux "the sieur Dufresne and his companion actors." Among those companions when Madeleine Béjart and Molière joined them were his wife, Madeleine de Varannes, his sister, Madeleine Dufresne, her husband, François de La Cour, Pierre Réveillon known as sieur de Chasteauneuf,[3] Jean-Jacques de Belair, and a youngster named René Berthelot. The newcomers – soon to be joined by the rest of the Béjart family who were preparing to leave Paris in early June – would complete the troupe.[4] Since nothing survives of its repertory, we can not even guess at the roles each actor played, but we can surmise that the company had lacked a leading lady. Playwright Jean Magnon, author of the *Artaxerxès* that had been produced by the Illustre Théâtre, dedicated his new play *Josaphat* to Épernon when it was published in 1647. He obviously had hopes that Madeleine would play another of his heroines. In the dedication he thanks the duke for his rescue of Mlle Béjart. "The protection and relief . . . that you have given to the most unhappy and one of the most worthy actresses of France, is not the least action of your life . . . You have taken that unfortunate woman from the precipice where her merit had cast her, and you have restored to the stage one of the most beautiful characters that it has ever borne. She has returned to the stage, my lord, only in the great hope of playing worthily one day her role in that illustrious play in which, under borrowed names, is to be represented a part of your life."[5]

The troupe did not, however, lack a leading man. The large and elaborate theatrical wardrobe of Pierre Réveillon, sieur de Chasteauneuf, indicates his function. His two embroidered silk suits with matching cloaks lined with velvet, his "antique" suits in black with gold and silver embroidery, red with gold embroidery, and green satin with silver lace are clearly examples of the finery expected of a *jeune premier*.[6] The newcomer Molière, whose costumes in any case were in the hands of a Paris money-lender, would not this time have a share in the heroes.

Paul Scarron's celebrated novel, *Le Roman comique*, describes a troupe of itinerant actors in the middle of the seventeenth century.

It was between five and six when a cart entered the market at Le Mans. This cart was drawn by four very skinny oxen, led by a mare whose foal cavorted around the cart like the little mad thing it was. The cart was full of chests, trunks and large rolls of painted cloths piled up like a pyramid. On the top sat a young lady dressed half in the fashion of the city, half in that of the country. A young man, as poor of dress as he was handsome of bearing, walked along side of the cart . . . An old man dressed more normally, although still badly, walked next to him. He carried on his shoulders a bass viol and, because he stooped a little while walking, from a distance he looked like a big tortoise walking on its hind legs . . . A provost's lieutenant . . . named La Rappinière accosted them and asked them with the authority of a magistrate what sort of people they were. The young man . . . said that they were French by birth, actors by profession; that his professional name was Le Destin, that of his old comrade La Rancune, and that of the young lady perched like a hen on the top of their baggage was La Caverne. This bizarre name made several of the locals laugh; at which the young actor added that the name "La Caverne" should not seem any more strange to intelligent men than "La Montagne," "La Valée," "La Rose" or

"L'Épine." The conversation was ended by sounds of blows and curses coming from in front of the cart. It was the servant of the tavern giving warning to the carter that his mare and his oxen were making free with a pile of hay in front of the door . . . And the mistress of the tavern, who loved the theatre more than sermon or vespers, and with a generosity unheard of in the mistress of a tavern, said the carter could let his animals eat their fill.[7]

For many years, partly because Scarron's novel was published beginning in 1651, while Molière was in the provinces, and partly because rags to riches is always a good story, the Moliéristes asserted that *Le Roman comique* was a *roman à clé*, and that Le Destin was Molière and La Caverne Madeleine. But the first piece of documentary evidence extant concerning Dufresne's augmented troupe demonstrates the distance between Scarron's ragtag band, living from hand to mouth, and the respectable and celebrated actors of the duc d'Épernon, who in May of 1646 contracted with three carters to move their many possessions from Nantes to Rennes. The troupe was making its way from Paris to the south via Brittany.

In spite of the labors of many in the archives and parish registers of France, a full chronology of Molière's travels in the provinces has not been achieved. Still, some patterns emerge and some generalizations are possible. The troupe of the duc d'Épernon was at the duke's service first. Épernon had his capital at Bordeaux and his castle at Cadillac on the banks of the Garonne outside of Bordeaux. It was in Agen, however, that he lived in high style with his mistress Nanon de Lartigue. The first surviving record of the presence of Dufresne's company in Agen is dated December 15, 1647; the actors were spending the Christmas and carnival seasons entertaining their patron.

Earlier that same year, in mid-July, the actors accompanied Épernon when he went to Toulouse for the official welcome of the comte d'Aubijoux, *lieutenant général* of the neighboring province of Languedoc. The governor of Languedoc was Gaston d'Orléans, the brother of Louis XIII, but he spent little or no time in his domain, preferring to leave it to the king's lieutenants. The actors entertained Aubijoux on behalf of the town of Toulouse, which rewarded them with a meager 100 *livres*.

On July 27 the troupe accompanied the count to the nearby city of Albi. The "consuls," or aldermen, of Albi promised greater recompense, but had to be reminded by the *intendant* of Languedoc to pay what they owed. From Carcassonne, he wrote on October 9: "Gentlemen, having arrived in this city I found the troupe of actors of Monsieur the duc d'Épernon who told me that your city had asked them to perform plays while Monsieur the comte d'Aubijoux stayed there, the which they did, without anyone having kept the promise that had been made to them which is that they were promised a sum of 600 *livres* and expenses for the transport of all their baggage. This troupe is made up of very honest people and very good actors who merit being recompensed for their trouble."[8] Two weeks later when the troupe arrived at Albi, after a stop in Toulouse, Dufresne, Réveillon, and Berthelot signed a receipt for 500 *livres* paid them by the city, not quite what had been promised, but better than what they got from Toulouse.

The last stop of 1647 was for the holiday and pre-Lenten festivities at Agen. From there, the troupe probably returned to Paris for the annual meeting of the actors at Easter, since Dufresne and his companions are next heard of in April, back in Nantes, where they stayed for several months. This time it was "le sieur Morlière" who represented the troupe before the town "*bureau*." He very humbly requested permission for the actors to mount the stage, but permission was denied. The governor, the duc de La Meilleraye, was ill, and there were to be no performances until news arrived of his convalescence. Evidently the governor got well, because a month later the town called in Dufresne and told him that the next day's performance was to be a benefit for the hospital. This was standard practice, and Dufresne agreed. That same day, May 18, Pierre Réveillon's daughter Isabelle was baptized and the witnesses included Dufresne, Du Parc (Berthelot has adopted his stage name), Madeleine Béjart, and Marie Hervé. The child's godfather was Louis Bouju, president of the Parlement of Brittany, a clear sign that these actors were not considered rogues and vagabonds by the good citizens of Nantes.

In August of 1648 a revolt known as the Fronde broke out against the policies of the Queen Regent, Anne of Austria, and her minister Mazarin. Named for the slingshot with which boys hurled rocks at stray cats, the Fronde hurled its missiles against the tax policies of Mazarin, a man who impoverished France and enriched himself beyond measure. Active opposition to Mazarin arose on August 27, the famous "day of the barricades," when Mathieu Molé, first president of the Paris Parlement, was arrested on the rue St-Honoré in front of the Maison des Singes. Other frondes broke out in other cities, most notably in Normandy, in Provence, and in Guyenne where the duc d'Épernon remained loyal to Mazarin. The final curtain of the Fronde did not fall until the peace of Bordeaux in July 1653.

What this meant for the actors of the troupe of Dufresne was an interruption in their normal pattern of travel. In 1648, they left no trace in

Bordeaux, Cadillac, Agen, Toulouse, or Albi. Bordeaux had risen against Épernon and the actors were not wanted. In fact, the only sign of them is a sad one. On November 1, in Poitiers, southeast of Nantes, the troupe buried Madeleine de Varannes, the wife of its leader.

In March 1649 the actors were at Cadillac and on May 4 they were paid 75 *livres* to perform for the comte du Roure, now *lieutenant général* for Languedoc, during his stay in Toulouse. This occasion was marked by the construction of a stage in the Hôtel de Ville. The actors then moved north, to Vienne and to Poitiers, where they were refused permission to play by the mayor and aldermen. The minutes read: "Monsieur the mayor announced that he had received a letter from the sieur Morliere, actor, who asked permission to come into the city with his companions for a couple of months, that he did not want to answer without conferring. It was enacted that Monsieur the mayor will go with Monsieur the lieutenant general to prevent the said actors from coming into the city, given the misery of the weather and the high price of grains."[9] Turned away by Poitiers, the actors moved to Narbonne, not the first time they had played in Languedoc, but the beginning of a new pattern.

In Narbonne Molière was godfather to a mysterious baby, perhaps belonging to a member of the troupe: "Jean son of Anne." Anne is without a surname and the other parent of the child is unnamed. Molière gave his name and quality as Jean-Baptiste Poquelin, *valet du chambre du roi*. Although he had, in exchange for 630 *livres*, given his father the right to pass the *survivance* of the office on to one of his brothers, there is no evidence that Jean Poquelin did so until 1657. "Jean Poquelin son of Jean Poquelin" succeeded his father on the *Etat des officiers de la maison du roi* in 1637 and continued to be listed until 1648.[10] In any case, Molière continued to style himself "*valet du chambre du roi*" in various Church and legal documents until his death. Actors were, of course, meant to be excommunicates, cut off from the sacraments of the Church. They often admitted to their profession when they were parents of a child being baptized, but not when they were godparents. Then they employed various unlikely qualifications: "*Noble damoiselle* Magdelaine de Varannes," "*honorable homme* Charles du Fresne," "Madeleine Béjart, *fille de noble* Joseph Bejar, *bourgeois de Paris*." A curious paragraph in a biography of Boissat, member of the Academy, and vice-bailiff of Vienne, makes much of the fact that this respectable gentleman entertained Molière, and treated him with honor, even though he was an actor. "He did not anathematize him, as did several others who affected a foolish and insolent severity. He even invited this man, eminent in his art, to dinner. He gave him a sumptuous meal. He did not include him, as an excommunicate, among the impious and scoundrels."[11]

At the baptism of poor Jean, son of Anne, Molière was joined at the font by a new member of the troupe, nineteen-year-old Catherine Leclerc de Rozé, the daughter of actors Claude Leclerc de Rozé and Nicole Ravanne. Raised in Paris by her mother and grandparents after the death of her father, she would soon marry Edme Villequin, sieur de Brie, change her stage name to Mlle de Brie, and eventually become celebrated as an ingenue leading lady. Her husband-to-be, who called himself "sieur de Brie" after his native district, was twenty-three years her senior; he joined the troupe probably in 1650 or 1651. No record has been found of their marriage, but their first child was baptized in Grenoble on August 16, 1652.

The year 1650 also marked the beginning of the Fronde of the Princes, an anti-Mazarin crusade led by some of the highest nobles of France, and especially by the prince de Condé, his brother the prince de Conti, their sister Mme de Longueville, her husband, and the prince de Marcillac, all of whom saw in the Fronde an opportunity to battle the growing power of the centralized monarchy. In January of 1650 they were arrested and imprisoned.

The actors, meanwhile, moved on from Narbonne to Agen, where on February 13, Dufresne appeared at the Hôtel de Ville to tell the council that he and his troupe were there by order of the governor, who had also ordered a stage to be prepared with a comfortably furnished gallery for himself in the *jeu de paume*.[12] In June civil war broke out in Bordeaux and through the southwest. The actors made their way east to Toulouse and from then on played most frequently, although not exclusively, in Languedoc. Their appearance in Agen in February 1650 was probably the last time they played for Épernon, an unpopular governor who resigned in July.

Life was not easy in most of France in 1650–1. Royal demands, fueled by the war with the Hapsburgs, increased exponentially; population and interest rates grew, as did inflation, eating away the savings of the people. The price of salt, taxed by the crown, went from seven to seventeen *livres* the hundred-weight. Tariffs and duties of all kinds rose. Famines and popular uprisings were frequent in both Guyenne and Provence, but Languedoc, well supplied with grain, and with a prosperous merchant class, was often an oasis of calm.

Languedoc extends from the Rhône to the Garonne; Bas

Languedoc is a plain some forty kilometers wide along the Mediterranean, from Montpellier to Narbonne, and probably the most attractive territory in France for a band of itinerant actors. Travel was as easy there in the seventeenth century as anywhere in the country. A post road ran from Pont St-Esprit, where the water coach from Lyon discharged its passengers, to Nîmes, Montpellier, Béziers, Narbonne, Carcassonne, and Toulouse, where one could take another water coach for Bordeaux. Nowhere else in France was there such a prolife-ration of cities so close together. The climate is temperate in the winter, hot and dry in the summer. The one problem for the actors was that they were in the land of the *langue d'oc* where the language spoken was not French.

Another myth must be challenged. Had Dufresne's troupe set up their trestle stage in the village squares as many have supposed, no one in those audiences would have understood a word the actors said. A few plays were written in the *langue d'oc*, but these were obscene farces in the old style, not the sort of thing at all for Dufresne's respectable troupe. The company might, of course, have followed the lead of the Italians and improvised, but it seems unlikely that these actors, most of them Parisians, knew the local language well enough to improvise in it. They were thus restricted to playing for the nobility or in the larger towns and cities with a French-speaking population.

Though the troupe had lost its patron, it was not long in finding another source of support. From October 24, 1650, to January 14, 1651, the États Généraux of Languedoc met at Pézenas and for a substantial part of that time the gentlemen of the États were entertained by the troupe of Dufresne.

Languedoc had certain privileges and freedoms not held by all the provinces of France. It was "distinguished from most of the other prov-inces of the kingdom conquered by force of arms, upon which the prince has the power to levy the taxes that seem good to him, without asking their consent."[13] Languedoc had the right to consent to be taxed and to decide how the royal taxes should be apportioned. For this purpose there met annually a body made up of twenty-three bishops and archbishops representing the twenty-three dioceses of the province, an equal number of noblemen, and sixty-eight members of the Third Estate, two from each episcopal city and one from each of the others. These 114 gentlemen sat for months on end under the leadership of their president-born, the Archbishop of Narbonne. The États did not always meet in the same place. Most often the site was Montpellier, but between

1650 and 1658 the choice fell three times on the small city of Pézenas, a few miles to the northeast of Béziers.

The German travel writer Elie Brackenhoffer describes his journey from Valros to Pézenas as "good road, agreeable weather, pretty countryside planted with olive trees." He dined in Pézenas, which he calls "one of the most beautiful places in all Languedoc; . . . it is almost square, closed off by walls and gates; it has beautiful streets and a rather large number of sumptuous and pretty houses that are marvelous to see. Here and there are beautiful fountains and rather large plazas where the inhabitants walk and divert themselves. The Hôtel de Ville also is magnificent . . . The people are friendly and respect strangers; the women are of a very remarkable beauty; they wear a provocative costume, almost half nude, so that one sees almost completely their shoulders and their naked breasts, which I have not seen anywhere in France but here."[14]

The actors were in Pézenas at the invitation of the gentlemen of the États Généraux who, when not wrangling about the apportionment of their annual "free gift" to the king, required entertainment. The arrival of the king's lieutenant general on October 27 was a special occasion that may have inaugurated the theatrical season. And Molière himself signed a receipt on December 17: "I have received of Monsieur de Penautier [treasurer of Languedoc] the sum of 4000 *livres* granted to the actors by the gentlemen of the estates."[15] This handsome sun suggests that the actors had been in Pézenas since the beginning of the session. They were not staying for the end, however, but traveling on for Christmas and carnival elsewhere, probably in Montpellier.[16]

The actors returned to Paris for Easter 1651. Jean Poquelin had prepared a "Memoir of what I have disbursed and paid for my eldest son to him and on his behalf," and Molière signed a "recognition" on April 4 before notaries agreeing that his father had, indeed, paid out 1,965 *livres* to him and on his account. Perhaps it was during this 1651 Easter visit that Edme Villequin, sieur de Brie, joined the troupe.

The Fronde was bloody and ruinous in the provinces from autumn of 1651 to autumn of 1652, and for several months in 1651 there is no trace of Dufresne and his actors. In January, 1652, however, the burlesque poet and musician Charles Coypeau Dassoucy, a friend of Molière's, wrote to him from somewhere in Languedoc but without any sure indication of where either writer or recipient was to be found. However, clearly they both had been at the États in Carcassone, and Dassoucy begs Molière's pardon for leaving him without saying good-bye. He was snatched away with such haste by the man obliging him with a ride that he barely avoided the wheels while entering the carriage. The obliging traveler was Monsieur "Fresart," possibly M. de Frézals, a councillor of the Parlement of Toulouse, who had been sent to the États on behalf of the Parlement to discuss the frivolous behavior of the États during this difficult period. Among their objectionable activities, according to the Parlement, was that "these gentlemen, more concerned for their diversion than for the relief of the people, in a continual comedy supported and paid for by the blood of the widow and the orphan and the substance of the poor, excite tears and draw forth sighs from the hearts of all the province . . . The expenses of the province would diminish by half if those that are only for private purposes were cut back."[17] Perhaps the Parlement had heard of those 4,000 *livres* paid out the previous year for three months of theatrical diversions.

The next sign of the troupe is August 12, 1652, eight months later, when the first child of M. and Mlle de Brie was baptized in Grenoble. From Grenoble the troupe passed to Lyon where it spent Christmas and carnival.

In February 1653 a new actress was added to the company, the third of "the three great actresses" who would accompany Molière to Paris in another five years. This was Marquise-Thérèse de Gorle, the daughter of a Swiss-Italian charlatan named Jacomo de Gorla, who had been a resident of Lyon from 1635. On February 19, the contract of marriage was signed between Marquise and René Berthelot, sieur Du Parc. The bride brought a dowry of 3,000 *livres*, the groom offered a contribution of 2,000 and promised to "dress and bejewel his wife with good clothing, rings and jewels according to her quality."[18] Molière witnessed the contract, as did Dufresne, Réveillon, and Joseph Béjart, the first certain evidence of his return to the profession. The ceremony of marriage was performed four days later.

At some time during this stay in Lyon, in the spring or summer says the popular wisdom, but more likely for carnival 1653, and before Mlle Du Parc joined them, the company may have produced Pierre Corneille's machine play, *Andromède*, first performed by the actors of the Hôtel de Bourgogne at the Petit-Bourbon in Paris during the chaotic month of January 1650, but before the arrest and imprisonment of the princes and the withdrawal of the king, the regent, and Mazarin from the capital. The music for *Andromède* was composed by Charles Coypeau Dassoucy, and the elaborate and spectacular scenes and machines were designed by Giacomo Torelli, the "magician of Fano," who worked for the French court from 1644 to 1660. The play was published first in August 1650, making it accessible to other troupes for performance, provided the music could be managed. It seems highly probable that if the play were mounted by the troupe of Dufresne, Dassoucy himself would have taken the music in charge. The only evidence for this performance, however, is a copy of the 1651 quarto edition in which someone, Molière himself according to certain scholars, has written next to the character names the names of actors from the troupe.[19] Andromède and Junon are assigned to Madeleine Béjart, Jupiter to Du Parc, Timante and Le Soleil to Joseph Béjart, and Persée to Molière. The other characters are to be played by Geneviève Béjart, now known as Mlle Hervé, Dufresne, de Brie, Mlle de Brie, and Chasteauneuf. Unexpectedly, the celebrated poet and pastry cook Ragueneau, whose daughter would later marry the actor La Grange and play minor roles at the Palais-Royal, is included among the troupe, as are the sieur and Mlle Vauselles, that is, Jean-Baptiste L'Hermite and his wife Marie Courtin, Madeleine's aunt. Two mysterious actresses complete the roster: Mlle Magdelon and Mlle Menou, both playing nymphs. Neither has adopted a proper stage name, suggesting they are company children. Very likely Mlle Magdelon was the seventeen-year-old daughter of the L'Hermites and Mlle Menou the ten-year-old Armande Béjart.

Andromède is no light undertaking. It has nineteen speaking roles, four singing roles, two choruses, eight dancing winds, and as many courtiers and followers as a budget permits. The settings include a vast mountain pierced by a grotto, a public plaza in a capital city surrounded by palaces, a delicious garden with statues and fountains, a storm with lightening and thunder, a giant head of Medusa backed by an agitated sea, a royal palace, and a magnificent temple. Many characters ascend, descend, or cross the sky, and the eight winds perform an aerial ballet.

Andromède is a carnival spectacular and really not a likely candidate for production by a small provincial troupe in the low season of spring and summer. No doubt a simplified version could have been done, but there seems little point in a production lacking dazzle. Corneille himself says that "my principle end here has been to satisfy the eye with the brilliance and diversity of the spectacle," and hopes that an abundance of theatricality will make up for any lack of genius in the text.[20] In any case, whether they produced *Andromède* or not, the troupe of Dufresne moved on from Lyon to Languedoc where they were to find a new patron.

On July 2, 1653, Armand de Bourbon, prince de Conti, then twenty-three years old, left Bordeaux for Cadillac and then Pézenas. For twenty-two months he had ruled Guyenne as head of the insurrectional government, but with the royal troops at the city gates, Conti fled. On July 20 in Pézenas he signed the Peace of Bordeaux, and the Fronde was finally over. Conti was the younger son of the Condé family; his older brother was the Grand Condé and his sister was Mme de Longueville. Conti was a brilliant student, educated at the Collège de Clermont in Paris and at the Sorbonne where he defended a thesis in theology. Deformed by a hunchback, he was marked for the Church, but never took holy orders. In 1653, wisely staying away from the centers of power, he settled with his household at the Grange des Prés at the gates of Pézenas and waited to make sure he had been forgiven by Mazarin.

The Grange des Prés, which Conti had recently inherited from his mother, was a manor house with outbuildings, three garden pavilions, and an expanse of vineyards and gardens behind a wall. It was more a gentleman's farm than a princely estate. When Conti arrived to take possession, the house had been rarely used since 1641 and the prince's secretary, Sarasin, had to borrow furniture from the neighbors to make the place habitable. The garden, on the other hand, was charming in the Italian style. It mingled a kitchen garden and fruit trees of all sorts with fountains and fantasies of topiary and with alleys of cedar and laurel opening onto long vistas of the plain of the Hérault.[21]

Conti had briefly lived the life of a worldly *abbé* in Paris and he was passionately fond of the theatre. Now cut off from the great world and with a fractious mistress on his hands, he was delighted by her suggestion that they find some actors to entertain them. The story is told by Conti's gentleman of the chamber, the abbé Daniel de Cosnac:

As soon as [Mme de Calvimont] was lodged in the Grange, she proposed to send for some actors. As I had the money for the *menus plaisirs* of this prince, he gave me the charge. I learned that the troupe of Molière and Mlle Béjart was in Languedoc; I sent for them to come to the Grange. While this troupe got ready to come following my orders, another arrived at Pézenas; that was the troupe of Cormier. The natural impatience of M. le prince de Conti, and the presents that this latter troupe made to Mme de Calvimont, got them hired. When I tried to explain to M. le prince de Conti that I had engaged Molière on his orders, he answered that he himself had engaged the troupe of Cormier and that it was more proper for me to go back on my word than he on his. However Molière arrived and having asked that he be paid at least what it had cost him to come, I could never obtain it, although justice was on his side; but M. le prince de Conti had found it good to be obstinate on this trifling matter. This bad business vexing me, I resolved to have them perform on the stage in Pézenas and to give them 1,000 *écus* [3,000 *livres*] of my own money rather than break my word. As they were ready to play in the town, M. le prince de Conti, who was put on his mettle by my action and pressed by Sarasin, whom I had interested in my cause, agreed that they should come once to play at the Grange. This troupe did not succeed during its first performance in the opinion of Mme de Calvimont, nor consequently in the opinion of M. le prince de Conti, although, in the judgment of all the rest of the listeners, it infinitely surpassed the troupe of Cormier, both by the excellence of the actors and the magnificence of their costumes. A few days later they played again, and Sarasin, praising them at great length, got M. le prince de Conti to agree that the troupe of Molière should be retained and that of Cormier excluded. Sarasin had supported and helped them in the beginning because of me; but then, having become amorous of Mlle Du Parc, he thought of helping himself. He won over Mme de Calvimont and not only dismissed the troupe of Cormier, but got a pension for that of Molière.[22]

The troupe was no longer the troupe of Dufresne, but now the troupe of Molière and Mlle Béjart or only of Molière. Of course, Cosnac was writing his memoirs after Molière had become celebrated. What Cosnac does not mention is any previous connection or friendship between Molière and the prince de Conti. Indeed, the story he tells makes a previous connection most unlikely. But La Grange and Vivot, in their preface to the 1682 *Oeuvres*, write that "as [Molière] had the advantage of attending all his classes with the late prince de Conti, the liveliness of mind that distinguished him from all the others earned for him the esteem and good graces of the prince who has always honored him with his good-will and protection."[23] In fact, Conti did not "always" honor Molière, but rejected him viciously, as we will see. Furthermore, Conti was nearly eight years younger than Molière, and while such a disparity in ages would not have been unusual in a Clermont classroom, in this case it seems unlikely. Conti did not enter Clermont until 1637, when Molière may have already left, and did not finish until 1644, when Molière was performing with the Illustre Théâtre.

Years later in 1671, when Conti was dead and Molière still living, the abbé de Voisin wrote that it was at the Grange des Prés that Conti and Molière became companions. Conti, he tells us, was not content merely to see the performances of his actors, but enjoyed talking with their leader about the theatre and reading aloud with him the most beautiful passages from plays both ancient and modern.[24] The stagestruck prince had, in fact, performed in a Clermont production in 1641, produced in the new theatre at the Palais-Cardinal.

Tired of Pézenas and Mme de Calvimont, Conti accepted an invitation from the comte d'Aubijoux, the king's lieutenant general in
Languedoc, to visit Montpellier for the opening of the États Généraux.
Conti was received with "all the magnificence possible," with banquets,
balls, and ballets. Plays were performed as well, undoubtedly by Conti's
troupe, both for its patron and in its accustomed role as entertainment
for the États. Conti had been invited for four or five days, but enjoyed
himself so much after the rural solitude of the Grange that he stayed for
two weeks. Unfortunately, without the restraint of his official mistress, he
allowed himself to be seduced by a prostitute and contracted "the hor-
rible disease that spoiled five or six of the best years of his life."[25]

From Montpellier the prince returned to Paris where he completed
his return to grace by giving up his various Church benefices and marrying Mazarin's niece, Mlle de Martinozzi. Among the groom's other
gifts to his seventeen-year-old bride were the bacteria he carried. He
received a dowry of 200,000 *livres* and the governorship of Guyenne and
was named general of the army of Catalonia, where he spent the
summer with his soldiers, not returning to Languedoc until the end of
November 1654.

His actors were still in Montpellier in January 1654. In March, Mlle
Du Parc gave birth to her first child in Lyon, although her presence in
the city where her parents lived does not necessarily imply that the whole
troupe was there. They were, however, definitely in Lyon toward the end
of that year, on the way back to Montpellier to entertain the États and
their patron Conti, there to represent the king, and in need of solace for
the death of his secretary Sarasin.[26]

A printed *livret* or program has survived from the carnival season of
1655 in Montpellier. Entitled "Le Ballet des Incompatibles donné à
Montpellier devant Monseigneur le Prince et Madame la Princesse de
Conti," it has been identified as Molière's earliest work, even though
regarded as of mediocre quality. The *livret* includes, along with names of
characters and dancers, two short *récits*, or sung passages, and several
hundred lines that were neither sung nor spoken but merely printed in
the program so that audience members could identify the characters.
These verses are also, according to Georges Couton, a kind of society
game in which comparisons are made between the dancer and the character he represents.[27] Molière may have written them, but so may
Guilleragues, the prince's new secretary, or one of the gentlemen
dancers, or even the prince himself.

The ballet begins with a song by The Night, followed by the entry of

Discord, danced by La Pierre, a musician and dancing master. Discord establishes the conceit of the ballet, that the characters of each entry will be incompatible, contrasts, or antitheses. Pairings in Part One include the four elements, Fortune and Virtue, an old man and two young men, and two philosophers and three soldiers.

Molière and Joseph Béjart danced a poet and a painter in the sixth entry, which also included Wealth as an alchemist. A single verse introduces all three: "Famous philosophers, who with such pure ardor / Search for the secrets of this vast universe,/ All agree that with our painting, / Our ingenious verses and our divine crucibles, / If there is a void in nature, / It must be in our purses."[28] Part One ends with a charlatan and Simplicity.

Part Two opens with a song by The God of Sleep, a somewhat dangerous conceit in a theatrical event, followed by the entry of Ambition. Ambition is followed by Dissimulation and two drunkards, one of them danced by Joseph Béjart. Molière, on his second entry, danced a "*harangère*," a fishwife, opposite Eloquence. Molière's verse this time is specific, and, if read ironically, may indicate that he had something to do with the text. "I make as fine verses as those I recite,/ And often their style excites me / To give to my muse a glorious employment. / My mind does not follow the rhythm of my steps:/ Far from being incompatible with this Eloquence, / Everything that he has not is what is always mine."[29] They are, thus, complements rather than rivals. The other entries of Part Two featured Wisdom and two lovers, Truth and four courtiers, Sobriety and four Swiss, and a bacchante and a naiad. All these characters were danced by men, a mixture of professionals, members of Conti's household, and representatives of the third estate. Only in the final entry did six women appear with the incompatible God of Silence. None of the women came from Molière's troupe; all were daughters of the Parlement. The verse for the Argencourt sisters proposes a solution to incompatibility: "If we were to take you in hand, poor God of Silence, we would soon teach you to speak."

Whether Molière was the sole author of the program verses or merely a contributor, the verses that refer to him suggest that by this time he had started to write. La Grange gives contradictory information about Molière's first full-length play, *L'Étourdi*. According to the preface to the 1682 edition of Molière's *Oeuvres*, it was first performed in Lyon in 1653;[30] in his *Registre*, however, written closer to the event, La Grange dates the first performance to 1655. The troupe spent the winter and spring of 1655 in Languedoc and the summer in Lyon and Dijon. It seems possible *L'Étourdi* was performed then, although in my opinion it was probably done first for the États Généraux in Montpellier. A date of 1655 is probable because, like Quinault's *L'Amant indiscret, ou le Maître étourdi*, Molière's play was written in imitation of an Italian play by Beltramo entitled *L'Inavvertito overo Scapino disturbato e Mezzetino travagliato*. Quinault's version appeared in Paris in 1654, where Molière could have seen it during an Easter visit. He helps himself freely as well to Tristan L'Hermite's *Le Parasite*, also played in Paris in early 1654.

L'Étourdi, like the piece it imitates, is a written-out version of a *commedia dell'arte* scenario. In form it is accumulative. What plot interest exists is based in audience anticipation of a sequence of tricks played on the old man, the blocking character, by the crafty servant, Mascarille. Each trick is then undercut by the blundering of Mascarille's master, Lélie. The play includes a number of conventional *commedia dell'arte* scenes and lazzi, well-enough managed. It is, as one critic rather scornfully puts it, "still an actor's play."[31] It bristles with stage life at those moments when its author allows two characters and an action to take the stage. Otherwise, it is a practical addition to the repertory of a traveling troupe, a conventional neo-Roman comedy that takes place in a conventional street with houses. It has ten speaking roles and can be done almost anywhere.

Its one eccentricity is the size of the role of Mascarille. The character is on stage for thirty-five of the play's forty-one scenes, and when he is on stage he dominates. Ten years later in *L'Impromptu de Versailles* Molière puts into the sarcastic mouth of his wife a line that deserves to be carefully thought about when relationships within the troupe are considered: "You should write a play that you could act all by yourself."[32] At the worst, *L'Étourdi* suggests a burgeoning ego on the part of its author and his "excited muse"; at the best, a concern that other members of the troupe are not as adept as he at comedy.

Molière left Paris in 1646 in the wake of Madeleine Béjart to become an unexceptional actor in the troupe of Charles Dufresne. Within two years, he was managing some of the troupe's business; within seven years the troupe had become that of Molière and Mlle Béjart; within less than ten years Molière was hob-nobbing with a prince of the blood, dancing in society ballets, and starring in plays he had written. Clearly a number of important developments had occurred. He had discovered that his true talent lay in comedy, although he had not yet given up hope of being recognized as a tragic actor. Several portraits of him painted in the 1650s, including one as Caesar and one as Mars, testify to that.[33] He had discovered the pleasures and no doubt the pains of responsibility and was making use of his education and his past experiences at court. And he had begun to write.

Madeleine, on the other hand, had begun to make money. In February 1655 she loaned 3,200 *livres* to one Antoine Baratier, a royal official of Montélimar, and on April 1 she invested 10,000 *livres* with the États de Languedoc.[34] That Madeleine had accumulated such large sums of money certainly tells us that the troupe had been successful. Conti, unlike some of their earlier patrons, did add them to his household and granted them a subvention of 5,000 *livres* to be drawn not from his private funds but from the funds of the province.[35] From 1650 to 1656 it seems likely that they were in residence for most or all of the session of the États de Languedoc. In 1650 the troupe received 4,000 *livres* for its services; in 1656 their fee was 6,000 *livres*. Away from the États, playing in the cities of the south, the troupe was at the mercy of the city administrators, who set their fees and determined their contributions to the poor tax. In Dijon, for example, in June and July 1655, the councillors set the entrance prices at twenty *sous* for new plays and ten for the others.[36] These were not Paris prices, but judging by Madeleine's prosperity, the actors were living well.

And they were generous. In the summer of 1655 Charles Coypeau Dassoucy, the poet and musician who had apologized to Molière in 1652 for not saying goodbye to him, arrived in Lyon. What charmed him the most was "the meeting with Molière and Messieurs the Béjarts."[37] "A man with a friend is never poor," in the opinion of the poet, who had Molière and all the house of the Béjarts for his. "I was richer and happier than ever," he writes, "for these generous people were not content to help me as a friend. They treated me like a member of the family." Dassoucy remained in Lyon in the company of the actors for three months and then accompanied them on the water coach down the Rhône. The actors were on their way to the États in Pézenas, and had invited Dassoucy to go along. "It's said," he writes, "the best brother is tired of feeding his brother at the end of a month, but these, more generous than all the brothers who have ever been, had me at their table for a whole winter, and I can say:

> That in this sweet company
> Where I fed harmoniously,
> In the midst of seven or eight dishes,
> Exempt from care and embarrassment,
> I sweetly spent my life."[38]

In all Dassoucy was with the troupe for six months, no doubt earning his keep as their musician, and at the end – having received generous gifts from the prince de Conti and Monsieur Guilleracque, president of the Cour des aides in Bordeaux – he took his leave in Narbonne of the actors, "these people, well worthy of representing in reality in the world the characters of princes they represent everyday on the stage."[39]

Dassoucy does not mention the death, early in 1656, of Pierre Réveillon, sieur de Chasteauneuf. He had been widowed in 1653 and was the father of four children. The troupe took responsibility for his estate and for Henry, Bernard, Isabelle, and Catherine. It was Charles Dufresne who packed the actor's costumes in two trunks, converted his money into a letter of credit, and arranged for trunks, letter, and children to be sent to Réveillon's sister in Paris. Nor did the actors forget the children. Seven years later, when thirteen-year-old Catherine was apprenticed to a dressmaker, it was Molière, de Brie, the Du Parcs, Louis Béjart, and several of the other actors of the troupe of the Palais-Royal who paid the fee of 120 *livres*. In 1673, when Catherine was married, Molière, his wife, and the de Bries signed the marriage contract.[40] Réveillon had been an important member of the company and was probably not replaced until Charles Varlet, sieur de La Grange, joined the troupe in Paris in 1659.

The actors had again joined their patron Conti in Pézenas for the meeting of the États Généraux where he represented the royal power. On November 9, 1655 an official delegation of deputies, including three bishops, three barons, and three representatives of the third estate, came to the hotel Alfonce where Conti was lodged to make a formal call. The prince unexpectedly greeted them at the courtyard door and announced that he was forced to meet them there because his room was in a state of extreme disorder. His actors were preparing to perform a play. After an exchange of compliments, the prince led his distinguished visitors to the street door and bade them farewell. The disgruntled dignitaries must have wondered at the prince's priorities.[41]

The actors stopped in Narbonne in late February 1656 on their way to wait for Conti in Bordeaux. The consuls of the town were happy to give them the right to play in the Grande Salle of the Hôtel de Ville. They were in Narbonne for several months and apparently in Bordeaux for much of the rest of the year; a letter from the king's lieutenant in Guyenne recommending the actors of the prince de Conti to the consuls of Agen notes that the troupe has spent some time in Bordeaux. From

Agen the actors went to Béziers for the 1656–7 session of the États. This was to be their last visit.

Returning to Paris from Bordeaux, the prince de Conti fell ill with what Cosnac calls a fever. Very likely the symptoms of syphilis had become increasingly troublesome both to Conti and to his wife. During his illness he was visited by the severe and zealous Papillon, bishop of Aleth, who converted him to godliness and recommended to him a director of conscience, the abbé Ciron. The pleasure-loving prince joined the Compagnie du Saint-Sacrement and repented for his past sins and errors including his love of the theatre. When the États met in Béziers in December 1656 the actors were no longer invited to make themselves at home in Conti's rooms, and a few months later the prince wrote to the abbé Ciron from Lyon: "There are some actors here who used to bear my name; I have had them told to stop it and you can be sure that I have taken care not to go see them."[42] According to Racine, Conti from this time on made war without mercy on the theatre and later, as governor of Languedoc, even forced one troupe to take refuge across the Rhône in Provence.[43]

Back in Béziers in 1656 the deputies were still disgruntled. A complaint was filed stating that "the troupe of actors that is in the city of Béziers distributed several tickets to the deputies of this company so they could enter the theatre without paying in the hope of receiving some gratification."[44] After a deliberation, the assembly of the États told the actors to take back their free tickets and, more importantly, forbade the treasurer either directly or indirectly to grant them any sums of money whatsoever. Conti's converted hand was probably at work, although another possible reason for this change of heart was the presence in the chair, replacing the ailing archbishop of Narbonne, of the bishop of Viviers, one Louys de La Baume de La Suze, who happened to be the brother of the countess of Modène, displaced in her husband's affections by Madeleine Béjart.[45]

Although La Grange in his *Registre* claims that Molière's second full-length play was done for the first time at the États de Languedoc, it seems more likely that it was performed simply for whatever audience cared to pay to see it. *Le Dépit amoureux* is a more complicated play than *L'Étourdi* and much less of a showcase for its author. No single role dominates, and every actor has at least one good scene, even the pedant and the bravo. Like *L'Étourdi*, it has a plot based on Italian models, especially Nicolo Secchi's *L'Interesse*, perhaps by way of D'Ouville's *Aimer sans savoir qui*, written in 1646. It is less dependent on Roman conventions than its predecessor and the women's roles are more important. Although the premises of the story are somewhat incredible and the exposition is definitely awkward, Molière handles a complex plot with considerable finesse. *L'Étourdi* is almost entirely limited to two-character scenes; *Le Dépit amoureux* has scenes with three and even four characters, some of which are good early examples of the rhythmic duets and trios and quartets the playwright later managed so brilliantly. The ending is typically and completely unrealistic, the sort of thing the neoclassical theorists warred against and Molière kept on doing.

Whatever the critics have thought of *L'Étourdi* and *Le Dépit amoureux*, and in general these plays have not been highly regarded since they lack the satire of manners and the philosophical edge prized by the literati, they are workmanlike, reasonably funny, and well-grounded theatrically. They are actable. They are, of course, derivative, but they were written hurriedly by a man who was occupied with co-managing a troupe, rehearsing daily, performing several times a week, and always facing the need to travel on.

After 1656, the actors did not return to Languedoc; they were unwelcome in an area increasingly dominated by the devout party and the Compagnie du Saint-Sacrament. In 1657 they appear to have spent most of the year in Lyon and Dijon. Regardless of what Conti may have told them, they were still calling themselves "the actors of Monseigneur le Prince de Conti." In Dijon the city council set their admission fee at fifteen *sous* for new plays and ten for the others and demanded ninety *livres* in poor tax. When the actors did not pay it, the council forbade them to perform and promised to fine them, break-up their stage, and expel them from the city if they dared to play. The tax was reduced to forty-five *livres*; the actors requested a further reduction since their expenses had been great and their profits small.[46] The council refused. The troupe left for Lyon, whether by choice or by expulsion is not clear. But profits were better in Lyon. A charity performance there on New Year's Eve brought in 271 *livres*.[47]

Chappeauzeau had encountered Molière and the others in Lyon, possibly in 1653. In 1656 he published a book about the city in which he writes: "The noble amusement of honest people, the worthy pleasure of the world of fashion and the wits, the theatre, although not established as in Paris, is none the less played here at all the usual seasons, and by a troupe that, itinerant as it is, is ordinarily just as good as that of the Hôtel [de Bourgogne] that remains in one place."[48]

If, indeed, they were as good as the "great actors" of the Hôtel de Bourgogne, then perhaps it was time to think about Paris. Their usual circuit through Languedoc was closed to them; Lyon was comfortable and welcoming, but not large enough to support them permanently. Their patron had become their mortal enemy, leaving them at the mercy of town councils like that of Dijon. What Molière certainly realized, however, is that provincial troupes could not simply arrive one day in Paris and expect to be welcomed. Actors, like everyone else, lived in a society that was increasingly insitutionalized and centralized. There were already three theatrical troupes playing in Paris, two French and one Italian, and in the minds of many that was probably two too many. Furthermore, without a patron, some great noble of France to lend his name and his prestige, establishment in Paris would not be easy.

In 1658 the actors spent Christmas and carnival in Grenoble. They then went to Paris for the usual Easter gathering. After Easter the troupe did not return to the south. Instead, it went to Rouen, much closer to its final destination. Thomas Corneille wrote from there to the abbé de Pure on May 19: "We are awaiting here the two beauties [Mlle de Brie and Mlle Du Parc] that you believe can compete this winter with [Mlle Baron's] brilliance." He goes on, "I have remarked in Mlle Béjart a great hope to play in Paris, and I have no doubt that when they leave here, the troupe will pass the rest of the year there. I wish that she would make an alliance with the Marais; that could change its destiny."[49]

An alliance may have been what Madeleine had in mind. More likely she hoped to replace the foundering troupe of the Marais. In either case, on July 12 in Rouen Madeleine Béjart signed a sublease of the Théâtre du Marais to begin on September 29, 1658, and end at Easter 1660. The rent was to be 3,000 *livres* a year, payable quarterly. Madeleine gave as her permanent address the house of Monsieur Poquelin under the pillars of the market in Paris.[50] The lease, however, was never taken up.

La Grange and Vivot write of this stay in Rouen: "In 1658, [Molière's] friends advised him to approach Paris by bringing his troupe to a neighboring city: this was the way to profit from the credit that his merit had acquired with several people of consideration, who, interested in his glory, had promised to introduce him at court. He spent the carnival season at Grenoble, which he left after Easter, and established himself at Rouen. He stayed there all summer; and after several trips he made secretly to Paris, he had the benefit of having his services and that of his comrades accepted by Monsieur, the only brother of the king, who,

having granted him protection and given his name to the troupe, presented him in this quality to the king and the queen mother."[51]

As do most of the biographical materials from the period, this account
stresses Molière's role in the troupe's establishment in Paris and ignores
the other members of what was, after all, a small republic. As orator and
spokesman of the company, and as its budding dramatist, Molière was
probably its most prominent and publicly recognized member in the
provincial cities where the troupe had played, and he did have certain
connections at court. Obviously the prince de Conti and his household
would not have sponsored him or any other actors. Gaston d'Orléans,
who had lent his name to the Illustre Théâtre, was patron of another
provincial troupe. The duc d'Épernon was in favor, but rarely in town.
But Daniel de Cosnac had left the prince de Conti to become almoner
in the household of the king's brother, whose former tutor, the philosopher La Mothe Le Vayer also probably knew Molière. Another likely
conduit to the court, however, was via the duc de Guise in whose household the comte de Modène now served as first gentleman of the
chamber. What this suggests – as does Thomas Corneille's letter and the
lease on the Théâtre du Marais – is that it was Madeleine as well as
Molière who finally brought the actors home to Paris.

CHAPTER FIVE

Return to Paris

In October 1658 the young king Louis XIV was in residence in Paris at the Louvre. On the 24th of the month he accepted the invitation of his brother Philippe, duc d'Anjou, to attend a performance in the Salle des Gardes of Corneille's *Nicomède* by a troupe of actors newly arrived from the provinces. The troupe was led by an actress, Mlle Béjart, who had – the king may have remembered – some sort of connection with the disreputable friends of his uncle Gaston d'Orléans and an actor named Molière whose reputation as a *farceur* had reached even Paris. The king knew that he was not supposed to appreciate farce, that it was no longer considered a genre appropriate to the fine French classical theatre, a gift to the nation of the late Cardinal Richelieu. But – like his father before him – when it came to the theatre, this monarch did not have especially elevated tastes. He was too well trained, of course, to show his faint disappointment when the *farceur* arrived on the stage in a conventional "Roman" tunic and plumes and began speaking Corneille's rounded periods with a strange, halting delivery.

Louis was twenty. He had been titular king of France for fifteen years, although the kingdom was governed by his mother, the dowager Anne of Austria (actually a princess of Spain), and her first minister, Cardinal Jules Mazarin (actually an Italian named Giulio Mazarini). France was a newly peaceable kingdom, its rebellious *frondeurs* largely forgiven if not forgotten. The "personal reign," when Louis would declare himself king of France in fact as well as in name, was three years in the future. The matter of greatest concern in the fall of 1658 was when the king would marry.

There was a fad in fashionable Paris mid-century for the *portrait parlant*, the portrait in words, and Louis sat for his to his cousin, the daughter of Gaston d'Orléans, known as La Grande Mademoiselle. This enamored princess wrote on October 7, two weeks before Molière played for his prince for the first time. "The stature of this monarch is as

2. *Louis XIV*, engraving by Poilly from a painting by Mignard

much above that of others as is his birth and his bearing," she begins. We must understand this stature to be figurative not literal, since Louis was a not especially tall man whose red heels were designed to make him appear more imposing. Mademoiselle continues: "His manner is lofty, bold, proud, and agreeable, with something both sweet and majestic in his look; he has the most beautiful hair in the world, both in color and in the way it is dressed. Beautiful legs, beautiful walk, and very agile. Finally, all in all, he is the best looking and the best made man in the kingdom." Louis was also, according to his cousin, an excellent dancer, good horseman and hunter, and a courageous and model warrior. He was not, however, especially outgoing. "At a first meeting, he is cold. He speaks little; but to persons he knows well he speaks well, correctly, and says nothing that is not to the point. He banters very agreeably, has good taste, discerns and judges the best in the world, is naturally good, charitable, liberal, acts like a king and takes no action that is not kingly . . . He has a very good head for business, speaks well in the councils, and in public when he has to." In love with Louis herself, she has little to say about his attraction to women, merely that "he is very suited to be a lover."[1] Portraits of the young Louis show a slender man with abundant black curling hair, dark, almond shaped eyes, well-defined protruding lips, and a swarthy complexion. His expression is unrevealing.

Facing this paragon from the stage was Jean-Baptiste Poquelin, sieur de Molière, home from the provinces after thirteen long years. He was thirty-six to his monarch's twenty, and no longer young. His various portraits done in the late 1650s by Pierre Mignard show that he had lost his early beauty and had become a pleasant-looking man, still healthy, with a great head of black curls, compelling dark eyes, and, indeed, very little neck. Like the king he was serious, too serious, according to the writer of *La Pompe funèbre* of Scarron, to replace that comical gentleman in Paris society.[2] Also like his future patron, he was not voluble. The actor La Grange, who knew him for fifteen years, described him very much as La Grande Mademoiselle described her cousin: "Although he was very agreeable in conversation when the people pleased him, he spoke very little in company, unless he found himself among persons for whom he had particular esteem. This suggested to those who did not know him that he was a melancholy dreamer. But if he spoke little, he spoke well."[3]

Donneau de Visé, writing during the quarrel of *L'École des femmes* in 1663, describes the dreamer seen through the eyes of a lace merchant on the rue St-Denis. Argimont, hearing "Élomire" is in his shop, rushes downstairs to see him and returns disconsolate to his visitor Oriane:

Madame, I am in despair, unable to satisfy you. Since I went down, Élomire has not said a single word. I found him leaning against my shop, in the posture of a man who dreams. He had his eyes fixed on three or four persons of quality who were haggling over the price of my lace; he appeared to be listening to what they said and seemed, by the movement of his eyes, to be looking into the depths of their souls to see there what it was they did not say. I even believe he had a tablet and that under cover of his cloak he wrote down, without being seen, the more remarkable things they said.[4]

This is the same Molière promoted to tourists in Pézenas today: the silent figure sitting in the corner of Gély's barber shop, watching the quaint manners of the provincials and noting them for future use.

Philippe, Louis's brother, known as Monsieur, was eighteen when he displayed his newest acquisition to his mother and brother: this troupe of actors newly arrived from the provinces. The likeliest conduit between Molière and Monsieur was Daniel de Cosnac, former intendant of the prince de Conti and partisan of Molière and his troupe, recently added to Monsieur's household. Undoubtedly Cosnac was there, crossing his fingers in a corner of the Salle des Gardes. Possibly Gaston d'Orléans and his daughter were there, since they had been with the court three weeks before at Fontainebleau. The prince de Condé, later to show himself sympathetic to Molière, was not there; he had not yet made honorable amends for his treasonous behavior during the Fronde. His brother the prince de Conti, who had been forgiven and who had also been at Fontainebleau, was certainly not there. He remained devout and opposed to the pleasure of the theatre. All eyes, of course, were on the king and his family, although the actors may have spared more than one glance for the Royal troupe of the Hôtel de Bourgogne, come to see what sort of rivals these provincials might be.

The Louvre had no theatre. Across the way, at the Palais-Royal, Cardinal Richelieu's magnificent Italian-style theatre was moldering in ruins, its roof collapsed. And a troupe of Italian actors playing their improvised farces had been granted use of the Salle at the Petit-Bourbon, a vast room transformed into a more or less satisfactory Italian-style theatre by Giacomo Torelli, the great Italian designer.[5] The king had to be content with a temporary stage mounted in the room on the ground floor of the Louvre known variously as the Salle des Gardes, the Salle des Cent Suisses, and the Salle des Caryatides.

Originally part of the magnificent Renaissance Louvre built by Pierre Lescot for Henry II, it featured a coffered ceiling with gilded beams and, supporting a musicians gallery, the Tribune des Caryatides by the sculptor Jean Goujon.[6] The room, designed to be used for royal occasions, was inaugurated at the marriage of Mary Stuart and the dauphin on April 19, 1558. Goujon, who had illustrated the first French edition of Vitruvius, took the idea for the caryatids from that Roman architect. The caryatids were, according to Vitruvius, women from the city of Caryu, which had allied itself to Persia. The Greeks razed the city, killed the men and took the women into slavery. These were led in triumph with their arms raised, bearing above them the weight of the injuries their husbands and relations had done. Architects included them in public buildings as examples to posterity of the penalty exacted for treason. Posterity in this case may also have remembered that four ringleaders of the League were hung and strangled in the Salle des Caryatides near the end of the Wars of Religion. The room had also been used for Huguenot services under Henry IV, and then to display his effigy.

After 1610 the room was rebuilt. The wooden beams of the coffered ceiling were bending badly because of the weight from the balls and ballets that took place in the room above. The room was given its present volume and the ceiling vaulted in stone, although the decor had still not been completed at the end of the century. Sauval, who saw it before 1660, says that the room once known as "the Grand Tribunal now serves as the Salle des Gardes to the queen mother's apartments." He adds that the caryatids "are at present hidden behind a stage newly built in that room."[7] Thus, the king and his guests, many of whom had betrayed the monarchy only a few years before, were not reminded of the sad fate of the women of Caryu.

The only description of what happened in the Salle des Gardes on that October Wednesday is offered by La Grange and Vivot in the 1682 preface. Very likely neither was there, but we can assume that La Grange heard the story often enough.

. . . October 24 1658 the troupe appeared for the first time before Their Majesties and all the Court, on a stage that the king had had built in the Salle des Gardes of the old Louvre. *Nicomède*, tragedy by Monsieur de Corneille the elder, was the play chosen for this brilliant debut. These new actors did not displease, and the charm and acting of the women was found especially satisfying by all. The famous actors who gave such a good account of themselves in those days at the Hôtel de Bourgogne were present at this performance. The play finished, M. de Molière came on the stage and after having thanked His Majesty in very modest terms for His goodness in excusing his defects and those of his troupe, that could only tremble before such an august assembly; he said that the hope they had had to have the honor to be able to divert the greatest king in the world had quite made them forget that His Majesty had at his service some excellent originals, of which they were only the very feeble copies; but since His Majesty had been kind enough to suffer their country manners, he begged him very humbly to agree to their giving one of these little *divertissements* that had acquired for him a certain reputation, and with which he had amused the provinces.

This compliment, only the substance of which can be reported here, was so agreeably turned and so favorably received that all the Court applauded it, and applauded even more the little comedy which was that of the *Docteur amoureux*. That comedy, that had only one act, and several others like it have not been printed: he made them from some comic ideas without revising them; and he found it appropriate to suppress them, since he proposed for the purpose of all his plays to oblige men to correct their faults. As it had been a long time since anyone had mentioned little comedies,[8] the invention appeared new, and the one that was performed that day diverted as much as it surprised everyone. M. de Molière played the doctor and the king esteemed him so highly for the way he managed the character that His Majesty gave the order to establish the troupe in Paris. The Salle of the Petit-Bourbon was granted him to perform alternately with the Italian actors. The troupe, of which M. de Molière was the chief, and which . . . took the title of Troupe de Monsieur, began to perform in public November 3, 1658, [actually November 2] and gave as novelties *L'Étourdi* and *Le Dépit amoureux*, which had never been played in Paris.[9]

The troupe in 1658 consisted of ten shareholders: Molière, the four Béjarts (Madeleine, Joseph, Louis, and Geneviève) Catherine de Brie and her husband Edme, sieur de Brie, Marquise Du Parc and her husband René Berthelot, sieur Du Parc, best known by his *farceur* name of Gros René, and the elderly Dufresne. It was a troupe with limitations. It had not replaced Chasteauneuf, the actor who had played the *jeune premier* and hero roles in the troupe of Dufresne from before 1647 until his death in 1657b. It was celebrated for its three beautiful actresses, but it still had no leading tragic actor of substance. Molière and Gros René were fine *farceurs* and Joseph Béjart had developed a comic specialty of hapless lovers – Lélie in *L'Étourdi* and Éraste in *Le Dépit amoureux*[10] – but Louis and Geneviève Béjart and Edme de Brie were only capable of minor roles.

It was also a troupe without its own repertory. During its years in the provinces, it had largely performed plays that had been printed and were thus in the public domain, seasoned with several short farces provided by Molière. Molière, himself, had written only two full-length plays, *L'Étourdi* in 1655 and *Le Dépit amoureux* in 1656. If one believes La Grange and Vivot, it was with these two novelties that the new Troupe de Monsieur made its debut before the Paris audience. In fact, La Grange and Vivot carefully gloss over the initial failure of the troupe to please with a series of tragedies by Corneille. Someone with authority in the company, perhaps Molière himself, still believed that the only theatre to be taken seriously was the tragic theatre. After all, one of the best-known portraits of Molière the actor is Pierre Mignard's image of him as Caesar in *Le mort de Pompée*, probably painted within the year before the troupe's return to Paris. Or perhaps Madeleine, whom Tallemant des Réaux had just described as "the best actress of all," was not yet willing to give herself up to farce and folly. And, after all, none of them knew at this point that Molière would write important comedies and great satires.

Le Boulanger de Chalussay puts a description of the inauspicious public debut of November 2 in the mouth of Élomire:

> We came back [to Paris], sure to do marvels there,
> We had Corneille by heart, all of us.
> And such was already the rumor of my fame
> That we were immediately given the Salle de Bourbon.
> There, with *Héraclius*, we opened a theatre,
> Where I thought all would be charmed and would idolize me.
> But alas, who would have thought it, by a contrary effect,
> For from being charmed, all were dissatisfied;
> I thought this first attempt would show me a master,
> Instead I was afraid to show myself on the stage.
> But I took heart and in my most lofty tones,
> I did the *harangue*, I did my best,
> But I was tempting fate uselessly.
> After *Héraclius*, they booed *Rodogune*;
> The same for *Cinna* and even the charming *Cid*
> Received, with *Pompée*, the same treatment.
> In obvious disgrace, not knowing where to turn,
> I was a thousand times on the point of hanging myself.[11]

Instead of hanging himself, however, the deflated tragedian remembers how he introduced the Paris audience to his own plays that succeeded with all the spectators: the bourgeoisie in the *parterre*, the fine ladies in the boxes, and even the fops on the stage. He recapitulates the high points of *Le Dépit amoureux*: Gros René and Marinette each returning the other's love offering (fifty pins and a piece of cheese), Albert drowning out the pedant with his mule bells, and the lover Éraste played by the stuttering Joseph Béjart.[12]

Instead of what Parisians considered second-rate tragedy, Molière and his actors reintroduced first-rate farce. According to La Grange, who entered the troupe in April 1659 but who summarized the previous season in his *Registre*, "*L'Étourdi* had a great success and produced for each actor seventy pistoles." *Le Dépit amoureux* did as well.[13] Without these two plays by Molière, the first season would not have been profitable. Of course, the troupe had the advantage of playing rent-free, once it had paid the entry fee to the Italian actors of 1,500 *livres* for a half-share in the fittings of the theatre. The Italians had been at the Petit-Bourbon off and on since 1645, so it was well-known to the Paris audience as a public theatre space, even though it was part of the royal palace complex with rather difficult access. The new Troupe of Monsieur had to take the *jours extraordinaires*, that is, Monday, Wednesday, Thursday, and Saturday. According to Chappuzeau, theatres avoided these days because Monday was the day when the coaches for Germany and Italy departed, Wednesday and Saturday were market days, and Thursday was devoted to promenades.[14] On the other hand, three companies played on the *jours ordinaires*, while the Troupe de Monsieur had the undesirable days all to itself. Less than a year later, however, the Italian troupe temporarily disbanded when some of its members returned to Italy, and Molière and his colleagues began to play on Tuesday, Friday, and Sunday in competition with the Hôtel de Bourgogne and the Théâtre du Marais.

If, unfortunately, we have no record of the first season, what exactly was played and how much each performance made at the box office, we fortunately do have such information for the second season of 1659–60 and all succeeding seasons. Among the changes that took place in the troupe in April 1659 was the entry of Charles Varlet, known as the sieur de La Grange, who finally replaced Chasteauneuf as resident *jeune premier*. La Grange may have looked the lover but he had the soul of an accountant, and he kept a personal daily record of what was performed, how much was taken in at the box office, and what the individual share was for each actor. He did this from his entry into the Troupe de Monsieur until 1685. According to La Grange's *Registre* for 1659–60, all of the plays listed as failures by Le Boulanger de Chalussay continued to be performed in the second season, most at least twice. None of them did very good business at the box office, although *Cinna* did reasonably well, especially when combined with *Les Précieuses ridicules*. The most frequently performed full-length plays were *L'Étourdi*, *Le Dépit amoureux*, *Sancho Panse*, *Dom Japhet*, *Dom Bertrand*, and *Le Mort de Crispe* (originally from the repertory of the Illustre Théâtre). Until the opening of Molière's new play *Les Précieuses ridicules* on November 18, no evening yielded as much as 400 *livres*; the most profitable was *L'Heritier ridicule* that brought in 393 *livres* on August 3.

It is significant that the first real success the troupe had was with a new *petite comédie*, that is, a farce. The troupe had decided to reform the repertory and had taken steps to change the composition of the company. The situation was unusual. The troupe at the Théâtre du Marais had failed in 1657 and the theatre had been closed for two years. At one point, of course, Madeleine and Molière had planned to take it over, but had received the offer to play rent-free in a court performance space, an offer that could not be refused. La Roque, who had led the Marais troupe before 1657, then decided to reorganize and reopen after the Easter break of 1659; he lured the Du Parc couple away from the Troupe de Monsieur, perhaps because Marquise was not happy with the decision to increase the emphasis on comedy. Like Madeleine, Marquise Du Parc was best in tragedy. At the same time, two actors long associated with the Marais, the famous *farceur* Jodelet and his brother L'Espy, joined Monsieur's company.

Jodelet brought a repertory with him, plays written for him by Scarron and Ouville. The troupe played them during the 1659–60 season, although they did not prove to be especially profitable. They were simply too old, too familiar. The presence of Jodelet was largely symbolic, a sign of things to come, a promise that a lighter repertory could be expected.

Also in April 1659 Dufresne retired and the troupe added La Grange and the Du Croisys. Philbert Gassot, known professionally as sieur Du Croisy, was a provincial actor who proved to be extremely useful. Unfortunately, the same cannot be said for Mlle Du Croisy who was reduced to a half-share in 1662 and who abandoned the stage in 1664. The troupe began the season with twelve actors, lost Joseph Béjart, who died in May, 1659, said farewell to Jodelet who died on Good Friday, 1660, and welcomed the returning Du Parcs.

Although under the aegis of Monsieur, and installed in a royal venue, the troupe during its first seasons saw little of their patron or his brother, and when they occasionally did perform for the royals, the actors gained nothing but glory. The queen and Mazarin were occupied with royal matchmaking, while the king was occupied with Mazarin's niece, the tempting Marie Mancini. In the same month that Molière and his colleagues took the public stage at the Petit-Bourbon, Anne of Austria took her son to Lyon to meet a possible bride, his cousin Marguerite of Savoy. The king of Spain, who wanted Louis for his princess Maria Teresa, announced that the Savoy marriage "cannot be and will not be," and sent his ambassador to Lyon to offer both marriage and peace. The queen was delighted by the marriage, Mazarin by the prospect of finally resolving the war with the Hapsburgs.

The court returned to Paris at the end of January 1659. Monsieur saw a performance of a "comic subject" at the Petit-Bourbon on February 15,[15] while the king saw the company perform on at least five other occasions in April and May. On May 18 Louis ordered especially for himself two farces: *Gros René écolier* and *Le Médecin volant*. He undoubtedly had a splendid time, may even have laughed aloud, but the royal purse stayed firmly closed. The court spent the summer at Fontainebleau, then departed for Bordeaux and Languedoc. Mazarin and his Spanish counterpart met on the border for nearly three months, working out the Peace of the Pyrenees. Louis and his mother visited the provinces of the Midi, arriving on January 18, 1660, in Aix where the prince de Condé made *amende honorable* for his treasonous defection to Spain. On June 9, 1660, the marriage of Louis XIV and Maria Teresa took place in Saint-Jean-de-Luz, in the presence of the whole French court. The discarded Marie Mancini was reduced to bearing the train of Louis's once-hopeful cousin Mademoiselle. Someone had an ironic eye.

The king returned in August 1660 with his new bride to Vincennes, preparing to make their official entry into Paris on August 25, 1660. The troupe of Monsieur played four times at Vincennes for Louis and the court; on August 30 they were called to the Louvre by Monsieur and on September 4 to the Louvre by the king. Again, nothing was offered in the way of remuneration. It was only after the actors lost their theatre in October that the king, who would bring them to play at court six times before the end of the year, including Christmas Day, offered the actors a "*gratification*" of 3,000 *livres*. Monsieur, however, although he had originally promised a "pension" of 300 *livres* a year for each actor, never paid a *sou* to anyone.[16]

Meanwhile, the actors settled in Paris. Molière and the Béjarts – Mme Hervé, Madeleine, Joseph, Louis, Geneviève, and Armande – took a sublease on a house known as the Image St-Germain located on the quai de l'École near the theatre. Joseph Béjart died there on May 25, 1659. He was taken ill during a performance of *L'Étourdi* at the Louvre on May 11, and "finished his role of the Étourdi with difficulty."[17]

When the sublease was up, Marie Hervé leased another house on the quai de l'École, the Maison de la Noble Épine with two buildings separated by a courtyard. The Béjarts and Molière were to have all but the second floor and the upstairs of the front building for 900 *livres* annual rent.

The actors, after thirteen years on the road, owned very little when they arrived in Paris. All of Joseph Béjart's possessions, according to the inventory made after his death, could be kept in two trunks. One contained his theatre costumes, the other his private wardrobe. He owned a saber and two epées, but that was all.[18] Luckily, one member of the troupe had connections in the furniture business. What the actors did to furnish their new apartments was buy and borrow furniture from Jean Poquelin, Molière's brother. When he died in 1660, the actors had to pay up or give back. Molière had borrowed a single bed, three-and-a-half feet wide, with foundation, mattress, featherbed, cover and hangings. He said he would return it. Madeleine had taken 893 *livres* 11 *sous* worth of merchandise and had paid 695 *livres* of the debt at the time Jean Poquelin died. She still owed, both for merchandise and for rental of several pieces, 212 *livres* that she said was actually the debt of her sister Geneviève. The Du Parcs owed 213 *livres* and La Grange 750 *livres*.

Molière's father was still living in the house he owned at the Image St-Christophe, under the pillars of the market. The other children were established in their own lives. Molière's sister Madeleine was married on January 15, 1651, to André Boudet, a *marchand tapissier*. His half-sister Catherine had entered a convent. In September 1654, perhaps as a thirtieth birthday gift, Jean Poquelin ceded his business to his son Jean, both men described as *marchand tapissiers* and *valets de chambre ordinaire du roi*. At the same time, the father leased most of his house to the son, reserving for himself a room in the front and use of the kitchen. In January 1656, just over a year later, Molière's brother Jean married Marie Maillard, whose family included a bureaucrat of the Chambre des comptes and a bishop. The bride brought a dowry of 11,500 *livres*.

Young Jean's star was in the ascendant, his father's was not. Perhaps his business, that had flourished in the war economy of the 1630s, foundered during the Fronde. Nothing tells us how he felt about his son Jean-Baptiste when the latter returned to Paris in 1658. Much has been made of the fact that Madeleine Béjart gave the house of "Monsieur Pocquelin, *tapicier, vallet de chambre du roi*" as her Paris address when she leased the Théâtre du Marais in 1558, the assumption being that this indicates a reconciliation between Molière and his father. Of course, the Monsieur Poquelin in question may just as well have been brother Jean as father Jean, and, in any case, at the time she signed the lease Madeleine was in Rouen where no one knew if she was actually welcome under the pillars of the market. It would be nice to believe that she was and that the Poquelins were present, at least for the opening night at the Petit-Bourbon: father, brother Jean and wife Marie, sister Madeleine and husband André. Molière's father did attend his marriage in 1662, but he also, in July 1664, entitled a memorandum "I have disbursed for Monsr Molière all the articles written here."[19] "Monsr Molière" from a father leaves a bitter taste.

Madeleine did not, in any case, take up residence in what she had declared to be her permanent Paris address. She, with the rest of her family, shared with Molière the house on the quai de L'École. Whether she was still sharing his borrowed bed is not known.

Tradition has it that at some point during the provincial years, Madeleine was replaced in the affections of her Jean-Baptiste by Catherine de Brie and that he also became enamored of Marquise Du Parc who did not, however, respond to his infatuation. Like the smitten Corneille, who wrote a charming poem to Marquise, remarking that time would eventually "wither your roses as it has wrinkled my forehead,"[20] Molière also left a memento in verse of her, but of the most conventional kind. Her "complexion effaces the rose and the lilies of our young Phylis." Her figure is "admirable," she is witty and her features are "embellished with a sparkling grace."[21] Nothing in the poem, apparently written as a lyric for some court performance, suggests any very strong feeling on the part of its author.

Nor, if his first biographer Grimarest is right – which he might or might not be – did Molière have any deep feelings for Catherine de Brie, although he did have a sexual relationship with her. According to Grimarest, she "amused him when he wasn't working." One of his friends, surprised that a man of such delicate tastes would sleep with her, asked why. "Is it for her virtue, her beauty, or her wit you love her? You know that La Barre and Florimont are among her friends; that she is not beautiful, that she's practically a skeleton; and that she has no common sense." "I know all that, Monsieur," answered Molière; "but I am used to her defects; it would be too much to get used to the imperfections of another; I have neither the time nor the patience for it."[22] This Molière is no lover, and what Grimarest suggests may be only too true: that most women would not have wanted to have an affair with him. He was increasingly a very busy man and one with ambivalent feelings toward the women of the troupe.

His great friend Chapelle recognized that someone in Molière's circumstances, living and working intensely with a small group of women, would have difficulty keeping separate personal and professional relationships. Early in the spring of 1659, Chapelle wrote him a letter, one of the few surviving examples of Molière's correspondence. The letter is written both to a playwright besieged by three actresses wanting better roles, represented as Jupiter besieged by three goddesses, and to a man secretly in love faced by a trio of women who are sexually jealous of him.

The spring weather, after a terrible winter, has raised the spirits of Chapelle, who wishes his friend could be there to share the beauty of the countryside. Since that seems not to be possible, Chapelle is sending Molière a copy of some verses he has just written about the green that "carpets the earth" in the spring:

> Young and feeble, it creeps low
> In the bottom of the meadows and has not
> Yet the vigor and the strength
> To penetrate the tender bark
> Of the willow that holds out its arms.
> The branch, loving and flowering,
> Weeping for her new-born charms,
> All sap and tears, begs him,
> And jealous of the grassland,
> In five or six days resolves
> To gain the summit.[23]

Chapelle adds that his friend should share these verses only with "Mademoiselle Menou" since "they symbolize her and you."[24] "Menou" was almost certainly seventeen-year-old Armande Béjart, whom Molière would eventually marry and with whom he was apparently already in love. In any case, Menou was assuredly not Madeleine Béjart, Catherine de Brie, or Marquise Du Parc, for Chapelle goes on to say of his verses:

You will certainly see that it is especially to the point that your women do not see them, both for what they contain and because they are . . . so very bad. I wrote them in response to that place in your letter where you specify the difficulties that your three great actresses give you over the casting of your roles. If I were in Paris we could resolve it together, match your roles to their character, and remedy this strife that causes you so much difficulty. In truth, great man, you must keep your head in order to manage theirs, and I compare you to Jupiter during the Trojan war. The comparison is not odious, and fantasy led me to follow it when it came to me. Just remember the trouble that the master of the gods had during that war . . . to subdue three goddesses to his will.

Chapelle again breaks into rhyme to remind Molière of Homer's tale of that terrible business. He ends:

There's the story. What do you think of it?
Don't you think that a prudent man
Will see from this that it is not easy
To get three women to agree.
Profit from this; above all
Stay neutral and keep Homer in mind,
Tell yourself that man hopes in vain
To be able to accomplish
What a great god could not do.[25]

When not rehearsing, performing, or managing his actresses, Molière was reacquainting himself with Paris. Although he had undoubtedly made a number of trips there during the annual Easter closings, he now had time to notice the changes in the city of his birth. Living on the river, Molière would have been most aware of new construction there. The first of the stone *quais*, the quai de Gesvres, had been completed in 1657. There was a new pont au Change from the Palais to the Châtelet. The pont Royal, burned in 1654 and carried away by a flood in 1656, was being rebuilt, as was the pont Marie, damaged by the flood of 1658. Construction continued on the Île St-Louis and in the Marais, although most of the great seventeenth-century mansions in those fashionable neighborhoods had been completed earlier. At various sites throughout the city, new churches advanced by infinitesimal degrees. However, the years of war and civil strife had not been years devoted to the aggrandizement of Paris which was still in many districts a medieval city, noisy, dirty, crowded, and somewhat dangerous, the city of Boileau's *Satire VI*. It was only in the next decade, the 1660s, that Louis XIV and his minister Colbert, especially Colbert, would begin the transformation of Paris.

The king was not really fond of his capital city; it made him nervous. Twice in the years of the Fronde, he had been forced out of it; once the *frondeurs* had actually invaded his bedroom. Nor was the Louvre a comfortable place for king and court. It was too small and usually under construction, and Louis was almost always to be found somewhere else, at the Tuileries if he was in Paris, or at Fontainebleau or Vincennes or later St-Germain-en-Laye or Versailles. Molière must have seen the irony of it. A troupe of nomadic actors is finally established in a theatre in Paris and finds itself at the beck and call of a nomadic king.

Perhaps, however, the frequent absence of the king was finally an advantage for the troupe that had, in its first years, to make its living by appealing to a Paris audience that was hard to satisfy. Made up of solid bourgeois men in the *parterre*, fashionable women in the boxes, and wits and fops on the stage, this audience finally liked nothing better than the chance to demonstrate its taste and engage in literary controversies. Molière was about to give the audience what it liked best.

His new play, *Les Précieuses ridicules*, was first seen on November 18, 1659, on a double bill with *Cinna*. Although the usual custom of doubling the price of admission to the *parterre* was not followed for the debut of what was, after all, an afterpiece, the profits were substantial: 533 *livres*, the best receipts so far in the season of 1659–60. Strangely enough, Molière's new play was not seen again for two weeks, probably because the troupe was also engaged in presenting a new full-length play, *Pylade et Oreste*, by Coqueteau La Clarière that disappeared from the repertory after the more or less obligatory three performances. This unsuccessful playwright was a protégé of the Corneilles who were contemptuous of Molière's successful farce and unhappy about the treatment their friend's play had received. Thomas Corneille wrote to the abbé de Pure: "Everyone says that they performed his play detestably; and the great number of people they have had at their farce of *les Précieuses*, after having cancelled his play, certainly shows that they are only fit to sustain trifles, and that the strongest play will fail in their hands."[26]

Corneillian pique aside, it is faintly possible that the delay in performing *Les Précieuses* a second time may have resulted from interference. According to the very minor writer Somaize, whose disgraceful plagiarisms make him a far from reliable source of information, a gentleman of quality, habitué of the salons, succeeded in having the play banned for several days.[27] Whether true or not, this anecdote does indicate that the play became a matter of gossip and speculation, precisely what a play needed for success in 1659. From its second performance on December 2, 1659, to the end of the season on March 12, 1660, Cathos and Madelon rejected their bourgeois names and honest suitors, declared their allegiance to Madeleine de Scudéry's romances, and pronounced themselves "furiously for" the pretentious rigmarole of Mascarille and Jodelet some thirty-three times.

Beginning with that second performance on December 2, which followed an old tragedy, Du Ryer's *Alcyonée*, the price of a standing place in the *parterre* was doubled to thirty *sous*. The box office took in 1,400 *livres*, almost triple the previous high.[28] The gazetteer Loret wrote in the *Muze historique* of December 6 that Monsieur's actors were performing a comical subject that "induces endless laughter." He seems a bit put out at having paid thirty *sous*, but admits that he actually laughed ten *pistoles* worth. The troupe finally had a hit, not an enormous hit, but a very satisfactory one that earned for the actors a nice income for the season of nearly 3,000 *livres*.

Except, that tragedy was still what mattered. Thomas Corneille may not have been right about the talents of the Troupe de Monsieur, but he was not alone in his opinion about the difference between a tragedy and a trifle. On December 12, leading into the high season of Christmas and carnival, the company produced another new tragedy, *Zénobie* by Magnon, which did absolutely abominable business for three days and did not even make expenses on the fourth. Only when it was joined by *Les Précieuses* on December 26 did an audience of any size come to see it.

Unlike Molière's earlier short plays, *Les Précieuses ridicules* is not an imitation of a *commedia dell'arte* scenario, although it was criticized for being one, that is, for being a farce, and even accused, in a most odd turnabout, of having been plagiarized from a play written earlier by the abbé de Pure for the Italian actors at the Petit-Bourbon. It was then itself plagiarized by the accuser. This was Molière's first experience of the bizarre literary politics of seventeenth-century Paris.

Very little is actually known of Baudeau de Somaize who made a career for a year or two of riding on Molière's coattails, a *"fripier de Parnasse,"* according to one anonymous pamphleteer, that is, someone who peddles the leavings of his betters.[29] In this case, what was peddled was an attack in the form of a play entitled *Les Véritables Prétieuses*, published January 7, 1660, probably commissioned or promoted by the publisher Ribou, who also tried to bring out a pirated edition of Molière's comedy. In April of the same year, Somaize produced a version of *Les Précieuses ridicules* in doggerel verse, then a *Grand Dictionnaire des prétieuses* that continued to exploit Molière's work.[30] On the grounds, I suppose, that it takes one to know one, this indefatigable plagiarist throughout his publications accused Molière of "pillaging" the work of others, though nowhere so blatantly as in the extraordinary preface of *Les Véritables Prétieuses*.

Molière, says his tormentor, mocks those who ape others without acknowledging that he is the greatest ape of all. He has "copied the *Prétieuses* of Monsieur l'abbé de Pure, played by the Italians, but also he has imitated like an ape – which is all he is capable of – the *Médecin volant* and several other plays of the same Italians, and not only the plays they have performed on their stage, but even their postures, ceaselessly counterfeiting on his stage both Trivelin and Scaramouche, but what can be expected of a man who gathers his glory from the Memoirs of Guillot Gorju, that he has bought from his widow and from which he adapts all his work."[31]

Like all vilification that seeks to be effective, there is a kernel of truth in what Somaize says. Molière had used a *commedia dell'arte* scenario familiar to the Paris audience for at least one of his little farces, *Le Médecin volant*; neither he nor anyone else could or would bother to deny that. The scenarios were not literary property; they were simple plot structures available to be used by clever improvising actors who added their own comic routines. Some elements of *Les Précieuses ridicules* are similar to comic devices used in the *commedia dell'arte*; the disguised valet, for instance, is a commonplace. However, his function in this play, to inflict humiliation on the provincial girls, is not at all a typical *commedia dell'arte* conceit. Also undeniable is the probability that Molière profited from the comic skills of the actors whose theatre he had shared for nearly nine months, especially those of the great comic mime Tiberio Fiorilli, Scaramouche. The other two claims, however, are far less likely. The actor Bertrand Hardouin de Saint-Jacques, who played farce at the Hôtel de Bourgogne as Guillot Gorju, had been dead for ten years. He was the last of the *farceurs* in the royal troupe and a reminder of the rowdy and obscene genre that had been banished from the French stage. Here Somaize is not only suggesting that Molière is a plagiarist, he is warning his readers that the play in question violates decency. In fact, if the doctrines of *bienséance* are strictly applied, the play does violate them, which is, one imagines, part of its point. Somaize could have mentioned, but did not, Jodelet, another famous *farceur*, who appeared in the play under his traditional character name and introduced into it a powerful note of vulgarity.

The accusation that Molière had stolen all or part of the play from an earlier work by the abbé de Pure is perfect fantasy. According to the second version of Somaize's *Dictionnaire des précieuses*, the abbé "gave" the Italian actors a play in 1656 entitled *La Prétieuse*. It was a *succès de scandale* and agitated all of Parisian preciosity until the ladies realized that the abbé was attacking only the "false" *précieuses*. Somaize obviously thought this was his best argument; he returned to it again and again and even passed it on to the gazetteer of *Le Muse royale* who repeated it while carefully attributing it to Somaize.[32]

The abbé de Pure, a prolific minor writer, was responsible for a four-part work that appeared between 1656 and 1658 entitled *La Prétieuse ou le Mystère des ruelles*. It is not a novel, but a "psychological and sociological study of preciosity, its diverse varieties, its conditions of life."[33] If we are to believe Somaize, however, this same abbé de Pure wrote a play with the same title that was not a wise and witty examination of Parisian society but a satire of the behavior of the very women whose cause he had espoused. And he wrote it in Italian.

Not to belabor the point, the abbé de Pure actually included this "play" in his larger work. It seems a young woman, Aurélie, is in love with a rather déclassé writer named Scaratide. Her friends arrange to have her affair imitated on the stage of the Comédie-Italienne. Although furious, she sees the point, but instead of marrying the young gentleman her friends have found for her, she joins the *précieuses* in a form of celibacy. Whether the Italian actors ever performed such a piece seems to me to be extremely doubtful, but in any case, it has nothing to do with Molière's *Les Précieuses ridicules*.

The larger question is what or who was behind this almost instantaneous attack. Unknown hacks like Somaize rarely worked alone, as Molière's further experience will show. It is tempting to think that the actors of the Troupe de Roi, concerned that their own profits might be affected, prompted Somaize to act. And, indeed, they may well have done, as they certainly were to do with other hack writers in years to come. Yet the argument, with its emphasis on apery, suggests the literary world eager to call attention to and reject the work of an actor, indeed, not even an actor but a *farceur*. For as Somaize says in the preface to his verse version, "there is always something good in every profession and to speak as the vulgar do, better to be first in the village than last in the city, better to be a good *farceur* than a bad actor."[34]

At the heart of Somaize's attack on Molière is the question of farce. Molière is not an actor but a *farceur*; he has stolen his play from the Italians, who are also *farceurs* and who play only farce, and from a play written by the abbé de Pure for those Italians and thus also necessarily a farce. Somaize, on the other hand, who writes a *critique*, a play in verse (which thus necessarily is not a farce), and two dictionaries, cannot be accused of plagiarism since he has transformed an example of an illegitimate genre into several legitimate genres.

Molière had to know that the literary establishment would be staggered by *Les Précieuses*. In a period of literary docility, where compliance with genre rules led to fame and the gates of the Académie Française, this "actor" had thumbed his nose at the system. Farce, as everyone knew, had its established bounds. A farce was short, one to three acts. It was written in prose. Its characters were taken from the lower classes: citizens, villagers, and peasants. Its subject matter was domestic, its tone rude and even obscene, its manner of presentation full of rough, physical action. It sought only to amuse, never to teach or correct manners, and that, of course, was why farce was no longer thought appropriate to the modern stage.

In almost every category, *Les Précieuses* is a farce. It is short, in prose, has bourgeois provincials and servants for its central characters, and ends with vulgarity, sexual equivocation, and physical violence. On the other hand, it is a scathing satire of the language and manners of certain upper-class Parisian women and certain members of the literary establishment, wildly entertaining, but with an unmistakable intention to condemn both fashionable literary production and the society that creates and consumes it. It uses the veneer of farce to create the appearance of comic detachment; it permits its author to camouflage his intentions and pretend that he is only making fun of provincial girls and lackeys who violate the natural social order, commonplace objects of mockery who bear no resemblance to the actual inhabitants of the *ruelles*. In his preface, Molière cannot think how anyone could possibly object to the satire in his play. Just as the truly brave and the truly learned take no offense at the *Docteur* or the *Capitan* of the *commedia dell'arte*, so the "true *précieuses* are wrong to be offended when someone makes fun of the *précieuses ridicules*."[35] The satirist wears the mask of the *farceur*.

The only evidence that bears on the manner in which the play was received by its satirical targets was not published until 1693 in the *Menagiana*, a collection of anecdotes about and "sayings" of the abbé Ménage, the model for the pedant Vadius in Molière's much later satire of literary Paris, *Les Femmes savantes*. In this particular anecdote Ménage is made to say:

I was at the first performance of *Les Précieuses ridicules* of Molière, at the Petit-Bourbon. Mlle de Rambouillet was there, Mme de Grignan, all the clientele of the Hôtel de Rambouillet, M. Chapelain and several other acquaintants. The play was performed to general applause, and, as for me, I was so satisfied with it that I saw immediately the effect that it was going to produce. At the exit from the theatre, taking M. Chapelain by the hand: "Monsieur," I said, "we have approved you and I all the nonsense that has just been criticized so ingeniously and with such good sense; but, believe me, if I may quote what St-Rémy said to Clovis, we will have to burn what we have adored and adore what we have burned."[36]

Clovis was the first king of France to be converted to Christianity; Saint Rémy converted him. Ménage may have been converted by Molière, but the anecdote does not say that Chapelain agreed with him, nor the ladies who gathered at the Hôtel de Rambouillet. Nor do we know what the abbé Cotin thought or the abbé de Pure or any of the exquisite or pedantic gentlemen who attended the famous Saturdays of Madeleine de Scudéry – whose novels *Le Grand Cyrus* and *Clélie* are clearly primary sources for the behavior and rhetoric of Molière's Cathos and Madelon.

In fact, the preface Molière wrote for the hasty and unwanted publication of his play in January 1660 calls Ménage's supposed satisfaction into question. Because Ribou had tried to publish a pirated edition of *Les Précieuses*, Molière felt obliged to protect his work and publish it himself, something no theatre troupe wanted to have happen with a play that was still attracting a large audience. In the preface Molière mentions all the things he could and should have done to prepare the play for publication, if he had had time. "I could have taken the precautions that Messieurs the authors, at present my colleagues, are accustomed to take on similar occasions." These precautions would include a dedication to some great lord, a preface expounding the etymology, origins, and definitions of tragedy and comedy, and, of course, verses from friends recommending the play: French verses, Latin verses, "I could even have had myself praised in Greek, everyone knows that a compliment in Greek has marvelous power at the front of a book."[37] This witty dart has every appearance of being aimed at Ménage himself, whom Molière later described as knowing Greek better than any man in France, or at those of his friends to whom he had offered dedicatory verse. Ménage was also a celebrated and determined combatant in the literary wars.

Even if there is no way to identify him or her or them, surely we can assume that Molière had seriously annoyed someone or ones who were hiding behind the unknown figure of Baudeau de Somaize. Not that the "quarrel" of *Les Précieuses* is important by comparison to later quarrels. It does show, however, that Molière was perfectly willing to risk a brawl. He already knew, if he knew anything, that the king would find this play perfectly to His Royal taste. And what he learned, if he did not already know it, was that nothing brought the Parisian audience to the theatre like controversy and scandal.

Molière was not without friends and supporters. We would be mistaken to assume that the Paris literary and artistic world consisted only of the *abbés* and academicians. Over the years Boileau would be drawn to Molière, as would La Fontaine. La Mothe Le Vayer the younger, son of the free-thinking philosopher who had supervised the education of the king and his brother, was Molière's friend. So was the painter Pierre Mignard and the "other Baptiste," Jean-Baptiste Lully, superintendent of the king's music. His closest friend was Claude-Emmanuel Luillier, known as Chapelle, illegitimate son of François Luillier, a patron of the philosopher Gassendi. Chapelle, like Molière, attended the Collège de Clermont where, according to Grimarest, the two met, although Chapelle was four years younger. But Chapelle was also a friend of Jean-Baptiste L'Hermite, who was married to Madeleine Béjart's aunt, and who had briefly acted with Madeleine and Molière in the provinces. However they met, the hard-working, solemn Molière remained close to the dissolute Chapelle who drank much, published little, and agreed with his other friend Bernier that "abstinence from pleasure is a sin."

It may have been Chapelle who gave Molière the first germ of an idea for *Les Précieuses ridicule*. Chapelle writes of going south with his comrade Bachaumont in 1656 to "take the waters" and recover from lives of debauchery in Paris. During their trip they supposedly encountered the composer Dassoucy in Montpellier, where that unfortunate free-spirit was about to be burned for activites that were anathema to women. The women in question are provincial bourgeoises like Cathos and Madelon, the prettiest and wittiest women in town, but actually neither very pretty nor very witty. Making fun of them, Chapelle concentrates on how little they know of the great world of literary Paris, even to the point of believing that the notoriously homely Madeleine de Scudéry, author of romance novels avidly consumed by both provincials and Parisians, was divinely beautiful.[38] Although Chapelle and Bachaumont did not publish their *Voyage* until later, Molière could earlier have heard from Chapelle this juicy tale about their friend Dassoucy and the silly women of Montpellier. The *farceur* would have seen the comic possibilities, the satirist a social lesion to be excised – but not a very great or serious lesion, merely eccentric behaviors that most of his Paris audience, male and female, bourgeois and noble, would have found distasteful or without value.

Molière also saw the opportunity for several very good roles – especially for himself and for Jodelet, whose special talents he wanted to use. Although still using the "mask" of Mascarille invented for *L'Étourdi* and *Le Dépit amoureux*, he creates an entirely different character, a valet who is not brighter than his master, but who "passes in the eyes of many people for a sort of wit." "Of course," the master adds, "there is nothing cheaper on the market these days than a wit. He's a madman who's got it in his head to play the gentleman."[39] Unlike the usual *commedia dell'arte* routine where the servant merely pretends to be a gentleman or nobleman, this servant thinks he is one – which, of course, is why he, too, is humiliated at the end of the play.

Mlle Desjardins, who would later have a play produced by the troupe at Palais-Royal, wrote a *Récit en prose et en vers* reporting on *Les Précieuses ridicules* to Mme de Morangis.[40] Her description of Molière as Mascarille may not be entirely accurate, but is certainly worth knowing about:

Now imagine, Madame, that his wig is so big that it sweeps the floor every time he makes a bow, and his hat is so small that it is easy to judge that the marquis more often bears it in his hand than on his head. His neck piece could pass for a good-sized dressing gown, and his canons [loose breeches] seem to have been meant as hiding places for children playing hide and seek . . . A torch made of ribbons emerges from his pocket like a horn of plenty, and his slippers are so covered with ribbons that I cannot tell you if they were made of Russian leather, English calfskin, or Morocco leather; but I do know that his heels were half-a-foot high and I found it hard to understand how such high and delicate shoes could bear the weight of the marquis, his ribbons, his canons, and his powder.[41]

The first full season ended on March 12, 1660. It was a busy week, a busy end to a successful year. The future of the company, while hardly assured, looked better than it had the year before, although Molière must have begun to recognize the extent to which that future of the company was going to depend on him. His earlier work had been derivative; but now he had written something original and successful. Expectations were high. He knew, must finally have admitted to himself and the others, that they were not going to excel in tragedy. They were going to specialize in comedy – his comedy. Madeleine had tried to help out; she had refurbished an old play for carnival, *Don Guichot, ou les Enchantements de Merlin*, but it had not pleased. The other actors were delighted with Molière; they had even voted him an extra 1,000 *livres* as a playwright's share. But no one suggested he might act a little less often or take a little less responsibility for the management of the troupe. He was thirty-eight, nearing forty or old age; he was unmarried, childless, and getting tired.

CHAPTER SIX

Husbands and wives

The next season did not begin auspiciously. On March 25, 1660, Good Friday, Jodelet died and was buried at St-Germain-l'Auxerrois. On April 3, Molière's brother Jean died and was buried in the Innocents, leaving an infant child, Molière's godson, and a pregnant widow. The troupe reopened its theatre on April 9 with *L'Heritier ridicule* and took in a disappointing 156 *livres*. They were, however, in the process of rehearsing two new plays. One, Gilbert's *La Vrai et Fausse Prétieuse*, was meant to capitalize on the still ongoing fad for lampooning preciosity. It achieved nine performances at average profits. Molière was also, however, in the process of creating another little comedy that opened on May 28. Entitled *Sganarelle, ou le Cocu imaginaire*, it functioned for the troupe in the same way as had *Les Précieuses ridicules*. Joined as an afterpiece to the comedies and tragedies – by now far more often the former than the latter – of the regular repertory, the *Cocu* had thirty-four performances in its first season and produced more than average revenues even in the dog days of July 1660, when all of the court and most of fashionable Paris were on the Spanish border at the king's wedding. The troupe raised Molière's author's share from 1,000 *livres* to 1,500, and invested in some new crystal chandeliers. By the end of July the newly married king was at the Château de Vincennes, on the edge of Paris, and overjoyed to see, for the first time, *Les Précieuses* and *Le Cocu*. On June 30, Molière received, from the hands of secretary of state Le Tellier, 500 *livres* "to give him a way to bear the expenses he has in this city of Paris where he has come by the order of and for the pleasure and recreation of the said Majesty, and this for the six first months of the said year."[1]

Wiser in the ways of Paris publishers, Molière applied for and was granted a privilege on 31 May for the publication of all of his unpublished works: *L'Étourdi*, *Le Dépit amoureux*, *Le Cocu imaginaire*, and the still unproduced *Dom Garcie de Navarre*. Seeing no illegal publications in the offing, Molière made no use of this privilege, but the same Ribou who had tried to publish a pirated edition of *Les Précieuses* was only biding his time. On July 25 he applied for a privilege for *Les Amours d'Alcipe et Céphise* by "M. Doneau" and on July 26 for an additional privilege for *La Comédie Seganarelle avec des arguments sur chaque scène by the sieur de La Neufvillaine*.[2] The first was a plagiarism of Molière's play with genders reversed, *La Cocue* instead of *Le Cocu*. The second was a piracy of Molière's play with the addition of short descriptions of the action. The obscure writers, far from denouncing Molière, praise him to the skies and "La Neufvillaine" defends his piracy by explaining that the play had so charmed him he had seen it six or seven times, had "accidentally" memorized it, had written a description of each scene for the entertainment of a country friend who could not get to Paris to see it, and now, with publication of "disfigured" versions threatened, he is persuaded of the necessity that "we be printed."[3]

This time Molière took action. There was nothing he could do about *La Cocue*, but he filed a complaint against Ribou for publication of the play attributed to La Neufvillaine. Sent by the provost of Paris to confiscate the pirated edition, the sergeant and the *commissaire* found in Ribou's shop only three or four copies of the press run of 1,250. Ribou insisted on the validity of his privilege. When asked where the rest of books were, Ribou admitted that he had received them, said that he had put them where he pleased, and laughed at the officers. Molière then took the matter to the king's privy council which again forbade Ribou to sell the book and insisted that he turn over to Molière either the 1,250 copies in question or their value figured at thirty *sous* each.[4] Whether he did so is not known.

Le Cocu imaginaire is both the debut of the mask Sganarelle, which Molière was to adopt for several years, and the first play of a series in which the character played by Molière is obsessed with a fear of being sexually betrayed, the others being *Dom Garcie de Navarre*, *L'École des maris* and *L'École des femmes*. This is not an original theme; Pantalones by the score had been cuckolded in the *commedia dell'arte*, and so had husbands in the Pan-European domestic farce. Molière, however, was to use this commonplace of comic plotting as the basis for studies of obsessive sexual jealousy. *Le Cocu imaginaire* is only the starting point. Molière has most ingeniously plotted a kind of round dance where four characters, a married couple and a pair of lovers, all believe themselves to have been betrayed, although none has been.

Once again, Molière has himself betrayed the rules of genre. Although written in verse and thus necessarily not a farce, the play features the plot of Sganarelle and his wife that could easily have come from any of the vulgar domestic farces of the late fifteenth and early sixteenth centuries. There is no evidence to prove it, but chances are the nameless "Wife" was played by a male actor, possibly Louis Béjart who later played Mme Pernelle in *Tartuffe*. The young couple, Célie and Lélie, are gently burlesqued; both speak the modish language of love, both becomingly swoon when they discover the faithlessness of the other. The play is not, however, an open satire of Parisian manners, and no objections to it seem to have been voiced. Of course, everyone who was anyone was out of town.

A new play by Gilbert, *Huon de Bordeaux*, opened on August 5 to mediocre business, but was kept in the repertory until after the king had seen it on September 4. In early October *Le Médecin volant* was added to the repertory of afterpieces and played three times. And then disaster struck. La Grange marks the date with a black lozenge:

Monday, 11th October. Monsieur de Ratabon, the king's Superintendent of Buildings, began the demolition of the Theatre of the Petit-Bourbon, without warning the Troupe that found itself very surprised to be without a theatre. Complaint was made to the king, to whom Monsieur de Ratabon said that the site of the hall was necessary for the construction of the Louvre, and that, since the interior of the hall, that had been fitted out for the ballets of the king, belonged to His Majesty, he had not believed he needed to consider the actors in order to advance the plan for the Louvre. The bad intentions of Monsieur de Ratabon were obvious.[5]

Monsieur, their nominal patron, came to the actors' rescue, and the king granted them the right to play at the Palais-Royal in the theatre built some twenty years earlier for Cardinal Richelieu. To the north of the Louvre, the Palais-Royal had passed to Louis XIII on Richelieu's death and become the home of the widowed Anne of Austria and her sons until they were driven out of Paris by the Fronde. The Palais-Royal then became the residence of the late king's sister, the exiled Queen of England, and her daughter, who became Monsieur's first wife.

The Grande Salle, designed by Lemercier and opened in 1641, had been a splendid court theatre, the first in France equipped for changeable scenery. The cardinal spent 300,000 *livres* on it, a third of which went for machines. It was not, however, furnished as a public theatre. The anonymous *grisaille* that shows the cardinal offering an entertainment to the royal family also shows open galleries along the sides of the room; and instead of a standing *parterre*, an essential feature if one wanted to attract the male bourgeois audience, the theatre at the Palais-Royal had

3. Louis XIII, Anne of Austria, and Cardinal Richelieu in the new auditorium of the
Palais-Cardinal [later the Palais-Royal].

a series of risers where benches could be placed for a seated audience.
Furthermore, nineteen years after its inauguration, the Grande Salle was
in ruins. Three of the unusually long beams that had supported the roof
had rotted and fallen down, leaving half of the room uncovered.[6]

M. de Ratabon was told to make "gross repairs," and he did. Rather
than fitting new beams and installing a new ceiling, Ratabon had a large
blue cloth stretched across the hole, with which the troupe was forced to
make do until 1671. The king, applied to, gave the actors permission to
remove the boxes and other useful interior fittings from the Petit-
Bourbon, although Carlo Vigarani, the successor to Giacomo Torelli,
refused to let them take any scenery, claiming that he wanted to use it at
the Tuileries where he was building the Salle des Machines. In fact,
according to La Grange, Vigarani had all of Torelli's scenery burned in
order to wipe out the memory of his predecessor.

Du Croisy was put in charge of getting the new theatre ready to
open.[7] He hired Charpentier the carpenter and Buret the joiner to
install the boxes, two rows of seventeen each, raise the stage, and make

a *parterre*. The work took three months at a cost estimated at 4,000 *livres*.[8]

The troupe survived on visits. Playing for the king or for Superintendent of Finances Fouquet, or for a variety of dukes, marshals, and plain messieurs, the actors took in 5,115 *livres* in "gratifications," 3,000 from the king. Each actor thus got 425 *livres* to see him or her through the three months without a theatre. The usual expenses for porters and ushers, music, posters, and candles did not apply. Nothing is known of how the theatre's employees managed the break, but the actors, considering they were three months without their usual shares and had to pay out thousands of *livres* for refitting the theatre, did not do badly. A full share for 1659–60 had been worth 2,995 *livres* 10 *sous*; the same for 1660–61 was worth 2,477 *livres* 6 *sous*.

Where was Molière during all of this? Playing his usual roles, one assumes, but not taking responsibility for the restoration of the theatre. Reimbursements are noted for L'Espy, La Grange, Du Parc, and even for Mlle de L'Estang who oversaw the box office, but not for Molière, not even for the six *livres* worth of upholstery fabric. According to faithful La Grange, the master was holding off the Hôtel de Bourgogne and the Théâtre du Marais, eager to enlist the stars of the Troupe de Monsieur under their flags. But "the Troupe of Monsieur remained stable; all the actors loved the sieur de Molière their chief, who joined to an extraordinary merit and talent the bearing of a gentleman and an engaging manner that obliged them to protest to him that they wanted to stay with him and that they would never leave him, whatever proposition might be made to them and whatever advantage they might find elsewhere."[9]

La Grange is absolutely right, of course; none of the actors left the troupe during this difficult time, but then it is hard to see why anyone would have wanted to. In the long run, the Grande Salle at Palais-Royal was going to be a much better theatre for them than the vast medieval space they were leaving behind. The king liked them and called them to court frequently. And they had a resident playwright who had just written several solid hits. But La Grange, as usual, misses no opportunity to establish Molière as the leader and soul of the troupe.

Of course, the leader was now writing a very large flop. While the men of the troupe oversaw construction, while Madeleine found him a new place to live, Molière was polishing his tragicomedy, *Dom Garcie de Navarre*. It was not a new play – he had already applied for a privilege to publish it – but it was an entirely different kind of play. If successful, it would overcome the image of the *farceur* who could only write and act low comedy.

Unfortunately, *Dom Garcie* was doomed. Probably first written when Molière was very young, the play was old-fashioned by 1661, a tragicomedy in the Spanish style based on an Italian play by Cicognini and reminiscent in form and style of Corneille.[10] The plot is repetitive, the verse conventional, but the play is not without interest for anyone trying to discover Molière. Dom Garcie is afflicted with violent jealousy. His beloved tells him in Act I what he must do to please her: he must "banish forever the fearsome monster that poisons your passion with its black venom."[11] This turns out to be very hard for Dom Garcie to manage, and instead of being a tragic-heroic sort of fellow, he finally becomes, well, just the least bit funny. Persuaded that he has been accusing Done Elvire unjustly, he resolves to commit suicide and to seek out

> The glorious means to exit from this life,
> Some great deed that signals my faith,
> So that in expiring for her, she will regret me,
> And be able to say, seeing herself avenged:
> "It was from his too great love that he injured me."[12]

There is a convoluted psychology in this that is intriguing and not unnatural, but the threat is unconvincing, which makes it hard to take the prince seriously. And then, too, Molière played the role himself, which was, according to Donneau de Visé's *Nouvelles nouvelles*, reason enough for the play's lack of success.[13]

At least one biographer of Molière believes that *Dom Garcie* was produced in order to give Madeleine Béjart a last starring role before she got too old.[14] Done Elvire would have been, had the play succeeded, a final "ray of glory," and perhaps a way to keep Madeleine occupied while her lover – her former lover? – pursued his interest in Armande. There is something a little unnerving in the thought of Molière making love to the mother on stage and the daughter off, masking his real jealousy of the one by acting it toward the other.

Madeleine and Molière were still apparently on good terms in January 1661, however, whatever his relationship with Armande at the time. The actors found their lodgings on the quai de l'École too far from their new theatre, but this time the Béjarts decided to live separately. At Christmas, 1660, Madeleine rented four rooms for herself and Molière in the *corps de garde* of the Palais-Royal, located directly across the street from the theatre. This was not a true apartment, but four separate rooms, one on the first floor and three on the second. Marie Hervé rented, also from Christmas but for only six months, part of a house on

4. *Armande Béjart*, drawing by Frederic Hillemacher, 1858.

the rue Fromanteau. Louis was living elsewhere, probably with a woman named Gabrielle Falletière, with whom he had a son baptized on July 6. Where Geneviève was living is not known; nor are Armande's whereabouts clear.

A year later, when the marriage contract between Molière and Armande was signed, Marie Hervé was back living with Madeleine, but Molière had rented his own apartment from October 1, 1661, on the rue St-Thomas-du-Louvre. This followed by nearly six months his request to the troupe, made at the beginning of the season, for a second share, "for himself or for his wife if he were to marry."[15]

How to try to understand what was going on in the first months of 1661? We might wonder if Marie Hervé and Madeleine decided to separate Armande from Molière for a time. That might explain Mme Hervé's rather unusual six-month lease. The absence of the family would give Madeleine and Molière the opportunity to live together alone, probably for the first time. But then why did Madeleine rent four rooms, one of them separated from the others? Did Molière demand two rooms of his own, one in which to write and one in which to sleep alone in that rather narrow bed he had borrowed from his brother? And what did Madeleine mean to suggest when, on June 7, 1661, she bought, from her aunt Marie Courtin and the latter's husband Jean-Baptiste L'Hermite, the very mill of La Souquette that the L'Hermites had been given by the comte de Modène, Madeleine's first lover and the likely father of Armande. She paid 2,856 *livres* for it. Was she so desperate at that point that she thought of moving herself and Armande away from Paris to the wilderness east of Avignon? Some have speculated that Madeleine, knowing she could not have Molière for herself, actually promoted his relationship with Armande, but the psychology of that seems unnecessarily bizarre. Much more likely is Madeleine's disbelief and despair followed by her gradual acceptance of the inevitable.

Molière was certainly thinking about marriage in the spring of 1661 while he was writing *L'École des maris*. It opened on Friday June 24 as an afterpiece to Gilbert's *Le Tyran d'Egypte*. As was often the case with a Friday opening, the box office was mediocre; the purpose of the Friday performance was only to advertise the actual opening on Sunday. As the word of mouth spread, earnings continued to increase, rising to 1,132 *livres* for the ninth performance on July 10. On July 11 the company departed for Vaux to play for Fouquet and then made its first visit to Fontainebleau where the king saw the new play on a double bill with *Le Cocu*. On the way back to Paris the troupe was stopped by the marquis de Richelieu and asked to play *L'École des maris* for the queen's ladies. Fouquet gave them 1,500 *livres*, Richelieu 880. *L'École des maris* was unusually popular with the women and aristocrats who sat in the boxes; La Grange notes on three occasions that fifteen, eleven, and nine boxes were taken, evidently worth remarking. Back in Paris, the troupe continued to perform *L'École des maris* throughout the summer.

L'École des maris is the third play in Molière's jealousy series, but the first one to feature a man obsessed with the fear of being cuckolded by

5. Molière as Sganarelle in *L'École des Maris*, engraving by Chaveau, 1661.

a much younger wife. It also features a debate between two brothers about the proper strategy for managing women.

Sganarelle, played by Molière, is the younger brother in age but the elder in spirit, bourgeois, conservative, fearful of the styles and manners of the new age. Ariste, played, probably, by the doyen of the troupe, L'Espy, is the older brother by twenty years, but liberal, fashionable, and kind. Each of the brothers has brought up one of the daughters of a mutual friend and each proposes now to marry the girl he has raised. Sganarelle keeps his Isabelle locked up and refuses her permission even to take a walk with her sister. He dresses her in "decent serge," like a bourgeoise, and sees to it that she applies herself to household matters; for pleasure, she is permitted to knit stockings. Ariste, on the other hand, believes that women should enjoy a bit of freedom. Virtue is not a matter of locks and grills; virtue comes from honor and honor is based upon the heart.

Ariste keeps his girl, Sganarelle loses his. The play demonstrates that Ariste's maxims are the ones to follow: young people should be instructed in a cheerful, pleasant way; they should be reproved softly; and they should not be taught to fear in the name of virtue. Furthermore, in Ariste's view, normal social intercourse is not a crime. Companions, diversions, dances, and plays are very proper to form the minds of young people. "The school of the world . . . teaches better, in my opinion, than any book."[16]

All that will have to change, Sganarelle reminds him, when you marry. Ariste doesn't see why.

> SGANARELLE
> What? if you marry her, she can claim
> The same freedoms she took as a girl?
> ARISTE
> Why not?
> SGANARELLE
> You would be so obliging
> As to let her have beauty marks and ribbons?
> ARISTE
> Of course.
> SGANARELLE
> You would permit her, this dimwit,
> To run to all the dances and salons?
> ARISTE
> Certainly.
> SGANARELLE
> And let all the fops pay visits?

ARISTE
Why not?
SGANARELLE
And gamble and give suppers?
ARISTE
Surely.
SGANARELLE
And your wife will listen to their sweet words?
ARISTE
She will.
SGANARELLE
And you will watch these dandies
And you won't get a bellyful?
ARISTE
That's right.
SGANARELLE
Go on, you're an old fool.[17]

Along with his fear of being cuckolded, Sganarelle reveals a deep contempt for women and especially for the one who outwits him. Sganarelle's last speech is more than a comic finale. He is angry and bitter, and everything he has feared about women has been proven true.

> This disloyalty amazes me;
> And I do not think that Satan in person
> Could be as wicked as this vixen.
> I would have staked my life on her:
> Anyone who trusts a woman after this is a poor fool!
> The best of them teems with malice;
> The whole sex was conceived to damn the world.
> I renounce it forever, this treasonous sex,
> And I take great pleasure in sending them all to the devil.[18]

Although the play clearly upholds Ariste's point of view, the two brothers are Jekyll and Hyde, opposites, but at two ends of the same spectrum. Ariste is certainly making the argument the fashionable audience wants to hear, and Ariste is upheld by the events of the play, but what Sganarelle feels cannot be dismissed. He has a precarious hold on a world that is slipping away; unlike his flexible brother, he can only hold on more tightly to what he believes to be real and valid. The belief that women are chattels whose value depends on their chastity is not just another example of Sganarelle's outmoded thinking. It protects him from what he privately fears the most: that he cannot depend on love to protect his honor, because he is not capable of inspiring love. He is

unlovable. This is the same fear that will motivate the actions of
Arnolphe and Alceste.

Love as Ariste defines it is not necessarily romantic or even sexual. He
believes that a woman will not dishonor a man who has won her heart,
but by that he seems to mean a woman who is grateful for good treatment. As he explains of his relationship with Léonor:

> A paternal command obliges her to marry me;
> But my plan is not to tyrannize over her.
> I know that our ages do not correspond at all,
> And I leave it entirely to her free choice.
> If an income of four thousand *ecus* in good investments,
> A great fondness for her, and my kindly cares,
> Can, in her opinion, make up for
> The inequality of age in such a union,
> She can marry me; if not, choose elsewhere.[19]

Ariste is a reasonable man, but not a passionate man; Sganarelle is the
opposite, passionate and unreasonable. Molière, who was passionate by
nature and reasonable by act of will, suspected that people like Ariste
could remain moderate because – as he was to say later – they had never
been in love. Not that Sganarelle is in love, either. That turn of events
comes only in the last of the cuckold plays, *L'École des femmes*.

Molière, however, was in love – with Armande, who was twenty years
younger than he. *L'École des maris*, when seen in that context, can be read
as a promise to Armande that their marriage will be of the kind
described by Ariste. Or, it can be read as a warning that she risks marrying a Sganarelle. Or, maybe both. He will try to be reasonable and
generous in spirit, but he is a jealous man and perhaps one who, in spite
of all his sexual adventures, believes himself to be unlovable. This would
not be unusual in someone who lost a mother at an early age and was at
odds with a father who, like so many of those Molière was to invent,
believed in absolute paternal power.

Once again in verse – so it cannot be accused of being farce – *L'École
des maris* is in fact not one. Unlike the earlier little comedies, this play
begins with a long discussion or argument between two characters who
represent conflicting points of view, a technique Molière used again in
L'École des femmes and *Le Misanthrope*. The plot is engaged when a neighbor, young Valère, reveals that though he has never spoken to her, he is
mad about Isabelle. Ergaste, Valère's valet, an intelligent cynic, recognizes that because of her severe treatment by Sganarelle, Isabelle is "half
won already." He has served twenty young hunters, and they have all

agreed that nothing gives them greater hope of success than brutal husbands and their bitter wives. Ergaste thus suggests to us that Valère, like his other masters, is a seeker after prey, and for the moment it would appear that Sganarelle's view of the world is more accurate than Ariste's.

On the other hand, Valère is not very aggressive. He has been mooning after Isabelle for four months, but has found no way to speak to her, only exchange looks, and he does not know if Isabelle returns his feelings. She does, of course. With her marriage to Sganarelle scheduled in a week, she sees her choice narrowed to "despair or Valère," and she turns out to be considerably more adroit than he in arranging things, even finding ways to use Sganarelle himself as her go-between.

Ergaste and Valère react quite differently to Isabelle's stratagems. Ergaste reads her as a trickster, better than he expected at the game of love, while Valère reads her as the innocent heroine he wants her to be. In fact, Valère is the innocent in this play, the one who believes the world resembles a romantic novel. Isabelle is a trickster and a good one, one point of the play being that Sganarelle's treatment of her has taught her to deceive. But we are nonetheless left wondering if, when she tires of him, Valère can expect the same. Her last stratagem, pretending to be her sister involved with Valère for more than a year, is "shameful," as she herself describes it. But having been raised to be deceitful, how can she ever be anything else? Léonor escapes from the romantic young fools at the ball, with their jokes about women who love old men, and comes home to the good old man she esteems and wants to marry. If Molière wondered which kind of husband he would be, an Ariste or a Sganarelle, he must also have considered what kind of wife Armande would be, a Léonor or an Isabelle.

The marriage contract was drawn up and signed in good bourgeois form on January 23, 1662, in Madeleine's apartment on the place du Palais-Royal. Molière's father was there and his brother-in-law, André Boudet. Armande was seconded by her "sister" Madeleine and her brother Louis. Marie Hervé, who claimed to be the mother of the bride, was the actual second party to the contract, describing herself as widow of "Joseph Bejard, living as a squire, sieur de Belleville" – a pair of lies that may have had as its purpose the hope of overshadowing the Poquelins. Armande's age, which must certainly have been known to everyone concerned, is given as "twenty years or thereabouts." The contract establishes a community of property between the spouses-to-be. Molière offers his bride a marriage settlement of 4,000 *livres*; Marie Hervé, who had no source of income other than what her children gave her, promises a contribution of 10,000 *livres*, one-third to the community and two-thirds to be the property of Armande. The 10,000 *livres* was paid; Molière signed a receipt for it on June 24.

The likeliest source of the 10,000 was Madeleine, who as early as 1655 was lending substantial sums of money. It was common for a portion of the bride's contribution to a community of property to remain legally hers, to be inherited by her children if she were to die. However, two-thirds is an unusually large portion to be reserved as personal property and might be taken to suggest that someone – Madeleine? – had doubts about the marriage. Or, perhaps, it merely reflects the financial difficulties Marie Hervé herself had experienced.

The religious union of Jean-Baptiste Poquelin and Armande Grésinde Béjart took place at their parish church of St-Germain-l'Auxerrois on Monday, February 20, 1662, and not on Mardi Gras as La Grange remembered it. Although Monday was not usually a working day, this one was. The troupe paid a "visit," and received 220 *livres*. La Grange marks the event in his *Registre* with a blue circle, but does not mention the name of the bride. At the end of the season, he notes that the troupe has been augmented by two actors, La Thorillière and Brécourt. He lists Mlle Molière as a member, but he does not indicate when she actually began to play. The Béjart women were not among La Grange's favorite people.

The last play in the jealousy sequence is the famous *L'École des femmes*, the play that did not star Armande as the innocent Agnès, although several generations of critics and teachers, longing for irony, have wished it had. It was also Molière's first enormous hit, the first of his "great" comedies, and the cause of a long and finally tedious literary quarrel. It resembles in certain ways the little comedies that preceded it, but it also represents a giant gain in Molière's authority as a playwright.

The troupe had just completed a run of fifteen performances of Boyer's *Tonnaxare*, one of its few successes written by someone other than Molière. Boyer received 150 *louis d'or* in a gold and silver embroidered purse just before Christmas. The day after Christmas 1662 *L'École des femmes* opened with earnings of 1,518 *livres*, the most taken in up to that point for a single performance, and continued through the end of the season with thirty-one performances at the Palais-Royal and a number of visits. On June 1, 1663, a reprise of *L'École des femmes* was joined by its *Critique*; this combination appeared at the Palais-Royal for thirty-two successive performances, with earnings going as high as 1,731 *livres*.

The play and its author apparently came under attack from the beginning. The satirist Nicolas Boileau Despréaux, who was to become a close friend of Molière's, possibly as a result of his support of *L'École des femmes*, wrote on January 1, 1663, only a few days after the play opened, his *Stances à M. Molière, sur la comédie de L'École des femmes, que plusieurs gens frondaient.*[20] Loret also noted that in spite of the *"frondeurs,"* everyone was going to see it.

L'École des femmes is a five-act play in verse, a true comedy by the rules of the day. It abides by the unities of time, place, and action, although with its tongue in its cheek. Its characters are appropriately non-noble, although rich, and its setting a neo-Plautine street. Unlike the characters in Roman comedies or in the Italian plays based on them, these characters are self-conscious about being out in the open. At the very beginning of the play, Chrysalde looks around and discovers that he and Arnolphe are alone and can talk without fear of being overheard. At the end, however, Chrysalde decides that the street is not an appropriate place to unravel mysteries, and leads everyone inside, a declaration, perhaps, that the playwright was through with Roman staging conventions.

Molière played Arnolphe, a rich *rentier* who bought some country property and wants to be known as M. de la Souche, Mr. Rootstock, or Mr. Stump. The phallic nature of the image conforms to Arnolphe's obsession and matches Arnolphe's humor, which is gross for a character in a true comedy. Although the costume is not identified in Molière's inventory, we know from various visual sources what it looked like. Arnolphe wore the narrow breeches of the previous reign with a long doublet, short cloak, square collar trimmed with lace, and a broad-brimmed black hat. If the painting entitled *Les Farceurs français et italiens* on display in the lobby of the Comédie-Française is credible, we can observe that the costume was golden brown, trimmed on the sleeves and vertical edges of the doublet and cape with gold braid. It resembles the costumes of Sganarelle shown in various prints and frontispieces, but is darker and without the baggy cap and ruff.[21] Arnolphe is to some extent a mask derived from the *commedia dell'arte*, but mostly he is an old-fashioned provincial Frenchman.

He is not a Parisian, because the plot of the play requires the kind of casual encounters that happen in a smaller place. The society Arnolphe and Chrysalde are part of is a small-town society, where everyone knows what everyone else is up to. The setting is not a village but a town like one of those Molière knew so well in the provinces, perhaps Bordeaux, a likely place for a sudden return from North America, or Rouen, slightly inland of Le Havre, and the perfect location if one wants to make jokes about the Corneilles.

The play, like its predecessor, opens with a kind of debate. Arnolphe is sure that he has found a way to avoid being betrayed by his wife. He will marry an innocent, a fool. "A clever woman," in his view, "is a bad omen."[22] He has made sure his wife will not be clever by taking her from her peasant mother at four and having her brought up in a little country convent as an idiot. A wife who knows nothing of the ways of the world will not know that betrayal is even possible. Now he has brought her to "this other house" he owns where no one ever comes and has put her in the charge of two simple servants.

But Arnolphe is betrayed by nature. While he is away, Agnès sees a beautiful young man, Horace. He finds a way into the house, and Agnès describes what happened to her agitated guardian:

> He swore he loved me with a peerless love,
> And said the nicest things in the world to me,
> Things that nothing can ever equal,
> And every time I heard him speak,
> This sweet sensation tickled me and down inside
> I felt some *je ne sais quoi* and I was very excited.[23]

The plot turns on the fact that Horace, son of a friend, chooses Arnolphe as his confidant. Arnolphe continues to prepare Agnès for marriage, while she plots to escape. All seems lost when Agnès runs away with Horace, and he confides his beloved to his dear friend Arnolphe. But the problem is solved by the appearance of Horace's father with his old friend Enrique, just back from America, who turns out to be Agnès's long-lost father. Arnolphe is foiled and everything ends happily for the young lovers.

What separates this play from the mass of Italian-style comedies it resembles is the characterization of the two principals. Arnolphe is not just a simple obsessive, nor is he a stereotyped conservative. He is a generous man, delighted to see young Horace, perfectly happy to lend him rather a lot of money. At his other dwelling he keeps open house. When he inquires about Oronte, Horace's father, he wants to know if his old friend is still *gaillard*, lively, maybe a bit of a libertine. Arnolphe, like Mr. Pinchwife in Wycherly's *The Country Wife* that borrows from *L'École des femmes*, does not dread betrayal because it offends morality, but because he knows how easily it can be accomplished.

Already, Arnolphe is much richer character than his predecessor

Sganarelle. He is also more inventive. Aware that his Agnès has been blemished by an experience he did not want her to have, he tries to mend matters by preaching to her a sermon on marriage and giving her a little collection of maxims that forbid her pleasures she, in fact, knew nothing about. He is here at his most officious. "Society is divided into two parts," he tells her, "but the two parts are not equal."[24] The husband is the all-powerful, the supreme authority, the one who governs. The wife is submissive, docile, humble and obedient. Arnolphe wants more from marriage than fidelity; he wants the pleasure of having absolute power over someone else. He wants to mold her soul like a bit of wax between his hands, form her as it pleases him.

Agnès is also an interesting character. She is, of course, not dumb at all; she is uninformed and uneducated. She can read and write, which many women of the period could not, but these skills serve the needs of the plot. As a result of her meetings with Horace and through the course of events, Agnès learns how disgracefully she has been treated. Realizing she has been kept in ignorance, she is even afraid to write a letter, unsure that she has the language in which to express herself.

After Arnolphe tricks Horace and retrieves Agnès the two confront each other, and Molière writes at the top of his form for the first time. Arnolphe begins in a bitter fury, asking where she could possibly have learned the language and ways of gallantry. Agnès cannot understand why he is upset; she is only doing as she was told, preparing to marry and save herself from sin. But "I intend to take you for my wife," says Arnolphe. "Yes," answers Agnès,

> But to speak frankly between you and me,
> He is much more to my taste than you are.
> With you marriage will be vexatious and painful,
> You paint a terrible picture of it;
> But he, he makes it seem so pleasurable,
> That he makes me want to marry him.[25]

This is a question of love. Love, according to Agnès, just happens, and it has not happened to her with Arnolphe. Why? Because he has done nothing to make himself lovable. And he should be aware that she now knows what he has made of her. She is ashamed to be like a dumb beast and will no longer be satisfied to be a fool. Arnolphe's fury can only be assuaged by beating her, but when he raises his hand to her, she says: "You can do that, if that will make you happy" – and he no longer wants to. He realizes that he is in love with her.

ARNOLPHE

Ah well, let us make peace. Come, little traitor,
I pardon you and give back my affection.
Consider the love I feel for you
And seeing me like this, love me in return.

AGNÈS

With all my heart I would comply if I could.

Arnolphe then tries to make himself lovable.

ARNOLPHE

My poor little chick, you can if you will.
Only listen to my amorous sigh,
See this dying look, contemplate my person,
And leave this snotnose and the love he gives you.
This is some spell he must have cast on you,
And you will be a hundred times happier with me.
Your great passion is to be well-dressed:
You always will be, yes, I mean it,
Endlessly, night and day, I will caress you,
I will rub you, kiss you, eat you.[26]

And Arnolphe thus reveals, just as we are beginning to feel the least bit of sympathy for this man who is almost frantic with love, that the root of his obsession is and always has been sexual. What he wants and now admits he wants is total possession of her body; he will caress her, rub her, kiss her, eat her, while still pretending that she is the one seeking sexual gratification. If she is looking for that *je ne sais quoi*, that little sensation down inside, Arnolphe wants to be the only one who can give it to her. But Agnès again stings him with her coldness, and he threatens her with a convent dungeon.

This scene is not comic, nor is it tragic as the genre was defined in the seventeenth century. It is deeply serious, although the rules do not permit comic characters to have such intense feelings. It goes well beyond the assigned purpose of comedy – to correct manners – in its revelation of the sexual jealousy of a unique character. In fact, the play is what Donneau de Visé calls it in the first volley of the literary war of *L'École des femmes*: a monster, neither one thing nor the other, and very unlike anything that had come before.

The quarrel of *L'École des femmes*, that is, the plays and pamphlets that rolled off the Paris presses in 1663 and 1664, was preceded by a *fronde*, a series of attacks on the performed play, probably instigated by the Corneilles. They had a very specific objection to a pointed dig in Act I, scene 1. Arnolphe has taken the name of M. de la Souche because it sounds better than his given name, Saint Arnolphe being the patron saint of betrayed husbands. Chrysalde has a hard time remembering his friend's new alias and, in any case, finds this habit of buying an old seigneury and adopting the particule to be an abuse, a pretense of nobility by someone who should be proud of being a bourgeois. He comments:

> I know a peasant called Gros-Pierre [fat Peter],
> Whose only property was a single quarter of land.
> He had a muddy ditch dug all around it,
> And from it took the pompous name of Monsieur de l'Isle.[27]

Molière had been smarting for two years, ever since Thomas Corneille had written the abbé de Pure that his troupe was capable of playing nothing but bagatelles, trifles like *Les Précieuses ridicules*. The abbé had not kept the judgment to himself. Now Molière was unable to resist the temptation to avenge himself on the brothers, nor did he keep silent about his plan. "Pierre" makes reference to the elder Corneille, the "great" Corneille, but the barb is aimed at his little brother Thomas, the writer of the letter, who wanted to be known as M. de L'Isle because he owned an orchard on the Île de la Litte in the Seine.

The king was exercised by the number of people who had usurped titles of nobility or bought them. An order of the previous year, 1661, had required all those claiming nobility to present evidence for their titles. La Fontaine was found lacking authority for his "de," and fined. Thus, Molière was not only making a nasty innuendo about the social status of the Corneilles, he was implying an irregularity that could have caused them real problems.

The Corneilles fought back, suggesting this new play was nothing more than another bagatelle and later prompting a young writer named Boursault, a protégé of Pierre Corneille's, to write, and the Royal troupe to produce, a polemical play entitled *Le Portrait du peintre*, meant to avenge "the outraged glory of the greatest men of our century."[28]

Georges Couton has devised a chronology of the quarrel and included selections from the various plays and pamphlets in his edition of Molière's works.[29] With one exception, Donneau de Visé's *Nouvelles nouvelles*, they all postdate not only the publication of *L'École des femmes* but the premiere of its *Critique* on June 1. Donneau's objections to the play are general. Never has he seen so many good things mixed with so many bad things; never have so many people rushed to see a play that they found *méchante*, not only bad but wicked. Donneau's only specific complaint is that Molière did not invent the action; he took it from Scarron's *La Précaution inutile* and Straparole's *Les Nuits facétieuses*.[30]

It was Molière himself who established the issues of the quarrel with his clever *Critique*. Eager to extend the run of *L'École des femmes*, and pay back Thomas Corneille, he let it be known as early as February that he was working on a new play in which he would list all the faults that had been found in his play and excuse them. What he put on stage on June 1 was a gathering of society men and women, whiling away the time between the theatre and supper. Uranie, a heavenly creature, and her cousin, the plain-spoken Élise, begin the play by discussing the *équivoques*, or puns, that Élise detests, finding them obscure and old-fashioned, *turlupinades* "collected from the mud in Les Halles or the place Maubert."[31] This appears at first to be irrelevant, but in fact the *Critique* is focused on the use of equivocation and ambiguity in the language and action of *L'École des femmes*.

The others arrive: Climène the *précieuse*, the Marquis, Lysidas the poet, and Dorante, the decent gentleman. Climène has just come from seeing *L'École des femmes* and is stricken with a *mal de coeur*, that wonderful French euphemism for nausea. Specifically, she has been put into this state by "*les enfants par l'oreille,*" "*la tarte à la crème,*" "*le potage,*" and the famous "*le,*" that is, by a number of moments in the play that can be taken to mean more than one thing. The first occurs when Arnolphe brags that Agnès is so innocent she asked if children were made through the ear; the second when he insists that she is unaware of rhyme. Alain, the male servant, is the one who explains that "the woman is the *potage* of the man," and that a man gets extremely angry when other men want to dip their fingers in his soup,[32] a metaphor that is repeated when Arnolphe offers to eat Agnès. And finally, there is the famous "*le.*" After Agnès admits that Horace took her hands and arms, Arnolphe want to know if he took anything else. Agnès tries to tell him that Horace also took "*le . . .,*" but Arnolphe interrupts and frightens her. As Agnès stalls, the audience fills in the missing word until she finally admits that Horace took *le ruban que vous m'aviez donné*, "the ribbon that you gave me."

Climène is outraged by this, furiously scandalized, but Uranie disingenuously proposes that the scene is simply about a ribbon. If Climène thinks otherwise, then Climène is the one with the dirty mind.

CLIMÈNE   Ah well! Ribbon if you like; but this "*le,*" where she stops, is not there for nothing. This "*le*" stimulates strange thoughts. This "*le*" is furiously scandalous; and whatever you say, you cannot defend the insolence of this "*le.*"

ÉLISE   That's true, cousin. I am on Madame's side against this *"le."* This *"le"*
is insolent to the last degree, and you are wrong to defend this *"le."*
CLIMÈNE   It is an obscenity that cannot be defended.
ÉLISE   What was that word, Madame?
CLIMÈNE   Obscenity, Madame.
ÉLISE   Ah! Good heavens! Obscenity. I don't know what that word means;
but I think it's awfully pretty.[33]

This little tease, Élise, was the first role Molière wrote for his young wife.

The Marquis – possibly Molière's role, since he does remind us of
Mascarille – has another objection to the play: the *parterre* laughed at it,
so it must be worth nothing. The writer Lysidas adds that in his opinion
the play is not properly a comedy, just another bagatelle. Anyone who
knows Aristotle and Horace will recognize that this play sins against all
the rules of art.

While Uranie and Élise mock the critics Dorante defends the play and
the playwright, openly speaking for Molière. Comedy, Dorante tells us,
is more difficult to write than tragedy. When you create a tragic hero,
you can do what you like, you only have to consult your imagination. But
the comic character has to be drawn from life, painted from nature. And
then, a comedy has to be funny, and "it's a strange undertaking to make
decent people laugh." As for the rules, Dorante addresses Lysidas:

It seems, to hear you talk, that these rules of art are the greatest mysteries in the
world; but they are only some convenient observations, that good sense has
made, about what can increase the pleasure one takes in these kinds of poems,
and the same good sense that made these observations in other times can make
them now without the help of Horace and Aristotle. I would like to know if the
greatest rule of all the rules is not to please, and if a play that has attained its
end has not followed a good course."[34]

Uranie hammers the final nail into the pedant's coffin by adding: "I've
noticed something about these men: it's the ones who talk the most about
the rules, and who know them better than anyone else, who write plays
that no one finds beautiful."[35]

By and large we do not know what objections had actually been raised
to *L'École des femmes* before the *Critique* was written. What Molière does
with the objections he raises – and counters – is accent the scandal. He
also defends his technique as a comic writer, praises the good taste of the
bourgeois audience, and lauds the intelligence and critical acumen of
the courtiers. All this is done directly through Dorante. He uses Uranie
and Élise, especially Élise, to mock the enemy forces: the empty headed
fops, the precious prudes, and – especially – the camp of the Corneilles.

George Couton makes an excellent case for believing that Lysidas is based on Thomas Corneille himself.[36] Molière does not introduce here the question of whether he wrote the *Critique* as a *pièce à clef,* a play that includes characters modeled on people known to members of his audience. He does have Dorante remark that characters in comedy must be drawn from nature, that a "portrait must be a good likeness." Apparently some people took Molière's portraits to be good likenesses, whatever the playwright intended. A fairly credible tale goes that the duc de La Feuillade thought the Marquis in the *Critique* was based on him. One day he encountered Molière and greeted him as a friend. When Molière bowed in return, the duke took his head and rubbed his face against the buttons of his doublet, all the while saying "*tarte à la crème, Molière; tarte à la crème.*" Since the duke's buttons were diamonds, Molière stepped away with his face running blood.[37]

The other issue that Molière does not introduce in the *Critique* is any affinity between his plays and himself, even though Donneau hinted at the association in his *Nouvelles nouvelles.* "In all his plays Molière makes such fun of cuckolds and depicts jealous men so naturally, he must be among their number . . . To do him justice, he gives no evidence of his jealousy outside of the theatre, he has too much prudence."[38]

Between the *Critique de l'École des femmes* and Molière's second and final response, the little play known as the *Impromptu de Versailles,* Donneau de Visé published his dialogue *Zélinde, ou la Véritable Critique de l'École des femmes* and the actors of the Hôtel de Bourgogne produced *Le Portrait du peintre* by Corneille's protégé, Boursault. Donneau's device this time is to have *L'École des femmes* criticized for its failures of technique by a man of common sense, a lace merchant from the rue St-Denis who goes to all the first nights and stands in the *parterre,* in other words, by the very sort of spectator Dorante lauds in *La Critique.* The specific objections to Molière's work are much the same. Boursault, on the other hand, stresses Molière the "painter" who burlesques so well all the *gros dos,* the big shots of the court.[39]

The published edition of *Le Portrait du peintre* may not be an accurate version of what was said and done on the stage; Molière's reaction suggests that it must have been more malicious and more personal. We know at least that Boursault did not include in the published text the vulgar *Chanson de la Coquille* that was sung during the performance. For the entertainment at Vaux-le-Vicomte on August 17, 1661, Fouquet's secretary Pellisson had written a prologue spoken by Madeleine Béjart, who emerged from a shell, costumed as a naiad. She was, perhaps, a little old to be playing a nymph, though her status in the company made it appropriate for her to speak the praises of the king in whose honor the party was given. The *Chanson de la Coquille*, used first by Boursault and reprised by Donneau de Visé, refers both to Madeleine's age and to her sexual history:

> Coquille dit-il si belle et si grande
> N'accommode pas mon limaçon.
> Coquille dit-il si belle et si grande
> Demande un plus gros poisson.
>
> [The Shell, says he, so beautiful, so big,
> Does not accommodate my snail.
> The Shell, says he, so beautiful, so big,
> Asks for a fatter fish.][40]

At least in the published version, Boursault makes no other personal references. However, judging from Molière's response, they must have been made.

The *Impromptu de Versailles* was played at Versailles for the first time on October 18 or 19, 1663, two weeks at most after *Le Portrait du peintre*. Molière had gone to see Boursault's little play, sitting on the stage where all could see him laugh and appear to enjoy himself. In fact, he was no longer amused by the quarrel, which had been going on for nearly a year, and was ready to have it over. The *Impromptu* takes aim at the actors of the Hôtel de Bourgogne, first by burlesquing them, then in a direct attack heavy with contempt.

L'Impromptu de Versailles is a mine (maybe a land mine) of information about Molière and his troupe, since he and his actors are the characters in it. The conceit is that he has written a new play to be performed that day before the king, but it has not been rehearsed. The actors are in revolt, not at all the docile worshippers of Molière pictured by La Grange. Madeleine thinks he is taking an unnecessary risk that may give more ammunition to his enemies. Armande thinks he should write a play just for himself or, even better, a play showing how lovers change when they become husbands, how a ceremony takes away all the good qualities of a woman. Everyone is distractible, including Molière, who begins to describe the play he did not write attacking the actors of the Hôtel de Bourgogne. In a series of caricatures, he burlesques them and their style, beginning with Montfleury, a very fat actor whom Cyrano compared to the Trojan horse full of 40,000 men or Saint Ursula hiding 11,000 virgins under her veil.[41] Molière makes fun of him for playing tragic kings. He then satirizes Beauchâteau and his wife, Hauteroche, and Villiers. In each case, he imitates the actor reciting a few lines from Corneille.

By this time, Molière had decided that the final cause of the attacks on him was the Hôtel de Bourgogne, the troupe that had the most to lose when a competitor met with great success. He has "Madeleine" interrupt the rehearsal to complain that his response is not sufficiently vigorous, that he should not spare a single one of the actors. This elicits from Molière in the character of "Molière" a long statement on the role the Royal actors have played in the quarrel.

You want me to be incensed and follow their example and burst out with invective and insults . . . Aren't they willingly ready for these kinds of things? When they deliberated whether they should perform *Le Portrait du peintre*, and some feared a riposte, didn't others answer: "Let him insult us as much as he likes, as long as we make money"? Is that not the mark of a soul very sensitive to shame? And wouldn't I avenge myself well by giving them what they want? . . . The great wrong that I have done them is that I have had the happiness to please a little more than they might have liked; . . . But let them do as they wish; nothing they undertake bothers me. They criticize my plays; so much the better; God keep me from making anything that pleases them. That would be a bad business for me. . . The actors have only unleashed him [Boursault] on me to engage me in a foolish war, and keep me, by this artifice, from some other works I have to write; . . . But finally I will make my declaration publicly about this. I do not intend to make any response to their critiques or counter-critiques. Let them find all the faults in the world in my plays, I agree with them. Let them seize them from us, turn them like a shirt collar, put them on their stage, and try to profit from whatever favor they find there . . .; I consent: they need them, and I will be perfectly happy to contribute to their survival, provided they will content themselves with what I can decently give them. Courtesy has limits; and there are things that make neither the spectators laugh, nor he of whom they speak. I abandon to them gladly my works, my face, my gestures, my words, my tone of voice, and my manner of acting, to use them as they please, if they can find some advantage in it; . . . But in abandoning to them all that, they must do me the grace to leave me the rest and not to touch on matters of the kind with which I am told they attack me in their plays. That is what I civilly request of this honest gentleman who has gotten involved with writing for them, and that is all the answer they will have from me.[42]

And, indeed, that was the last word Molière had to say. *L'Impromptu de Versailles* had nineteen performances between its opening and the first of January; after that it was rarely seen. Molière's detractors persevered for another four or five months, both on the stage of the Hôtel de Bourgogne and in print. Donneau de Visé continued to be the one most given to personal innuendoes. In his *Réponse à l'Impromptu de Versailles, ou la Vengeance des marquis*, probably produced at the Hôtel de Bourgogne within days of the first performance of Molière's *Impromptu*, Donneau describes the scene at the Hôtel when Molière came to see *Le Portrait du peintre*. There were thirty-one cuckolds in the audience that day, thirty who applauded everything and one who tried to laugh, but without much inclination.[43]

The most blatant attack on Molière did not come from the stage, however. Montfleury, who was evidently vastly unamused by his competitor's parody of him, denounced Molière to the king. According to a letter from Racine to the abbé Le Vasseur in November 1663, "Montfleury has made a petition against Molière and sent it to the king. He accuses him of having married the daughter, and of having formerly slept with the mother."[44] He adds that no one listens to Montfleury. Certainly the king didn't. On February 28, 1664, Louis XIV was godfather to Louis Poquelin, the first child of Molière and Armande.

Aside from a few hints suggesting that Molière would not have written so constantly about jealousy and betrayal if he had not experienced them, and a rather stereotypical husband-wife exchange in *L'Impromptu*, nothing in the written record of the quarrel of *L'École des femmes* allows us to assume that Molière and Armande were anything but content in the first two years of their marriage. Molière successfully detached his young wife from the Béjarts. Armande made her debuts as an actress and as a mother. The theatre was thriving, artistically and financially. And the Sun King continued to shine.

CHAPTER SEVEN

The courtier

On August 17, 1661, a very hot day, Louis XIV and his court left Fontainebleau at 3:00 in the afternoon and arrived at 6:00 at the château of Vaux-le-Vicomte, the newly completed country estate of the king's Superintendent of Finances, Nicolas Fouquet. Fouquet was giving a party for 6,000 guests beginning, of course, with His Majesty the king, the dowager Queen Anne of Austria, the king's brother Monsieur, his wife Madame, and all the court. Only the queen Marie Thérèse, heavily pregnant, was absent.

The evening began with a promenade to admire the fountains and waters.[1] The gardens at Vaux were the first important creation of André Le Nôtre, a vast expanse of *parterres*, avenues, *allées*, perspective vistas, canals, basins, fountains and cascades. After the gardens, the guests were shown the château itself, a masterwork of the fashionable Paris architect Louis Le Vau with decor by the painter Charles Le Brun. A lottery with prizes for all was followed by a collation prepared by Vatel of "delicate and rare" foods served on gold plates.[2] Supper music was provided by Jean-Baptiste Lully and twenty-four violins. After supper, the guests repaired to the pine grove, where a stage had been erected, and were entertained by a ballet devised by Beauchamps and a comedy written for the occasion by Molière. This was followed by a magnificent display of fireworks.

The king left at 2:00 in the morning, even more suspicious of his minister than he had been when he arrived. Mme de La Fayette wrote of the occasion: "For a long time the king had said that he wanted to go to Vaux, the superb house of this superintendent; and, although prudence should have prevented [Fouquet] from showing the king something that so clearly indicated the misuse of state money, and also the king's decency should have kept him from going to visit a man whom he planned to destroy, nonetheless, neither the one nor the other considered it."[3] According to the abbé de Choisy, Louis was angry enough to arrest

Fouquet on the spot, both because of the minister's arrogance in displaying his ill-gotten luxury and because he had permitted Le Brun to put a recognizable likeness of Louise de La Vallière, Louis's mistress, in an allegorical painting. However, the queen mother persuaded her son not to take an ill-considered and scandalous action.[4] The indiscreet superintendent was not arrested until September 5.

The first of Molière's court entertainments was thus written neither for his patron nor his patron's brother, but for the presumptuous minister who employed not only the king's playwright, but the king's architect, painter, gardener, cook, musician, and dancing master. Constructed by as many as 18,000 workmen between 1657 and 1660, Vaux was the too obvious symbol of Fouquet's ambition and greed. Everywhere the jealous young king turned his eyes he saw Fouquet's emblem, a busy squirrel, and Fouquet's motto: *quo non ascendet?* To what heights may I not climb? Fouquet's climb was ending, but not before he had shown his master an example of how to give power and glory visible expression through the arts. Fouquet fell, but Le Vau, Le Nôtre, Le Brun, Lully, and Molière rose to almost unimagined heights as providers of the royal pleasures and purveyors of the royal image. Had there been no Vaux, chances are there would have been no Versailles.

Exactly how Fouquet came to choose Molière to devise the entertainment for his fête is not clear. Possibly Jean de La Fontaine, a client of the superintendent, recommended him. It was La Fontaine who, describing his patron's party to his friend Maucroix, remarks that he was delighted with Molière, "for he is my man,"[5] and reminds Maucroix that they had agreed that this writer was going to restore to France the good taste and the style of Terence. At some point, of course, La Fontaine and Molière became friends. Fouquet had first asked the troupe to play for him in Paris in the fall of 1660, while the Palais-Royal theatre was being rebuilt. The actors were also invited to perform at Vaux on July 11, 1661, barely a month before the great day, perhaps as a form of tryout.

In any case, Molière had only two weeks to write and stage his entertainment for Vaux. "This is, I believe, something totally new," he wrote, "that a comedy be conceived, written, learned, and performed in fourteen days."[6] The little play, entitled *Les Fâcheux*, has almost no plot but simply recounts the tribulations of a young man whose rendezvous with his beloved is continually interrupted by a series of irritating bores. The young man was played by La Grange, the beloved by Catherine de Brie, and most if not all of the irritating bores by Molière, himself.[7]

La Fontaine's letter to Maucroix continues with a detailed description of the performance at Vaux. The theatre among the pines was illumined by a hundred torches. The ballet began with a display of machines devised by Torelli and painted by Le Brun. A very realistic rock was transformed into a shell and from the shell emerged Madeleine Béjart, costumed as a naiad, to speak a prologue in honor of Louis written by Fouquet's secretary, Paul Pellisson. The nymph predicted that if the king were to so order, the trees would speak and the statues walk. At her signal, the statues turned on their pedestals and from them issued fauns and bacchantes to dance the first ballet entry. La Fontaine remarks that it was very amusing to see a statue give birth.[8]

Unlike the prologue, the play requires no spectacle. To say that *Les Fâcheux* is slight is to overestimate its weight. Theatrically, the most interesting thing about it is Molière's conceit of playing multiple roles. Like *L'Étourdie*, it is designed to display the talents of its author. Historically, it has a certain importance since it was the first of Molière's *comédie-ballets*, an invention mothered by necessity. "It will not be out of place," writes Molière in the preface, "to say a word or two about the ornaments that were mixed with the play. The plan was to give a ballet as well; but, as there was only a small number of excellent dancers selected, the ballet entries had to be separated, and the conclusion was to put them between the acts of the play in order to give the dancers time to return in other costumes. So that the thread of the play would not be broken by these sorts of intermezzi, it was decided to connect them to the plot as best as could be managed and to make a single entity of the play and the ballet."[9] The result was not entirely successful in the view of Molière; time was short and no single vision ruled. Nonetheless, the mixture was found agreeable and would serve as a model for similar entertainments that could be contemplated at greater leisure.

The king liked it. A week later the troupe was called to Fontainebleau where, on his name day, August 25, the feast of Saint Louis, the king saw *Les Fâcheux* a second time. In fact, what the king saw was not exactly the same play. Molière writes, in the dedication to the printed edition, that he has a special reason to dedicate this work to His Majesty, who gave him the idea for what has become the best scene in the play. According to an anecdote recorded by Ménage, the king encountered Molière after the performance at Vaux and pointed out to him M. de Soyecourt, later royal *grand veneur*, or chief huntsman, saying "there is an original you haven't yet copied." Molière is then supposed to have within forty-eight hours written the scene of Dorante, who is obsessed with hunting and insists on telling the frustrated lover at huge and tedious length about his pursuit of a buck.[10]

Les Fâcheux opened in Paris on Friday, 4 November, and did reasonable if not unusual business through the Christmas season, in spite of La Grange's serious illness that kept him off the stage for two months. Molière had it published almost immediately, on February 18, 1622, suggesting that he thought it had exhausted its welcome; however, it continued to be part of the stable repertory of the troupe for a number of years.

In his clever dedication to the king, Molière remarks that he had never done anything so easily or quickly or joyfully as obey the command of his sovereign, "that leads me to conceive what I would be capable of executing in the way of a whole play if I were inspired by such orders. Those who are born in a high rank can have the honor of serving Your Majesty in great positions, but, as for me, all the glory that I can aspire to is to entertain you. There are the bounds of my ambition; and I believe that it is not useless to France only to contribute to the diversion of her king."[11] The king apparently agreed.

After the death of his brother Jean in April 1660, the title of *tapissier du roi* was restored to Molière, thus giving him a useful entrée at court where he was not, however, universally welcomed. He was, after all, an actor. La Grange writes in the preface of 1682 that "his work in the theatre did not keep him from serving the king in his office of *valet de chambre*, that he discharged very diligently." He was esteemed by the king and by "the most enlightened courtiers" and "was known at the court as a civil well-bred man . . . who accommodated himself to the humor of those with whom he was obliged to live."[12] Reading between the lines, we might suspect that there were some less enlightened courtiers and court officers who were not at all pleased to share with an actor their opportunities to encounter the king, and that Molière did a great deal of accommodating.

Several anecdotes, true or not, nonetheless illustrate the kind of problems Molière must have had with some of his colleagues at court. One appears for the first time in 1732 in Titon de Tillet's *Description du Parnasse français*. "Here is something I learned from the late Bellocq, *valet de chambre* of the king, a man of great wit who made very pretty verses. One day when Molière presented himself to make the king's bed, R . . ., another *valet de chambre* of His Majesty, who was supposed to make the bed with him, turned brusquely away, saying that he would not do it with an actor; Bellocq immediately advanced and said, 'Monsieur de Molière, may I have the honor of making the king's bed with you?'"[13]

What may be an elaboration of this anecdote – or, perhaps, an invented tale, or even possibly a true story – is the celebrated incident of the king's *en-cas de la nuit*, first told in the *Mémoires* of Mme Campan, lady-in-waiting to Marie-Antoinette. Mme Campan had collected a number of historical anecdotes from the reigns of Louis XIV, XV, and XVI. This one had great appeal to the nineteenth century and is the source of the famous painting of *Molière à la table de Louis XIV* by Ingres.

A bit of background is necessary to understand the anecdote. Mme Campan explains that before the revolution the royal servants took certain precautions. Clean linens kept in the rooms of the king and queen in case Their Majesties might want to change formed the *paquette d'en cas*, while a bowl of bouillon, a cold roast chicken, and bottles of wine, barley water, and lemonade, the *en-cas de la nuit*, were on hand should royal hunger occur unexpectedly.[14]

The source of the anecdote was an old doctor, M. Lafosse, who had told it to Mme Campan's father-in-law. The doctor was

a man of wit and of honor, and incapable of inventing such a story. He said that Louis XIV learned that the officers of the chamber having demonstrated by offensive behavior how injured they felt by having to eat at the table of the Contrôleur de la Bouche with Molière because he was an actor, that celebrated man abstained from presenting himself at that table.

Louis XIV, wanting to put an end to this outrage that should not be offered to one of the great geniuses of his century, said one morning to Molière at the time of his *petit lever*: 'It's rumored that you don't eat well here, Molière, and that the officers of my chamber don't find it proper to eat with you. Perhaps you are hungry; myself I wake up with a very good appetite: sit down at this table and let someone serve me my *en-cas de nuit*.'

Then the king, cutting his chicken and having ordered Molière to sit down, served him a wing while taking at the same time one for himself, and ordered that the most notable and favored persons of the court be introduced.

'You see me,' said the king to them, 'giving something to eat to Molière, who my *valets de chambre* do not find to be good enough company for themselves.' From this moment, Molière had no need to present himself at the service table; the whole court rushed to invite him to their tables.[15]

Arguments have been made for and against the likelihood of this anecdote being true. However, Louis XIV did have a doctor named Chaban de Lafosse and, although he rarely ate with anyone else, even members of his own family, on one occasion as a young man Louis invited his hostess, the wife of the superintendent of the Jardin Royal, to join him

at his private table. That incident was recorded by the indefatigable
Loret on June 14, 1659.

Had Molière been only a writer, a denizen of Parnassus like his friends
La Fontaine, Boileau, and Racine, he would have posed no problem at
court. But he was and continued to be and refused to cease being an
actor. Furthermore, his life was notoriously irregular. In consequence, he
was an obvious example of why actors were marginal in French society,
both excommunicated by the Church and denied the full privileges of
citizenship by the state.

On the other hand, Louis fully understood the power of the arts and
their potential for creating a royal image. He needed Molière to help
envision and produce the festival he had in mind that would efface the
memory of that humiliating evening at Vaux-le-Vicomte. He also understood the power of the symbolic gesture, so an invitation to Molière to
sit at his table and join him in a symbolic chicken wing would not be out
of keeping with Louis's way of doing things. After all, in February of
1664, the king graciously consented to be godfather to Molière's first son.

So far as we know, Molière was not involved in the first great theatri-
calized event organized to display the image of Louis as the Roi Soleil,
the Sun King. This was the Carrousel des Tuileries, an equestrian
extravaganza held on June 5–6, 1662. We need not speculate about the
king's reasons for organizing, funding, and participating in this kind of
event, for his motives are clearly explained in the *Mémoires* written for the
edification of his son. Louis believed that a monarch should provide
"public amusements that belong not so much to us as they do to our
court and to all our people."[16] The king also believed in the "free and
easy access of subjects to the prince." He noted, however, that the monarchy had become too familiar during the regency of his mother and
Mazarin and that correcting this lapse required strictness on the one
hand and the provision of pleasures to be shared on the other. These
pleasures would serve to charm a disaffected nobility and produce a
polite familiarity between king and courtiers. What's more, he was
certain that his subjects in general enjoyed spectacles, would be
delighted by seeing their monarch ride, fence, and dance, and would
think well of him for being skillful.

Beyond these practical advantages, Louis saw what symbolic advantage could be gained from his personal participation in events such as
the Carrousel of the Tuileries, the occasion when he adopted the
emblem that was to symbolize his personal reign for the next fifty-three
years. Considering the function of an emblem, Louis reflects: "I believed

that, rather than settling on some private or lesser thing [might the reference be to Fouquet's squirrel?], it should represent in some way the duties of a prince and always stimulate me to fulfill them."[17] So, he chose as his symbol the sun, the "noblest of all" symbols, because it is unique and brilliant, and because "of the light it imparts to the other heavenly bodies that seem to pay it court." This metaphor is both accurate as regards the solar system and illustrative of Louis's perception of the relationship of king and courtiers. The king, like the sun, was to be regarded as the source of life and joy so long as he, like the sun, ran a steady and invariable course. Of course, Louis also knew that, unlike the moon that shares the sky with countless stars, the sun is alone in the heavens.

What sort of courtier was Molière? He was certainly not among those in the first range of the planets around the Sun King. But he was someone with a presence at court and with access to His Majesty. He was useful and agreeable, not aggressive or combative in his behavior, but rather someone who preferred to retreat when challenged and take his revenge later, from the stage. He was, as we have seen, quiet in company, but nonetheless politically skillful, able to navigate successfully for many years the tempestuous waters of the court.

In her wonderful film *Molière*, Ariane Mnouchkine imagines the actor/playwright as courtier. Her Molière adopts the elaborate court dress of the marquises he satirizes, appearing in satin doublets glittering with gold and silver thread, with gigantic breeches and knots of ribbons at elbow and knee. She even invents a scene in which Boileau tries to read his friend some lines from a new satire, but Molière is too busy trying on wigs to listen.[18] Various anecdotal paintings, mostly done in the nineteenth century, also show Molière in the guise of a nobleman.

But would the appropriation of aristocratic dress and manners have been a politic choice for a bourgeois actor and *valet de chambre*? The few portraits of Molière done later in his life – unfortunately undated – do not show him in elaborate court costume. Indeed, Molière is typically represented in a shirt with some sort of dressing gown over it, reading or writing. In some cases, however, he is wearing a full period wig.

Perhaps the best evidence of the figure Molière cut at court comes from the inventory made after his death. Following a long and fascinating description of his costumes, the lawyers entered his personal wardrobe:[19]

Item, a doublet, breeches of ordinary material with a satin vest lined
    with padding and a silk stocking . . .   15 *livres*.

Item, a doublet and breeches of black Holland cloth, a pair of silk
stockings . . .   10 *livres*.

Item, a doublet and breeches of brown drugget, a doublet lined with
black taffeta, a pair of wool stockings and one of worsted . . .
       15 *livres*.

Item, a doublet and rhingrave breeches of musk Holland cloth with a
white vest of Chinese satin, the garters and stockings in silk with
satin decoration . . .   25 *livres*.

Item, a dressing gown of striped brocade, lined with blue taffeta . . .
       25 *livres*.

He also owned shirts, of course, two dozen of good Holland linen and
six old ones, eighteen night shirts, fourteen camisoles and eight pairs of
underdrawers, along with handkerchiefs, nightcaps, cravats and neck
bands, all worth together some 229 *livres*. The most expensive item in the
inventory of Molière's wardrobe: his two dozen linen shirts valued at 96
livres.

The Molière of the inventory was a fastidious man, well supplied with
personal linen of high quality. He was not ostentatious in the least. His
most expensive suit of clothing, the only one in a color other than black
or brown, the only one garnished with ribbons, was still worth a mere 25
livres. To put that in perspective, we can contrast Molière's best suit with
the inventory made in 1670 of the wardrobe owned by Charles Varlet de
La Grange. The fashionable clothes worn on stage by this *jeune premier*
were worth 5,235 *livres*.[20]

The image of Molière at court, then, is of a politic man of the middle
class, decently and respectfully dressed in the typical costume of the
middle class, with good linen showing at neck and sleeve and an occasional touch of color or lace. Nothing in Molière's personal wardrobe
violated the sumptuary ordinances continually passed though frequently
ignored. As a man of the theatre, he surely knew the value of contrast,
knew that a dark and quiet figure caught the eye against a background
of gaudy and glittering colors.

A year after the Carrousel of the Tuileries, in the summer of 1663,
Louis issued the first two lists of men of letters who were to receive royal
"gratifications." Not since the death of Richelieu, twenty years earlier,
had writers attracted royal notice and royal support. The king asked
Chapelain, member of the Académie Française from the beginning, to
identify those writers deserving royal endorsement. Molière, probably to
the surprise of the many enemies he had made with *L'École des femmes*,

was on the list. Chapelain notes that the playwright knows the rules of comedy and follows them naturally. His best plays have invented plots, but judiciously invented. His "*morale*," that is, his view of life, is good, verisimilar, but he needs to guard against the use of farce and buffoonery.[21] Louis, of course, unlike the elderly academician, found nothing wrong with farce and buffoonery.

Molière responded to the honor and to the 1,000 *livres* that would eventually accompany it with a graceful *Remerciement au roi*. This brief and witty "thank you" was published as a pamphlet, made part of public discourse, and praised by Robinet who asked, "Do you have the *Remerciement* [Molière] has written about his pension as *bel esprit*. Nothing has been found so elegant and pretty."[22]

This little occasional piece cleverly expresses how Molière, during the time he was favored, both praised his monarch and shared with his young king a realistic appraisal of the situation in which they found themselves. Because it is largely unknown, I shall offer here a rather detailed account of it.

Molière's "thank you" begins with a conceit. The poet awakens his muse and scolds her for not having thanked the king for his favors. But, better late than never, he concludes, sending her off to the Louvre dressed as a marquis. A muse in her natural state would shock the court, it seems.

Thalia is advised to wear the largest possible necktie and the smallest possible doublet, a hat with at least thirty plumes, and an elegant cloak caught up at the back by a ribbon. Upon entering the Salle des Gardes, she should take a turn around to see who's there, hailing loudly anyone she thinks she recognizes by their name and not their rank. This "familiarity" gives an "air of quality," or so the poet assures her.

It is now time for action. If the way is clear, the "marquis" should merely scratch on the door of the king's chamber; if the way is blocked, however, Thalia must climb up on something, wave her hat, call her name loudly to the usher, and then throw herself into the crowd, cutting off the important people, elbowing the others out of the way, fighting like the devil until she comes face to face with the doorkeeper. If he proves inexorable, the poet advises his muse to plant herself in the doorway and refuse to move. That way, when someone approaches whom the usher must admit, he will have to let the "marquis" in as well.

Much of this vision of the court is repeated elsewhere in Molière's works, especially in *L'Impromptu de Versailles*. But the final stanza is more revealing of the actual position Molière held. Once in, the muse should try to press forward, but if that proves impossible she should simply wait for the Prince to come past. "He will know your face / In spite of your disguise." Then she is to make her compliment. Now, says the poet, you could make an extensive speech, and he launches into a sample full of clichés and syntactical tangles. But, he concludes:

> Great princes enjoy nothing more
> Than compliments that are short;
> And ours has other things in store
> Than listening to your long report.
> Praise does not touch him, nor flattery move him;
> As soon as you open your mouth to approve him,
> His favor and grace to praise with your art,
> He understands your guile
> And sweetly beginning to smile
> In a way that charms the heart,
> He will pass by like a dart,
> And that will have to suffice.
> There's your compliment concise.[23]

Two things stand out in this clever and graceful bit of courtly writing. One is the picture of Molière quietly waiting to be recognized by the king who knows his face. The other is the assumption underlying the fictional event of the "compliment" that the king is too occupied with the real business of ruling to take time for ceremony, just as Molière is too absorbed with the real business of entertaining the king to take the time to express his thanks in person. All that is necessary between them is a glance of understanding.

The king not only added Molière to his pension list, he supported the troupe as well. Between the spring of 1659, when La Grange began to keep his accounts, and August 1665, when the king regularized his support, the actors received in all from the royal purse some 31,800 *livres*, an average of about 6,000 a year for entertaining the monarch.[24] The first payment was made in October 1660, following a number of performances given gratis. From the summer of 1660 until the spring of 1662, the troupe was called to court, whether at the Louvre, Vincennes, or Fontainebleau, only for single performances. Beginning in May 1662, however, the king invited them to make extended visits commencing with a week in May and seven weeks in August at St-Germain-en-Laye. In 1663, after Molière received his "gratification," the actors were invited to Versailles for the first time. In May of 1664, of course, Versailles became the magical island where Louis, with the help of

Molière, Lully, Beauchamps, and Vigarani would erase forever the memory of the night he was merely a guest at Vaux.

Before those enchanted evenings in May 1664, which were to be a turning point in Molière's relationship with the king, he devised the afterpiece known as *L'Impromptu de Versailles* to mark the troupe's first stay in October 1663 at the king's country retreat and *Le Mariage forcé*, the second of his comedy-ballets, for the court's carnival festivities of 1664. *Le Mariage forcé* is chiefly interesting for its lively satire of pedantry. The *Impromptu*, on the other hand, offers another fascinating glimpse of Molière at court.

The conceit of the piece is metatheatrical. The actors play themselves and their situation. Called to court and required to present a new play, "Molière" frantically tries to conduct his grumpy colleagues in a rehearsal, interrupted by a busybody courtier. Aside from a number of entertaining and revealing interchanges among the actors, the play includes several references to the king.

Early on, Molière creates a particularly interesting relationship between the play and the monarch, who is absent in the stage fiction though present in reality. When the character "Mademoiselle Béjart" suggests that when the king orders him to do the impossible, "Molière" should make a respectful excuse, "Molière" answers that "kings like nothing so much as prompt obedience, and what they don't find at all amusing are obstacles . . . They want their pleasures and they never want to wait for them; and the least prepared for are always the most agreeable. We must never think of ourselves when they want something from us: we are here only to please them; and when they order us to do something, it's up to us to take advantage of whatever they want. It's better to do what they ask badly than not do it soon enough; and if one has the shame of failure, at least one has the glory of having obeyed their orders."[25]

This could be taken several ways, but we must assume that Molière did not mean it to be taken literally. "Kings" might pettishly prefer something poorly done to pleasure deferred, but his king, whose artistic judgment and taste were beyond question, would surely not allow himself to be ruled by such arrogant impatience.

A bit later on, "Molière" is distracted from the rehearsal when "Mademoiselle Béjart" wants to know why he did not write on this occasion a satire of the actors of the king's own troupe. At the request of "Mademoiselle de Brie," who claims she has never heard about this project, "Molière" gives a summary of what he thought of doing. He envisions a situation where a playwright, who is thinking of offering them his new play, interviews a troupe of actors newly arrived from the country. "And who among you plays the kings?" he asks. When the actor is pointed out, the poet is nonplused. "Who? This handsome young man? Are you joking. A king should be big, fat as four men, a king – my word – should have a proper gut on him, a vast circumference to fill a throne as it should be filled. What a business to have a king with the figure of a lover!"[26]

This satire of Montfleury, the stout tragedian of the Hôtel de Bourgogne, is also an appreciation of Louis and a sly suggestion that the rival troupe, although patronized by the king, was not paying attention to the new image of monarchy that king conveyed. "I, on the other hand, am aware of the distinction between 'kings' and 'my king'" is what Molière is whispering behind his hand.

At the end of the play it is Molière's king and not some generic "king" who sends a messenger to say that His Majesty, from the kindness of his personal heart, will be happy to put the new play off until another time and will be content to see today whatever you can perform.

The real Louis, unfortunately, did not always show the consideration of the fictional Louis; the real Louis seems to have enjoyed the conceit without taking the hint. Molière had time to versify only the first third of *La Princesse d'Élide*, the centerpiece of Louis's *Plaisirs de l'île enchantée*, and in the preface to the 1666 edition of *L'Amour médecin*, a comedy-ballet devised for the king at Versailles in September 1665, its author notes that it was "proposed, written, learned, and performed in five days."

Rushed or not, *Les Plaisirs de l'Île enchantée* marked both Molière's triumph as a courtier and client of the king and the beginning of his long and bitter struggle to persuade the king to permit public production of *Tartuffe*. The troupe performed four times at Versailles between May 7 and May 13, 1664, although only *La Princesse d'Élide*, the baroque fairy-tale Molière wrote especially for the occasion, was presented during the three days of the official fête. *Les Fâcheux* and *Le Mariage forcé* served as grace notes, while *Tartuffe* was, as Georges Couton so eloquently describes it, "like an abscess, purulent, nauseating, amidst the splendid scenery" of the great outdoor theatre.[27]

Versailles in 1664 was still a modest country retreat, although work had begun on the park and the expansion of the château. The number of guests invited to Versailles on the occasion of the first great fête held there was also modest: 600 compared to the 6,000 invited to Vaux by Superintendent Fouquet. The official description of the *Plaisirs*, published by Robert Ballard with engravings by Israël Silvestre, notes that Versailles was a country house with all the charms one desired in such a spot transformed into a perfect enchanted palace by the adornments of art.[28] Although the palace was not large, the anonymous author found it charming in every way. Its surrounds were notable for beautiful walks, flowers, and especially for an orangerie and a menagerie, in which were to be found several star-shaped courts with pools for "aquatic animals." Aside from Louis XIII's Renaissance château, that still forms the center of this vast monument to Bourbon ambition, we would find it hard to recognize the Versailles of 1664. For purposes of the *Plaisirs*, the building site became a giant theatre, a kind of theme park or fairground. Unlike Vaux-le-Vicomte, which was complete in every detail, Versailles was still nothing more than an idea. The enchanted isle was the work, not of Le Vau, Le Brun, and Le Nôtre, but of Carlo Vigarani, an Italian scenic designer and engineer. The magnificent buildings, the *allées* and courts, the tilting ground, the theatre – all were temporary theatrical illusions.

Although the party lasted from May 5 to May 14, the actual *Plaisirs* were performed on three successive evenings, May 7–9. The king had put the enterprise in the hands of the duc de Saint-Aignan, first gentleman of the chamber, requesting that he find some theme that would unite the various events. Saint-Aignan and Vigarani chose as their motif the story of Alcine the sorceress from Ariosto's *Orlando furioso*. Alcine keeps in her palace, by means of magic charms, a group of knights led by Roger who amuse themselves by tilting at the ring and by a ballet and play.

Molière was commissioned to write and produce the play. The actors from the Palais-Royal participated in other ways as well in the *Plaisirs*. They actually left Paris for Versailles on April 30, a week before the entertainments began.

The guests arrived on May 5 and 6. On the evening of May 7, they gathered at a circle where four great *allées* met, the circle marked by high hedgerows, each *allée* ending in an archway thirty-five feet high festooned with gold and decorated with the king's arms. The weather was unusually fine for May, although a little wind was blowing, threatening the curtains, the wooden buildings, and the thousands of candles and torches that illumined the scene. The heavens, however, were impressed by the power of His Majesty and the decorations stood against the wind.

The first evening was devoted to a tournament and a collation. At 6:00 p.m. the herald entered followed by three pages with the king's page, M. d'Artagnan, richly dressed in the king's livery, presenting the king's sword and shield, glittering with a jeweled sun and bearing the motto: *nec cesso, nec erro,* "I do not slacken, I do not lose my way." Trumpets and drums announced the entry of the dukes themselves, each representing a mythical knight, followed by the king representing Roger, mounted on "the most beautiful horse in the world," dressed and armed as a Greek warrior. Ten knight-contestants entered after Louis, each also representing a character from *Orlando furioso*. Behind the warriors came Vigarani's first great set piece, the chariot of Apollo, eighteen feet high, twenty-four feet long, shimmering with gold and all the colors of the rainbow. Apollo himself rode on top of the chariot, with the four Ages at his feet. Representing Apollo was – Charles Varlet de La Grange of the troupe of Monsieur. Representing the Ages were Mlle Molière, Mlle de Brie, Hubert, and Du Croisy. Time drove the chariot that was pulled by four giant horses, while the Twelve Hours and the Twelve Signs of the Zodiac walked alongside. Bringing up the rear were the knights' pages, bearing their swords and shields, and a troop of twenty shepherds carrying the materials needed to set up the lists for the tilt. The procession made its way around the circle, the knights saluted the two queens in whose honor the fête was supposedly being given, and all the participants took their places, the king in the middle opposite the dais, the dukes to his left and right, the ten knights with their pages along the sides of the chariot.

"When all were in place there was a profound silence," broken by Mlle de Brie representing the Age of Brass. She and the other actors spoke the tributes written by M. de Périgny to the queens. And then the tournament began. All admired the quickness and grace of His Majesty, but he did not win. The finalists were the duc de Guise, the marquis de Soyecourt (the model for Molière's hunter-bore), and the marquis de La Vallière, who received the winner's diamond-studded sword and buckler from the hands of the queen mother. This marquis was the brother of the king's mistress, Louise de La Vallière, in whose covert honor the party was actually being given. To the suspicious modern eye, his triumph appears to have been another coup de théâtre, predetermined and not fortuitous, although even a cynical historian of the late twentieth century would rather not believe that the marquis, representing a flower of chivalry, took a diamond sword and buckler in return for the honor of his sister.

Night fell as the tournament ended, the musicians entered, and the supper was served. The Four Seasons appeared: Mlle Du Parc as Spring, riding a beautiful Spanish charger, "with the sex and the advantages of a woman, but showing the facility of a man," Du Parc as Summer, on an elephant, La Thorillière as Autumn on a camel, and Louis Béjart as Winter, on a bear. They were followed by forty-eight costumed servants bearing baskets filled with delicacies and Vigarani's second showpiece, a mountain shaded by trees, magically moving through the air, bearing Pan and Diana represented by Molière and Madeleine. The actors presented the feast to the queen, a great table was unveiled, the court supped and then returned, in decorated carriages, to the château.

On the second evening the party assembled at a second circle, in line with the first and like the first surrounded by hedgerows, but closer to the lake where the palace of the sorceress Alcine awaited. The conceit of the second event was that Roger and the knights had prepared an entertainment for the queen (given that Alcine's magic floating island was parked off the coast of France). Within the second of the magic circles, a theatre had been constructed. The wind was a problem, but the king ordered the circle to be roofed with a sort of fabric dome to protect the candles and torches. Israël Silvestre's engraving shows in considerable detail the stage with its trompe l'oeil vista of what appears to be a natural *allée* leading to a lake and the floating palace of Alcine. The royal family sits in armchairs with the king opposite the vanishing point of the perspective. Courtiers stand behind and to the side of the royal party, or sit with the ladies of the court in five rows of raked benches. On stage the actors of the Palais-Royal are resplendent in their Roman costumes, the "classical" dress usually worn only in tragedy, but here appropriate to neoclassical romance.

La Princesse d'Élide is based on a Spanish model, Moreto's *El Desden con el Desdan*. It has a simple fairy-tale plot. The king of Élide has a daughter who scorns love. She adores only hunting and the forest, a sort of female Hippolytus. Her father wants her to marry and for this purpose holds a tournament and calls three princes to court. The princes are put through their knightly paces on the assumption that one will please the princess, and she will choose him to be her husband.

Eurale, prince d'Ithaque is madly in love with the princess and wants to win the contest. After observing her, he concludes that the way to do it is to pretend to be as disdainful of love as she is. After a series of comic misunderstandings orchestrated by Moron, the court jester, the lovers are – of course – united while the other princes are contented by two convenient cousins.

In his previous comedy-ballets Molière's comic action was interrupted

by romantic or pastoral ballet entries, danced by courtiers and professional dancers and loosely connected to the plot. For the *Princesse d'Élide*,
however, Molière himself devised the comic interludes that featured his
character Moron and Moron's parallel love affair with Philis. The most
famous of the interludes is Moron's adventure with a bear that he turns
into an encounter between a prince and his subject:

Ah! Monsieur the bear, I am your servant with all my heart. Please, spare me. I
assure you that I'm not a tasty morsel, I'm nothing but skin and bones, I see
people down there [i. e., in the audience] who would suit you better. Eh! eh! eh!
Monseigneur, gently, if you please. La! la! la! la! Ah! Monseigneur, how handsome Your Highness is and what a great figure! He has such a gallant air and
such a small waist. Ah! Beautiful fur, beautiful head, beautiful eyes, so large and
brilliant! Ah! beautiful little nose! beautiful little mouth! pretty little teeth! Ah!
beautiful throat! beautiful little paws! handsome little claws! Help!!![29]

While some in the audience must have appreciated Moliere's observa-
tion that the king, like the bear, could be dangerous, Louis surely enjoyed
this parody of the sort of rank flattery he encountered daily. He must
have enjoyed even more the opening scene when Arbate, the prince
d'Ithaque's wise tutor, speaks to him of the necessity for a prince to be
in love. When Euryale orders Arbate to scold him for his weakness,
Arbate counters that to be truly great and generous, a young prince must
fall in love. "I believe," he says, "that one can expect anything of a prince
as soon as one sees that his soul is capable of love . . . Love goads the
heart to noble acts. All the greatest heroes have experienced it. I have
seen you grow before my eyes, My Lord, and I have seen your virtues
flower. My eyes have recognized in you the blood from which you spring.
I have discovered in you a mine of wisdom; I find you handsome, you
have a grand air and a proud soul . . . but I was uneasy when you didn't
fall in love."[30]

Once again, Molière speaks behind his hand. The sentiments are
unexceptional so long as the audience is reminded of the legitimate
union of Louis and his queen. What everyone knew, of course, was that
Louis was not, had never been, in love with her but was mad about Mlle
de La Vallière, his mistress since 1661 and mother of his children. The
queen was miserable about it, the queen mother was furious. During
Lent two years before, Anne of Austria had brought the preacher and
moralist Bossuet to court to warn the king off the primrose path. Louis
was not amused, and Bossuet found himself unwelcome at court for
many years. As Georges Couton points out, the young Louis, when faced
with a choice between the preachers and the poets, chose the poets.[31]

6. *Les Plaisirs de l'Île enchantée, seconde journée*, engraving by Israel Silvestre, 1664.

Journée
sur lequel la Comédye, et le Ballet
furent représentéz.

et secudis, Cum Privilegio Regis.

Molière's boldness in praising the king's adultery publicly and in front of his wife and mother was perhaps more rash than bold. Although the line "my eyes have recognized in you the blood from which you spring" was undoubtedly meant as a compliment to the queen mother, it might also have been taken as a reminder of the rumors that circulated for so many years linking Her Majesty to her minister Mazarin. Molière was certainly aware of the queen mother's ambivalence toward him. On the one hand, she had always loved the theatre, especially the Italians and the opera. On the other, she was extremely pious and increasingly influenced by the conservative religious faction led by the Compagnie du Saint-Sacrement that had joined in the furor against *L'École des femmes*. In the dedication to *La Critique de L'École des femmes*, Molière envisioned a queen mother in whom religion and the theatre were compatible, a queen mother "who proves so well that true devoutness is not contrary to decent diversions; who . . . does not disdain to laugh with the same mouth with which she prays so well to God."[32] What he may not have known nine months later was that Queen Anne had found a lump in her breast and knew she was dying. Had he been aware of that, perhaps he would not have been so reckless as to have included among the theatrical pleasures of May 1664 the first performance of *Tartuffe*.

More fuel for the fire that was smoldering was the casting of *La Princesse d'Élide*. It was with this play that Molière introduced his wife, Armande, to the court in a starring role. Although she had appeared among the ensemble in both afterpieces to *L'École des femmes*, she was now judged ready for center stage. What might have created a minor scandal, however, was the casting of her mother, Madeleine Béjart, as Philis, Molière-Moron's beloved in the parallel plot. Molière thus called attention not only to the king's irregular love life, but to his own as well.

The third day of the *Plaisirs de l'Île enchantée* was the most spectacular. The court found itself on the banks of a lake upon which floated three islands. On the center isle, a large rock was defended by a flock of different animals. On one of the smaller isles, the king's orchestra appeared; on the other his trumpets and drums. Alcine, the sorceress, entered from behind the rock, borne by a sea monster of "prodigious grandeur" and accompanied by two nymphs riding whales. As they approached the shore, they spoke a dialogue provided by Périgny that predicts the events to come, that is, the liberation of the knights. Alcine was represented by Marquise Du Parc, the nymphs by Catherine de Brie and Armande. The rock then opened to reveal Alcine's palace and the ballet began. This was not a court ballet but a theatrical ballet, danced by professionals. The conceit of the ballet was Alcine's efforts to guard the palace against the intrusion of the fairy Mélisse with the ring that would free Roger and the others. The ballet characters were giants and dwarfs, moors, and demons. In the final entry, Mélisse, disguised as Atlas, put the ring on the finger of the choreographer Beauchamps, dancing Roger, and the palace was reduced to ashes by grand and magnificent fireworks.

Although the *Plaisirs* were finished, the fête was not. On Saturday June 10 the king and the courtiers held another tournament; this time the king won. On Sunday the king took everyone to see his menagerie, notable especially for its "incredible number" of rare birds. In the evening the actors gave a reprise of *Les Fâcheux* with its ballets. On Monday there was a lottery that everyone won. The prizes were jewels, furnishings and silver. And although it is usual for fate to decide such things, in this case fate agreed with the wishes of His Majesty when it dropped the *gros lot* into the hands of the young queen. Following the lottery there was another tournament. It was after this tournament, on Monday evening, that the actors played *Tartuffe*. The next evening, after still another tournament, the final theatrical event was a reprise of *Le Mariage forcé*. The next morning the king left for Fontainebleau. On Saturday the *Gazette* reported that the king had forbidden any further productions of the play entitled *L'Hypocrite*, adjudged "injurious to religion and capable of producing very dangerous effects."[33]

In spite of this lapse in courtly acumen, the king was pleased with Molière and awarded him an extra 2,000 *livres* for the *Princesse d'Élide*. Nor was Molière's work for Louis XIV finished. Still to come were ten entertainments prepared for the king and the court. Still to come was the decision by the king to patronize the troupe and add it to the pension list. Although the controversy over *Tartuffe*, that lasted until well after the death of the queen mother, was bound to affect the relationship between the king and Molière, to all appearances Molière remained in favor.

Between July 1664 and February 1672 the troupe played at court two or three times a year with the exception of 1669–70, when it was called five times to St-Germain-en-Laye and once to Chambord. Many of the visits were long: three weeks at Fontainebleau in July and August 1664, nearly three months at St-Germain-en-Laye in 1666–67, ten days at Versailles in July 1668, three weeks at St-Germain for carnival of 1670, twenty-five days at Chambord in October 1670, fifteen days at St-Germain in 1672. Several of these visits were for important court festivals and included the presentation of new entertainments.

The *Ballet des muses*, which celebrated Christmas of 1666, carnival of 1667, and the end of court mourning for Anne of Austria, included two or three works by Molière: *Mélicerte*, incomplete and possibly never produced, the *Pastorale comique*, which may have replaced *Mélicerte* but has not survived, and *Le Sicilien, ou l'Amour peintre*, a farce added to the final performances. The *Ballet des muses* was a monumental undertaking with thirteen *entrées*, fourteen with the addition of *Le Sicilien*. All the theatrical troupes – the Italians, the royal troupe of the Hôtel de Bourgogne, and the actors from the Palais-Royal – participated along with courtiers, court musicians, and a regiment of professional dancers. Théophile's *Pyrame et Thisbé*, honoring Melpomone, muse of tragedy, and performed by two courtiers, made up the second entry while the ninth was an improvised affair celebrating Polymnia, muse of eloquence, with three Italian actors playing Latin orators and three of the Burgundians Greek philosophers. Molière and his troupe performed the third entry consecrated to Thalia, muse of comedy. The other entries were danced. The king appeared in the fourth entry as a dancing shepherd, in the sixth as a ridiculous poet, and in the eighth – devoted to Erato, muse of romance – as Cyrus, the hero of Mlle de Scudéry's popular novel. When *Le Sicilien* was added, the king also danced a moor of quality in the masquerade finale, along with Madame and Mlle de La Vallière.

Le Sicilien is a useful farce with a typical plot, ornamented with music, dance, and Mediterranean exotica. The rivals are a French gentleman and a Sicilian; the French gentleman has a Turkish slave valet; the beloved is a Greek slave. Molière played not the wily valet Hali but the jealous Sicilian owner of the beauteous Isadore, played by Mlle de Brie. Little can be derived from the surviving *livret* of the *Pastorale comique*, but the cast list tells us that Molière himself played Lycas, a "rich shepherd," and Lycas is, interestingly, a singing role that has two scenes with another rich shepherd, Filène, played by the professional singer Destival. The songs might be characterized as "patter songs"; they are certainly not love lyrics. In the first, Lycas is a kind of chorus or echo to Filène, but in the second, the two share the lyrics equally. Very little evidence survives to enable us to characterize Molière as a singer, but this scene suggests that he could hold his own in a kind of musical comedy.[34]

Mélicerte is an unfinished "heroic pastoral" in verse, written, like *La Princesse d'Élide*, to show off the charm and talent of a debutante, in this case the boy Michel Baron. It may, in fact, never have been produced at all, but in intention, at least, it is a courtier's play, an opportunity to communicate with the king as Molière had done in his earlier plays written for the court. Molière wrote for himself the role of Lycarsis, a herdsman, who announces to his colleagues that the king is going to honor them with his presence for the feast of Pan. The king is described in a relatively banal way; he has a certain "*je ne sais quoi*," he's a "master king," "the best in the world."[35] The courtiers are described more imagistically, but still conventionally, as a heap of glittering flies on a honeycomb. Since the play was never finished, we will never know if Molière actually proposed to put a king onstage in a pastoral comedy, but in what exists of *Mélicerte*, there is nothing that can be read as a private message from Molière to Louis XIV.

There may however be a message in *George Dandin*, written for *Le Grand Divertissement royal de Versailles* held to celebrate the peace of Aix-la-Chapelle and inaugurate the gardens and fountains of Versailles. The magnificence of the park and the supper and even of the theatre can be taken for granted. What seems paradoxical is the play, a sour note in the harmony of pleasures provided. Although a comedy-ballet, the *Grand Divertissement* lacks unity. The ballet, with lyrics by Molière and music by Lully, is a pastoral opera that ends in a conflict between Amour and Bacchus. The comedy is perhaps the most cynical play Molière ever wrote about one of his favorite topics: marriage.

Less than a year had passed since first president Lamoignon of the Parlement of Paris had forbidden a public presentation of *Tartuffe*. The king had promised to look into the matter, but had taken no action. Molière had been seriously ill, his own marriage was in jeopardy, and he was in no mood to provide baroque frivolities. Thus, on that superb stage to that brilliant assembly he presented the story of a rich peasant who has committed the error of marrying the daughter of a noble house fallen upon hard times. The daughter, who has nothing but contempt for her husband, betrays him openly with a young gallant. After Dandin tries and fails to persuade the girl's parents of their daughter's deceit he concludes that "when one has, like me, married a wicked wife, the best course of action is to go and throw yourself in the water head first."[36] He leaves the stage to the sound of the fountains and the waters.

Beside presenting images of impoverished and morally bankrupt aristocrats and a peasant brought down by social climbing, Molière also introduces a central female character who actually does betray her husband. This is his second such character, the first being Alcmène, the wife of Amphitryon, who betrays her husband unknowingly with Jupiter disguised as his rival. *Amphitryon* preceded *George Dandin* in Molière's repertory. It opened at the Palais-Royal, so cannot be considered as a commission from the king, but it was played before the king at the Tuileries during the carnival diversions of 1668. The two plays make an informative contrast.

Many historians and critics have suggested that Molière's version of Jupiter's adventure with Alcmène should be seen as analogous to Louis's adventure with Athénaïs de Rochechouart, marquise de Montespan. The argument is that just as Molière celebrates the king's love for Louise de La Vallière in the *Princess d'Élide* so he endorses the king's new affair in *Amphitryon*, especially at the end of the play when Jupiter appears as himself to reassure the man he has cuckolded, to "restore your heart to the state it should be in, and reestablish peace and quiet in your house." He continues: "My name, that the whole earth incessantly adores, suppresses the rumors that could break out. There is nothing at all dishonorable about sharing with Jupiter. And without a doubt it can be only glorious to see yourself the rival of the king of the gods."[37]

The analogy holds, but not the conclusion. Unlike her predecessor Louise de La Vallière, Mme de Montespan was married, and Molière is satirizing and not sanctioning Louis's behavior. Jupiter is clearly a sexual predator and his justifications are undercut by Amphitryon's silence and by the reactions of his valet, Sosie, played by Molière himself. Although Amphitryon has no response when first Mercury and then Jupiter reveal the identity of his wife's seducer, Sosie remarks that "Lord Jupiter knows how to gild the pill." Sosie is also less than impressed by Mercure who, disguised as a second Sosie, has tormented and beaten him. Mercure echoes Jupiter when he claims to Sosie that "the beatings of a god do honor to those who endure them." Sosie is unconvinced and, as the messenger god ascends to heaven, mutters: "I've never in my life seen a god more devilish than you."[38]

A final ironic moment in the scene includes Jupiter's announcement that the house of Alcmène and Amphitryon will be blessed by the birth of a son "who . . . will fill all the vast universe with his deeds" and his prediction of great wealth for them, a sign to everyone that they are sustained by Jupiter.[39] These auguries strangely foreshadow the joy of the marquis de Montespan's father who, upon hearing that his son had been cuckolded by the king, cried out: "Finally Fortune enters our house." The lady's father was apparently also beside himself with delight. A popular ballad notes that when he learned that his daughter was pregnant by the king, "he took his theorbo and sang Alleluia."[40]

If we look at *George Dandin* with its immediate predecessor in mind, we will read it as more than just another cuckold farce. *Amphitryon* is the story of a great lord betrayed by a god; *George Dandin* is the story of a peasant betrayed by a courtier – another analogy that deserves notice. This is not the place to discuss in detail Armande's behavior after 1664, but whether or not she had actually deceived Molière, her conduct had certainly given rise to a great deal of gossip and speculation and the two were living separately. Molière had written a whole series of plays about men who feared betrayal; now he began to write about men who had been betrayed, about the women who betrayed them, and about the men who preyed upon the women.

Alcmène may be the innocent prey of Jupiter, but Angélique in *George Dandin* is a more equivocal character. On the one hand, she actively participates in an illicit liaison, on the other she is presented as the victim of an arranged marriage to a man she despises. Her attitude is understandable: "I have no intention of renouncing the world and burying myself alive in a husband. What? Just because a man decides to marry us, everything must be over and we must break off all commerce with the living? . . . What a joke! I have no desire to die so young . . . I want to enjoy the beautiful days of my youth, take the sweet freedoms permitted me, see the world, and taste its pleasures."[41] But she is also the devious, sly, and hypocritical "crocodile" her husband accuses her of being. On balance, audience sympathies are with Dandin.

Angélique is looking for trouble and finds it in Clitandre, another sexual predator. Unlike the eager and innocent lovers of Molière's early plays, Horace, for example,[42] Jupiter and his human counterpart take great pains to seduce married women – as does the king, as do the courtiers buzzing around the honeycomb Armande. The message, then, from the poet to the patron is a simple one: innocent and youthful love can be sanctioned, but a liaison that parts husband and wife is another matter. With *George Dandin* the poet-courtier does not mask the misgivings of the poet-moralist or the despair of the poet-husband.

CHAPTER EIGHT

Enemies

Molière had fought and won his first great battle. He had defeated the pietists, the *précieuses*, and the Parnassians who, for their various reasons, had attacked his *École des femmes*. Flags flying and, one might say, thumb to nose, he entered the fray a second time, and found himself unhorsed. From May 17, 1664, when the *Gazette* announced that the king had forbidden further performances of a play entitled *L'Hypocrite*, until February 5, 1669, when *Le Tartuffe ou l'Imposteur* opened at the Palais-Royal, Molière battled doggedly – and for a long time unsuccessfully – for the right to produce his play. Unlike the earlier conflict fought largely in the literary lists with pamphlets and plays, the war of *Tartuffe* took place at court and in the cabinets of the powerful. Its skirmishes were rarely public, and its details remain obscure.

Still another war broke out sixteen months later when Molière fired a first shot into the citadel of the Paris faculty of medicine. This was *L'Amour médecin*, written for a court festival, but a great favorite with Paris audiences. Although Molière's attacks on medicine created less scandal than his perceived attacks on religion, the two controversies can be fruitfully considered together. Molière thought of them as related. In the petition he addressed to the king, on the day *Tartuffe* finally opened in Paris, he proposes an end to both:

A very estimable doctor, whose patient I have the honor of being, promises me and will swear before notaries to keep me alive another thirty years, if I can obtain for him a favor from Your Majesty. I told him, as for his promise, I would not ask so much of him, and I would be satisfied with him if he were to be so obliging as not to kill me. This favor, Sire, is a canonship in your royal chapel at Vincennes . . . Dare I ask this other favor of Your Majesty the very day of the great resurrection of *Tartuffe*, brought back to life by your kindness? I am, by that first favor, reconciled with the devout party, and I would be by the second with the doctors. This is without a doubt too much favor for me all at once, but perhaps not too much for Your Majesty.[1]

Before departing for the wars, let us stop for a moment to assess the state of things at the Palais-Royal between the spring of 1664 and the winter of 1669. The troupe was more or less stable. At the beginning of the 1664–5 season the men included Molière, Louis Béjart, Du Parc, de Brie, Du Croisy, La Grange, La Thorillière, and – newly entered – Hubert. The women were Madeleine Béjart, Geneviève Béjart (known as Mlle Hervé), Mlle de Brie, Mlle Du Parc, Mlle Du Croisy, and – admitted in 1663 – Mlle Molière, Armande. Du Parc died in November 1664 and Mlle Du Croisy, never more than a bit-part player, was relieved of her share. The resulting roster remained unchanged until 1670 with the exception of Marquise Du Parc, who left the troupe, this time for the Hôtel de Bourgogne, at Easter of 1667.

The years between Easter 1665 and Easter 1668 were rather lean ones. The troupe spent a lot of money in the spring of 1665 on new settings for *Dom Juan*, which did not have the extensive run needed to recoup the extraordinary investment. The next season was the least profitable in the history of the company, in part because Molière's illness combined with the death of the queen mother on January 20 created an unwanted vacation of nearly two months during the period of the holidays and carnival, usually the most lucrative time of the year.

Molière himself was relatively inactive throughout the season of 1665–6. *L'Amour médecin*, which he described as "a sketch, a little impromptu," was his only new work between the final performance of *Dom Juan* on March 20, 1665, and the opening of *Le Misanthrope* on June 8, 1666. The two major premieres during 1665 were Mlle Desjardin's *La Coquette, ou le favori*, that ran for thirteen performances but made very little money, and Racine's *Alexandre*, meant to see the troupe through the Christmas season. However, Racine, not liking the tragic style of the actors at the Palais-Royal, permitted the Burgundians to produce the same play a week later. After three more performances the Palais-Royal, without a novelty for the holidays, closed its doors.

They remained closed until February 26. Rumor had it that Molière was desperately ill, possibly dead.[2] Then Anne of Austria died on January 20, plunging Paris into mourning until the burial on February 12. Shortly thereafter, rumor had it that Molière was not dead and on February 21 Robinet announced that the God of Laughter, the French Momus, had escaped the gluttonous gullet of Fate and would soon be back on stage.[3]

The following season, 1666–7, was more successful. Molière provided two new plays, *Le Misanthrope* and *Le Médecin malgré lui*, substantial if not exceptional hits, while the troupe's long stay at court for the *Ballet des muses* brought in 12,000 *livres* in clear income to the actors. However, the next season was once more rather unprofitable. Robinet remarks on April 16, 1667, that Molière again had been rumored to be dying,[4] and La Grange notes a number of "interruptions" that help account for the low income. The only real hit of the season was *Amphitryon* which opened on January 13 and was offered continuously until the end of the season on March 18.

The 1668–9 season was also marked by "interruptions" of a week to ten days until the opening of *Tartuffe* on February 5, 1669. *Tartuffe*, of course, was a huge success and the actors' shares the highest they had ever earned.

Whether Molière was acutely ill in January 1666 – or merely ailing and furious with Racine who had left the troupe without new material for the holidays – there is no way to know. I think it likely he was both ill and furious, but mostly furious. In any case, he was well enough on January 19 to arrange for a new apartment and sign a lease for five years to come. Nor do we know his condition in April of 1667 or in August of that same year when La Grange and La Thorillière went to Lille to find the king and beg for *Tartuffe* while Molière went to his hideaway in the Paris suburbs. There is no doubt that he had been – and would continue to be – ill. By 1666–7 he was almost certainly infected with the tuberculosis that would kill him in 1673. However, a heretical possibly might also be entertained. There is a suspicious correlation between Molière's absences from the stage, the shortened run of *Dom Juan*, and the king's unwillingness to lift the ban on *Tartuffe*. Before April 1665, when *Dom Juan* closed never to reopen, what La Grange calls "interruptions" did occasionally occur,[5] and Molière periodically took a week or ten days off when he was finishing a new play. However, after the "failure" of *Dom Juan* (of which more later), Molière began to be absent from the stage of the Palais-Royal for significant periods of time: a month in April and May of 1665, long breaks in June, July, and August of the same year, and the very long break, from December 7, 1665 to February 21, 1666, that most biographers assume represents the first critical episode in Molière's illness.

In the next season, Molière had only two vacations, a week in July and two in March, but something was amiss since the troupe took a double Easter holiday, forty-six days rather than the usual twenty-three to twenty-five. He opened the new season, but played rarely in May and took time off in June and July. After the second interdiction of *Tartuffe* on August 6, 1667, and an "interruption" of seven weeks, Molière played six times and then did not appear again until January 2, 1668. The season of 1668–9 included six "interruptions" and a short vacation until the successful opening of the third *Tartuffe* on February 5, 1669.

Following that longed-for event, the pattern changed and Molière had very few respites. Even in his final season, when his health was supposedly failing, he was "indisposed" only twice, on August 9 and 12.

Although we know from a number of sources that Molière was ill during the last years of his life, the specific references to his being near death all come from the gazetteer Robinet whose weekly *Lettres en vers* provide snapshots of the Paris theatrical scene in the 1660s and 1670s. But it is well within the realm of the possible that Robinet's columns were for sale and that what appears in them depends by and large on what the subject pays to have said. I want to propose as a conceivable interpretation of the chronology I have sketched above that Molière was engaged in a strategy designed to encourage the king to approve production of *Tartuffe*. In any case, its opening in February 1669 appears to have achieved a remarkable remission. Perhaps there was a bargain struck. "All right, Molière," we might have Louis say. "You win. But if I let your *Tartuffe* go on, you must promise me no more 'interruptions,' no more vacations, no more substitutions. It will be Molière first, last, and always." "Fine," says Molière, "sure," knowing as he says it that he will live to regret it.

All of this was still before him on May 12, 1664, when he presented the first three acts of his new play *Tartuffe* to the king and his guests at Versailles. This performance raises several questions, first among them being "why?" Why would Molière perform an unfinished and potentially scandalous play on such an important occasion? The only likely explanation is that the king asked to see it and Molière complied.

The play was controversial before it was performed publicly. No doubt several readings had taken place, one probably for Louis.[6] In any case, the *dévots*, the extreme Christian party, knew about it and knew that its presentation at court was imminent. On April 17 the Compagnie du Saint-Sacrement, a secret society of powerful courtiers and parlementarians, deliberated on how to "procure the suppression of the evil play of *Tartuffe*." The gentlemen decided that each one would "speak to his friends who had some credit at court to prevent the performance."[7] The king apparently did not listen to advance warnings and the performance went on.

Five days later the *Gazette*, while congratulating His Majesty for condemning the Jansenists, also praised him for "forbidding performance of a play entitled the *Hypocrite*, that His Majesty, fully enlightened in all things, judged absolutely injurious to religion and capable of producing very dangerous effects."[8] This overstates the king's point of view. Clearly Louis had been forced quickly to recant his support for Molière's new play, but probably not because he was concerned with its dangerous effects. A more diplomatic, but still ingenuous, reading of his action was contained in the official account published by Ballard later that year:

> His Majesty had a play entitled *Tartuffe* performed that the sieur de Molière had written against the hypocrites; but although he had found it very diverting, the king perceived so great a resemblance between those whose true devotion set them on the path to heaven and those whose vain exhibition of good works did not prevent them from committing bad ones that his very scrupulous concern for religious matters could not permit this resemblance between vice and virtue . . . and while not doubting the good intentions of the author, he had forbidden it in public and deprived himself of this pleasure, in order that others, less capable than he of making a just discernment, not be abused by it.[9]

We can only speculate about what actually went on at Versailles after the performance on May 12. Apparently one of the players was the Archbishop of Paris, Hardouin de Péréfixe, former tutor to the king. At least, it was reported to the assembly of the Compagnie du Saint-Sacrement on May 27 that it was M. de Péréfixe who had informed the king, perhaps "fully enlightened" him, concerning the bad effects *Tartuffe* might produce.[10] Another influence may well have been the queen mother, who had always been pious. She was, after all, Spanish. In May of 1664, moreover, she knew she had a tumor in her breast. She was deeply concerned that her son was faithful neither to his wife nor to his church; only a few weeks before he had declined to take communion at Easter, insisting that to do so would be hypocritical.[11] The great festival in which *Tartuffe* played only a minor role was overtly meant to honor the queens, but the queen mother surely recognized that Louis's mistress Louise de La Vallière, a woman she had never officially "met," was the true focus of the celebrations. Given these circumstances, given all the various ways in which the young king was defying his mother, it is credible to suppose that Anne of Austria, under the influence of Bossuet and the other *dévots*, asked her son as a favor to prohibit *Tartuffe*, and that her son granted her appeal. *Tartuffe* would not have been very high on Louis's list of priorities.

The second question that engages us is why *Tartuffe* was the cause of such strife. Louis, himself, was somewhat bewildered by the fuss. According to Molière's own preface, a week after *Tartuffe* was banned a play entitled *Scaramouche ermite* was performed at court by the Italian troupe. "The king, as he was leaving, said to the great prince [undoubtedly Condé]: 'I would really like to know why the people who are so scandalized by Molière's play have nothing to say about this one of Scaramouche'; to which the prince replied: 'The reason for that is that Scaramouche's play mocks heaven and religion, which these gentlemen care nothing about; but Molière's play mocks them; that's what they can't abide.'"[12] Apparently, in this first version Tartuffe himself was costumed as a priest in a soutane or at least as a *petit collet*, a wearer of the "little collar," one who has taken minor orders and dresses so as to be identified as a churchman. This gave opponents evidence for their assertion that Molière was attacking the Church itself and not just the hypocrites who used the Church for their own purposes.

Molière had supporters as well as adversaries; the prince de Condé was one of Molière's most powerful and persistent champions. He was also the brother of Molière's former patron, the prince de Conti. Unlike his brother Conti, who was converted to fundamentalist Catholicism, Condé remained a free thinker until the very last years of his life. He commanded three performances of *Tartuffe* during the years it was banned, including one given after the archbishop of Paris had pronounced that anyone who saw *Tartuffe* was liable to excommunication.

This delight in *Tartuffe* may have been merely aesthetic; it may have been philosophical; it may also have been a deliberate gesture to underline the difference between the two brothers, Condé and Conti. Condé would go another twenty years before taking Easter communion, the minimum sacramental act required of a Christian. Conti lived under the guidance of his personal director of conscience, examining each thought and action for evidence of impiety. And it was, after all, Conti, former pleasure-seeker and former patron of Molière, who had – following the prompting of his director of conscience the abbé Ciron – reneged on his patronage and let it be known that "his" actors were no longer to bear his name. If there was an event in Molière's own life that motivated him to write *Tartuffe*, it was probably Conti's betrayal.

Conti became a member of the Compagnie du Saint-Sacrement with such luminaries of the conservative church as Bossuet and Lamoignon, first president of the Parlement of Paris. The goals of the society were charitable and social and included the oversight and reform of manners and morals. Unfortunately, in this last arena the members of the Compagnie often went too far. Conti, himself, procured the arrest of a woman in Bordeaux in 1658 for *mauvaises moeurs*, bad behavior. When she protested, the Procureur Général investigated and concluded that she had been the victim of an illicit congregation that was compromising domestic peace.[13] In 1660 a scandal erupted in Caen, in Normandy, when the Compagnie was the subject of an exposé by one Du Four, abbé d'Aulnay, who accused this devout gang of introducing themselves into families and religious communities to hunt down those tainted with Jansenism, while they themselves departed from the straight and narrow, opening a wide and spacious way to salvation.[14] The gentlemen were, in other words, hypocrites. An inquiry into Du Four's charges resulted in an act of Parlement. Secret societies were forbidden. Of course, first president Lamoignon, who presided over Parlement the day the act was passed, was himself a member of the Compagnie du Saint-Sacrement, so no action was anticipated. The Compagnie was "officially" disbanded in 1666, but undoubtedly survived, driven even further underground.

George Couton has noted that one verse of *Tartuffe* unmistakably links its title character to the Compagnie. In line 1248 Tartuffe assures Cléante, his victim's brother, that he will use Orgon's property "Pour la gloire du Ciel et le bien du prochain," for the glory of God and the good of one's fellow men. This phrase recurs so frequently in the Statutes of the Compagnie that Couton regards it as almost a motto.[15] The inescapable conclusion is that Molière knew something of the secret Compagnie – more than he should have known – that identified his target, at least to those who were in the line of fire. That in itself is enough to explain the devout reaction to his play.

Molière probably had several specific objectives: privately he was avenging himself on his faithless patron while publicly he was attacking the members of a secret society who burrowed like termites into the fabric of the city and the court, defending Church and aristocratic power and privilege. He believed that he could count on the support of the king who was clearly uneasy about the growing power of the cabal. He was right, but only in the very long run.

In the short run, the play remained under interdiction. Loret writes in his *Muze historique* of May 24 that Molière has been making trip after trip to plead for his "persecuted work," but without success. Boileau published his *Satire II. À M. de Molière* on July 12, defending his friend, but Molière's pleasure in being publicly praised was doubtless attenuated when there appeared on August 1 a vicious attack by a Paris priest, Pierre Roullé, *curé* of Saint-Barthélemy, against "this man, or rather Demon clothed in flesh and dressed like a man and the most signal scoffer and freethinker who ever was in the centuries past, who has had enough of impiety and abomination to bring from his diabolical mind a play ready to be rendered public by putting it on the stage to the derision of the whole Church and in contempt of the most sacred character and of the most divine function and in contempt of what is most holy in the Church, founded by the Savior for the sanctification of souls, who wants to render the usage of it ridiculous, contemptible, odious."[16] Roullé thinks Molière should be burned in expiation of this crime of divine *lèse Majesté*, but he recognizes the godlike mercy the king has shown by giving the insolent wretch the opportunity to do solemn and public penance for the rest of his life and to cease creation of his licentious and libertine poetry. As Roullé's vitriol dripped off the press, Molière was entertaining the king and his honored guest, the papal legate Cardinal Chigi, at Fontainebleau with four performances of the *Princesse d'Élide*. Lionne wrote to the duc de Créqui that this *fort galante* play was given in place of *Tartuffe*, which the king had entirely suppressed out of piety.[17] Cardinal Chigi had no such scruples and while in Paris invited Molière to read the play to him. The cardinal was called away in the middle of Scene 3 to attend some ladies who had come to ask for indulgences. His holy duty done, he returned laughing to Molière and requested another scene.[18] This anecdote is affirmed by Molière, himself, who includes among his arguments in favor of *Tartuffe* the approbation of "Monsieur le Légat."[19]

This reference occurs in what is known as the *Premier Placet présenté au Roi*. Not printed but apparently circulated, since three manuscript copies are to be found in seventeenth-century collections,[20] Molière's petition is a direct and forthright response to the "injuries" and "calumnies" in Roullé's pamphlet.

Molière argues that since the duty of comedy is to correct men while diverting them, he had thought it appropriate to render this service to the honorable people of the kingdom. His play would "proclaim" the hypocrites, much in evidence and very dangerous, and show "all the covert deceptions of these counterfeiters of devotion." He insists that he has made every effort to distinguish the "unadulterated hypocrite" from the truly devout. Nonetheless, "the tartuffes have underhandedly had the cunning to get themselves into Your Majesty's good graces and the originals have finally had the copy suppressed."[21]

A later edition of Ballard's *Les Plaisirs de l'Île enchantée* adds to its original description of the king's reasons for banning *Tartuffe* the following: "He forbade this play until it was entirely finished and examined by people capable of judging it."[22] Molière seems to substantiate this when he says that the initial blow was softened by the way in which the king had explicated his motives. "I thought," he adds, "that this relieved me from any cause to complain."[23] But now, in spite of this, in spite of approval from Cardinal Chigi and other prelates, Molière finds himself viciously attacked by a local parish priest who has never seen the play. Molière begs the king to permit the play to defend itself and its author, that is, to permit its public performance. He puts his interest into the king's hands and respectfully awaits the king's pleasure. He had a long wait.

Molière may have gone too far; he comes close to accusing the king himself of hypocrisy, proscribing in public what he applauded in private. Perhaps, too, the king was simply not in a position to alienate the devout party or perhaps he was still abiding by the wishes of his mother, whose death impended for several years. In the meantime, the issue was kept alive by private performances.

The first and one of the most important of those private performances took place at Villers-Cotterets in late September 1664 at the command of Monsieur, the king's brother. This was still a performance of the first three acts,[24] and the king was possibly present.[25] In November the troupe was summoned to Le Raincy, the country house of the mistress of the prince de Condé. According to La Grange, this was the first performance of *Tartuffe* in five acts,[26] although a year later another performance took place at Le Raincy and Condé's son, the duc d'Enghien, wrote to M. de Ricous to arrange things. According to this letter, *Tartuffe* was not yet complete since Enghien asks if the fourth act is finished and can be performed.[27] This was the last known performance before the Paris opening of the retitled *L'Imposteur* on August 5, 1667.

Before that second public performance, however, Molière took another giant risk. He offered to the Paris public his version of that most baroque of all fictional characters, Don Juan. The "quarrel" that followed was, like the quarrel of *Tartuffe*, rather humdrum: one pamphlet attacking *Dom Juan*, two defending it. But by the time the polemics appeared, the issue was moot. The play had disappeared from the Paris stage for the lifetime of its author. Again, as in the case of *Tartuffe*, the real action took place elsewhere.

Dom Juan, ou le Festin de pierre was a familiar title. The story was first introduced by the Italian *commedia dell'arte* troupe and was imitated in two French versions by Villiers and Dorimond. Molière's version owes something to his Paris predecessors and also to the so-called Cicognini version written in Italian, but nothing directly to Tirso de Molina's original Spanish play, *El Burlador de Sevilla*. The French *Festins* were all spectacle plays with multiple settings, and that seems to be what Molière and his actors, in great need of a hit, prepared their audience to see. Loret published the usual puffery in his *Muze historique* the day before the opening. The "dreadful" stone guest, writes Loret, who has been so popular on the Italian's stage, is about to appear on ours. The "rare mind" of Molière has treated the subject in such a way as to appeal to serious people, and with his usual fine style. This remark was meant to counteract the general perception that people went to see the various *Festin de pierre* plays only for the moving statue of the Commander and his horse. The actors, Loret hears from those who have seen rehearsals, do marvels and the scene changes, which are so adored by the bourgeois audience members, will include "a surprising effect."[28]

The scene changes represent a real departure for the troupe. Although the actors were accustomed to transposing plays and comedy-ballets written for the court to their Palais-Royal stage, these did not usually include changeable scenery. For *Dom Juan*, however, which did not open at court, the troupe bought a new set of decors. According to a contract signed with the painters Jean Simon and Pierre Prat on December 3, 1664,[29] the settings for *Dom Juan* included a palace setting with a garden visible behind, a country hamlet with a backdrop of the sea, a forest with a temple painted on the shutter, the inside of the temple, a room, and a city with a port visible behind. All the settings began with wings eighteen feet high at the front, diminishing as they went upstage in order to force the perspective. For painting all of this scenery plus *bandes* and *frizes* to conceal the tops of the wings, and new decor for the proscenium, and what appear to be new stage boxes, Simon and Prat charged 900 *livres*. This sum does not, of course, include what was spent for carpentry nor for the "surprising effect" mentioned by Loret, probably the appearance, transformation, and disappearance of the Spectre in Act V, scene v.

Although the expense of the new decors was onerous, the troupe anticipated recouping costs and eventually making money. The play opened on February 15 after a week's interruption and ran until the Easter closing, fifteen performances. The gross receipts were high, rising to a new maximum of 2,390 *livres* on February 24, then dropping off as the Lenten season deepened. The profit to the actors, while good, was affected by having to pay for the production, and certainly the troupe expected to reprise the play after the Easter break and continue to reap the harvest of its investment. Unfortunately, the play disappeared after its fifteenth performance.

This took place in spite of the bowdlerizing of the famous scene of the beggar, performed as written only on opening night.[30] Thanks to a pirated edition that appeared in Amsterdam in 1683, we do possess the original text.[31] The section that Molière agreed to remove follows the beggar's offer to pray for Dom Juan if the latter will give him alms. Dom Juan ironically assumes that the beggar must be prosperous if he spends all his time as he says, praying to heaven. "Alas," answers the beggar, "most of the time I don't have even a bit of bread to put in my mouth." Dom Juan finds it strange that the beggar's prayers have been so poorly rewarded. This is followed by the offending exchange:

DOM JUAN . . . Ah ha! I will give you a gold coin if you will blaspheme.
LE PAUVRE Oh! Sir, do you want me to commit such a sin?
DOM JUAN It depends on whether you want a gold coin or not. Here's the one I'll give you, if you blaspheme. Come on, blaspheme!
LE PAUVRE Sir!
DOM JUAN Or you can't have it.
SGANARELLE Oh, come on. Blaspheme a little. There's nothing wrong with that.
DOM JUAN Take it, here it is; take it, I tell you, but first blaspheme!
LE PAUVRE No, sir! I'd rather die of hunger.
DOM JUAN Go on, then . . .[32]

This was the end of the cut, but Dom Juan's speech continued with "I will give it to you for the love of humanity," also controversial and scandalous, "love of humanity" being taken as the antithesis of "love of God."

Dom Juan, like *Tartuffe*, shows Molière gambling with fate. Like its predecessor, it is a play about hypocrisy. Dom Juan, on the surface a baroque prince who has freed himself from the constraints of an ordered but moribund society, is hypocritical to the core. His apparent allegiance to libertinage itself is only a veneer. In fact, he owes allegiance to nothing; he is a hollow man.

At the beginning of Act IV, Dom Juan, "playing the hypocrite," reports to his father that he has seen the light. He promises to do public reparation, to show the world how he has changed, and he begs his father to help him find a director of conscience, someone to guide him on the path he has chosen.[33] His apparent sincerity even convinces his servant Sganarelle, only too familiar with his master's usual behavior. Of course, as soon as his father leaves the room, Dom Juan disabuses the valet. He is delighted, he says, to have a witness "to the depth of my soul and the real motives that oblige me to do things." Sganarelle is shocked.

"What? You believe in nothing, and yet you propose to set yourself up as a devout man?" Dom Juan sees no reason why he shouldn't.

There are so many like me, who adopt this profession and wear this mask to abuse the world . . . There's no shame in it; hypocrisy is a fashionable vice, and all fashionable vices pass for virtues. The role of devout man is the best of all the roles that one can play today, and professing hypocrisy has marvelous advantages. This is an art in which the impostor is always respected; and even when he is found out, no one dares say anything against him. All the other vices of men are exposed to censure, and anyone is free to attack them; but hypocrisy is a privileged vice that holds its hand over the mouths of everyone and enjoys sovereign impunity.[34]

They all stick together, he says. The truly pious are the dupes of the others, the ones who have by means of this stratagem redressed the "disorders of their youth." And he will do the same, but he will not give up his usual habits. If someone finds him out, why, the whole cabal will defend him.

This is the way to do with impunity whatever I want. I'll set myself up as a censor of the actions of others, judge everyone badly, and have a good opinion only of myself. If anyone offends me, I shall never pardon him, I shall secretly preserve an irreconcilable hatred. I will be the avenger of Heaven, and under this ample pretext, I will press my enemies, I will accuse them of impiety, and I will loose upon them the zealots who, without knowing why, will publicly accuse them, overwhelm them with insults, and damn them with their private authority. This is how to profit from human weakness and how a wise man accommodates himself to the vices of his century.[35]

That this speech refers directly to the prince de Conti seems obvious. Conti's conversion was not believed in universally. The king detested him, his own brother disliked him, and Molière certainly had no reason to respect him. Molière must have believed, moreover, that Conti's position at court was weak, and, indeed, this tirade was not an issue either at the time of the first performance or in 1682 when the publishers were forced to reprint twenty-one pages and rebind the book, principally because of cuts made by the censors in the third act.

Dom Juan is, of course, a seducer and an atheist. Acts I and II largely concern the first of these activities, Act III the second. The encounter between Dom Juan and Sganarelle in Act III, scene i on the subject of what the master believes can be profitably read as a parody of a dialogue between a sinner and his director of conscience, and as another attack on Conti and those like him. Because he puts the servant and clown Sganarelle in the position of the director of conscience, the one who defends the existence of God, Molière was once again accused – and rightly so, I should think – of mocking the fundamentalist faction of the Church. Does Dom Juan believe in Heaven, Hell, the devil, the afterlife? He doesn't want to say. "Yes, yes. Ha, ha, ha." "A hard man to convert," remarks Sganarelle. "How about the *Moine bourru?*" The *Moine bourru* or the Angry Monk was meant to run through the streets at Advent, making frightening noises. Sganarelle's belief in him, as in the *loup-garou* or werewolf, is equal to or maybe greater than his Christian belief; Molière thus equates belief and superstition. Finally Dom Juan admits that he believes that two and two are four and four and four are eight and Sganarelle launches into his sermon:

I've never studied like you, thank God, and no one could boast of ever having taught me anything; but with my small intelligence, my small judgment, I see things better than all the books, and I understand very well that this world we see is not a mushroom that popped up in a single night. I would like to ask you who made these trees here, these rocks, this earth, and this sky up above, or if all of that caused itself? Take you, for example, there you are: did you make yourself, didn't your father have to make your mother pregnant to make you? Can you see all the inventions that make up the man machine without admiring how they are arranged? These nerves, these bones, these veins, these arteries, these . . ., this lung, this heart, this liver, and all these other ingredients which are there and which . . . Oh, damn it, interrupt me, please! I can't dispute if no one interrupts me.[36]

Dom Juan does not want to dispute. Dom Juan is waiting for the fool to finish his argument. Sganarelle's final point is that there is something in man which all the scholars cannot explain. "I have something in my head that thinks a hundred different things in a minute, and makes my body do whatever my head wants. I want to clap my hands, lift my shoulders, raise my eyes to the skies, lower my head, move my feet, go right, go left, forward, back, turn . . ." And spinning, he falls down. "Good! Your argument has broken its nose," points out Dom Juan.[37] This scene was allowed in 1665, but not in 1682.

One would think that *Dom Juan* would have been found more offensive than *Tartuffe*, but perhaps it was so specific to Conti that the others of the devout party, who were sorry they had permitted him to join the Compagnie du Saint-Sacrement, decided not to make an example of it. Perhaps Molière was able to persuade the king not to take action. Perhaps the king was prepared to bargain this time and understood that the troupe simply could not afford to have the first run of the play aborted. *Dom Juan* was never performed for the court and there is no evidence that the king ever saw it. Perhaps that, too, was part of the bargain. Unlike *Tartuffe*, which had the king's imprimatur, *Dom Juan* was strictly between the troupe and the Paris audience. No one, this time, could accuse Louis of hypocrisy.

Or maybe one can. On August 14, 1665, five months after the truncated run of *Dom Juan*, the troupe was summoned to St-Germain-en-Laye. La Grange writes: "The king said to M. de Molière that he wanted the troupe to belong to him in the future and had requested it of Monsieur. His Majesty at the same time gave a pension of 6,000 *livres* to the troupe which took its leave of Monsieur, asking for his continued protection, and took the title: La Troupe du Roi au Palais-Royal."[38] This suggests that some arrangement had been made between Molière and his patron or, at least, that Molière remained in or had been restored to royal favor.

For his next war, Molière chose a much less powerful enemy: the doctors. He attacked, however, with the same degree of bitter irony that characterizes *Dom Juan*. In fact, his first volley against the doctors comes in *Dom Juan*, at the beginning of Act III, when Sganarelle steals a doctor's hat and robe and explains that he has been prescribing for the peasants. Dom Juan sees no problem with this, since "medicine is one of the greatest of all human errors." Molière's specific target is "emetic wine," a powerful purgative, the use of which was then being debated by the Faculty of Medicine. One exchange from this scene is worth quoting:

SGANARELLE There was a man who was in agony for six days; no one knew what else to prescribe for him, all the medicines did nothing. Finally someone said, "Give him emetic wine."
DOM JUAN He recovered, did he?
SGANARELLE No, he died.
DOM JUAN An admirable effect.
SGANARELLE What? For six whole days he could not die, and that killed him instantly. What could be more efficient?[39]

A more concerted attack on the doctors came in Molière's next play, a little farce entitled *L'Amour médecin*, written for performance at court on September 14, 1665. It was the first command performance by the newly adopted Troupe de Roi au Palais-Royal. Molière describes it as "a simple sketch, a little impromptu," proposed, written, rehearsed, and performed in five days.[40] And, indeed, the play, in three swift acts, is a farce in the Italian manner and largely of historical interest, although it was very popular during Molière's lifetime. It is, like its two predecessors, a portrait of hypocrisy. Medicine is an illusion; doctors are no better than charlatans, alchemists, or astrologers. As M. Filerin, the doyen of the doctors in the play, says: "Thanks to Heaven people are infatuated with us, so let us not disabuse them, let us profit from their stupidity. We are not the only ones, as you know, to prey on human weakness . . . but the greatest weakness of men is their love for life; and we profit from that, with our pompous rigmarole, we know how to take advantage of the veneration for our profession that the fear of death gives."[41]

Four doctors are called in to treat Lucinde, the daughter of Sganarelle, who is fallen into melancholy. All that is wrong with Lucinde is that she is in love, but her father will not allow her to marry, not wanting to provide a dowry. The doctors are M. Tomès, M. Des Fonandrès, M. Macroton, and M. Bahys. They "consult," they bicker, they are scolded by M. Filerin for their unprofessional behavior. Finally, in a typical denouement, Lucinde's lover arrives disguised as a doctor and Sganarelle is tricked into accepting the marriage.

What was unusual about this production was that each of the fictional doctors was modeled on a well-known physician. Molière was constantly accused of writing *pièces à clef* with characters that could be recognized by those "in the know." In this instance, however, the models were definitely identified because the actors playing the copies wore portrait masks.[42] According to Brossette, Boileau collaborated with Molière in devising the character names. Des Fonandres meaning "killer of men" was Des Fougerais, Bahys, "one who barks," was Esprit who stuttered, Macrotan, "one who speaks slowly," was modeled on Guénaut, and Tomès, "one who draws blood," on Daquin. Brossette identifies the model for Filerin as Yvelin who was physician-in-chief to Madame, the king's sister-in-law.[43] Guénaut was the queen's doctor, Esprit head doctor for Monsieur, and Daquin one of the king's eight official doctors. Des Fougerais had no court appointment, but was celebrated anyway.

We usually assume that Molière's dislike and mistrust of doctors arose from his own experiences with them during his illness, but this first full attack on the medical profession was written before he fell ill.[44] He had, however, endured two deaths in the fall of 1665 that may have aroused his spleen. His close friend the abbé La Mothe Le Vayer died in September, possibly as a result of treatment with emetic wine, and his son Louis died in November; Molière may have blamed the doctors for either death or for both.[45]

He also had a personal reason to dislike Daquin who had been his landlord. On September 2, 1661 Molière rented an apartment in a newly built house owned by Daquin on the rue St-Thomas-du-Louvre, that ran between the rue St-Honoré and the Seine opposite the Palais-Royal. There he brought his young wife in February 1662, there they were living when their son was born in February 1664. In May of that year the family subleased from another tenant of Daquin's what was probably a larger apartment, but the move may have had other motives as well.

There are two versions of the story. The more credible one appeared in *Élomire hypocondre* in 1670. Daquin supposedly asked the actor to vacate his apartment, without giving a reason. Molière offered to pay more and the lease was renewed, but the offended tenant was merely biding his time. Armande had Mme Daquin expelled from the theatre, to the delight of Molière, but Daquin, a royal physician, did not take this insult lightly. To his extreme chagrin, Molière was forced to apologize, which increased his thirst for revenge.[46]

Also according to Le Boulanger de Chalussay, the lesson Molière learned from the Daquin incident was that Aesculapius had more credit at court than Momus. However, unlike the furors roused by *Tartuffe* and *Dom Juan*, the reception of *L'Amour médecin* was almost uniformly positive. The *Gazette*, so happy to commend the king for his interdiction of *Tartuffe*, found *L'Amour médecin* to be "very agreeable."[47] M. de Langeron observed the comic effect of the masks, remarking that while doctor Guéneau laughed, doctor Esprit did not.[48] Condé's son, the duc d'Enghien, wrote rather a long account of the play to the queen of Poland. It was not, he noted, especially funny as described, but "nothing could be funnier to see."[49]

By the time Molière wrote his second play attacking the doctors, *Le Médecin malgré lui* that opened on August 6, 1666, he had certainly experienced their treatment first hand. Probably because it opened in the dog days of August, the play was not very profitable at first. It was a serviceable afterpiece for *Le Misanthrope*, but rarely did well by itself. Robinet stresses its power to cure disease through laughter, including his own migraine.[50] But the play was also regarded as a bagatelle, funny, witty, yet lacking the caustic and personal undercurrents that the audience now expected of Molière. The point, of course, was clear and hardly novel: any clod can become a better doctor than the doctors. The play owes a great deal to the farce of the Italians and especially to the second zanni of the Italian troupe that shared the theatre at Palais-Royal, the great Arlequin Domenico Biancolelli, but it may also owe something to Molière's own experiences. Although medical jargon and dog Latin are both commonplaces of farce, Molière's version in this play is unusually specific. After proposing that the muteness of the heroine results from the action of "certain humors," Sganarelle launches into shreds of Latin, half remembered from church and his grammar school, and then explains to the enchanted father:

these vapors of which I speak pass from the left side, where the liver is, to the right side, where the heart is, while the lung, that we call in Latin *armyan*, having communication with the brain, that we call in Greek *nasmus*, by means of the vena cava, that we call in Hebrew *cubile*, find the said vapors in its way, filling the ventricles of the shoulder-blade; and because the said vapors . . . follow this argument, I beg of you . . . and because the said vapors have a certain malignity . . . listen to me, I conjure you . . . have a certain malignity . . . pay attention, please! . . . which is caused by the accretion of the humors engendered in the concavity of the diaphragm, it so happens that these vapors . . . *Ossabandus, nequeys, nequer, potarinum, quipsa milus*. And that's precisely why your daughter is mute.[51]

There is a point to all this, buried in the nonsense. The "vapors" impede the action of the lungs. As in Toinette's diagnosis of Argan in *Le Malade imaginaire*, the lungs are the problem. Sganarelle's speech mimics what the patient, what Molière himself, hears when he asks his doctor what causes the fever, the cough, and the bloody phlegm, his *fluxion du poitrine*, his inflammation of the lungs. The answer is, of course, that there is no answer, something Molière had already learned.

Tuberculosis was common in the sevententh century. It was known as phthisis, scrofula, bronchitis, consumption, and, to be sure, inflammation of the lungs. The disease had been recognized as far back as history is recorded. Hippocrates, himself, knew it to be prevalent and incurable, and he advised doctors to avoid treating tubercular patients since they were sure to die and damage their doctors' reputations.[52] The Greeks, like Molière's doctor Mauvillain, prescribed a milk diet and fresh air, while the Romans believed in asses milk, a well-ventilated sick room, and long sea voyages like the one that supposedly cured Cicero.[53] At least Molière could console himself that the remedy he chose – a milk diet and a dwelling outside Paris – was both classical and non-invasive and for a time even effective.

Exactly when Molière leased his apartment in Auteuil is unknown, although he was certainly a tenant there in August 1667 when he witnessed the impertinent behavior of his landlord's gardener.[54] A likely time for him to have made the move was during the first known acute episode of his illness at the end of 1665 and the beginning of 1666.

Molière and Armande, presumably after Daquin demanded an

increase in their rent, subleased from Nicolas de Boulainvilliers an apartment in a second building owned by Daquin. The sublease was to begin at the third quarter of 1664 and run for three years. However, less than two years later, Molière and Armande rented another apartment on the rue St-Thomas-du-Louvre, apparently because Boulainvilliers gave up his lease. They lived there briefly, or perhaps not at all, since they sublet it in January and rented for five years yet another apartment on the same street, the third and fourth floors in a building owned by the widow of Antoine Brulon. The rent of this apartment was just over half that of the previous one, 550 *livres* a year instead of 1,000. One possible explanation is that the difference went to pay the 400 *livres* yearly rent on the apartment in Auteuil.[55]

This little apartment became Molière's retreat from Paris, from Armande, and from the overwhelming pressures of his profession. It was where he could recover his health; it was also where he could entertain his friends, enjoy the peace of the countryside, and write without interruption. It was probably where he finished *Le Misanthrope* in the spring of 1666. Linked to Paris by water coach, Auteuil was not exactly the desert wilderness Alceste offers and Célimène rejects, but it was as close to solitude as Molière could manage. The new Paris apartment was almost a return to the communal living of the provincial days. Geneviève Béjart and her husband were upstairs, the de Bries were downstairs, Madeleine and her mother were sometimes in the guest room, and Marquise was next door. The common wisdom is that Molière and Armande were separated in 1666 and reconciled at some appropriate time before the birth of their third child in October 1672, but that seems like a modern way of understanding what happened. Nothing suggests that any recognized separation took place, but rather that Molière withdrew to the extent that he could from a world that gave him no pleasure. He was sick, he was bitter, and he was disillusioned, a perfect frame of mind for completing his masterpiece.

We shall consider that masterpiece in a later chapter. For now, we must return to the history of *Tartuffe*. In the summer of 1667 Molière clearly believed that he had the king's permission to produce a new version of his outlawed play. He had finished it, which was one of the king's conditions. He had changed its title to *L'Imposteur* and the name of its hypocritical false *dévot* from Tartuffe to Panulphe. Even more to the point he had "disguised the character in the costume of a fashionable man," given him "a small hat, a great wig, a large collar, a sword, and lace on everything."[56] Finally, he had softened various things and carefully cut "anything that I judged capable of furnishing the shadow of a pretext to the celebrated originals whose portrait I was trying to paint."[57] The queen mother was deceased, the Compagnie du Saint-Sacrement officially disbanded. However, the cabal was not dead but only sleeping and the king was out of town.

L'Imposteur opened on August 5, 1667. This was not an auspicious time to open a new play. The army was in Flanders and a survey of the troupe's usual earnings in August indicates that theatre-going was not high on the list of social priorities in the late summer in Paris. But perhaps that was the point, perhaps Molière believed that with *le tout Paris* out of town, the *dévots* would be less inclined to react. If that is what he hoped, he was wrong. The play opened on Friday, the usual day to introduce a new play so that word of mouth could spread and bring in a full house on Sunday. The box office took in 1,890 *livres* at the first performance, promising a profitable run. Except – there was no second performance. On August 6 "an officer of the Parlement came on behalf of the first president M. de Lamoignon to forbid the play." La Grange and La Thorillière went on behalf of Molière to present a second petition to the king, who was besieging Lille. La Grange writes: "we were very well received. Monsieur protected us as usual and His Majesty sent word that on his return to Paris he would have the play *Tartuffe* examined and that we would perform it."[58]

Meanwhile, back in Paris, Molière sought remedy from the most powerful protection available: the young Madame, wife of his nominal patron Monsieur.[59] The lady, who was eager to see the play, sent the abbé Delavau, one of her gentlemen, to make known the king's intentions to Lamoignon. Delavau's mission failed, although the first president agreed to call on Madame. When he did so, four or five days later, the subject of the play never came up.

Molière's next step was to go himself to see Lamoignan, introduced by their mutual acquaintance Boileau who describes the interview:

... Molière explained the subject of his visit; M. le Premier Président answered him as follows: Monsieur, I hold your merit in great esteem; I know that you are not only an excellent actor, but also a very clever man who does honor to your profession and to France, your country; however, with all the good will in the world, I cannot permit you to play your comedy. I am persuaded that it is very well-written and very instructive, but actors are not meant to instruct mankind on matters of Christian morality and religion; it is not the business of the theatre to preach the gospel. When the king returns, he will permit you, if he finds it *à propos*, to perform *Tartuffe*, but I would abuse the authority he has done me the honor to confide in me during his absence, if I were to grant you the permission you request.[60]

Molière was disconcerted by this response, which was not what he expected. He tried to insist that his play was perfectly innocent, that he had taken every precaution to treat the subject with delicacy. Unfortunately, says Boileau, he was so angry that he could only sputter and, after listening to him for a moment, Lamoignon excused himself, saying that he was afraid he would be late for mass.

On August 11 another blow fell. Hardouin de Péréfixe, archbishop of Paris, issued an order. A play has been performed on one of the stages of this city, he begins, a play that under the pretext of condemning hypocrisy exposes people of the most solid piety to the jests and calumnies of the freethinkers. To prevent this, the archbishop forbids "all the people in [his] diocese of Paris to perform under whatever title this play, to read it or hear it read, in public or in private, under pain of excommunication."[61]

On August 20 appeared on the bookstalls a *Lettre sur la comédie de l'Imposteur*. It was unsigned and possibly written in collaboration with Molière himself since it is very detailed.[62]

Parts 2 and 3 make up the only published defense of the play before Molière's preface of 1669. Part 2 clearly reflects on the reasoning of Lamoignon, "the strange disposition of the mind" of certain people who, finding no specific evil in the play, "condemn it in general, solely because religion is mentioned in it and because the theatre, they say, is not a place where [religion] should be taught."[63] On the contrary, proposes the anonymous author, "pagans, who had no less respect for their religion than we have for ours, had no fear to put it on their stages . . . they wisely believed there was no better way to persuade people of the truth of it than the spectacles that were so popular. It is for that reason that their gods appeared so often on the stage, that the denouements, which are the most important parts of the poem, almost always are the work of some divinity, and that there is not a single play that does not include . . . exemplary proof of the clemency or the justice of Heaven toward mankind."[64] This *à propos* passage of course calls attention to the denouement of *L'Imposteur/Tartuffe* with its *rex ex machina* and the clemency of Louis XIV.

The letter seems to have had no effect, nor did Molière's second petition, even though it ends with what might be regarded as a threat: "I respectfully await what Your Majesty will deign to pronounce on this matter; but what is very certain, Sire, is that I will no longer think of writing plays, if the tartuffes have the advantage."[65]

The travelers return, the troupe reopens its theatre at the Palais-Royal and Robinet notes that Molière, "taking courage in spite of storms and squalls," has returned to the stage.[66] The return was brief. The "god of laughter" was going to demonstrate in action that he meant what he had said. From October 9 to December 31, 1667, Molière's plays did not appear in the repertory.[67] The troupe was summoned in November to Versailles; Molière did not go. In January 1668 he opened *Amphitryon*, the story of a man betrayed by Jupiter. In July the troupe contributed only the caustic comedy *George Dandin* to the *Grand Divertissement Royal de Versailles*, a striking contrast to its participation in the *Plaisirs de l'Île enchantée*. August, September, October, and November were marked by interruptions and vacations. Finally, it seems likely that Molière and the king came to some understanding, for on February 5, 1669, *Tartuffe* began its Paris run.

It was the most successful and profitable of all of Molière's plays. Robinet describes the excited audience that mobbed the theatre: "Curiosity," he says, "like nature abhors a vacuum." People risked being smothered in the press, cried out "I'm suffocating, I can't stand it! Alas, Monsieur Tartuffius, must wanting to see you cost me my life?" He continues:

> This Molière, with his brush,
> Has made a speaking portrait of [Tartuffe],
> With so much art, so much justice,
> And, finally, so much delicacy,
> That he charms the truly devout
> While enraging the frauds.
> And the rest of the characters,
> The thing is manifest,
> Are so well cast,
> So naturally played,
> That no comedy has ever
> Been so applauded.[68]

Two weeks later Robinet identifies the actors and notes that Her Majesty the Queen had commanded a performance and "laughed long to see the Hypocrite get what he deserved."

For Molière the victory was bitter and incomplete. In a preface written for the first edition of the play that appeared on March 23, he lists all the enemies he has made writing plays. The marquises, the *précieuses*, the cuckolds, and the doctors have suffered in silence and have even pretended to be amused, but the false *dévots*, those who have "hidden their own self-interest in God's cause," have taken up arms against the performance, which has been subjected to the same scrutiny as the text. According to these hypocrites, even the expurgated play is "full of abominations, and nothing is to be found in it that does not merit the fire. Every syllable in it is impious; even the gestures are criminal; and the slightest wink of an eye, the slightest shake of the head, the slightest step to the right or the left hides a mystery that only they can explicate to my disadvantage."[69]

The actors had their most profitable season in the lifetime of Molière thanks to *Tartuffe*: 5,477 *livres*, 3 *sous* per share, more than double the income of the previous season when Molière and his repertory were frequently unavailable. For Molière himself, however, this success could not make up for nearly five years of failure marked by persecution, character defamation, loss of prestige and income. The continued support by the king of his Troupe du Roi au Palais-Royal could not hide the decline in Molière's personal influence at court. He was no longer just a source of pleasure to Louis, an entertainer who could be relied on when a festival was in view. He had become a problem, someone with an agenda, not someone who could be greeted with a wink and a nod. "What about my play, Sire?" "Any decision about my *Tartuffe*, Your Majesty?" Molière's was one voice among many, a special pleader like all the others.

In 1664, he was a rising star. In 1669, he was disillusioned with king and court, but inescapably caught up in a system of patronage. There are two ways to read the denouement of *Tartuffe*. The first way is relevant to the time when it was written, probably in the summer of 1667 when production of *L'Imposteur* was pending and when Molière had reason to believe that the king had chosen to sustain his cause and was prepared to oppose the power of the devout party. Under such conditions, we can understand Molière's claim in the Exempt's speech in Act V:

> We live under a Prince, the enemy of fraud,
> A prince whose eyes can see into every heart,
> And who cannot be deceived by all the art of the impostors.[70]

If the production of *L'Imposteur* had been allowed, the lines would ring with sincerity. But when the action of Lamoignon was endorsed by the king (or at least not reversed), this paean to Louis's perspicacity must have sounded hollow indeed to its author. The preface of 1669 contrasts strikingly with the speech of the Exempt and suggests an alternate reading. In the speech the king can easily tell the difference between the true and false *dévots*, in the preface the false *dévots* still have power, including the power to entice the truly religious to their party. In the speech, the king has a superhuman ability to avoid such a trap and see through the lies of the impostors. In the preface the king is powerless, his judgment of the play meaningless to affect its reception. For those aware of the history of *Tartuffe*, the denouement could only have been ironic.

Molière continued to write for the court. Indeed, all of his new works between March 1669 and March 1672, with the exception of *Les Fourberies de Scapin*, were commissioned by the king. Of these only *Le Bourgeois gentilhomme* has remained consistently in the performed repertory. The others – *Monsieur de Pourceaugnac, Les Amants magnifiques, Psyché*, and *La Comtesse d'Escarbagnas* – all either comedy-ballets or spectacle plays – are considered minor works and rarely or never performed in the modern theatre. His last two plays, *Les Femmes savantes* and *Le Malade imaginaire*, were written after his break with Lully and his isolation from the court and are among his greatest. We might say, then, that Molière continued to honor his contract, more for the sake of his troupe than for his own sake, but not with enthusiasm. Only at the very end of his life, when the king's patronage was doubtful and the approval of the Paris audience all important, did his full genius reappear.

CHAPTER NINE

Friends

One morning in early autumn, while the days are still long and the weather fine, four friends set off from Paris to see "the new embellishments" at Versailles and hear Polyphile read his just completed "Adventures of Psyché." Polyphile is joined in the expedition by Acante, Ariste, and Gélaste. Traditionally, the four friends, characters in La Fontaine's *Les Amours de Psyché et Cupidon*, are identified as La Fontaine himself, Boileau, Racine, and Molière.[1] Without taking these identifications too literally, or assuming that these fictional characters are meant to be biographical, we can still contemplate the possibility that Gélaste is in some measure a reflection of Molière and Molière's ideas as seen through the eyes of his close friend La Fontaine.

La Fontaine's four characters, though legitimate denizens of Le Parnasse, the Paris literary scene, are set apart by their distaste for the academic. "If by chance they hit upon some point of science or of literature, they take advantage of the occasion; without, however, dwelling too long on any one thing, but rather leaping from one idea to another, like bees that encounter different kinds of flowers in their paths."[2] The same could be said of the four models. Not yet the serious men of letters nor the academicians that three of them would one day be, La Fontaine was writing charming tales and fables, Boileau satires, and the other two plays. All were irrepressible. An anecdote reported by Racine's son Louis, in his *Mémoires sur la vie et les ouvrages de Jean Racine*, describes how his father and his father's friends used to meet frequently for a meal at a famous bistro. Exchanges of wit were the order of the day and faults in syntax or taste were "severely punished." A copy of a poem, *La Pucelle*, by the politically powerful but artistically mediocre academic poet Chapelain lay on the table, and the guilty party was assigned to read a certain passage. A grave fault could cost the condemned man twenty verses, while an entire page was considered a death sentence.[3]

7. *Nicolas Boileau*, engraving by Bouys.

In La Fontaine's conceit, the four friends, arriving at Versailles well before the midday dinnertime, go first to admire the king's menagerie, filled with birds and mammals from distant lands. Next they make a tour of the Orangerie, amazed by certain trees that have survived for more than a hundred winters. During their dinner, they praise the monarch for his intelligence and heroic qualities, while pointing out that even

8. *Jean de La Fontaine*, from a painting by Hyacinth Rigaud, 1696.

Jupiter could not continually apply himself to the conduct of the universe. Rulers need some recreation, and their ruler has chosen to relax by building palaces, an appropriate hobby in their view. After which, they return to the palace and admire the tapestries and Chinese silks in the king's bedroom. Finally, they are conducted to the grotto of Thetis in the garden to rest during the heat of the day. A thousand jets of water cool the air, but the friends find the spot a little damp. Telling their guide

9. *Jean Racine*, from a painting by Hyacinth Rigaud, 1696.

to reserve this pleasure for the German tourists, they look for a sheltered corner to begin their reading.

Based on Apulius, La Fontaine's story retells and embellishes the legend of the unfortunate Psyche who attracts the amorous attention of Cupid and the awful enmity of Cupid's mother, Venus, unable to tolerate the unimaginable and inexpressible beauty of the young princess. When Cupid abducts Psyche and wafts her to his palace in the sky to be his wife, part of the bargain he makes with her is that she must never try

10. *Claude-Emmanuel L'Huillier dit Chapelle.*

to discover who he is or see his face. But, egged on by her jealous sisters, who insist the husband she has never seen must be a beast or a monster, Psyche – armed with a lamp and a dagger – creeps to the side of her sleeping spouse. Instead of the dragon she fears, the light reveals a young man so beautiful that she knows at once he can only be Cupid. Stooping to see him more clearly, she lets fall on his thigh a drop of burning oil from her lamp. Waking, the god sees Psyche, her lamp, and the dagger she has let fall from her trembling hand.

And here Polyphile stops the reading. "Excuse me," he pleads, "from reading the rest; you would be overcome with pity at the tale I have to tell you. . . . I haven't the right talent to continue a story that ends like this one."[4]

Acante wants Polyphile to continue, but the writer refuses. What satisfaction will his listeners have in weeping for the suffering of the beautiful girl? Acante is perfectly willing to weep, even happy to weep. "Compassion also has its charms, that are no less than the charms of laughter. I even think that they are greater and that Ariste agrees with me. Be as tender and moving as you wish, both of us will listen to you the more willingly."[5]

This is the cue for Gélaste, who defends, in the debate to come, the superiority of comedy. Molière did not himself write very much of what we call "dramatic theory," although he does defend comedy in various prefaces as a corrective of manners, usually in response to anti-theatrical polemics that assert that the theatre is a threat to society. Gélaste takes a different tack in his defense of the comic, one that cannot be provably attributed to Molière. Yet who better than the one the gazetteer Robinet christened *le dieu du ris*, "the god of laughter," to speak for the power of laughter, to say "I would rather be made to laugh when I should weep than weep when I should laugh."[6]

Acante suggests that they stroll on through the garden, the heat of the day being past, although he suspects that Gélaste would prefer to spend his time with some Psyche than with trees and fountains.[7] Letting this pass, Gélaste, knitting his brow, declares that he must cure the others of the error of thinking laughter a lesser pleasure than tears. But, argues Ariste, "pity is, of all the emotions aroused by discourse, the most noble, the most excellent, if you will, and I even maintain the most agreeable: there is an audacious paradox!" "Oh immortal gods," cries Gélaste, "are there men in the world mad enough to sustain such an extravagant opinion? I do not say that Sophocles and Euripides do not divert me more than many makers of comedies; but things being equal, would you leave the pleasure of seeing a funny fellow like Phormio trap two old men in order to go weep with the family of King Priam?" Yes, Ariste would. But for Gélaste, things being equal, he sustains that "the healthier people always prefer comedy to tragedy . . . Ah, my friend, don't you see that one is never tired of laughter? One can tire of gambling, rich food, women; but of laughter, no. Have you ever heard anyone say, 'we've been laughing for a whole week; I beg you, let us weep today?'"

Ariste accuses his opponent of frivolity. Where is the usual defense based on comedy as a corrective of manners? But Gélaste ripostes with

Homer, not the classical theorists. "When Achilles is surfeited with the fine pleasure of weeping, he says to Priam: 'Old man, you are miserable and that is the condition of mortals, they pass their life in tears. The gods alone are exempt from misfortune, and live above in comfort, without suffering.' How will you answer that?"

"I answer," says Ariste, "that mortals are mortals when they weep for their own pain, but when they weep for the pain of others, they are like gods." But, answers Gélaste, "the gods never weep. Their portion is laughter . . . Blessedness consists of laughter."[8]

Ariste would continue, but Polyphile stops the debate by indicating Acante, patiently waiting to show his friends the marvels of the king's garden. As Book I ends, they find themselves in a leafy *salon*, a leftover from one of the great royal festivals. There they seat themselves on the grass next to a little canal and Polyphile continues his reading.

Whether Molière ever spent the day at Versailles with Boileau, La Fontaine, and Racine is not, finally, an issue. He was a friend of all three, at least until his notorious break with Racine at the end of 1665, and his relationships with them place him in the context of literary Paris.

The four men represent two different generations. La Fontaine, born in June 1621, was the elder of Molière by some six months. Boileau, born in 1636, was nearly fifteen years younger than Molière, while Racine was almost exactly three years younger than Boileau. Boileau, like Molière, was a native Parisian, born in the enclosure of what is now the Palais de Justice where his father was clerk of the Conseil de la Grand'Chambre. Racine was born in La Ferté-Milon, seventy-six kilometers from Paris, a journey that, in 1683, took Racine and his family from Wednesday morning until supper time on Thursday.[9] La Fontaine, who was allied by marriage to Racine's family, was from Château-Thierry, on the border between Champagne and Île-de-France. Both had family backgrounds similar to Boileau's: papa Racine was a functionary, controller of the traffic in salt, while papa La Fontaine had the more elegant title of Councilor of the King and Master of Waters and Forests. He had married well, the daughter of a rich wholesale merchant, and the family lived in a vast and elegant house. Racine was orphaned at the age of three and taken by his grandmother to the Jansenist abbey at Port-Royal, where his aunt was a nun. He was educated there and at the Collège de la Ville de Beauvais. La Fontaine studied at the excellent Collège de Chateau-Thierry and possibly continued his education at a Paris school. Boileau began his education in Paris at the Collège d'Harcourt and continued it at the Collège de Beauvais. He then "undertook" the law and was received at the bar in December 1656. La Fontaine also studied law and was received as an *avocat* in the court of the Parlement of Paris, thus qualifying to inherit his father's office. Molière, as we have seen, had some connection to the law as well.

One aspect of their lives La Fontaine, Boileau, and Racine did not share with Molière; all were attracted at some point and for various reasons to the Church. La Fontaine actually joined the order of the Oratoire and studied theology for eighteen months. Boileau was "tonsured," that is, took minor orders, in 1662 and had a "living," the Priory of Saint-Paterne, with an income of 800 *livres* a year. Racine, who had been brought up in an intensely religious family and atmosphere, spent months in Uzès, in the south of France, tonsured and dressed in black from head to toe, hoping that his uncle, the Reverend Father Sconin, could promote for him a benefice from the Bishop of Soissons. The quality of his piety is open to question, however. Already close to La Fontaine, Racine writes to him in November, 1661, shortly after his arrival in Uzès, that the women of the town are "brilliant, and dressed in the most natural way. As for their persons, one could say, with Terence, "Their complexion is natural, and their bodies firm and full of juice.'" However, he will not continue, since to do so might interfere with his purpose. He has been told to be blind, "but if I cannot be that, then at least I must be mute; for, you see, one must be a monk with the monks, as I have been a wolf with you and the other wolves, your comrades."[10]

By 1661, then, Racine knew La Fontaine. The older man had married, in 1647, Marie Héricart from Racine's native town of La Ferté-Milon. She was lively and frivolous, but she bored her husband, who, in any case, was not tempted by marital fidelity. Tallemant des Réaux, the great gossip of the day, who knew La Fontaine, Maucroix, Furetière, and others of the Parisian literary circle known as La Table-Ronde, writes of La Fontaine under the heading "Racan and other dreamers." This "literary lad," according to his wife, was so absent-minded that he could go for three weeks without remembering he was married. Another anecdote suggests, however, that his memory loss may have been deliberate. "When someone says to La Fontaine, 'So and so is flirting with your wife,' he answers, 'Upon my word, let him. I don't care at all. He'll be as bored with her as I am.'"[11] This was not a marriage to keep La Fontaine at home. In 1657, burdened by the debts left him by his father, the La Fontaines annulled their community of marriage and the no-longer-so-young "lad" entered into an exchange of pensions with Fouquet, the royal Superintendent of Finances. La Fontaine undertook a *pension poé-*

tique to be paid four times a year in epistles, ballads, and odes. Fouquet was to furnish a more material sort of pension, which – apparently – he did. La Fontaine was also to compose a work in praise of the glories of Fouquet's paradise, Vaux-le-Vicomte. This patronage was arranged by the poet's old friend from La Table-Ronde, Pellisson, now Fouquet's private secretary. From that time on, La Fontaine spent most of his time either at Vaux or in Paris.

Considering that the remains of Molière and La Fontaine (or what are optimistically assumed to be their remains) now share a burial site in Père Lachaise cemetery, the details of their friendship are few. One anecdote, that exists in several versions, suggests that Molière was slightly protective of his ingenuous friend. Louis Racine, who did not himself know La Fontaine, nonetheless testifies in his *Mémoires* of his father that at dinner with Racine, Molière, and some others, La Fontaine was being teased and called *"bonhomme,"* a term conveying credulity and even simple-mindedness. He accepted the badgering with his usual good humor, but Molière spoke up, saying: "Don't mock the *bonhomme*; he may outlive us all."[12] In another version, Molière is said to have remarked: "Let our witty ones flutter about as they will, they will not efface the *bonhomme.*"

The *bonhomme* was, like Molière, a swimmer in the seas of patronage. Unlike Molière, cynical after betrayals by Conti and the king, La Fontaine seems to have been truly devoted to his patrons, especially Fouquet. After Fouquet's arrest in September 1661, La Fontaine wrote an *Ode au roi* defending the superintendant, but it had no effect on Louis, assuming he read it. Fouquet was tried in November 1664 and condemned to life imprisonment on December 20. In April of the following year Molière's troupe, perhaps at the prompting of La Fontaine, took the bold step of producing Mlle Desjardins' play, *Le Favori*, with a central character clearly modeled on Fouquet. The play is yet another appeal for clemency for the former minister, but this does not seem to have interfered with Louis' enjoyment when it was played for him at Versailles on June 12.

After Fouquet's arrest, his court poet found himself without funds and suspected by Colbert of who knows what kind of treachery. In addition, La Fontaine was condemned to pay a heavy fine for having usurped the title *écuyer*, "squire," and used it in signing two contracts.[13] He chose as new patrons the duc de Bouillon and his wife, who owned the château in Château-Thierry. In an *Épitre* addressed to the duke, La Fontaine makes a pathetic appeal, swearing that he, "the least proud, the least vain of men," had never even thought of applying the word "squire" to himself and had signed the documents without reading them. "I was then in Champagne," he writes, "sleeping, dreaming, going about the countryside."[14] The duke apparently spoke to Colbert, the fine was rescinded, and La Fontaine dedicated his *Psyché* to the Duchess, who remained his patron for many years. The Duchess, one of the notorious Mazarinettes, nieces of Cardinal Mazarin, was famous for her romantic intrigues. She was not, as were her sisters Olympe and Marie, a favorite of the king, who disliked her but thought that she would be suitable to introduce the dauphin to the arts of love. The Bouillons were not, perhaps, a very politic choice as patrons of an impecunious poet, but the pretty, frivolous duchess was a faithful friend.

A more seemly though not very lucrative arrangement was the post La Fontaine secured in July 1664 with the dowager duchesse d'Orléans, widow of Louis XIII's brother Gaston. With the office came a commission certifying that Jean de La Fontaine, that "least proud, least vain of men," was now a gentleman. The lady was the opposite of the delightful duchesse de Bouillon, a sad, dour and devout person in mourning for her favorite daughter, but the appointment gave the poet a certain status and a reason to be in Paris.

One of La Fontaine's duties as gentleman in waiting was to keep an eye on the dowager duchess's dog, Mignon, who had a bad habit of collaborating with the enemy bitches in the other wing of the Luxembourg palace, the enemy being the Grande Mademoiselle, daughter of Gaston d'Orléans by his first wife. The ladies did not speak.

During the eight years La Fontaine spent in service to the old duchess he published his adaptations of Ariosto and Boccaccio, three volumes of his *Contes et nouvelles en vers*, a *Fables choisies*, the *Amours de Psyché*, a *Recueil des poésies chrétiennes et diverses*, and a second collection of fables. It was one of the most productive periods of his life. But as his work progressed, his life disintegrated. Shortly after he left the Luxembourg, he became the permanent house guest of his friend Mme de La Sablière, a woman who was living separately from her husband. Her circle included not only La Fontaine, but Bernier, the doctor and popularizer of Gassendi, who was also her guest, Chapelle, possibly Molière and Boileau, possibly the courtesan Ninon de Lenclos. According to Perrault, who was also a habitué, La Fontaine's neglect of his private affairs meant that his friends had to come to his rescue, and it was Mme de La Sablière who provided for him for the next twenty years. From his early days as the resident poet at Vaux, La Fontaine had descended to being supported by a rich bourgeoise. Nonetheless, his work continued to grow in depth and complexity.

Molière died shortly after his friend became Mme de La Sablière's guest. The possibility certainly exists that he was not entirely taken by the lady and her appropriation of La Fontaine. She is a not unlikely model for Philaminte in *Les Femmes savantes*, a character whom Molière thoroughly savages. She was definitely "master" of her house, she was passionate about astronomy, she studied mathematics and did dissections, and she had her circle or *salon* of literary men. Boileau lashed out at her in his *Satire X:* "This *savante* . . . why is it that her eye is dim and her complexion dull? Because she has spent the night, astrolabe in hand, on the roof looking at Jupiter."[15]

La Fontaine, however, was constant in his praise of her and sincere in his gratitude. He was sixty-two when he was finally admitted to the Académie Française in 1684, at about the same time as Boileau. His entry discourse was most unconventional: an *Épitre* in verse addressed to Mme de La Sablière. The most moving part of it, however, is the old poet's recognition of his own mortality. "Since my muse, as well as my days, sense the inevitable course of their decline, and since the flame of my reason is going to be extinguished, should I use up what remains in complaining, and, prodigal of the time left me by fate, lose it in regretting what I have lost. If Heaven reserves for me still some spark of the fire that burned in me in my season of youth, I should use it, wise enough to know that the most beautiful sunset is neighbor to the night."[16]

La Fontaine left nothing behind about his friendship with Molière, unlike Boileau who lived until 1711 and was given to reminiscences in his old age. Many of these were recorded by his amanuensis Brossette or by Louis Racine, who interviewed him when he began to write the biography of his father. According to Brossette, Boileau and Molière were introduced by Boileau's brother in the last half of 1663.[17] Boileau had called himself to the attention of the older writer earlier that year with the publication of a poem entitled *Stances à M. Molière*, praising his *École des femmes.* "Let the envious grumble," Boileau writes; "they have proclaimed loudly on all sides that you charm the vulgar in vain, that nothing about your verses is pleasing. If you knew how to please a little less, you would not displease them so much."[18]

Boileau continued his praise of Molière in his *Satire II*, probably written in 1663 although not published until 1665. In it the poet begs Molière to teach him how to rhyme, something the "master" seems to do effortlessly. *Satire II* plays with a conventional conceit, a war in the land of Rhetoric between Rhyme and Reason, and tells us little about the relationship between the two men beyond the fact that Boileau and his circle admired the playwright.

In his old age, Boileau saw himself as having tried, never successfully, to perfect his friend's work. Although he esteemed Molière infinitely, he told Brossette that Molière was guilty of negligent versifications and irregular denouements.[19] On one occasion, after he had pointed out to the playwright several examples of "jargon," Molière told Boileau to go ahead and correct the faults, while he "went out for a moment with his wife." But, although Molière approved of the changes, Boileau was sorry to discover that he did not include them when the plays were printed.

Nor did Molière take heed of Boileau's new ending for *Tartuffe*. According to Brossette, Boileau thought "that it would have been perfectly easy for M. Molière to end *Tartuffe* with a happy and natural denouement. For instead of introducing the casket with the papers against the state, and without introducing a king's officer, and without employing the authority of the king, he could, after the discovery of the imposture of Tartuffe, have brought on stage all the characters of the play to deliberate on the proper punishment for the rascal."[20] Orgon, the most injured, would call for extreme measures. The maid would "say very comic things." Finally, the decent man would propose showing contempt for such low and shameful behavior and chasing the scoundrel away. Boileau then wants a scene where everyone methodically beats Tartuffe, followed by the entry of Mme Pernelle, still defending his honor and virtue. Boileau claims that Molière did change the ending, but – the king hearing of the change – he was forced to leave it as it had been. This conflicts with another comment, that Molière would realize his idea and his plan only once, after which he would never correct it. Boileau seems to have been just the least bit jealous of his vastly more creative friend and not entirely aware of the pressures that the playwright experienced. Molière appears to have been patient with Boileau and to have tried to find ways to appear to appreciate the younger man's critical enthusiasm. Boileau, near the end of his life, needed to believe that he had been an important factor in Molière's success.

Paradoxically, that older Boileau, the spokesman for *purisme* and *classicisme*, the defender of traditional forms, was in his youth a fierce iconoclast, opponent of preciosity, and audacious critic of his elders and supposed betters.

The fifteenth child in a family of sixteen, Boileau added the modifier Despréaux (meaning "of the meadows") to his name to distinguish himself from his brothers, and especially from his brother Gilles, a minor writer but major player in the political skirmishes that were a constant feature of life on Le Parnasse. This adopted patronymic – that employs the *particule* – was meant to suggest, as were many of those adopted by actors, a noble connection.

Boileau had a difficult childhood. His mother died when he was eighteen months old, and he later told Louis Racine that he had resided, until he was fifteen, in a sort of drafty hut constructed above the attic of his father's house. When he was about ten, he was "cut for the stone," that is, he underwent one of the only successful surgical procedures that had been developed by the mid-seventeenth century, removal of a kidney stone. He continued to experience kidney stones until he was forty. He also suffered from some sexual anomaly, perhaps as a result of his early surgery, and was apparently impotent.[21] He told his friend Racine that he would never want to live his life over again if it meant beginning it with as painful a childhood.[22]

Boileau never married, nor does he seem to have had a "penchant" for women. The most venomous of his satires is *Satire X, Contre les Femmes*. Not only was he sexually dysfunctional, he may also have been rather ugly. A poem of some 200 lines, all rhyming in "eau" and "ique" (i.e., with "Boileau" and "critique") was circulated in 1664, calling attention to his piggish eyes, yellow skin, nose round as a turnip, spindly legs, and hunched shoulders, "like a camel."[23]

Although he was admitted to the bar, there is little evidence of Boileau's having practiced law. He survived nicely on the income from 36,000 *livres* inherited from his father along with his living from the Priory of Saint-Paterne. In the earliest stages of his career, he was the shadow of his brother Gilles, a satirist who attacked some of the most redoubtable academic writers of his time while allying himself to Chapelain and the abbé d'Aubignac, strong supporters of the powerful minister Colbert. It was Chapelain who succeeded in forcing the Académie Française to accept Gilles Boileau as a member, despite his extreme youth – he was only twenty-eight – and over the opposition of Ménage and the *précieuse* party.

According to Tallemant, Gilles Boileau's attack on Ménage came about because the great man treated the neophyte like a little boy. When Gilles Boileau asked Ménage to read a Latin elegy he had just written, Ménage put it to one side while handing the lad a copy of his own newest work, a Latin elegy dedicated to Queen Christine of Sweden, telling him to read it and learn more from it than from all the ancients.[24] The young man, who naturally had a caustic wit, was only too happy to apply that wit to Ménage's model, and Ménage's enemies were only too happy to circulate the result. This was a typical skirmish in the literary wars of the day, wars in which Molière himself began to participate in a small way after he became friends with Nicolas Boileau.

Their friendship may have been strained in 1663 when Colbert, now firmly in power as an advisor to the king, issued a list of writers who were to receive royal pensions. Molière was on the list for 1,000 *livres*, Racine – who had yet to write his first play – was on a slightly later list for 600, the Boileau brothers were not on any list, in spite of Gilles Boileau's presence amongst the immortals and in spite of the fact that Chapelain, who had been Gilles Boileau's patron, was the "pontiff" upon whose advice Colbert had acted. "Muse, let us change our tune," wrote in response the younger Boileau, who had followed his brother into battle as a satirist. In *Satire II* he realizes the genre is fatal to the author, no matter how much it amuses the reader. "A boring elegy, a stiff panegyric, can rot at leisure at the back of a bookstore . . . with no enemies but dust and worms." But an author who makes his readers laugh will make enemies of those very readers when they "see themselves reflected in his mirror."[25] Boileau continues by mocking Chapelain's *La Pucelle*, universally considered to be perfectly awful.

Some biographers have suggested that Molière may have been involved in several anonymous publications that circulated following the first pension lists, maligning both Chapelain and Colbert. This proposal rests on the assumption that Molière was among the habitués of the Croix-Blanche, a tavern on the rue de Bercy near the marché St-Jean where the brothers Boileau, with Racine and Furetière, plotted their attacks on Chapelain and Colbert. What little evidence exists, however, connects him rather to the Croix-de-Lorraine, frequented by a coterie of philosophical libertines and bons vivants.[26] Molière was too aware of the precariousness of his connections at court to risk not only his own pension but the position of his troupe as well by taking part in an attack on the powerful Colbert.

Boileau, who was fifteen years younger, without family or professional responsibilities, not on the pension list, and with a comfortable private income, had less to lose. Forty years later he remembered contributing only one or two "pleasantries" to *Chapelain décoiffé*.[27] On the other hand, he and his brother Gilles were apparently the primary authors of the much more dangerous pamphlet known as *Colbert enragé*. According to a contemporary observer, Colbert discovered the guilty parties and called the elder Boileau to account in a stormy interview. In 1665, however, the pension list included the name of Gilles Boileau, who had "hastened to disavow" any connection with "this indecent piece" and "charitably made it known to Chapelain that his brother Despréaux was the author of it."[28] Attacks on Boileau mounted in the middle 1660s after the publication of his first seven satires. An anonymous pamphlet entitled *Discours satyrique au cynique Despréaux* focused on the literary hoodlums, the "cabal of malicious wits," who controlled satire. This cabal certainly was meant to include Molière. Another *libelle*, the *Satyre de Satyres*, charged Boileau with making a demigod out of a *farceur*. Cotin accused Boileau of being the instrument of Molière's vengeance; according to still another anonymous author, Molière was, from self-interest, trying to destroy the reputation of the good writers in the mind of His Majesty.[29]

At least one of these anonymous *libellistes*, the neophyte Edme Boursault, had been involved in the theatrical war of *L'École des femmes*; he was the author of the *Portrait du peintre*, a *libelle* in dramatic form, played at the Hôtel du Bourgogne in October 1663. Others were written by or prompted by the various great men of letters whom Boileau had goaded: Cotin, Quinault, Chapelain, the abbé du Pure. Cotin actually put his name to the most credible of the attacks on Boileau, the *Critique désintéressée sur les satyres du temps*. Years later, Molière – prompted perhaps by Boileau – would get even.

By then, however, Boileau had truly changed his tune. Beginning in his middle thirties, the *enfant terrible* began to maneuver for a secure position in the world of letters. Instead of plotting mischief with his libertine cronies at the Croix-Blanche, he began to frequent the *salons*. He sought the patronage of the king's second official mistress, Mme de Montespan, and her sister Mme de Thianges. He became a protégé of Premier Président Lamoignan, the very pillar of Parlement who closed Molière's production of *Tartuffe* in August 1667. And, finally, Boileau renounced his benefice of the Priory of Saint-Paterne and gave all the proceeds of his living to charities. He was positioning himself to become what he did become: a conservative man of letters, an academician with a court appointment whose opinions – both literary and otherwise – were of the most orthodox.

From the satire he turned to the less frivolous form of the *épître* and then to what would be the work of which he was most proud: his *Art poétique*, the rules of poetry written in perfect alexandrine couplets. This was published in 1674, as were his translation of Longinus and his first *épîtres*. It was in 1674, as well, that he was finally presented at court and received a royal pension and a privilege to publish all his work, honors long delayed because of the enmity of Chapelain and Colbert. His achievement is symbolized by a gift presented to the young duc de Maine, son of Louis XIV and Mme de Montespan, in 1675. A painting, it shows the prince with his mother, with Mme de Thianges, his aunt, and with the duc de La Rochefoucauld and his son. Behind this noble grouping and separated by a balustrade stand three men of letters: Boileau, Racine, and La Fontaine.[30] By then Molière was dead.

The reformed Boileau continued to know Molière; the two were certainly friends still in March 1672 when Molière produced *Les Femmes savantes* with its character Trissotin, a clear caricature of their old enemy Cotin. However, a number of contemporaries noticed that after Molière's death, Boileau was less complimentary than he had once been. The eulogist, who once wrote "If you knew how to please a little less, you would not displease so much," now asserts in his *Art poétique* that Molière had been too much a "friend of the people," had replaced what was "agreeable and fine" with buffoonery, and had "shamelessly allied Terence and Tabarin." In his bid to become the law giver of Le Parnasse, Boileau no longer recognized the author of the *Le Misanthrope* in Scapin's lazzi of the sack.[31] Desmarets de Saint-Sorlin was among those who objected, speaking in the voice of the dead Molière: "Cowardly heart who pursues the living and the dead, you adored me living; now that I sleep you . . . blacken my genius with the title of buffoon."[32] Pierre Bayle also wrote, in a letter to his father, that a clever satirist will never attack someone who is sharper than he is and the proof of this is that "Boileau followed this policy with Molière whom he flattered profusely in one of his satires." But, Bayle adds, "since his death, Boileau has audaciously published what he has found to be faulty in Molière's plays."[33] Attacking an actor of Molière's prowess, someone who could put you on stage and mock you for all the world to see, would be more an act of madness than an act of courage according to Bayle.

Perhaps this is why the literary satirist strongly advised the theatrical satirist to quit the stage because of declining health. "The profession of actor exhausts you; why don't you renounce it?" he asked, according to Louis Racine. "Alas," answered Molière, "I'm prevented by a point of honor." At that Boileau's true feelings emerged. "What point of honor? What! You dirty your face with the mustache of Sganarelle in order to come onto the stage to be beaten? There's a fine point of honor for a philosopher like you."[34]

Boileau remembered this conversation long after Molière's death, perhaps because it suited him to believe that the friend of his youth was more philosopher than performer on the public stage. Molière's "point of honor," which probably referred to his consciousness of his importance to the lives and incomes of his colleagues and employees, would not make sense to Boileau who had no responsibilities for anyone other than himself.

But Boileau was a paradoxical personality, especially in his relationships. Although he had been close to Molière, in 1700 he wrote to Brossette that the two *plus beaux esprits* of the century were Racine – in later life his closest friend – and not Molière, as one might also have expected, but Molière's own best friend, Chapelle.[35] This judgment alone expresses the paradox.

Unlike the four friends of *Psyché*, all of whom were or became celebrated, Chapelle was a marginal character, a libertine, a notorious drinker and carouser. Educated at the same school as Molière, Chapelle studied medicine, but like Boileau was not obliged to earn his living; his father legitimized him and gave him an income. His work was as ephemeral as his life; the only moderately important thing he wrote and published was the record of his travels through Italy and the South of France. He was involved in any number of anonymous pamphlets fired off in the endless literary wars. He was, to be frank, a tavern wit, but one to whom Boileau as well as Molière remained faithful.

An anecdote demonstrates the power Chapelle had over his friends, who were all concerned about his passion for wine. Boileau met him on the street one day and began to talk to him about the problem. Chapelle assured his friend that "I feel the truth of your arguments; I am resolved to change, but so you can finish persuading me, let's go in here; you can talk at your ease."[36] Chapelle ushered Boileau into a tavern and ordered a bottle of wine and then another. Boileau, carried away by his discourse against wine, drank with him until finally the preacher and the convert were equally drunk. True or not, the anecdote points to a Boileau with ambivalent feelings towards a man and life-style that both attract and repel him. Perhaps it was that very ambivalence that held the interest of Molière, even after Boileau embarked on a course that would lead to the court, the Académie Française, and the role of pontiff of the literary world of Paris.

Racine, on the other hand, was only briefly close to Molière, whom he treated very badly. Boileau forgave him his trespasses, which were considerable, but Molière did not. Racine brought himself to the attention of the Paris literary establishment in 1660, when he was only twenty-one years old. An orphan, Racine was talented, well-educated, and very ambitious, but without financial resources. Although he knew La Fontaine as early as 1661, he was not part of the circle around Fouquet. When he heard that Fouquet's secretary Pellisson had been imprisoned in the Conciergerie, his response was a cruel joke. Apparently, though very young, Racine was clever enough to foresee the fall of Fouquet and the rise of Colbert.[37]

His first literary effort was an ode entitled *La Nymphe de la Seine* in honor of the entry of the king and his new wife Marie-Thérèse into Paris in August 1660. This ode he sent to Chapelain, as "Secretary-General of Le Parnasse," who responded: "the ode is very beautiful, very poetic, and there are many stanzas that could not be improved. If one were to look back over the few places marked, one could make a very beautiful piece of this."[38] Racine's first plays, written at about the same time, were received less enthusiastically by the Hôtel de Bourgogne and the Théâtre du Marais, although the young playwright consoled himself by remarking that "the actors at present like nothing but gibberish, unless it comes from one of the great authors."[39]

Four years later, however, after a stay in Uzès with the uncle who had hoped to procure for him some sort of religious benefice, Racine managed to achieve what Boileau did not: a place on the list of men of letters who were to receive an annual pension from the crown. Colbert's purpose in establishing this stable of royal pensioners was the glorification of the monarchy, so we should not be surprised that a satirist was excluded. Why Racine, with no body of work to speak of, was included is a more interesting question. The answer undoubtedly lies in his assiduous licking of Chapelain's boots. When Chapelain let it be known in June 1663, shortly after the first pension list was drawn up, that verses celebrating the king's recovery from roseola would be welcome, Racine – who was not on the June list – was only too happy to oblige. What's more, he again submitted his ode to Chapelain who wrote to Colbert about this "young man named Racine . . . who has polished his work according to my advice."[40] The result: in August of 1664 the name "Racine" was present on a list of *"Gratifications aux savants et hommes de lettres"* posted in the royal accounts.

By that point, Racine was acquainted certainly with Molière, probably with Boileau, in both instances through the offices of La Fontaine. He had accomplished his objective with Chapelain – a reliable if not ample income – and he had *entrée* at court and was admitted to the king's *lever*. Now he could begin to make a place for himself in less magisterial circles. Boileau expressed contempt for Racine in some unpublished verses, but understood nonetheless why the indigent young man needed to promote himself so vigorously. And Racine joined Boileau and the others in tavern games and anonymous attacks. Though aiming for the heights, he was not averse to amusing himself in the foothills. His intention was to make his reputation first as a playwright, although he would never have assumed that playwriting alone would make possible his full ascent.

Since the Hôtel de Bourgogne and the Marais had not welcomed his first dramatic efforts in 1660, his turn to the company at the Palais-Royal in 1664 is understandable. In a letter to the abbé Le Vasseur, written in November 1663, Racine remarks that his new play, *Les Frères*, is not going very well. "I finished the fourth act on Saturday, but unfortunately I don't like it at all, no more than the others, all the drawn swords."[41] In the next paragraph he mentions that he encountered Molière at the king's *lever*, "who was praised by the king, and I was very happy for him: and he was very happy that I was present."

According to Boileau the play, known variously as *Les Frères ennemis* and *La Thébaïde*, was Molière's idea. Boyer had written a very bad *Thébaïde*, on the subject of the civil war in Thebes after the exile of Oedipus. Molière is said to have proposed to Racine that if he would *rajuster* Rotrou's *Antigone*, he would wipe out Boyer's version.[42] "Readjusting" the work of others was a favorite sport in the theatre of the day, so there is nothing inherently unlikely about the idea that Racine was motivated by previous versions of a story that intrigued him. Nor is it inherently unlikely that Molière might have advised him to write it, although there seems to have been only one reason for him to have done so.

Marquise Du Parc inspired many literary gentleman, including Racine, but not, it appears, Molière himself, who wrote no starring roles for her. Yet the troupe was eager to retain her. Racine's play offered her the important role of Antigone, and, in fact, she was already cast and the production promised in December, 1663.[43] Her presence at the Palais-Royal also would have been an inducement to Racine, who would later write *Andromaque* for her, to give the troupe his *Frères ennemis*.

He had to wait nearly six months to see it produced. It may be that Molière held it until Boyer's play was produced at the Hôtel de Bourgogne. Or perhaps production was delayed because the troupe was already committed to a carnival spectacle, *Bradamante ridicule*, that the actors were ordered to play by the duc de Saint-Aignan, who gave the company 100 *louis d'or* for the extraordinarily expensive costumes. The audience for the opening of this parody included the king, one of the rare times he attended a public theatre.[44]

Molière knew the duc de Saint-Aignan well; the two were collaborating on plans for the *Plaisirs de l'Île enchantée*, the king's great festival at Versailles, that would take place the following May. M. de Saint-Aignan was also one of Racine's prime targets as he maneuvered for patronage. In November of 1663 he noted that the duke had found his ode, *La Renommée aux Muses*, very beautiful and had asked to see his other work and to meet him.[45] Apparently the duke also liked the play, the first edition of which was dedicated to him.

This curious juxtaposition of Racine and Saint-Aignan with Molière suggests that the duke may have applied a certain amount of pressure on behalf of a young protégé. Nonetheless, the troupe was occupied with other work until June. For more than three weeks in May, the actors were at Versailles. When they returned, they prepared for the debut of the new playwright.

The play was a failure. Opening night brought in meager receipts that then fell off sharply. The addition of well-known farces as afterpieces helped a little, but not enough to bring profits up beyond the average level. Still, the troupe allowed the play to run for twelve performances and revived it after a month away with the court at Fontainebleau, where they had played it for the king. The play then entered the repertory, unusual for a failure, and was performed occasionally during the remainder of the season and even during the following season.

Most failures in the seventeenth-century French theatre disappeared quickly. Racine got more than fair treatment from the actors at the Palais-Royal, but as he was to show later on, he was not mollified. June was not the best time to open a new play, to be sure. The theatre high season, the time when troupes made most of their money, was from All Saints, November 1, to the Easter break that took place after the first three weeks of Lent. Still, it was usual at the Palais-Royal to open a new play in June. Among Molière's own works that debuted then were *L'École des maris* (June 24, 1661), which did excellent business, and the *Critique d'École des femmes* (June 1, 1663), which did even better. Audiences were usually smaller in the summer; the courtiers were often away in their domains or out of town with the court. But good plays could attract decent houses, at least through June and into July.

Racine's second play, *Alexandre*, was given a more favorable position in the schedule; it opened at the Palais-Royal on December 4, 1665, to excellent receipts for the first four performances. At the fifth performance, the box office fell off. The day before, it seems, the actors of the Hôtel de Bourgogne had given a private performance of the same play for the comtesse d'Armagnac. On the day of the sixth performance La Grange made the following entry into his *Registre*: "This same day, the Troupe was surprised that the same play of *Alexandre* was performed on the Stage of the Hôtel de Bourgogne. As this was done with the complicity of M. Racine, the Troupe did not believe the author's shares were owing to the said M. Racine who had used it so badly as to have given and taught the play to the other actors. The said author's shares were redivided and each of the twelve actors had for a share forty-seven *livres*."[46]

With his dubious maneuver, Racine lost 564 *livres*, almost as much as his year's pension, and the friendship of Molière, who had treated him with such benevolence. Why he made this choice has been discussed endlessly without any very satisfying conclusion being reached. At the time, the two companies were engaged in one of those little wars so dear to the hearts of their audiences: two plays with the same title offered in competition. In mid-October, the Hôtel had produced Quinault's *La Mère coquette* and a week later the Palais-Royal had responded with another *Mère coquette*, this one by Donneau de Visé. At the end of November, Robinet in his weekly rhyming letter, announced that since neither of the mothers had carried the day, two rival *Alexandres* were now in prospect. The Burgundians, hearing of the plan to produce Racine's new play, had decided to revive an old play by Boyer entitled *Le Grand Alexandre*. It failed miserably.

Whether the Hôtel came to Racine or Racine to the Hôtel is not known, but the negotiations must have taken place either before or, more likely, at the time of the opening at the Palais-Royal. The actors needed at least ten days to learn and rehearse the play, which they performed first on December 14.

Racine, from the beginning, would have preferred the tragedians of the Hôtel de Bourgogne to the Palais-Royal troupe that was celebrated for comedy. One can only too easily imagine the young writer, so desperate for recognition, seeking out Montfleury and Floridor with news of his unexpected success, suggesting that the failure of Boyer's play need not mean the failure of the Hôtel to prevail. One can also easily imagine that Montfleury, Floridor, and the others, still smarting from Molière's attack on their tragic style in the *Impromptu de Versailles*, were willing to violate the unwritten rule of the theatre that a troupe enjoyed exclusive rights to any play they originated until that play was published. The actors of the Hôtel knew they could do a better job of a tragedy than that buffoon Molière and his bunch. Montfleury, in particular, whose style was as pompous as his girth was enormous, must have longed to get even with the man who wrote "a king has to be as big and fat as four men."

Racine was clearly enticed by the bubble reputation, the idea that the Hôtel de Bourgogne was definitely the best of the theatres for tragedy, but there may have been something else at work that has been overlooked. It seems that Racine had very strong views on how his plays should be acted. According to Boileau, Racine recited his own work "marvelously well," and took a very active role in rehearsing the actors.[47] When the experienced Mlle Du Parc, who defected to the Hôtel de Bourgogne at the end of the 1666–7 season, played the title role in Racine's *Andromaque*, the author taught her the role and "made her repeat it like a schoolgirl."[48] A more detailed picture of Racine's way of dealing with actors is drawn by his son Louis. Although he is writing of a somewhat later time in Racine's career, the playwright's attitude toward the actor seems much the same. Speaking of Mlle Champmeslé, the second of the tragedy queens whom Racine loved and for whom he wrote his great female roles, Louis Racine says "that woman was not born an actress. Nature had given her only beauty, a voice, and a memory: as to the rest, she had so little intelligence, that she had to be taught the meaning of the verses she had to say, and given the inflections. Everyone knows what a talent my father had for declamation, the true inclination for which he could give to actors capable of acquiring it . . . He formed La Champmeslé, but with a great deal of difficulty. He first got her to understand the verses that she had to say, showed her the gestures, dictated to her the inflections that he even notated. The scholar, faithful to her lessons, although an actress by art, on the stage appeared inspired by nature."[49]

Molière gives a picture of himself as a director in the *Impromptu*; he does ask an actor to stand aside, observe him, and imitate him, but he does not try to impose his playwright's will on the minute details of the performance. He speaks for the most part to his actors as professionals who know how to do what he asks them to do. If the neophyte Racine – who blamed them for the failure of *Le Thébaïde* – attempted to teach the actors at the Palais-Royal how to act or tried to impose on them the tragic style in vogue at the Hôtel de Bourgogne, a certain lack of sympathy between author and actors seems inevitable. Marquise Du Parc, of course, was unhappy with her roles at Palais-Royal and in love with Racine, so perhaps she was willing to put up with his condescension for her and her craft.

Racine's contempt for actors was not unusual in the society, although it may have been in a playwright who wanted to sell his work to them. However, he had been raised by the Jansenists at Port Royal to believe that the theatre was iniquitous and actors deservedly excluded from the communion of the faithful. A Jansenist *libelle* had accused him of being a public poisoner while his aunt, who was prioress of Port Royal, wrote to him "in the bitterness of my heart" that so long as he did not break off his commerce with the actors "that dishonors you before God and before men" she would refuse to see him or speak to him, knowing him to be "in a state so deplorable and so contrary to Christianity."[50]

Louis Racine notes that relations between his father and Molière were "chilly," which he attributes to the defection of Mlle Du Parc to the Hôtel de Bourgogne in 1667 and not to his father's betrayal. He insists that his father spoke well of Molière's work on the occasion of the failure of *Le Misanthrope* – which, of course, did not fail – and that Molière defended Racine's only comedy, *Les Plaideurs*.[51] But perhaps here is a case where Grimarest reports a more probable state of things: "Many people imagine that Molière had a private relationship with M. R***. I have not found that to be true, in the research that I have done; on the contrary, the age, the work, and the character of these gentlemen were so different that I cannot believe that they would have sought each other out; and I do not think even that Molière had a high opinion of R***."[52] It would be surprising if Molière had anything but a very low opinion of Racine, because they did, briefly, have a friendship – until Racine demonstrated just how little that friendship meant when he saw an opportunity to advance his own interests.

Boileau apparently managed to stay friends with both, although his very close relationship with Racine took place after Molière's death. La Fontaine, the *bonhomme*, was sleeping and dreaming as usual and paying little attention to poetic and theatrical politics. Chapelle probably took Molière's side; at least Racine was disconcerted when Chapelle remained noncommittal about his *Bérénice*. "Tell me as a friend," said Racine, "your feelings. What do you think of *Bérénice*?" "What do I think of it," said Chapelle? "Oh, Marion weeps, Marion shrieks, Marion wants someone to marry her."[53]

Racine gave up writing plays for the public stage after *Phèdre*, first performed on New Year's Day, 1677. His son refers to this retirement as "the happy moment when the great religious feelings that had filled my father in his youth, and that had been for a long time asleep in his heart . . . suddenly awakened."[54] Whatever the accuracy of this reported conversion, the reborn Racine did seek a pious wife and broke with all that "pernicious society of the theatre." His son goes on to tell us that when his father resolved to marry, "neither love nor self-interest played any part in his choice; in such a serious matter, he consulted only reason."[55] Reason told him, however, to marry a young woman with a good deal of property. He, himself, continued to receive his pension as a man of letters, by then increased to 2,000 *livres* a year; in addition he enjoyed various court offices, including that of royal historiographer worth 6,000 a year. The fact is that he died a "fabulously rich man."[56]

Louis Racine asserts that his father was not present at Auteuil the night of the "famous supper," another glimpse of the friends together. He is undoubtedly correct, since Molière did not lease his retreat on the Seine outside of Paris until January 1666 at the earliest, a month after Racine's treachery. But Boileau was certainly there and La Fontaine possibly. Racine's empty place was filled by Chapelle. Two versions of the evening exist, one by Grimarest and one by Louis Racine, who confirms that, improbable as it may seem, the event did take place.[57]

It was Chapelle who invited a group of convivial friends to dine and drink at Auteuil. Molière was following his doctor's advice and drinking nothing but milk. The guests also included "the other Baptiste," Jean-Baptiste Lully, composer and director of the king's music, the comte de Jonsac, a gentleman rhymer to whom Chapelle had addressed his verses on the gathering at the Croix-de-Lorraine, and M. de Nantouillet. Grimarest's informant was probably Michel Baron, Molière's protégé, who was very young but nonetheless present on the insistence of Lully, while Louis Racine had heard the story from Boileau.

In Grimarest's version, Chapelle and his guests arrive at Auteuil, hoping to sup with Molière. The latter, telling them that his health does not permit him to entertain them, drinks his milk and goes to bed, leaving Chapelle and the young Baron to do the honors.

The wine puts Chapelle into a bad mood. "*Parbleu*," he complains, "I am a great fool to come and get drunk here everyday, just to do honor to Molière; I am sick and tired of this business; and what annoys me is that he believes that I am obligated to him." The company, almost all drunk at that point, agree. They keep on drinking and little by little the conversation shifts. Around three o'clock Chapelle says, "how little our life means. How full it is of setbacks. For thirty or forty years we are on the lookout for a moment of pleasure that we never find. In our youth we are harassed by our damned parents, who want us to stuff our heads with a lot of nonsense." After a sour review of his own education, Chapelle raises his voice against the opposite sex. "All these women," he says, "are animals who are the sworn enemies of our repose. Yes, *morbleu*, sorrow, injustice, unhappiness on all sides in this life." Jonsac agrees with him and adds: "Let us leave it . . . Let us go drown ourselves together. The river is at our door." Nantouillet is in accord, arguing that there is no better time to die than with good friends. Besides, news of their death will make quite a stir. As the suicidal drunks head for the river, Baron runs to awaken Molière. In the meantime the group reaches the river-bank, finds a boat, and prepares to head for deep water. Some domestics and neighbors try to fish them out and the indignant gentlemen draw their swords and chase their rescuers back to Molière's house, where the playwright asks what in the world is going on. "Listen, my dear Molière," says Jonsac. "You're an intelligent man. See if we are wrong. Exhausted by the troubles of this world, we have made our plans to pass to the other: the river appears to us the shortest way to get there."

"What's that! Gentlemen," answers Molière, "you have formed such a beautiful plan without including me? What, you want to drown yourselves without me? And I thought you were my friends." "Damn right," says Chapelle, "we're doing him an injustice. Come on and drown yourself with us." "Oh, but wait," answers Molière. "This is not something to undertake at the wrong moment; this is the last act of our life, it must not lack merit. Someone might be malicious enough to give a bad report of us if we were to drown ourselves now: it would certainly be said that we had done it at night, like common suicides, or even like common drunks. Let us seize a moment that does us the greatest honor. Tomorrow between eight and nine in the morning, sober and in front of everyone we will go to throw ourselves head first into the river." Lully strongly approves; "Molière always is a hundred times more intelligent than we are. . . . Let's go to bed. I'm sleepy." [58] In the morning the sheepish friends decide to continue to suffer the miseries of their lives.

Molière was often annoyed with Chapelle and unable to understand how a man of such intelligence could have so little self-control. There was, according to Molière, no passion less worthy of a gentleman than the passion for wine. "Chapelle," he adds, "is my friend, but this unhappy penchant spoils for me all the pleasures of his friendship."[59] He also warned Baron not to imitate Chapelle who would sacrifice his friends for the sake of a witticism. Nonetheless, Molière had a spare room set aside for Chapelle in Auteuil and appears to have continued his relationship with his oldest friend until his death.

Some of Molière's other friendships are less well documented, either because the friends were less celebrated or because they were not part of the literary world that published every letter, anecdote, and reminiscence. He was apparently close to the physician Jacques Rohault, like Chapelle and Bernier a former student of Gassendi, who wrote a *Traité de physique* found among Molière's books at Auteuil. Other names connected to Molière include the skeptical philosopher La Mothe Le Vayer and his son the abbé La Mothe Le Vayer. The former was the tutor of the king's brother, Monsieur, and for a time of the king himself. The latter, a minor literary light and one of the habitués of the Croix-de-Lorraine according to Chapelle, died in September 1664. Molière wrote a sonnet addressed to the senior La Mothe Le Vayer on the death of his son. Whether the verses were written before or after the death of his own son a few weeks later is not known. In the sonnet he advises the old man to let himself weep and to ignore the precepts of a philosophy that would have one accept the death of a beloved son with dry eyes. A year later one of the doctors who had treated the abbé La Mothe Le Vayer was a target of Molière's satire in *L'Amour médecin*.

Another celebrated friend was the painter Pierre Mignard, who did a number of portraits of Molière, beginning in 1657 in Avignon. Ten years older than the actor, Mignard appears to have been more a family friend than a tavern acquaintance or a frequent guest at Auteuil. His daughter served as godmother to Molière's second son, Pierre, and Mignard himself was the executor of Madeleine Béjart's estate.[60] Around 1661 the painter was given a very important commission: to paint the fresco that would decorate the dome of the new church of Val-de-Grace, founded by Anne of Austria as a thank offering to the Virgin for the unexpected pregnancy that resulted in Louis XIV. Construction was slow, but Queen Anne did see the fresco in progress before she died in January 1666. It represented her, in a glory surrounded by more than 200 saints, offering the new church to God.

The fresco, the largest in the world, was first seen by the public in September 1666. It evidently aroused either the envy or the wrath of Charles Le Brun, who "having the confidence of Colbert, reigned over the arts with the authority of a despot."[61] A pamphlet war broke out and Molière took part in it with an ode of 366 lines entitled *La Gloire du Val-de-Grace*, published in April 1669. It seems to have been an answer to a poem by Charles Perrault, who was both a poet and chief clerk under

Colbert with responsibility for the royal building program. Perrault was also charged with having forced Mignard, against his will and on pain of exile, into the newly founded Académie Royale de Peinture et de Sculpture to take orders from Le Brun.

Molière was bold enough to direct his words to Colbert himself, in a deviation from his earlier courtier's caution. While praising the minister for sharing the taste of his master the king and for his hard work and "vigorous genius," Molière clearly expresses doubts about Colbert's politics of patronage. "Great men, Colbert, are bad courtiers," he writes with surprising familiarity, "little given to discharging the duties of the sycophant. They give themselves wholly to reflection, which is how they achieve perfection . . . Who gives himself to the court robs his art. A mind divided rarely fulfills itself. And the arts [*emplois de feu*] ask everything of a man. The artist should not leave the cares of his profession to go every day to wear out your doorkeeper."[62] While quite obviously accusing Colbert's favorite, Le Brun, of being a careerist, Molière is also reflecting on his own choices. The tone of "who gives himself to the court robs his art" is very different from the graceful *Remerciement* to the king written five years earlier.

Molière, finally, chose to remain on the periphery of literary Paris. His friends and associates are now seen to have been giants of the age, but in Molière's lifetime only Racine scrambled to the heights of Parnassus and was invited into the Académie Française. In general, those of Molière's generation whose ambitions were focused on a career in literature, the Chapelains and Cotins and de Pures, left no work of substance. They fulfilled the terms of their contract as royal pensioners with fulsome flatteries of the monarch, and passed their time in literary squabbles and *salon* swaggerings.

Molière had neither the time nor the temperament to be a Parnassian. He was far too occupied as a playwright, actor, and leader of a company. Nor does it seem that Molière was especially interested in using his stage as a battlefield in the literary wars. His early *Précieuses ridicules* takes aim at the romantic novels of Madeleine de Scudéry and the effect of those novels on silly women, while sideswiping the gentleman amateur poets and *salon* habitués. Still, by using provincial girls and valets pretending to be gentlemen, Molière is able to argue, however unconvincingly, that he is not maligning literary Paris.

This argument is less credible when the question is of *La Critique de l'École des femmes*. The punning marquis is not a lackey pretending to be a marquis and the women are true Parisians. The play does attack the poet Lysidas, modeled, according to the abbé d'Aubignac, on the younger Corneille, Thomas, who had called Molière's *Précieuses ridicules* "a bagatelle."[63] But the "war" in which *La critique* was a sally was really more a theatrical than a literary quarrel, although Boileau was pleased to call attention to himself by taking a small part in it.

Molière then ignored literary Paris for some years. The satire of pedantry in *Le Mariage forcé* is clearly inspired by the *dottore* of the *commedia dell'arte*. *Le Misanthrope*, performed in June 1666, is set in Paris society, the play's targets largely drawn from the lesser nobility – those useful *petits marquis* – and the upper bourgeois/officer class. The famous scene of the sonnet introduces Oronte, a poetic haunter of court and *salons*, who insists, however, that he is an amateur whose "little sweet nothings" were tossed off in a quarter of an hour. There are certainly connections between the world of *Le Misanthrope* and Le Parnasse, but the focus is elsewhere.

Only with *Les Femmes savantes* does Molière openly engage the enemy, especially Boileau's *bête noire* Cotin. The issue would seem to have been almost moot by the time the play was produced in March 1672, since Boileau had found patrons and was on his way to a royal appointment, while Cotin and Ménage, the other target, had lost their pensions and, thus, their royal patronage. However, the play was not new in 1672; Molière may have begun it as early as 1668 and he definitely received permission to publish it in December 1670.

Cotin and Ménage were old and without the patronage and salon backing that might make mocking them dangerous. Cotin had engaged in any number of literary wars over the years, some of which had peripherally involved Molière. Why the playwright finally decided to retaliate from the stage is not clear, but his satire is unusually venomous, given that the targets of it were such easy marks.

In general, Molière's portraits, when taken from life, were veiled and the author insisted that he had no particular models in mind. No one believed him, but no one could prove that his satirical attacks were personal. He broke this pattern first in *L'Amour médecin* with the use of portrait masks of the four fashionable doctors and then in *Les Femmes savantes* with character names: Trissotin (three-times-the fool) but originally Tricotin,[64] and Vadius, a pun on Aegidius Menagius (the latinized form of Gilles Ménage). To confirm the identification, Molière took two examples from the published works of Cotin and had Trissotin recite them as his own, while he introduced Ménage, best known as the translator of Diogenes Laertes, as someone "who knows Greek as well as any man in France." Molière's specificity was defended by Donneau de Visé in the *Mercure galant*, who noted that "Aristophanes did not destroy the reputation of Socrates when he made fun of him in one of his farces."[65]

The play's satire is focused on the bourgeois women who want to be taken for intellectuals, while the two old pedants form a decorative centerpiece, a comic interlude in Act III, not unlike other scenes in Molière, especially the scene of the madrigal in *Les Précieuses ridicules*. Trissotin presents his banal sonnet, *To the princess Uranie on her fever*, and the three women, Philamente, Bélise, and Armande, fall about in ecstasy. Satire becomes farce when the women choose as their favorite phrase *quoi qu'on die*, "whatever you say," a meaningless filler employed for the sake of the rhyme. Repeating *quoi qu'on die* over and over, the women turn themselves into a flock of silly ducks.

When Vadius arrives the two men of letters at first exchange elaborate compliments. Then Trissotin asks Vadius what he thinks of a "little sonnet on the fever of the princess Uranie." Vadius finds it "miserable," and the exchange of compliments is quickly balanced by an exchange of insults in which the two Parnassians reveal their true colors. "Peddler of rhymes, disgrace to the profession", "Dealer in second-hand writing, impudent plagiarist"; "Do you remember your book and how badly it did?"; "Your bookseller ended up in the poorhouse"; "My glory is established: you defame it in vain"; "Yes, yes, I refer you to the author of the *Satires*."[66] And thus Molière brings the quarrel back to Boileau.

According to Grimarest, the play did not appeal to the court audience. "What does it matter to me," said the marquis de***, to see a pedant ridiculed?" "And where did he unearth these fools of women whom he treats as seriously as if they were a good subject," added the comte de***. "There's nothing to laugh at in all that for the courtiers or the common people."[67] The world of the play, bourgeois and bookish, is narrow, and much of the satire lacks the universal application of Molière's better-known plays. The first run of *Les Femmes savantes* began well, with eight of the eleven performances before the Easter break doing more than 1,000 *livres* in box office revenue, but profits quickly fell off when the play was revived to inaugurate the new season.

Boileau took a certain amount of credit for *Les Femmes savantes*, a play that may reflect his attitudes and interests as much as those of its author. It was Boileau who had begun his satire on women at about the same time Molière began the play, which is unusually misogynistic. It was Boileau who claimed to have "given" Molière the scene between Trissotin and Vadius which he had witnessed when it was played in reality between his brother Gilles and Cotin.[68] Perhaps it was Boileau who finally persuaded Molière to take the play, the only one in his repertory after *Le Misanthrope* "completely finished," that is, written in verse and in five acts, out of his fabled trunk and stage it, maybe even against his better judgment.

In general, though, Molière kept his private friendships separate from his work in the theatre. He did not take his revenge on Racine or correct the drunken libertinism of Chapelle from the stage. The evidence, though unreliable and anecdotal, is consistent; Molière was a discreet and faithful friend with a few intimates whom he endorsed and endured. Quiet in company, always observant, sober and sensitive, he smiled and nodded and went his own way. He revealed himself rarely even to his friends and then only when his emotional distress was extreme. The cause of that distress was not the failure of a play or the failure of friendship but the failure of love, the unraveling of his marriage to Armande Béjart.

CHAPTER TEN

Marriage (and love)

In January, 1666, Molière rented a new apartment for his family on the rue St-Thomas-du-Louvre; at the same time, he probably leased for himself a hideaway in Auteuil where he could escape from the pressures of family and profession.[1] He was struggling for *Tartuffe*, his health was questionable, and his marriage was seemingly troubled. Leaving Armande behind in the midst of her family and the troupe, Molière – as often as he could – took the water taxi to Auteuil where he could follow the milk diet prescribed by his doctor, write in peace, and talk with his friends.

Molière and Armande were never legally separated, as were, for instance, La Fontaine and his wife. Legal separation in the seventeenth century was usually a matter of money, when one spouse was deeply in debt and the other sued for "separation of goods" in order to protect his or her property. Money does not seem to have been an issue in the Molière marriage, however; the problem was the relationship itself and, apparently, from 1666 or 1667 through 1671, the two lived separately for the most part, she in Paris, he in Auteuil.

Although we only know for certain that Molière was in Auteuil by August 1667,[2] the likely time for the beginning of his stay was the winter of the previous year when he was trying to cope with the consequences of a debilitating chronic illness and finish *Le Misanthrope*. The most significant evidence suggesting that his marriage was in particular trouble at that point is the relationship he creates between Alceste and Célimène in the play he was writing, which ends with her refusal to join him in his solitude.

In the winter of 1666, Armande was the mother of six-month-old Esprit-Madeleine and was probably playing Lucinde in *L'Amour médecin*. Gossip accuses her of having had several extramarital liaisons, although the names cited by the anonymous author of *La Fameuse Comedienne*, the *libelle* that appeared in 1688, can be questioned, particularly that of the comte de Guiche, about whom Armande was supposedly "mad" after she met him at Versailles in May 1664 during the *Plaisirs de l'Île enchantée*. If that was indeed the case, then Armande was naive rather than predatory. Even the pamphleteer points out that the comte de Guiche was "a man for whom the happiness of being beloved by women counted for little good fortune."[3] In 1658 the comte de Guiche had had a openly homosexual relationship with Philippe d'Orléans, the king's adolescent brother;[4] in 1663–4 he was in exile, although he may have returned to court before May 1664. Another of Armande's supposed lovers was the abbé Richelieu, whose place in the *galanterie* is confirmed by Tallemant. But the abbé Richelieu left Paris for the army in April 1664 and died in Venice the following January. Armande's last supposed lover was the comte de Lauzun, celebrated as the man the king's cousin was later prevented from marrying. The *libelliste's* story is that Armande, "irritated by the coldness of the comte de Guiche, threw herself into the arms of the comte de Lauzun."[5] She may have done so. But all of this is meant to have happened around the time that Armande made her court debut in *La Princesse d'Élide,* nearly two years before her husband's escape to Auteuil.

The anonymous chronicler also charges her with having made use of the services of the wife of the porter at the Palais-Royal as a procuress. Nothing supports this accusation that Armande sold her favors; indeed, she and her husband were prosperous, on the way to being wealthy, and Molière was clearly a generous man. The image of the enchanting young actress enjoying her fame is not unattractive, even if it leads to the possibility that she did not remain entirely faithful to her aging, overworked husband, but that she turned to prostitution is beyond improbable.

Although no evidence suggests that Armande's behavior was especially egregious in early 1666, what did happen in February of that year was the meeting of Molière with Michel Baron, later the chief source of information for Molière's first biographer, Grimarest, who devotes a number of pages to the relationship of the boy and the older man.[6] Baron, the orphaned son of a theatrical couple, was twelve when he appeared in Paris with a children's troupe managed by Mlle Raisin, widow of the organist of Troyes who had astounded the city and the court in 1662 with a fraudulent magic spinet.[7] The children's troupe, known as the Comédiens de Monsieur le Dauphin, borrowed the theatre at the Palais-Royal for three days in February 1666. Baron was an immediate success; Robinet wrote in his gazette of February 22 that the boy,

like his mother, had the power to charm and that one day he would certainly be perfect in the lover's role.[8]

Molière, although unwell, made the effort to see the performance and
was enormously impressed. He invited the young actor to supper,
bought him a new suit of clothes, kept him overnight, and give him six
gold pieces "to spend on his pleasures." He then arose very early the next
morning, at 4:00 according to Grimarest, and went to St-Germain to get
an order from the king delivering Baron from his five-year obligation to
the children's troupe. When he returned he asked the boy what he most
wished for. Baron answered: "to be with you for the rest of my life." "Ah,
well," said Molière, "the thing is done."[9] According to Grimarest,
Molière took great pains to teach the boy good manners, and began to
train him as an actor. However, Armande "could not endure" her
husband's kindness to the child, nor did the child have "all the necessary
prudence to control himself with a woman for whom he should have
shown respect."[10] Baron found himself "loved by the husband, even necessary to his productions, the pet of the whole court," but took little or
no care to please Armande, who "forgot herself one day and gave him
a slap over some trifle."[11] The boy was so stung by this that he left
Molière and returned to Mlle Raisin.

This must have taken place in the fall of 1666, when the troupe was
in the midst of preparing for the *Ballet des Muses* at court. Molière's contribution was to be *Mélicerte*, a "heroic pastoral" that – according to
Grimarest – was to include a major role for Baron, that of Myrtil, the
lover of the title character. Molière is supposed to have said to
Armande, "Is it possible that you have had the imprudence to strike a
child as sensitive as you know this one to be; and at a time when he is
charged with a role of 600 lines in the play we must perform incessantly
before the king?"[12] The role, as it exists, is not 600 lines, but perhaps it
was meant to be. Molière never finished the play. It remains a fragment
of two acts supposedly performed at court first on December 2, 1666.
According to La Grange and Vivot, who published it for the first time
in the 1682 edition of Molière's works, "only two acts were finished
when the king asked for it. His Majesty having been satisfied with it . . .
M. de Molière did not finish it."[13] But the possibility also must be
entertained that Molière simply gave up on *Mélicerte* after Baron's deser-
tion interrupted his plan to introduce his new protégé to the court as he
had done with Armande in *La Princesse d'Élide*. "Heroic pastoral" is
hardly the sort of thing one expects Molière to be writing, especially one
based on Mlle de Scudéry's *Grand Cyrus*. Nor is it inherently likely that

Louis was satisfied with a play that leaves all its plot threads hanging in mid-air.[14]

Grimarest says that Baron promised that he would perform the role in *Mélicerte* but adds that he had the audacity to ask the king for permission to leave the troupe. This would suggest that the unfinished *Mélicerte* was possibly included in the *Ballet des Muses* only during December and was replaced by the *Pastorale comique* in January when Baron left to rejoin Mlle Raison. But we have only the testimony of La Grange that *Mélicerte* was ever performed at all, and La Grange was ever careful of the reputation of Molière.

Some scholars have doubted that Myrtil was being written for Baron, just thirteen years old. Yet the role makes no sense unless a very young actor was destined to play it. The character is not old enough to get married and still occupied with games, although he is uncommonly bright according to his father, Lycarsis, the role Molière was writing for himself.[15] The nymphs Éroxène and Daphné want the boy to choose between them and engage himself to one of them with a future marriage in view. Myrtil finds nothing especially odd in the idea of an engagement, but he must reject the nymphs since he is in love with young Mélicerte. His father, shocked, bursts out: "What's that? How can a snot-nose like you know what it is to love?" The boy answers that "without knowing what it is, my heart knows how to do it."[16]

The usual plot is reversed. Instead of a beautiful girl with rival suitors, as in, for instance, the *Princesse d'Élide* or Molière's later *Les Amants magnifiques*, here a beautiful boy is pursued by several women.[17] The boy, though still a "snotnose" and occupied with games, is not without erotic feelings. On his first entrance, he is speaking to a sparrow he plans to give to his beloved. "Innocent little animal," he begins, "do not complain of the loss of your freedom. Your fate is glorious. I caught you for Mélicerte. She will kiss you, take you in her hand, press you to her breast. . . . What king, alas! happy little sparrow, would not want to be in your place?"[18] The sparrow may be innocent, but the boy is less so.

Molière writes for himself and Baron a stereotypical father-and-son relationship, at first reminiscent of that between Harpagon and Cléante. Unlike Harpagon, however, Lycarsis does not want to marry his son's beloved; in this case, he has promised the nymphs to promote their cause to Myrtil if the loser will take him instead. When Lycarsis interrupts a love scene between Mélicerte and his son, Myrtil defies his father and then begs him not to employ his natural rights. "Life is a gift I have received from you," he says, but "if you take Mélicerte from me, you take my life as well."[19] Again unlike Harpagon, Lycarsis is moved by his son's obvious distress and persuaded by the intensity of his love for Mélicerte. "Who would have believed it of this little rascal? What love! What rapture! What a way with words for someone his age!"[20] And he agrees to find Mélicerte's aunt and plead his son's case.

This scene, unlike any other in Molière between father and child, may be taken as a clue to his feelings for the young Baron. However, *La Fameuse Comédienne*, which was published fifteen years after Molière's death, suggests that they may have been more than paternal. The anonymous pamphleteer writes that as a means of assuaging the pain caused him by the indifference of Armande, he "took it into his head to attach himself to the young Baron, in the hope of finding more constancy in men than in women."[21] Baron, we are told, lived with Molière as his child, was spared nothing, and was instructed in all the arts of the actor, all of which agrees with what Baron told Grimarest some years later. But the *libelliste* adds that just as Armande had betrayed him, so did Baron. "It was written in the heavens that [Molière] would be cuckolded in every way."[22]

As Yves Giraud says in his article on the pamphlet, "we are no longer hagiographers."[23] That Molière might have had erotic feelings for a beautiful and seductive boy should not scandalize us, any more than does Shakespeare's love poetry addressed to a young man. But we also need not assume that the relationship was homosexual in the modern sense. Another clue in *Mélicerte* may help us conceive how Molière understood feelings and behavior that were both paternal and erotic. Lycarsis, who is plain-spoken to the point of vulgarity, explains the elegance of his son's language by the presence of an Athenian philosopher who stayed with them for twenty months and, finding Myrtil "*joli*," had the whim of "filling him with the spirit of his philosophy."[24] This might be taken to refer to the classical Athenian or Platonic ideal wherein a man was the mentor of a boy in many domains including the sexual. Molière may be dividing himself into the *pater familias* with life and death power over the child on the one hand and the wise and loving teacher on the other.

Or, as the scene between Lycarsis and Myrtil also suggests, Molière – going though an especially difficult and lonely time – may have simply found himself unexpectedly moved and somewhat obsessed by the orphaned waif. Armande apparently was less than enchanted by her husband's new protégé; whether her animosity was sexual or a more complex response to her spouse's generosity – both financial and emotional – to the interloper is hard to assess. That Molière retreated with

Baron to Auteuil is both highly probable and understandable. What happened there between them is unknown.

The boy was clearly there on the occasion of the famous supper when he caught the eye of Jean-Baptiste Lully, notorious for his "Italian tastes," that is, for having sexual relations with boys. Molière, ready to retire for the night and possibly trying to protect Baron, begged the company to excuse the lad from an all-night debauch, but Lully insisted that the party would be no good without him, and the boy stayed on downstairs.[25] It was on this same occasion that Chapelle supposedly delivered his misogynistic diatribe against women.

As in most of Europe before the eighteenth century, male-male sexual relationships in France usually took place between older men and boys, although the subject has been less studied in France than in Italy, England, and the Netherlands. According to most recent research, "homosexual sodomy, especially between men, was indeed quite common before the early eighteenth century. At the same time, there were few people . . . who engaged exclusively in same-sex sexual relations. In the case of men who had sex with both men and women, the relationship between age and sexual behavior was very important. Older men could penetrate both women and younger men without losing their sense of masculinity. Passive . . . intercourse did not make younger men any less manly, either."[26] Lully, for instance, married and had six children in the first six years of his marriage. It may be pertinent, however, that his wife was only fifteen when they married, and that no more children were born after she reached twenty-one.

By and large adult men did not have intercourse with each other, although there were exceptions. For the most part, men of like interests associated with each other, and may have taken their sexual pleasure at social gatherings, "debauches" in the parlance of the day. The very young Lully knew the libertines who drank together at the Cabaret de Bel-Air and the Croix-de-Lorraine, where Molière also came later according to Chapelle. The group included Dassoucy, the musician Chapelle supposedly encountered in Montpellier being accused of unnatural behavior by a group of disgruntled women, as well as Cyrano de Bergerac, "atheist in religion and heretic in love," and Des Barreaux, the king of the libertines. Atheism, freethinking, and male-male sexuality were inextricably linked in the seventeenth-century mind, and Molière was, of course, accused of all three.

Whatever Molière's feelings for Baron, there seems to be no doubt that he was – unlike Lully – substantively heterosexual. So was Baron, who has been, however, described as "not insensible to any temptation of the flesh." He was labeled his mother's son, she a famous *demimondaine*, he with a hereditary tendency to debauchery, "in spite of all of Molière's cares."[27] What must be kept in mind is that before the eighteenth century, same-sex sexual relations were regarded as a sin, like gambling and drinking too much, and not a culture or way of life. Although the laws against sodomy were punitive, very few people were actually accused of it and even fewer punished for it. Lully's close friend Chausson was burned alive on the Grève in Paris for sodomy with the son of a noble family, but the issue was class as much as morality.

As well as being a sanctuary for Molière and his protégé, Auteuil was also the site of a supposed conversation between Molière and his friend Chapelle on the subject of his marriage. The conversation is not especially credible, since the source, once again *La Fameuse Comédienne*, is suspect, but the scene is irresistible to biographers, partly because it creates a character psychology that seems compatible with Molière's plays, especially with *Le Misanthrope*, and partly because it is so very well-written.[28]

Chapelle comes upon Molière in his Auteuil garden "in one of those fullnesses of heart so well known to those who are in love."[29] Chapelle, "who believed himself to be above these sorts of things," wants to know why someone "who knows so well how to paint the weakness of other men" should himself exhibit the most ridiculous of all weaknesses: loving someone who does not love him in return. "As for me," he says, "I swear to you that if I were unhappy enough to find myself in such a state, and if I were strongly persuaded that the person I loved was granting favors to others, I would have such contempt for her that it would cure me infallibly of my passion."[30] He goes on to point out that since the present case involves a wife and not a mistress, Molière is fortunate to have the option of taking his revenge by having Armande imprisoned for adultery. "That will be a certain means of putting your mind at rest."[31]

"I see," answers Molière, "that you have never been in love and you have taken the appearance of love for love itself."[32] He agrees that he has studied human weakness, but personal experience convinces him that not all weaknesses can be overcome. "I was born with the utmost disposition for sexual passion," he says, "and, as all my efforts have not been able to conquer the penchant I have for love, I have tried to be happy, that is to say, as much as one can be with a sensitive heart."[33] What follows is clearly based on *L'École des femmes*. Molière describes how he raised Armande to be the kind of wife he needed, innocent and untouched by self-interest, ambition, or vanity. "As she was still young when I married her, I did not perceive her bad inclinations, and I believed myself a little less unhappy than most of those who take on such obligations." But after marriage, "I found in her so much indifference that I began to perceive that all my precautions had been useless, and that what she felt for me was far from what I needed to be happy . . . I attributed to her nature what was an effect of her lack of sexual feeling for me." When the rumor reached him that she was having a passionate affair with the comte de Guiche, he was forced to realize the truth. He has tried desperately to change, but cannot conquer his feelings, and he has had "the vexation of realizing that a woman without great beauty, who owes what little intelligence she has to the education I gave her, could destroy in an instant all my philosophy." When he confronted her, "her presence made me forget my resolutions, and the first words she said to me in her defense left me so convinced that my suspicions were unfounded, that I asked her forgiveness for having been so credulous." But nothing changed. Now he is determined "to live with her as if she were not my wife. But if you knew what I suffer, you would pity me; my passion has come to such a point that I even feel compassion for her, and when I consider how impossible it is for me to overcome what I feel for her, I tell myself that perhaps she has the same difficulty suppressing the penchant that she has to be a coquette, and I find myself more disposed to be sorry for her than to blame her. You will no doubt say to me that one must be a poet to love that way? But, for me, I believe that there is only one kind of love, and that people who do not have a weakness like this have never truly loved: everything in the world is related to her in my heart; my mind is so occupied with her that nothing can divert me in her absence; when I see her, an emotion and ecstasy that I can feel but never express takes away my power of reason; I have no eyes for her defects, I only see what is lovable in her. Isn't this the extreme of madness? And don't you admire the way that my reason shows me my weakness, without being able to triumph over it?"[34]

    There are clear parallels between the *libelliste's* version of Molière's passion for Armande and Molière's attribution, although couched in coded language, of similar feelings to Arnolphe and Alceste. Two interpretations are possible. The simplest, and perhaps the most probable, is that the anonymous writer simply mined the plays and transferred the predicament of Molière's characters to their creator. Yet, the other interpretation is worth examining, that Molière was more than the contemplative observer of human passions the hagiographers of the nineteenth century wanted to make him out to be. Without assuming any exact correspondences between artists and their creations, we can still conjecture that every artist finds ways to express his or her own emotions and – yes – passions. The plays of Molière return over and over to sexual jealousy and sexual need, to doubts about being loved, and to fraudulent marriages. These are not unique human experiences, and nothing proves that Molière's relationship with his wife was, well, disappointing. But perhaps the *libelliste* gets some of it right. In any case, the voice he gives Molière is too haunting to be dismissed outright. "I am thus determined to live with her as if she were not my wife. But if you knew what I suffer, you would pity me."

Grimarest's early biography includes a different version of Molière's confession. According to him, Molière would not have revealed his deepest feelings to Chapelle who was too much a friend to everyone to be a true friend to anyone. Rather, it was to the painter Mignard and the doctor Rohault that Molière spoke about his painful marriage. "I am the most unhappy of men," he said, "and I have only what I deserve. I did not think that I was too austere for domestic society. I believed that my wife should subjugate her behavior to her virtue and to my expectations; and I really feel that in her present situation, she would have been even more unhappy than I am if she had done so. She is lively and has wit and she is sensible of the pleasure of making good use of it. All that makes me suspicious in spite of myself. I criticize, I complain. This woman who is a hundred times more reasonable than I am wants to enjoy her life. She goes her own way: and assured of her innocence, she disdains the prudence I ask of her. I take this negligence for contempt; I would like some marks of affection in order to believe she feels some for me, and that her conduct be more correct so that my mind would be at ease. But my wife, always cool, and free from care, who would be exempt from all suspicion by any man less uneasy than I am, leaves me without pity to my troubles; and occupied only with the desire to please in general, like all women, without having any special intention, laughs at my weakness."[35]

Grimarest's Molière seems convinced that his wife is only a pleasure seeker and that he is unjustly suspicious. He is jealous, to be sure, but far more rational about it than the anguished Molière of the *libelle*. Grimarest ignores any parallel with *L'École des femmes*, but seems to be influenced by *Le Misanthrope*, painting a husband desperately trying to convince himself that his wife has not actually been unfaithful. The implications are not unlike the climactic moment in *Le Misanthrope* when Alceste says to Célimène: "Force yourself to appear faithful and I will force myself to believe you are so." The Molière of the *libelle* also shares with his characters a strong sexual energy; at the heart of his misery is his failure to gain sexual satisfaction from his marriage. In Grimarest's account of Molière, on the other hand, the playwright only wishes – euphemistically – that his wife would show some "marks of affection."

Although both Grimarest and the pamphleteer must be basing their "confessions" largely on gossip and on various anti-Molière pamphlets and plays, they also reflect the general understanding of the period that Molière's plays mirror his life. *Le Misanthrope* is of particular interest, of course, because it is the only one of Molière's major plays that has a love affair at its center and because it was written, or at least finished, during the time we presume Molière's marriage was disintegrating. According to Brossette, Molière read the first act of *Le Misanthrope* to an assembly in 1664.[36] The completed play was performed on June 4, 1666. Between the end of the December 1665 and the beginning of June 1666, the troupe played only twenty-five times and many of those performances were of plays not by or featuring Molière. So, it seems possible to imagine that he spent most of the spring of 1666 writing in Auteuil.

While it would be foolish to think that Alceste and Célimène are direct imitations of Molière and his wife, it would be naive to assume that their experience does not inform the play. Had there been no Armande, there could have been no Célimène, nor could Molière have created a relationship with such complexity and such a depth of ambivalence without his own adventure of deeply loving someone who might or might not love him in return. Act IV, scene iii is one of the greatest scenes ever written for a pair of precarious lovers; it begins with Alceste in a state of furious hyperbole and ends with Alceste pleading with Célimène to pretend fidelity. What is different about this scene from most of Molière's writing is its intimacy and its degree of revelation. Alceste commences with high rhetoric: no horror of which the human soul is capable can compare to her treacheries; not fate, not the devil, not the Heavens in their wrath have ever produced anything as wicked as Célimène. He is completely transported by jealousy, beside himself that she has written a love letter to Oronte, consumed by rage. Her cool response: "Have you lost your mind?"[37]

He is unable to evoke from her any emotion. Accused of betraying him, of having pretended to love him, of trying to evade the issue with silly lies, she answers that "what you believe matters very little to me."[38]

It may not matter, but she knows only too well how to increase his misery. She tells Alceste that she receives the attentions of Oronte with great pleasure, that she admires what Oronte says and esteems what he is. And then she tells Alceste to leave. Her language and syntax are simple and even blunt; in response he foregoes some of his formal eloquence and gradually speaks from his confused heart:

> Heaven! Can anything more cruel be contrived?
> Was any heart ever treated like this?
> I am rightly furious with her,
> I come here to complain, but I'm the one who is scolded!
> My pain and my suspicions are pushed to the limit . . .
> And yet my heart is still so cowardly
> That it can't break the chain that attaches it to her,
> Nor can it defend itself with noble contempt
> Against the ungrateful object that it loves too much.
> Traitress, you know this perfectly well, and you
> Use my extreme weakness against me,
> And keep for yourself the prodigious excess
> Of this fatal love born of your treasonous eyes.
> At least defend yourself against this crime that crushes me,
> Stop pretending that you are guilty,
> Prove to me that the letter is innocent,
> My love will come to your assistance;
> Force yourself to appear faithful,
> And I will force myself, I will, to believe you are.[39]

But even this confession does not move her. Her reasonable response, "why, if my heart were engaged elsewhere, wouldn't I simply say so," rouses from Alceste only that it is "his destiny to love her" and that "his soul is abandoned to her faithfulness." He will continue on to the bitter end, if only to see just how base and treacherous she can be. She answers simply and correctly: "No, you don't love me as one ought to love."[40]

This line Molière has used before, in his first play exploring sexual jealousy, when Elvire says to Dom Garcie that he will please her only "when you learn how to love me as one ought to love."[41] Molière knew how one ought to love, but also knew how hard it was to translate that knowledge into action and feeling. Alceste, years after Dom Garcie, still has not learned. Célimène's cool reason drives him into a fantasy where he wishes her miserable, without name, rank, or property, so he can sacrifice everything for her and so she will owe everything to him. Although the circumstances differ, the need to dominate and control that was so obvious in Arnolphe is revealed again in Alceste.

Alceste's deeply sexual jealousy is reminiscent not of Grimarest's Molière, seeking affection and attention, but of the Molière of the *libelle*. Sexuality is the central subject of much of seventeenth-century French drama, although sexual feeling is disguised and coded. Even Molière, with his distaste for preciosity and contempt for Mlle de Scudéry and her *carte de tendre*, uses the code word "*tendresse*" to express the physical sensations of sexual attraction.[42] The male body, especially the aristocratic body, in France in the mid to late seventeenth century is not sexually explicit or even gender specific. It is seriously distorted by clothing. Unlike the male costume of Shakespearean England, with its focus on the pelvis and penis, the male costume of baroque France completely conceals the body under an avalanche of lace and ribbons. Men are visually feminized by their clothing and symbolically feminized by their presence in the *salons*, their interest in poetry and the arts, and their obsession with preferment at court. Nothing about them openly suggests sexuality. Women's clothing, on the other hand, distorts the body less and can reveal the breasts. Tartuffe pretends that the sight of Dorine's uncovered breasts presents an occasion of sin, and provides a concealing handkerchief. Women were assumed to be obsessed with romantic love and also assumed to be too easily aroused sexually, but Célimène makes the point that women "have to make an extreme effort when they resolve to confess that they are in love, since the honor of the sex, enemy to our passions, is strongly opposed to such admissions."[43] The society was ambivalent about "love," meaning sexual desire for another; it was an experience to be sought and a sin that endangered the soul. The king pursued sexual fulfillment with enthusiasm, the Church condemned it even within marriage where, in any case, it was rarely to be found. On the comic stage most love is puppy love and harmless, as it usually is in Molière, when plots revolve in proper neoclassical fashion around sons or daughters in love and fathers who wish to arrange their marriages elsewhere. But sexual love is seen as the cause of great unhappiness, as it is in *Le Misanthrope*, or even as extremely dangerous, as it is in Racine's *Phèdre*.

Molière seems to have done something unusual for his time; he married a woman with whom he was in love, who aroused him sexually. This in itself may explain why a *libelliste* would imagine the scene in which Molière confesses that his nature is deeply sexual and that his marriage has not fulfilled his needs. It is also an interesting contrast to the persona created by Louis Racine for his father, whose character Phèdre still symbolizes female sexual obsession: "I do not pretend to sustain that he was always exempt from weakness, although I have never heard anyone mention any, but (and my piety does not permit me to be unfaithful to the truth) I dare sustain that he never knew from experience these troubles and these transports that he depicted so well." Rather, he "followed the maxim that he put in the mouth of Burrhus: 'one does not love if one does not want to love.'"[44] Molière would almost certainly have disagreed.

Love is usually not an issue between Molière's married couples, more frequently encountered in the late plays than in the early ones. Infidelity, not love, is the subject of *George Dandin*. Orgon and Elmire may have once loved each other, but Orgon shows no interest in her illness, nor does he emerge from the table as quickly as we might expect of a man who loves his wife. Madame Jourdain is thoroughly fed up with Monsieur, Chrysale and Philaminte agree about nothing, and Argan is married to the greedy and fraudulent Béline.

There is another play about marriage and love, rarely produced and infrequently discussed, yet it may – like *Mélicerte* – yield some points worth noticing. *Amphitryon* is unusually interesting as a kind of minuet of marriage, in which Alcmène assumes she is with her husband Amphitryon when, in fact, she is with Jupiter in disguise, while her lady's maid Cléanthis plays out a parallel plot with her husband Sosie and his double Mercure.

Several moments in *Amphitryon* are revealing. The first is Jupiter's speech on the subject of husbands and lovers. On the one hand, the speech is a clever equivocation. Jupiter, who appears to be Alcmène's husband Amphitryon, wants her to regard him as her lover. The audience, knowing him to be Jupiter, recognizes that he is telling the truth, while she regards him uneasily. The distinction he makes between the way a husband feels and the way a lover feels reflects society's assumptions, but may also refer to Molière's self awareness of his own dual role. What Jupiter says is that his ardor and passion surpass those of a mere spouse. "You see a husband, you see a lover. But, to speak frankly, only the lover matters to me. When I'm near you, I feel the husband is an impediment. This lover, jealous to the last degree, wishes your heart to abandon itself to him alone."[45] The lover wants her ardor to be pure, to owe nothing to the bonds of matrimony, nor to a sense of duty that every day poisons the sweetness of "the most dear favors." Alcmène's response – not unlike Célimène's to Alceste's diatribe – is that if anyone were to hear him, they might believe that he was not entirely sane.

Nonetheless, when she describes the events of the evening to the real

Amphitryon, she tells him that his love was never so tender and so passionate. What she refers to is his discourse of love; of the physical consequences she says, merely, "We were served. We supped together alone. And, supper finished, we went to bed."[46]

In contrast to his master, Mercure, the false Sosie, has refused to speak "sweet nothings" to Cléanthis, claiming that fifteen years of marriage has "exhausted his vocabulary."[47] If she wants that sort of thing, she should take a lover. Shocked, she reminds him that she is an honest woman; he takes for his motto "less honor, more peace and quiet." The role of Cléanthis was invented by Molière in order to further develop the contrasts between love and marriage; she does not appear in Plautus or in earlier French versions. Cléanthis was very probably played by Madeleine Béjart,[48] while Molière apparently played Sosie.[49]

When Cléanthis encounters the real Sosie, she is furious: "When I expressed the feelings in my heart, to all my discourse you were like a stump, and never a sweet word from your mouth."[50] In both relationships, the masters and the servants, verbal lovemaking is taken as a key sign of feeling, so it is not surprising that the false Sosie who refuses to make love with language also refuses to take his place in the bed that "the laws of matrimony obliged him to occupy." The scene is a delightful tangle of mistaken identities and false assumptions, but it also underscores one of the themes introduced earlier in the play: sexual relations in marriage are legally obligatory and the refusal of one spouse to engage in them is grounds to end the marriage. But for the women, the physical act of making love has meaning only when it is engendered by the rhetoric of love. It is the golden tongue of Jupiter that wins the day for him.

A scene in *Le Bourgeois gentilhomme*, produced in October 1670, is often taken as a last word from Molière on the subject of his obsession with his wife. Cléonte, the young lover of the piece, has just been snubbed by his beloved, Lucile, played by Armande. "I love nothing in the world but her," he says, "I have nothing but her on my mind; she is all my care, all my desire, all my joy; I speak of nothing but her, I think of nothing but her, I dream of nothing but her, I breathe nothing but her, my heart lives entirely in her: and here's the thanks I get for so much love! I go two days without seeing her, for me two centuries: I meet her by chance; my heart leaps at the sight, joy breaks out on my face, I run delightedly toward her; and the faithless hussy turns away from me and passes by as if she had never seen me before in her life."[51] His servant Covielle suggests that Lucile is not worth loving. Everything about her is mediocre. "First of all, she has little eyes." "That's true," answers Cléonte. "She has little eyes; but they are full of fire, the most brilliant, the most piercing in the world . . ." "Her mouth is big," counters Covielle. "Yes; but . . . this mouth inspires desire, this mouth is the most attractive, the most amorous in the world." "She's not very tall," Covielle persists. "No; but she is very nicely proportioned." "She affects a kind of nonchalance in her speech and her actions." "That's true, but so gracefully, and her manners are so engaging that her charm insinuates itself into the heart." "As for her wit . . ." "Ah, she has wit, Covielle, the finest, the most deli-cate." "Her conversation . . ." "Her conversation is charming." "She is always serious." "Is there anything more impertinent that these women who laugh at everything?" "But finally she is the most capricious person in the world." "Yes, she is capricious, I agree; but caprice is becoming in a beauty, one can suffer anything from a beauty." Covielle gives up: "I see that you are ready to love her forever." "Who me? I'd rather die. I'm going to hate her as much as I have loved her." "And how are you going to do that, since you find her so perfect?" "That's what will be so remark-able about my revenge; that's how I will show the strength of my heart, to hate her, to leave her, even though she is so beautiful, so charming, so lovable."[52] But Cléonte does not leave Lucile, nor did Molière leave Armande, at least not permanently.

The last half of the decade of the 1660s, although full of professional and personal conflict for Molière, was also a time of relative stability for the troupe at the Palais-Royal. There were twelve actors in place at the beginning of the 1665–6 season: Molière and Armande, Madeleine, Geneviève, and Louis Béjart, M. and Mlle de Brie, Du Croisy, Hubert, and Mlle Du Parc. M. Du Parc had died the previous October; he was not replaced. In March 1667, Mlle Du Parc left the troupe for the Hôtel de Bourgogne, lured away by Racine who wanted her for *Andromaque*. She also was not replaced. Molière had written roles for both of them, but Du Parc's brand of old-style farce, played in white face as Gros-René, was not to the taste of the times. Mlle Du Parc had played some ingenue roles, for instance Célie in *Le Cocu imaginaire*, and Léonor in *L'École des maris*, as well as fashionable Parisiennes, although her real forté was as a tragedy queen. She also was not replaced.[53] Her loss was more damaging personally to Molière than professionally to the troupe; once again he had been betrayed by his former protégé Racine.

Marquise Du Parc died shortly after her triumph in *Andromaque*, on December 11, 1668, either in childbirth[54] or as the result of an abortion. She had apparently become the mistress of Racine who, according to later testimony, never left her bedside. The gazetteer Robinet wrote, on the day of her funeral, that the poets of the theatre pressed around her cortege, one of whom, "the most interested, was half-dead himself.[55]

In November 1679, eleven years later, the poisoner La Voisin testified to the Chambre Ardente that Racine had poisoned Mlle Du Parc out of jealousy. The accusation was taken somewhat seriously, but did not result in any action against Racine. La Voisin's "colleagues" were also quick to testify that Mlle Du Parc was one of the circle of society women and *dem-imondaines* who were intimate with La Voisin. Since Marquise was the daughter of a charlatan who sold patent medicines on the street in Lyon, such an accusation would not have seemed improbable.

Although there is no proof, one reading of the evidence, such as it is, that makes some sense is to assume that Marquise Du Parc was pregnant by Racine, that she (or he) got a drug meant to produce an abortion from La Voisin or one of the others, and that the drug caused her death. La Voisin also accused Racine of stealing from Marquise as she was dying, of taking from her finger an expensive diamond.[56] A more romantic interpretation of that gesture, if it happened, would be to suppose that the despairing lover was reclaiming a gift he had given her, perhaps after her great success in *Andromaque*, as a memento of their happiness. Of course, this was Racine, who was not noticeably romantic.

Molière not only lost old comrades during the 1660s, he also lost a sister and his father. Madeleine Poquelin, six years younger than her brother and married to *tapissier* André Boudet, died in May 1665. Jean Poquelin died less than four years later, in February 1669, at the age of seventy-three.

The elder Poquelin, so prosperous during the 1630s when he supplied the royal army with beds and bedding, had a relatively difficult old age. He must have thought that he had made wise provisions; in 1654, while his eldest son, the actor, was still a vagabond in the south, Jean Poquelin made an arrangement with his other remaining son. He ceded to the younger Jean all the merchandise listed in an inventory made privately between them, valued at 5,218 *livres*, 10 *sous*, 5 *deniers*. In return, the son gave his father the 218 *livres*, 10 *sous*, 5 *deniers*, and gave up his claim to the 5,000 *livres* owing him from his mother's estate. In addition, Jean rented to his son his house at the Image Saint-Christophe, under the pillars of Les Halles, for 500 *livres* a year, reserving for himself a room in the front part of the building and shared use of the attic and the kitchen.[57] It would seen that Jean Poquelin meant to retire.

Although he owned the house and could look forward to a small income from the rental and from his office as *tapissier du roi*, he had no capital. In 1651 he had to borrow money for the 5,000-*livres* dowry of his daughter Madeleine. In February of 1655 Catherine Poquelin, his daughter by his second marriage, wanted to join the order of Visitation nuns. The dowry again was set at 5,000 *livres* and the family of the girl's mother agreed that it could be paid from her dowry, which – unfortunately – Poquelin no longer had. He was again forced to borrow the money and this time have the loan guaranteed by his son and son-in-law.[58]

When the son married at the same time, it was his father's merchandise, passed to him privately the previous September, that made up the bridegroom's contribution to the community of the marriage. The elder Poquelin may not, in fact, have retired at all, but may merely have appeared to retire in order to advance his son's marriage. In late 1657 he certainly was in business; he took an apprentice in October of that year and in January of the year following he signed an agreement with two colleagues to share equally in profits from furnishing merchandise to the king.[59] As late as 1663 court accounts show 370 *livres* paid to Poquelin and Nauroy for rental of chairs, cushions, and tapestries for a ball at the Louvre and a ceremony at the church of the Feuillants,[60] and Molière himself paid 100 *livres* a year to his father to take as an apprentice in 1664 a ten-year-old, Jean Rondeau.

In 1658 a long-standing family dispute was settled and the Maison de l'Image Véronique, the house that had belonged to the first Jean Poquelin and his wife Agnès Mazuel, was sold and the profits divided. Jean Poquelin used his share to pay most of the loans he had taken out for his daughters' dowries. The remainder was paid by Molière after his father's death.[61]

In April 1660, brother Jean – having just renewed his lease of his father's house for five years – unexpectedly died, leaving a small child and a pregnant wife. The little family moved to her brother's house on the rue de Cygne and at some point Madeleine Poquelin and her husband, André Boudet, took over the lease of the Maison de l'Image Saint-Christophe, while Jean Poquelin moved away to the rue de la Comtesse d'Artois. There was to be no sharing a kitchen with the Boudets. In January 1667, nearly two years after Madeleine's death, her father and her widower "settled accounts," the issues being her dowry, never fully paid, the rent of the Maison de l'Image Saint-Christophe, "occupied by Boudet," and some merchandise confided by Boudet to Jean Poquelin. The father-in-law profited by 1,359 *livres*.[62]

The family seems to have accepted the return of their errant son and brother in 1658 with equanimity. Molière's brother sold and loaned furniture to the actors, his father attended his marriage to Armande. Yet when Jean Poquelin was in need of a substantial sum to repair his property in 1668, his eldest son found a circuitous route by which to loan him the money.[63] Scholars have often commented on Molière's thoughtfulness in sparing his father the embarrassment of knowing that he owed 10,000 *livres* to his son, yet somehow that motive does not ring especially true.

When Jean Poquelin's property was inventoried after his death, his papers included a "Memoir of what I have disbursed and paid for my elder son, both to him and to those whom he ordered me to pay." To this was attached a "recognition," signed by Molière before a notary and dated April 4, 1651, agreeing that his father's memoir was correct. This recognition applied to the 630 *livres* for which Molière apparently gave up the *survivance* of his father's office and his claim to the money owed him from his mother's estate, and to debts paid by his father after the failure of the Illustre Théâtre. But the total had mysteriously risen from 1,074 *livres* to 1,965 *livres*, all but 630 of which he still supposedly owed his father. He swore that he had in fact paid what he owed and that he knew nothing of various other sums his father claimed to have paid out on behalf of "Monsr Molière." His brother had received 5,000 *livres*, accounted for by the inventory given him when he married. His sisters had also received 5,000, at least in principal. He had apparently received 630 *livres*.

Nonetheless, the black sheep made it possible for his father to repair his decrepit house. Why he did so surreptitiously is a puzzle. Many surviving documents suggest that Jean Poquelin was not an overly conscientious accountant. Nor was there the slightest chance that he could ever pay back a loan of 10,000 *livres* or even pay the annual interest of 500 *livres*. If he thought he owed the money to someone other than his son, perhaps he would have tried. At the least, Molière would not have had to deal with his father on the subject or listen to his excuses. The house must have been in very poor condition to need 10,000 *livres* in repairs. In fact, 10,000 would have paid for a complete reconstruction. However, Jean Poquelin did not live long to enjoy it. A few months after the second loan contract was signed, he was dead.

Jean Poquelin left a small estate. His personal property was meager: some furniture, much of it "as is," some scraps of tapestry and upholstery fabric, one good black bourgeois suit, six pairs of raggedy men's underdrawers.[64] Everything was assessed at 892 *livres* 10 *sous*. He had 815 *livres* in cash on hand, and a stack of old debts, some owed him for thirty years. His house under the pillars was the estate's major asset, but the asset was diminished by the 10,000 *livres* borrowed to reconstruct it. By law Jean Poquelin's estate was to be divided three ways, one third to his son, one third to the children of his daughter Madeleine, and one third to the children of his son Jean. The surviving parents of those children were present at the inventory, but knew nothing of Molière's role in the loan that reconstructed the Maison de l'Image Saint-Christophe. Nor did they know that when they agreed that the rental income of the house should go to pay the arrears of interest and future interest owed to Jacques Rohault, they were actually agreeing to pay it to Molière.

By 1668 Molière was certainly well-off, rich enough to have given his father 10,000 *livres*, perhaps in return for a deed to the property. But that would have created a family scandal, since the other potential heirs would have lost their right to the only thing of value Jean Poquelin owned. Nor would Poquelin necessarily have accepted a gift from his son. Nor, finally, would Molière necessarily have felt that a gift would be appropriate, given his treatment by his father. A loan, channeled through a friend, would save the decaying property and his father's face, without his having to become involved.[65]

The house was rented in August following Jean Poquelin's death in February for 1,150 *livres* a year and remained in the family as a rental property until after the death of Molière's daughter Esprit-Madeleine in 1723. In 1724 her husband sold her half of the house for 8,200 *livres*.[66] During all those years, the rent continued to pay the interest due on the loan Molière had made to his father.

Jean Poquelin died on February 25, 1669, twenty days after his son became the most talked about man in Paris, twenty days after *Tartuffe* was finally performed on the public stage. Robinet wrote forty-four lines of doggerel praising it on February 9, another thirty on February 23. There is no way of knowing if the playwright's father read either. The 25th was a Monday, a day off, but the company gave a private performance for 550 *livres*. On Wednesday, the day of the funeral, Molière was at liberty.

Exactly how rich Molière had become by 1668 is not easy to calculate. Our two principle sources of information, the *Registre* kept by La Grange and the various surviving account books from the court of Louis XIV, do not always agree. Still, a reasonable estimate is possible.

We know, from La Grange, what an actor's share in the Palais-Royal troupe was worth from 1659 to 1673, the year of Molière's death. And we know that in the early years, the other actors voted Molière gifts when one of his plays attracted good audiences. At the end of the second full

Paris season, after the success of *Les Précieuses ridicules*, Molière also asked for and received from the troupe an extra share "for himself or for his wife if he should marry." He did marry, of course, and that extra share went to Armande when she joined the troupe. Beginning with *L'École des femmes* in 1662, Molière also took a regular author's share from first runs of his new plays and from the royal pension and various special payments and gratifications. He also received an annual 1,000 *livres* from the king in his quality as *beau esprit*, and presumably made a certain income from the sale of his published plays.

For instance, in the season of 1664–5, an actor's share was worth 3,011 *livres* 11 *sous*. Molière and his wife held two regular shares. In addition, Molière received two extra shares as author for the first runs of two new plays: *La Princesse d'Élide* and *Dom Juan*. *La Princesse* was only moderately successful and it was expensive to produce; each share's profit was 508 *livres* 16 *sous*. *Dom Juan* did much better and yielded 1,021 *livres*, 5 *sous*. The author's shares for the two new plays would have been 3,060 *livres* 2 *sous*. For the year, Molière and Armande would have had a minimal income from the theatre of 9,083 *livres* 4 *sous*, but that does not take account of the possibility that Molière also received extra shares of the more than 13,000 *livres* received that year from various royal visits.[67]

By the end of the decade, financial matters were more regularized. In the season of 1668–9, the troupe had eleven shares. The royal pension had been awarded on the basis of twelve shares and was being paid at 6,000 *livres* a year, or 500 per actor. The extra 500 was awarded to Molière as an author's share. He introduced three new plays during that season. *L'Avare* was essentially a failure, its first run broken after only four performances. *George Dandin* was treated, in the public theatre, as an afterpiece without increased ticket prices and, probably, without author's shares. But *Tartuffe* was the great financial as well as artistic success of Molière's career. Its first run lasted for twenty-eight performances; each share profited by 2,652 *livres* 15 *sous*.

If Molière was still receiving two shares as author, then his reward for *Tartuffe* would have been 5,305 *livres* 10 *sous*. This, added to his and his wife's regular shares, makes a total of 16,259 *livres* 16 *sous*. Plus, he had his pension of 1,000 as a literary man, an extra 500 from the troupe's pension, and probably an extra share of the *gratifications* the troupe received that season.[68] And whatever he made from publications. And, by this point, interest from money he had loaned or invested.[69] An income of 20,000 *livres* a year is probably a fair estimate. The vagabond had become a wealthy man.

CHAPTER ELEVEN

Last act

Louis XIV had begun his personal reign on March 10, 1661, after the death of his mentor, Cardinal Mazarin. The kingdom was at peace, a not entirely satisfactory state of affairs for a young king avid for glory. Various small interventions did not really create the kind of military prestige Louis sought. It was the death of the Spanish king in September 1665 that gave the French king his opening. He was married to a Spanish princess who had given up her rights to the various Spanish thrones, but only in return for a dowry of 1,500,000 *livres* that had never been paid. The French had no immediate designs on the Spanish crown, but they did worry about the Spanish Netherlands on their northern border, a weak point or "gate," as Cardinal Richelieu had put it, into France.

Several provinces of the Spanish Netherlands had a rather unusual inheritance law: a daughter of a first marriage took priority over a son of a second marriage. The new king of Spain, a sickly child, was the product of his father's second marriage, while the queen of France, Marie-Thérèse, was born of his first. Louis used this to establish a French claim for indemnity. His ministers raised an army of 60,000 men and in May of 1667 Louis led that army into the Low Countries and took Lille and a number of other smaller cities. In February of the following year the prince de Condé took the Franche-Comté, and in May the war, known as the War of Devolution, ended with the Treaty of Aix-la-Chapelle.

The Dutch were not happy with this result and Louis concluded that war was inevitable. Preparations for the Dutch war took four years, however, and during those years apparent peace reigned. The king's propaganda machine ground into action and Louis was lauded at every possible opportunity and in every possible form. "There are no limits to the glory of the Prince of the French, it reaches everywhere, and in all nations the truth of his history will surpass all the fictions of ancient times."[1] Thus begins the *livret* or printed program of *Le Grand*

Divertissement Royal de Versailles, held in mid-July of 1668 to celebrate "Peace" and "Victory," whose statues ornamented the garden theatre.

Even Molière wrote one of his very occasional "occasional" verses, a sonnet entitled *Au Roi sur la conquête de la Franche-Comté*. It has a graceful but not fulsome conceit. The king's victory was swift, faster than a torrent, the wind, the lightning. The poets' songs are not so quickly made, "and you spent less time at your conquests than it will take us to properly praise them."[2]

Le Grand Divertissement Royal was the first of a number of royal occasions between 1668 and 1672 when a play or comedy-ballet was expected from Molière. In all he wrote six court entertainments during this interval between the wars and two plays for the Palais-Royal. The latter were *L'Avare* (September 9, 1668) that failed immediately, and *Les Fourberies de Scapin* (May 24, 1671), that did almost as badly. For the king he wrote a series of bourgeois comedies that contrast strikingly with the pastoral ballets that served them as ornaments. These were *George Dandin*, the bitter story of a rich peasant betrayed by his aristocratic wife (Versailles, July 15, 1668), *Monsieur de Pourceaugnac*, the satire of a provincial lawyer duped by an Italian *fourbe intriguant* straight out of the *commedia dell'arte* (Chambord, October 6, 1669), *Le Bourgeois gentilhomme*, probably the best known of all the comedy-ballets (Chambord, October 14, 1670), and *La Comtesse d'Escarbagnas*, a slight and plotless satire of a pretentious provincial "snobette" (St-Germain-en-Laye, December 2, 1671). *Dandin* failed at the Palais-Royal but was retained in the repertory and *La Comtesse* was never performed in Paris. The other two were successful.

Molière was also responsible for a romantic comedy, *Les Amants magnifiques*, seen only at St-Germain-en-Laye in February, 1670, and for the vastly expensive and popular *Psyché*, produced first at the Salle des Machines at the Tuileries on January 17, 1671, and then transported to the refurbished Palais-Royal. This was the penultimate and most spectacular of the great court spectacles; the following year the king was preparing to go to war and the *Ballet de ballets*, given in honor of Monsieur's new second wife was – with the exception of Molière's sketchy *Comtesse d'Escarbagnas* – made up entirely of fragments from entertainments given in previous years.

The taste of the age for music, dance, and spectacle comes as a surprise to those who believe that the French theatre of the seventeenth century was strictly "classical," with small casts and single settings. While it is true that the commercial theatres usually chose plays that could be performed by the sharing company and in stock scenery, their reasons were practical and not necessarily aesthetic. Theatrical financing of the period made it difficult for a troupe to accumulate money; in general, expenses were paid daily and the remaining profits divided among the sharers. Furthermore, most companies played a rotating repertory, and unless a new play was a great success, the stage had to be refitted at least once a week and frequently for each performance. New scenery was expensive, and the machines necessary for full baroque splendor were beyond expensive and mostly beyond the means of the actors. The Marais had, for a time, specialized in machine plays, but neither the Palais-Royal or the Hôtel de Bourgogne had tried to rival it.

Matters changed somewhat when Molière began his sequence of court entertainments in 1668. *George Dandin* and *Monsieur de Pourceaugnac* may have appeared at the Palais-Royal without their musical ornaments, but the other two were fully mounted. *Le Bourgeois gentilhomme* requires nothing particular in the way of scenery, but music and elaborate costumes are essential. Robinet's report on the Paris opening assures his readers that the production is "almost" as it was at Chambord, with ballet entries, "harmonious concerts, and all the diverse ornaments."[3] The Turkish ceremony was, of course, included, although the *Ballet des nations*, an elaborate finale, was not.

Daily expenses rose to 300 *livres* per performance of the *Bourgeois gentilhomme* mostly for musicians and dancers.[4] Fortunately, very little other outlay was required; the king had paid – dearly – for the first performance at Chambord a month earlier, including 4,400 *livres* for the actors' costumes. The royal *État des dépenses* does not indicate what costumes the actors might have been given permission to use at the Palais-Royal, but clearly the troupe did not start over and recreate the production between the last court performance on November 13 and the Paris opening on November 23.

The *Bourgeois gentilhomme* relied on costumes and music while *Psyché* was a fully mounted baroque spectacle that, if it was not a masterpiece for its author(s), was a triumph for the troupe of the Palais-Royal. It was the most elaborate court production of the century and a great success transported to the public stage. It was the final collaboration between Molière and Jean-Baptiste Lully and it may also have been one cause of a rift between them.

Often ignored as "just a machine play" and because Molière was only partly responsible for its text, *Psyché* deserves more attention. It was an enormous undertaking for Molière as a producer. It was performed in Paris, not at Versailles or St-Germain, and in an elaborate baroque theatre with machines, purpose-built for court spectacles. In a scaled-down version, it was one of Molière's greatest successes at the Palais-Royal. It ran for thirty-eight performances through a late Paris summer, from July 24 to October 23, 1671, and was reprised successfully for carnival 1672 and again for the Christmas season of 1672–3, always with ticket prices doubled.

An unreliable eighteenth-century source, *Les Anecdotes dramatiques*,[5] reported that *Psyché* began with a kind of contest promoted by the king among Molière, Racine, and Quinault to see which of them could suggest the best use for a celebrated setting of hell left over from *Ercole amante*, performed in 1662. Supposedly Racine suggested the story of Orpheus and Eurydice, Quinault proposed the kidnaping of Persephone, but Molière carried the day with the tale of Psyche and Cupid. A more likely source for the idea is the publication in January 1669 of *Les Amours de Psyché et Cupidon* by Molière's friend La Fontaine. Quinault, later to write the libretti for most of Lully's operas, actually collaborated with Molière on the text of this "*tragi-comédie et ballet*," as did the doyen of French playwrights, Pierre Corneille, known for *Andromède* and other machine plays.[6]

The celebrated setting may have been used, but not with a view to economy. Court accounts are incomplete, but it can be said with some assurance that *Psyché* at the Tuileries cost Louis hundreds of thousands of *livres* at a time when a worker's income was about 300 *livres* a year. The *État officiel de la dépense* includes 44,983 *livres* in expenses for the stage and decors, but another account includes an additional 77,924 for decors and machines. Costumes cost 48,833 *livres*, wax, tallow and oil a mere 15,255.[7]

What did the king get for his money? He got eight settings of more or less standard baroque scenery: a sea port, a cypress alley, a rocky desert, a palace, a landscape with river, a garden, hell, and the heavens. He got perspective vistas, including one with three sets of wings. He got flying machines, both clouds and chariots. He got a wave machine, a river god, and a boat. He got Jupiter, Venus, Cupid, and lots and lots of *putti*. He got zephyrs, furies, and imps. He got Bacchus, Silenus, Egyptians and Maenads. He got Momus with a bunch of Pulchinellos, and Mars with a troupe of warriors. And he got Apollo, the Muses, and a chorus of 300 divinities standing on cloud machines.

The entertainment lasted for five hours. The ambassador from the court of Savoy wrote enthusiastically: "I have never seen anything here better executed or more magnificent and these are things that cannot be done elsewhere because of the quantity of dancing masters, seventy of whom danced together in the last entry. What is also marvelous is the quantity of musical instruments, of instrumentalists, and of singers, more than 300, all magnificently dressed. The room is superb . . . the stage spacious, marvelously well decorated; the machines and changes of scenery magnificent and well managed . . .; but for the last scene, it is the most astonishing thing ever seen, for in an instant appear more than 300 persons suspended or in the clouds, or in a glory, and making the most beautiful music in the world with violins, theorbos, lutes, harpsi-chords, oboes, flutes, trumpets, and cymbals." Magnificent though it was, the gentleman also thought it rather sad that the French should be reduced "in these sorts of things to the sentiments of the Italians," that is, to producing something visually very like an Italian opera.[8]

The French were thinking about that, too; the king had in 1669 granted a *Privilège* to one Pierre Perrin, permitting him to establish an Academy for the production of operas in the French language so that His Majesty's subjects might develop a taste for music and gradually become proficient in "one of the most noble of the liberal arts." [9]

The success of *Psyché* may have been one of the things that prompted Jean-Baptiste Lully to begin his assault on the opera privilege. Perrin's predicament was another. A minor poet and writer of lyrics both sacred and profane, Perrin joined with the composer Robert Cambert to create *Ariane*, which was rehearsed but never produced for the public, and *Pomone*, which was – after Perrin and Cambert were joined by two scoun-drels named Sourdéac and Champeron who took over "administration" of the project. *Pomone* was introduced at the transformed Jeu de paume de la Boutaille on the rue Mazarine on March 3, 1671, less than two months after *Psyché* had been seen at the Tuileries. Although Perrin's libretto was generally considered to be awful, the theatre itself, the machines and decors, the music and dance excited general admiration and the new academy was successful enough to arouse envy and appre-hension in its competitors. The Marais, equipped for spectacle, coun-tered with the *Amours du Soleil* and the *Amours de Bacchus et d'Ariane*, ornamented with music, machines, and ballets.

The Palais-Royal had no machines, but the actors realized that the time had come to rebuild the stage to accommodate them. On March 15 a deliberation was held, and it was decided to reconstruct and redec-orate the theatre. For over ten years the company had survived with its damaged ceiling replaced by a "great blue cloth suspended from ropes."[10] Now, so that they could compete successfully with the theatre palace on the rue Mazarine, the actors ordered a new ceiling, a third tier of boxes, new seat covers, and fresh paint. A month later, the theatre refurbished, the actors deliberated again and agreed to produce *Psyché*. The theatre cost the troupe 1,989 *livres* 10 *sous*, half of which was paid by the Italian company that shared the space. Preparations for *Psyché*, paid for by Molière and his companions, alone cost 4,359 *livres* 1 *sou*, a pittance compared to what the king had spent, but more than an average year's share for the actors.

Meanwhile Perrin, still holder of the opera privilege, was in very serious financial difficulty, with the unpaid musicians, with Sourdéac and Champeron, and with a creditor named La Barroire who had pursued him in and out of debtor's prison for years. This "uncivil war," as Robinet called it, began to make it obvious that Perrin was not the right person to establish the superiority of French musical theatre. Colbert took action and saw to it that Jean-Baptiste Lully was given the opportunity to buy the privilege from Perrin.

Molière may have wanted to buy that privilege himself. In 1688, after Lully's death, a *libelle* appeared reporting "what happened when Jean-Baptiste de Lully arrived in the Elysian Fields."[11] With Lully's life on trial before Persephone and the judges of the underworld, Molière steps forward and testifies that the great success of the first opera had both frightened him and awakened his cupidity. Fearing that his theatre would be deserted, he thought of making himself "the master" of this new institution. "As I needed a musician to execute this project, I cast my eyes on Lully and told him what I was thinking, persuaded as I was that the relationship we had had for years in collaborating on the pleasures of the King, and the marvelous success of the charming spectacle of *Psyché* . . . were infallible guarantees of our mutual understanding in the future. I told him what I had in mind, he applauded my plan, he promised me fidelity and even inviolable subordination. We made up our agreement, we settled on our responsibilities and our shares, and we took an oath to go together . . . to ask the King for the privilege to perform the operas. There was my mistake, Madame! . . . I slept tranquilly sure of the good faith of this treaty when Lully, more wide-awake than I, played his hand two days before the one upon which we had agreed; he went to the King to ask for the privilege for himself alone."[12] This Lully obtained, and it included rigorous conditions that forced Molière to battle for the right to perform some of his own work.

There is nothing inherently improbable in this anecdote. Perrin was a writer, not a composer, and had gone to Cambert for assistance. The refurbishment of the Palais-Royal lends further credence to the possibility that Molière did imagine himself the holder of the privilege. In any case, the final statement in the *libelle* is true, whatever the merit of what precedes it. Lully did want all the other theatres to be limited to two singers and to plays with no more than two songs. He clearly had in mind competition from the Palais-Royal where, for the first time in the summer of 1671, singers had agreed to appear openly on the public stage and in costume. Before *Psyché*, singers had performed only from boxes furnished with grills or lattices. Furthermore, the musical component of the Palais-Royal production was substantial: eight singers, sixteen dancers, fifteen instrumentalists, and assorted graces, amours, and zephyrs. The machines required three extra operators and the cast three extra dressers. Little wonder that Lully hoped to prevent this sort of thing from happening again.

When Lully's formal *Privilège* was issued in mid-March 1672 it merely forbade the production of plays entirely set to music without the written permission of Lully. Molière still had some credit with the king. However, the battle raged on and Lully was able to persuade His Majesty to impose, on August 12, a limit on the other theaters of six singers and twelve musicians. The troupe at the Palais-Royal continued to perform both *Psyché* and *Le Bourgeois gentilhomme*, presumably with Lully's scores, but whether ignoring or conforming to his limits cannot be conjectured.

In July Molière decided to reprise *Le Mariage forcé* and use it for the necessary interlude in *La Comtesse d'Escarbagnas* that he was introducing at the Palais-Royal. *Le Mariage forcé* (1664) was the first collaboration between Molière and Lully done for the king, but it had not succeeded with the Paris public. In 1668 it was reduced to a one-act afterpiece and played without music or ballet. When it was reprised in 1672 it included new interludes composed by Marc-Antoine Charpentier that require only three male singers, a counter-tenor, a tenor, and a bass.[13] The usual assumption is that there had been a break between Molière and Lully and that the latter was no longer welcome at the Palais-Royal. The other possibility is that he was simply too busy to bother with such a small matter. He was preparing his first production for the temporary theatre Vigarani was constructing for him in a tennis court on the rue Vaugirard. This pastiche was to include interludes and divertissements from *Le Bourgeois gentilhomme*, *Les Amants magnifiques*, *La Pastorale comique*, and *George Dandin*.

When *Psyché* was reprised for the Christmas season of 1672–3, La Grange notes that the troupe spent 1,100 *livres* putting the scenes and machines in order and finding new singers and dancers to replace those who had "gone elsewhere."[14] "Elsewhere" was undoubtedly the rue de Vaugirard. *Psyché* opened on November 11 to run in competition with Lully's *Fêtes de l'Amour.*

Molière again used the services of Charpentier to write the music for the interludes and divertissement of *Le Malade imaginaire*, his final play. Lully was once more otherwise engaged, writing and rehearsing his first grand opera. There was no royal entertainment in the winter of 1673, whether because the court was in mourning for the duc d'Anjou or because the Dutch war was far from won. Or perhaps the king thought that since he had provided for the professional production of musical spectacles, he need no longer produce them at court. Lully's privilege indicates how the king's mind – or Colbert's mind – was working: "to compensate for the great expense that [Lully] will undergo . . . for the stages, machines, decors, costumes, and other necessary things, We permit him to give to the public all the plays that he will compose, even those that have been performed before Us."[15] The Paris public was now expected to pay for the king's pleasures.

Molière also turned to the Paris public. The days of personal patronage were ending, and the king sought his glory on the battlefield rather than the dance floor. Molière would continue to receive his pension as one of a regiment of artists recruited to bear arms on behalf of the king's image. The troupe would continue to receive its subvention in return for regular appearances at court. But the taste of the town was now as important as the taste of the patron, and the town liked farce, especially farce seasoned with satire. They seem especially to have enjoyed the combination of satire and scatology that Molière contrived when he mounted an attack on the doctors.

Medical satire and parody was hardly new in Molière's work; he had started out by making French versions of Italian farces like *Le Médecin volant*. His *L'Amour médecin* (1665) with its satirical portraits of four court physicians, was a staple of the repertory at the Palais-Royal, as was his more farcical *Médecin malgré lui* (1666), featuring the masque Sganarelle. But in 1669 his attack sharpened in *Monsieur de Pourceaugnac*. This ingenuous provincial lawyer, come to Paris to wive him wealthily, or so he thinks, falls into the clutches of his fiancée's lover and a scheming Neapolitan who hand him over to a fidgety apothecary and two sadistic doctors. The apothecary provides the farce, but the doctors are almost too sinister to be amusing.

The usual assumption is that as Molière's health waned, his attitude toward doctors, who were unable to offer him a cure, became more aggressive. We know that Molière died of a tubercular hemorrhage; we know that he was ill in the winter of 1666; we know that he called attention to his cough in *L'Avare* in September 1668. We need not, however, assume that he was desperately ill for all the last seven years of his life. A description from *Monsieur de Pourceaugnac* of the title character, played by the author, is often cited as proof that Molière had deteriorated physically by the fall of 1669, three-and-one-half years before his death. The Premier Médecin calls his colleague's attention to the character's face, to "these wild, red eyes, this great beard, this constitution of the body, thin, pocked, black and hairy."[16] But this is a description not of the actor, who was normally clean shaven or had a small mustache, but of the character – a yokel from darkest Limoges.

To the Premier Médecin's description of Pourceaugnac is usually added Le Boulanger de Chalussay's description of Molière in *Élomire hypocondre ou les médecins vengez*, published in 1670, and cited as further evidence that Molière was in failing health. The cough is mentioned several times, but more to the point is the scene in which Élomire tries to get his wife to agree that he is ill. He enlists his servant, Lazarile, on his side. The scene is worth quoting in full, since usually a few lines from it are presented out of context.

ÉLOMIRE
Lazarile, isn't my face pale?

LAZARILE
Yes, Monsieur.

ÉLOMIRE
The mirror has told me the same thing;
And these arms that not long ago were like legs of mutton,
How do they look to you?

LAZARILE
Like nothing but bones,
And I think that soon, as dry as old skeletons,
They'll serve in place of castanets.

ISABELLE
Lazarile.

LAZARILE
Madame?

ISABELLE
You must learn that a servant
Who mocks a master gets to feel the broom; . . .
What! your master is thin and pale, you say?

LAZARILE
If he is not so to my eyes, let me be beaten.

ISABELLE
   How can he be so to your eyes, if he is not so to mine?
ÉLOMIRE
   But, my wife, perhaps you have weak eyesight?
   For, after all, Lazarile . . .
ISABELLE
   Lazarile and you,
   If you think you are thin and pale, are both mad;
   You sleep like a pig, you eat the same;
   What in the world could make you thin and pale?
ÉLOMIRE
   Fine, I will be whatever color you want;
   And even if you want, I will be fine and fat.
   But what matters to me is I think I am sick,
   And whoever thinks he is sick, is sick.
ISABELLE
   Whoever persuades himself
   That he is sick when he is healthy like you,
   Is on the high road to the madhouse. [17]

At which point Lazarile changes his tune and agrees with Isabelle. His master is not so much ill as crazy.

Élomire later tells the charlatans, Bary and l'Orvietan, that he had been ill, as Molière had been, but that he had regained his health, become "more fine and fat than ever," and was enjoying a long and successful run of his *Amour médecin* when, one evening, returning from the theatre, he was accosted by a hidious phantom. Since then, he has suffered like the damned and the result: "these sunken eyes, this pale face, this body . . . that is almost nothing more than a moving skeleton."[18] This time Isabelle is not present to disagree. Lazarile suggests that his master has been bewitched by the vengeful doctors, but the charletans are sure they can cure him, even if he is possessed by a devil.

Le Boulanger de la Chalussay titled his satire *Élomire hypochondre*. Pourceaugnac's doctors (mis)diagnose him as having hypochondria, or melancholy. Although *hypochondre* did not mean, in the seventeenth century, exactly what "hypochondriac" means in English today, nonetheless, to take Élomire and his symptoms literally, as many have done, is to ignore the sense of the two scenes which is that his symptoms are imaginary. Élomire is not a living skeleton. However, Élomire's insistence that whoever thinks he is ill, is ill leads us to entertain the possibility not that Molière was already wasted and in the last stages of consumption in 1670, but that he may have been a victim of melancholy, what we would now recognize as depression, often accompanied by physical symptoms as painful as they are ephemeral.

Would a skeletal man with sunken eyes, in the final wasting stages of consumption, have written for himself, in 1670, the enormous role of Monsieur Jourdain in *Le Bourgeois gentilhomme*, surely a fine and fat fellow, who fences and dances and cavorts in the Turkish ceremony, and rarely leaves the stage? Would he have written, in 1671, for himself the role of Zéphire in *Psyché* – who flies? Or the role of Scapin with lazzi and physical comedy throughout? Not until *Le Malade imaginaire* in 1673 does one of Molière's roles reveal him to have been physically incapacitated. Argan spends most of the play in a chair or in bed.

What the reasonable Molière has to say directly about health, disease, and medicine at the end of his life he puts in the mouth of Béralde, Argan's brother, in that same *Malade imaginaire*. Medicine, according to this man of moderation, is one of mankind's greatest follies, and belief in doctors one of mankind's greatest weaknesses. Doctors know what to call diseases in Latin and Greek, they know how to define them and classify them, but they know nothing at all about how to cure them. When someone is sick, the thing to do is – nothing at all. Rest. Be patient. Let nature heal. "Almost everyone dies of the remedies and not of the diseases."[19] An anecdote suggests that this attitude reflects both Molière's own point of view and the practice of his doctor and friend Jean Armand de Mauvillain. Supposedly both the actor and the doctor were at court for the king's dinner. His Majesty called to Molière: "Look, isn't that your doctor? What does he do for you?" "Sire," answered Molière, "we reason together; he orders remedies for me; I don't take them, and I get well."[20] Mauvillain was considered a heretic by his colleagues and was actually suspended from the Faculty of Medicine for four years for snatching off the Dean's hat during a heated discussion.[21]

Also, Molière's personal feelings about doctors and medicine should not be exaggerated. Clearly he had had some unpleasant experiences, but several of his good friends were doctors, including Bernier and Rohault. He thought well enough of Mauvillain to petition the king on behalf of the doctor's son. Jean Donneau de Visé, who knew Molière well, writes in the *Mercure galant* a few months after his death that "if [Molière] had had time to be ill [that is, had not died so quickly], he would not have died without a doctor. He was not himself convinced of all that he said against the doctors." Donneau de Visé suggests that Molière shared his own faith in natural and herbal remedies. "It is established fact that there are such remedies; the animals find them and cure themselves: so, since men know perfectly well the herbs that poison, why should they not know those that have the virtue of curing them."[22] But he reports that Molière, during an "oppression," did have recourse to bleeding.

Donneau de Visé also reminds us that Molière's intentions were not always vengeful. Doctors were funny for several reasons. They spoke a mysterious jargon, easy to mock; they wore pretentious costumes and rode around Paris on mules; they were not very effective and there were not many of them, only 110. Making fun of them was also one way to lessen the fear they must have inspired in most people.

The medical satire in *Le Malade imaginaire* is lighter than in *Monsieur de Pourceaugnac*, more tempered by farce. The play does, however, include a moment when Argan's terror of death is deeper than mockery, when he is rejected by his doctor who predicts certain death in four days. Like the moment in *L'École des femmes* when Arnolphe promises Agnès anything if only she will love him, like the moment in *Le Misanthrope* when Alceste begs Célimène to lie, this moment shatters the comic surface of the play and may well reflect the darker side of Molière.

In *Le Malade imaginaire*, as in *Les Fourberies de Scapin*, Molière flirts with his own death. In the latter play, performed in spring 1671, Scapin has himself carried on stage at the end with a vast bandage on his head, begging forgiveness of those he has offended. While walking along the street, we are told, he was struck by a stonemason's hammer, falling from the sky, which broke his skull and exposed his brain. This homage to Cyrano de Bergerac, who died from a similar accident, is a comic recognition that Molière has liberated the "scene of the galley" from Cyrano's *Le Pedant joué*. But while the audience is enjoying that self-referential joke, it also is not entirely sure that Scapin's final *fourberie* is going to work. The furious Géronte, earlier the victim of Scapin's sack, will forgive the dying rascal, but only if he really dies.

In *Le Malade imaginaire* Argan pretends not just to be dying but to be dead in order to test the feelings of his wife and daughter. Apparently lifeless in his chair – the very chair on display today in the upper lobby of the Comédie-Française – he watches their reactions. Béline, the wife, is hugely relieved to be rid of the burden of her disgusting husband, always coughing and spitting, always in a bad mood, wearing everyone out, and yelling at the servants day and night. This is certainly one possible version of Molière, himself, at home, ill and ill-tempered. Béline was not played by Armande (though the character may have represented her feelings or, more likely, how Molière was afraid she felt). Armande played rather the daughter Angélique, who is overcome at her father's death to the point of renouncing the world and her lover, Cléante. Her distress is expressed in formal language, difficult to play with emotional conviction, however the psychology of the moment, her regret that she opposed her father who died before she could mend the breach, is universally intelligible. How Armande played the scene after Molière's death is hard to imagine.

Molière knew what he had and knew he would probably die of it. The milk diet he apparently followed, combined with his retreat to Auteuil and his generally moderate style of life, seem to have kept him in reasonably good health for a number of years. He was not well, but he was not acutely ill. Tuberculosis does not necessarily run an uninterrupted course. Although it was then not curable in the modern medical sense, some who suffered from it were cured and some treatments were deemed to be effective. Molière was enough of a classicist to know that his doctor had ancient authority for the milk diet he recommended and that Galen in the second century advised above all rest in a cool and well-ventilated room. Molière may even have known that Cicero believed that a long sea voyage had cured him in the first century before Christ, but a long sea voyage was not easily available to a seventeenth-century Parisian, and Auteuil had to do.

Before World War II, when medicine was as much art as science, many writers on tuberculosis suggested a connection between the disease and certain mental states. As late as 1926, one authority writes: "There is no disease in which the mental and moral characteristics of the patient are so profoundly modified, and with which psycho-neuroses are so constantly associated, as chronic pulmonary tuberculosis."[23] These "psycho-neuroses," or "neurotic phenomena" were said to range from unwarranted feelings of vitality and well-being to nervous irritability to hypochondria to hysteria to melancholia. Because so many celebrated writers and artists of all kinds have had tuberculosis, a *post hoc propter hoc* fallacy developed and tuberculosis was actually considered a source of artistic genius. The consumptive artist became a kind of romantic icon in the nineteenth and early twentieth centuries.

Nothing about Molière suggests the frail Chopin, the delicate Brontës, or the prostrate, wasted Aubrey Beardsley. On the afternoon of his death, he played Argan, a role that makes minimal physical demands on an actor but requires vast vocal and emotional energy. On the other hand, he was late in his life apparently irritable, depressive, and even obsessive-compulsive. The stress of his illness may have created or fed

these psychological states, but they seem unlikely to have been caused –
as was once thought – by the "toxins" of his disease.

Our sense of Molière's personality in the last three years of his life
comes from Michel Baron, who returned to the Palais-Royal in 1670 and
whose memories were recorded by Grimarest thirty years later. This is
not inviolable evidence, but it is better evidence than most of what we
have. Baron was no longer a child; he was seventeen. He continued to
live with Molière in Paris and Auteuil, and he was with him when he
died. The anecdotes he tells are not necessarily complimentary; they
have never been thought well of by the hagiographers. But they are full
of life and personality.

Baron remembered, for instance, Molière's irritation with him when
he returned empty-handed from Jacques Rohault. He had been sent to
borrow a hat to be used as a costume piece for the Philosophy Master in
Le Bourgeois gentilhomme, a character modeled on Rohault, but he made
the mistake of telling Molière's old friend why the hat was wanted.[24]
Molière was not pleased.

Also through Baron we glimpse Molière the obsessively fussy house-
holder. No one could satisfy him. "A window opened or closed a moment
before or after the time that he had ordered it put Molière into a convulsion; he was petty on such occasions. If someone had moved a book,
it was enough to put him off his work for two weeks; there were few
domestics with whom he did not find fault; and the old servant La Forest
was caught as often as the others, although she should have been accustomed to that fatiguing orderliness Molière exacted from everyone. In
his view this was a virtue, to the point that those of his friends who were
the most orderly, and the best organized, were those he esteemed the
most."[25] If this is an accurate picture of Molière at home, Armande's
reluctance to join him in his wilderness is perfectly understandable.

But above all, Baron remembered Molière's generosity. Some of the
melancholy Alceste and the hypochondriacal Argan lived in him, but not
the miserly Harpagon. Baron had experienced Molière's bounty
himself; he remembered the new suit and the six gold pieces given to the
orphaned child he had been. And he remembered that Molière had
helped him borrow the money he needed to buy costumes from a retir-
ing actor.[26] But he had not fully absorbed the lesson. Shortly after he
returned to Paris, a provincial actor named Mignot who played as
Mondorge came to Auteuil to ask Molière for help on the grounds that
they had been together in Languedoc.[27] He and his family were in
"frightful misery." Baron saw him first, took him to the kitchen for a

meal, and then reported his plight to Molière who remembered him as a very decent man. Molière declared that Baron should decide on an appropriate sum to give the actor, and Baron suggested that four *pistoles* would be enough for Mignot to join a troupe. "All right," said Molière, "I am going to give him four *pistoles* from me, since you judge that to be appropriate: but here are twenty more that I am giving him from you: I want him to know that he is obliged to you for the service I render him. I also have a costume that I think I have no need for, that can be given to him as well."[28]

This costume, to help poor Mignot reestablish himself, had cost 2,500 *livres* according to Baron and was almost new. A costume that expensive could only be for tragedy, so we can infer that Molière by 1670 no longer played any tragic roles. Le Boulanger de Chalussay is still mocking him in 1670 for his failure as a tragic actor, but the last tragedy introduced by the troupe was Corneille's *Tite et Bérénice*, played in alternate weeks with *Le Bourgeois gentilhomme* from November 1670 to March 1671. No new tragedy was introduced, no old tragedy was performed in the final two seasons before Molière died.

Baron's return to the troupe was only one of the important changes made in 1670. Louis Béjart, a serviceable comic actor, retired with a pension after twenty-five years and, at the age of forty, bought a commission in the army. His share went to Baron, who was only seventeen. Then at the end of July the troupe added M. and Mlle Beauval, actors who had performed for a number of years in the provinces.

Adding actors in the middle of a season was most unusual and speaks of a sudden need. Jeanne Beauval was the one needed. She received a full share; her husband received a partial share and played minor roles. Some actors could leave the troupe without leaving a gap that had to be filled; this was true of Louis Béjart, for instance. Others were essential to the continuation of Molière's repertory and had to be replaced.

In this case, what seems likely is that the actress to be replaced was Madeleine Béjart. By the summer of 1670, Molière was at work on *Le Bourgeois gentilhomme* which includes a role that must have been originally intended for Madeleine, the maid Nicole, who is very much like Dorine in *Tartuffe*. Madeleine almost certainly had appeared as Aristione, a leading role in *Les Amants magnifiques*, the court entertainment seen at St-Germain in February 1670, but never transferred to the Palais-Royal. And she must have continued to play through the spring and summer, since the repertory includes a number of performances of *Tartuffe*, *L'Avare*, and *Pourceaugnac*, all plays that relied on her in important roles.

In early August, however, there was an interruption of one week before play resumed with *L'École des maris*.

Although she retained her share until her death in February 1672, Madeleine probably did not play after Jeanne Beauval joined the troupe. Her failing health may explain why the Beauvals were engaged in mid-season. It may also explain why the troupe ceased to perform tragedies. Madeleine was a tragic actress who also played Molière's sensible maid-servants and *suivantes*. Mlle Beauval was strictly a comic actress best known for her infectious laugh – which Molière capitalized on in *Scapin*.

There are a few glimpses of Madeleine after the troupe's return to Paris. She was clearly instrumental in arranging for that return and she even modified a text for performance by the troupe, although it was not successful, but then she seems to have lost authority. In the provinces she was a leader of a troupe known by her name, but in the worlds of *salon* society and court patronage there was no place for an actress and cer-tainly no place for a bourgeois woman whose reputation was stained by scandal. Molière had his court appointment and his literary friends; Madeleine had her family and the troupe.

She was a good business woman, but the troupe's business was done by the men, L'Espy, Hubert, or Du Croisy. She was a great tragedienne, but the troupe was not good at tragedy.[29] She was Molière's lover, his wife in all but name for nineteen years, but he married her young daughter and then withdrew to Auteuil. We would not be surprised if she became bitter, but there is no way to know.

She lived for many years on the rue St-Honoré in the Corps de Garde du Palais-Royal, in the rooms she rented in 1660 for herself and Molière. He left to begin his married life, she stayed. Sometimes her mother lived with her as did, before their marriages, her sisters Geneviève and Armande and occasionally their brother Louis. They were all living there when Molière's marriage contract was signed in Madeleine's apartment. Sometimes she lived on her own. Legal documents place her "vis-à-vis Palais-Royal," through July 1670. By the end of November 1671, however, she was living with her family on the rue St-Thomas-du-Louvre in the maison Brulon.[30] She made her will there on January 9, 1672, lying in bed in a room in Molière's apartment overlooking the court.[31]

Madeleine was unmarried, supposedly childless, and well-to-do. She owned property and she had accumulated a substantial amount of money. Not only did she keep the mill of La Souquette until her death, she also associated herself in a tannery business in Paris.[32] Unlike

Molière and Armande, she did not live luxuriously. Her possessions were laid out for inventory in two rooms, a chamber and antechamber on the fourth floor.[33] In the antechamber were found the usual kitchen furnishings, the whole lot worth 58 *livres* 17 *sous*. In the chamber there was a bed with its furnishings worth 35 *livres* – a nice contrast to Armande's bed, valued a year later at 2,000 *livres* – an ebony cabinet, and six chests full of clothing. None of the garments are specifically identified as costumes, but most of the pieces sound like a theatrical wardrobe, brightly colored and expensive. They include a jacket in gold brocade with false lace, a peasant bodice in silver cloth with its green satin skirt, trimmed with lace, a cherry taffeta skirt with a green satin doublet, a skirt in silver cloth with its apron of white satin and an apron in gold moiré. Decorative aprons were the sign on-stage of a *suivante* or lady's maid.

Some of the clothing was probably old; a dress of flesh-colored taffeta with two pairs of sleeves was valued only at 4 *livres*. Her jewelry was modest. The most expensive items in the inventory were a set of tapestries valued at 350 *livres* and silver valued at 948 *livres*. Cash on hand, however, totaled 17,809 *livres*. There were no debts and Madeleine's affairs were in order. Unlike Molière's father, who left a jumble of papers permitting the reconstruction of his professional life, Madeleine left only papers related to unfinished business.

Not all of the money owing her had been collected. A surprising discovery in the inventory of her papers are two documents indicating that she had, on more than one occasion, loaned money to Esprit de Rémond, comte de Modène, her former lover. One contract was dated January 7, 1662 and signed "Roquemartene," who had received "for and in the name of Mons. de Modène" 1,000 *livres* "to be used in the affairs of the said sieur de Modène." This was not a "constitution of interest," but a simple loan, meant to be repaid within two months. Apparently it was not. The other loan, for 3,000 *livres* and channeled through a third party, was made in August 1671 for the purpose of saving Modène from debtor's prison, or at the least from the embarrassment of being taken to court. An old creditor started legal action and Madeleine, acting through a family friend Romain Toubel, paid off the debt.[34] After her death Molière and Armande began legal action of their own to reclaim this and other moneys owed her.

The comte de Modène returned to Paris in 1664; for eighteen years he had been in the provinces or abroad. After a brief sojourn at the Hôtel de Guise, he moved in with his old friends Jean-Baptiste L'Hermite and Marie Courtin and saw to the publication of his three volumes on the duc de Guise's adventure in Naples. On August 4, 1665, he served as godfather to Esprit-Madeleine, the second child of Armande and Molière; Madeleine was the godmother.

All the mysteries of Madeleine's life are linked to Modène. What happened to their daughter Françoise? Was Modène Armande's father? Why did Madeleine buy the mill of La Souquette? Why was Modène the other godparent of Esprit-Madeleine Molière? Modène's biographer is forced to conclude that Modène was Armande's father and that, as so often happened, the grandparents were called on to be godparents as well. Nonetheless this nineteenth-century moralist is shocked that Molière would agree to the desecration of the sacrament of baptism. "How could Molière, whose first child had been held over the font in the name of the king and Henrietta of England, consent to have for godfather of his daughter the former lover of Madeleine and to revive in the eyes of all and especially in the eyes of his wife the distant past that was better forgotten? Why would he expose himself, especially in the middle of a conjugal crisis, why would he give Armande this proof of his lack of moral fiber?"[35] He is unable to entertain the possibility that Molière, a man whose morality was *not* of the nineteenth century, might have been wryly amused by the sight, at the font, of Madeleine and her two former lovers promising to make sure that the child followed Christ in all things.

The following year Modène married Madeleine's cousin, Madeleine L'Hermite, the daughter of Marie Courtin, another former mistress. He was fifty-eight, older than his new mother-in-law; his bride was thirty. She also had been born out of wedlock, although her parents married within a month of her birth. Marie Hervé, the mother of the Béjarts, was her godmother, but in spite of that and of the bridegroom's presence at the christening of Esprit-Madeleine, neither Molière nor the Béjarts figure as witnesses to the contract or the act of marriage. If Madeleine Béjart had had ambitions to rekindle her relationship with Modène, which seems doubtful, her hopes were at an end.

In early January 1670 the Béjarts lost their mother. Marie Hervé died, not in Madeleine's apartment opposite the Palais-Royal, nor in Geneviève's on the rue St-Thomas-du-Louvre, but on the rue Fromanteau in an apartment she was sharing with her son Louis. She had been the most supportive of mothers, godmother to her oldest daughter's illegitimate child, guarantor of leases and loans for the Illustre Théâtre, and faithful follower through all the years of exile. The troupe marked her death with an interruption of two weeks. Although she died in the parish of St-Germain-l'Auxerrois, she was buried at St-Paul in the Marais, the family parish, where her daughter Madeleine had inscribed: "Here lies the body of Marie Hervé, widow of the honorable Joseph Bejard, deceased the 9th of January 1670 at the age of 73."[36] Marie, who had been born August 1, 1593, was actually over seventy-six. Either her children did not know her real age, or Madeleine was still leaving evidence that her mother could reasonably have given birth as late as 1642.

Molière wrote almost nothing about mothers and daughters. Fathers and daughters, yes. Fathers and sons, yes. But very few mothers occur in his plays, and those that do are usually step-mothers, whether wicked like Béline or agreeable like Elmire. In his last years, however, he did write two mother-daughter relationships; in at least one instance the mother was played by Madeleine and the daughter by Armande.

Les Amants magnifiques may well be the least known of Molière's plays; certainly it is one of the least produced. It was written for the *Divertissement Royal* of February 1670, performed five times at St-Germain, dismantled and forgotten until it was briefly reprised in 1688. Armande played the beautiful young princess Ériphile and Madeleine her mother Aristione. Two princes are rivals for Ériphile and her mother tries to persuade her to make a choice between them, but the girl is in love with Sostrate, a mere general of the army and not royal.

Aristione knows her daughter. She tells Iphicrate, one of the rival princes: ". . . you have heard it said that the mothers must be cajoled to obtain the daughters; but here, unfortunately, all that is useless, and I have promised to leave the choice entirely to the inclination of my daughter."[37] The prince answers with an interesting compliment, if we interpret it as coming from Molière to Madeleine. "I seek the princess Ériphile only because she is of your blood; I find her charming because of all she has from you, and it is you that I adore in her."[38] The answer is also interesting. Aristione will allow herself to be praised for her sincerity, for her accomplishments, for her merit and virtue, but not for her charm or her beauty, not with a daughter like hers. The prince retorts with that terrible cliché: "But if you liked, the princess could pass as your sister."

The answer of Aristione/Madeleine: "Good heavens! Prince, I don't believe in all that nonsense to which most women subscribe; I want to be a mother, because I am one, and to want not to be one would be in vain. This title does not shock me, since, by my consent, I exposed myself to receive it. There is a weakness of our sex from which, thank heavens,

I am exempt; and I do not occupy myself, as so many foolish women do, with disputes about age."[39]

It is hard to imagine Madeleine speaking these lines without having consented to their implications. Either they represent her point of view, in which case they are a public admission that she is Armande's mother, or they are to be taken ironically and represent an attack by Molière on her policy of pretending to be Armande's sister. As for the rest of the speech, again either he is representing her true feelings about aging, or attacking her for still trying to compete with her daughter as an actress and a woman. If the speech is meant to be taken ironically, it shows Molière to be crueler than we would like to think of him as being. If the speech is taken as a representation of what Madeleine felt about the situation, we can derive from it some sense of the kind of relationship the two old lovers and colleagues had come to after nearly thirty years.

Madeleine died slowly, of what there is no way to know. She was bedridden by January 9, 1672; on February 14 she had difficulty signing a codicil to her will because she was weak, but also because her sight was affected – that suggests the possibility of diabetes. She remained, however, mentally acute. Sometime before her death she had officially recanted her profession in writing, following the formula "I, the undersigned, promise to renounce and do renounce from this time forth the profession of actress."[40] The beautiful redhead, *femme galante*, and tragedy queen had begun to worry about her immortal soul.

Her will suggests she was trying to make up for years of indiscretion and neglect of religion. She commends her soul to God, in the name of the Holy Trinity, and begs for the infinite mercy of the redeemer. She asks to be buried at St-Paul, with her family, and directs her executor to establish two requiem masses a week in perpetuity and to organize a fund to give in perpetuity alms to five poor persons in honor of the five wounds of Christ. These poor persons are to be selected by her sisters and by the eldest of the children of Mlle Molière, that is, by Esprit-Madeleine. After establishing trust funds paying 400 *livres* a year for Louis and Geneviève and Armande, Madeleine leaves the rest in trust to Armande to be used for more pious works.[41]

A month later, truly on the point of death, Madeleine changed the latter provision and left the residue of her estate in trust to Armande without conditions, to use as she pleased.[42] The painter Pierre Mignard was named to take charge of Madeleine's money and invest it for Armande and the others. As each of the recipients of 400 *livres* died, his or her income was to revert to the residual trust that was, after

Armande's death, to be paid to Esprit-Madeleine. By these convoluted means, Madeleine was able to leave her estate to her goddaughter/granddaughter.

Her sister Geneviève also had a child – who would inherit only if Esprit-Madeleine did not live to do so. Geneviève, who had been a small-part actress since the formation of the Illustre Théâtre, was six years younger than Madeleine. She had remained single, but on June 30, 1664, at the age of forty, she signed a marriage contract with Jean de Courbes, a painter. The whole family turned out for the occasion, which took place, oddly enough, in the dwelling of the L'Hermites. The wedding never happened. A few months later, in November of 1664, Geneviève signed another marriage contract, this time with Léonard de Loménie, a bourgeois from Limoges who called himself sieur de La Villaubrun. The ceremony was performed on November 27. The couple signed a lease for the fifth floor of the maison Brulon on the rue St-Thomas-du-Louvre on January 19, 1666, the same day that Molière and Armande rented the third and fourth floors in the same house. Geneviève and her husband were parents of one son, Jean-Baptiste Loménie, whose godfather is obvious. Léonard died in the spring of 1672, shortly after Madeleine Béjart, and Geneviève remarried quickly, in September, this time to Jean-Baptiste Aubry, son of the Léonard Aubry who had saved the Illustre Théâtre from the left bank mud and Jean-Baptiste Poquelin from debtors' prison. He was thirty-six, she was forty-eight. In all three marriage contracts, Geneviève offers only her own money and property; in the contract with Loménie, for instance, she offers 500 *livres* cash and 3,500 *livres* worth of costumes, linens, and furniture.[43] She was never given the kind of dowry Armande had, 10,000 *livres* from the family, presumably from Madeleine.

Some biographers of Molière have suggested that Esprit-Madeleine was raised by her father in Auteuil to save her from being "contaminated" by her mother. And perhaps, as a very young child, she was sent out of Paris to be nursed. Most children were, and it seems unlikely that Armande, who missed few performances, would have had time to nurse an infant or care for a toddler. But there is evidence that the girl may have been in Paris, one of the troupe's children, by the time she was four. We know that Molière cast one of the Beauval children, Louise, in *Le Malade imaginaire* and used the child's own name, Louison, for the character. Three children are needed in *Monsieur de Pourceaugnac*; two under seven and one of four; they are called Françon, Jennet, and Madelaine. Among the troupe's children were François Gassot, the son of Du Croisy, then

11. *Esprit-Madeleine Molière*, from a painting by Mignard.

seven, Thérèse-Jeanne Lenoir, the daughter of La Thorillière, who was six, and Esprit-Madeleine Molière, who was four. Another item that suggests that Esprit-Madeleine was at home at the Palais-Royal is the presence, among her mother's costumes for *Psyché*, of "a little child's costume for the same play, with a pink skirt and a green taffeta bodice, decorated with false lace."[44] She was five, nearly six, when the play opened at the Palais-Royal, possibly playing one of the little graces attending on the child Cupid played by eleven-year-old Pierre Lenoir.[45]

Esprit-Madeleine and her mother were not on good terms in later years. As a young woman she lived, apparently by choice, as a pensioner in a convent on the rue St-Honoré, and she sued her mother for an accounting of the estates of her father and Madeleine.[46] Perhaps this unhappy outcome was the result of Armande's second marriage and new baby son. Perhaps the two had never really been close. In *Psyché* Zéphire/Molière says to Cupid of his mother, the goddess Venus: "Your mother is like all beauties, who do not love grown children."[47]

Sometime in the early 1670s Molière and Armande began to live once again as a couple. According to Grimarest, they were "reconciled" thanks to certain friends.[48] The outcome of this "reconciliation" was their third child, Pierre, born on September 15, 1672. It was also at this time, says Grimarest, that – to render more perfect their union – Molière quit his milk diet, began to eat meat, and destroyed the perilous balance of his health.

In the fall of 1672 Molière moved. After eleven years on the rue St-Thomas-du-Louvre, he rented an apartment on the rue de Richelieu, not as convenient, but more elegant and away from the troupe and the family. The rue de Richelieu ran (and runs) along the western edge of the gardens of the Palais-Royal. Molière's new dwelling was north of the present site of the Comédie-Française, diagonally across the garden from his theatre located on the southeastern edge of the property.[49] His apartment had access to the garden, so the walk across it, past the Rond-d'Eau, the great basin, was not far. Or he could, if he was not feeling well, take his sedan chair.[50]

The apartment included basements – renter's choice of two large or two small – a kitchen, a stable – the first time Molière had somewhere to keep a horse and carriage – two full floors, four *entresols* or mezzanines, and an attic. The rent was 1,300 *livres* a year, an increase of 750 *livres* over what he had been paying on the rue St-Thomas-du-Louvre.[51]

The new lease was for six years; Molière was not expecting to die. He signed in Auteuil, Armande signed in Paris. She was pregnant with their third child, Pierre-Jean-Baptiste-Armand, who was born on September 15 and died less than a month later, on October 11, in the grand new apartment.

Less than six months after Molière occupied it, the apartment and its furnishings were recorded in detail in the inventory made after his death. It was, as the stage direction in *Élomire hypocondre* said it should be, *fort parée*, very elaborately furnished. The "apartment of the said lady widow" contained a bed, rather plain, a chaise longue, tables, many chairs, some with feather cushions, an armoire, a strong box, two harpsichords (one large, one small), two clocks, a great mirror, several sets of tapestries, and seven paintings. In another room, presumably the *salon*, were a great many books, more than eighty, including the Latin classics, the works of La Mothe Le Vayer and Corneille, and forty volumes of French, Italian, and Spanish plays. Another 120 volumes of plays, history, poetry and philosophy were found elsewhere. In the salon was also the couch with eagles' feet and domes, with gilded sculptures in relief, hung with gold and green taffeta, decorated with every sort of loop and fringe and tassel. It was by far the most expensive thing Molière owned. Also in the room: Turkish carpets, both for tables and floors, gilded chairs with striped taffeta cushions, three sets of tapestries, a small mirror, fire screens, window curtains, and alcove curtains, hung to provide a warm area around the fireplace in winter. In another room were two simpler beds and several paintings: a Holy Family, two landscapes, and a scene from *L'École des maris*.

The elaborate bed brings up again that puzzling question about Molière: was he, as he is painted in both *Élomire hypocondre* and Grimarest's biography, a man who loved show, who lived like a nobleman and dressed like one, too. He did, indeed, have in Paris those mirrors and paintings and tapestries mentioned by Le Boulanger de Chalussay, but not at Auteuil. Nor does his inventory confirm that he had himself dressed like a "Grand Seigneur," by a valet, and would not even arrange the folds of his own cravat.[52] He owned rather a remarkable amount of personal linen, but his private wardrobe was not elaborate at all. At Auteuil he slept in a bed valued at 150 *livres*. He had several tables, six armchairs, another thirty-three books, curtains to keep off drafts, a few dishes and utensils; these were not the rooms of a bourgeois living nobly. The grand *salon* on the rue de Richelieu with the great matrimonial bed was very likely for show, for Armande. Molière, when he was in Paris, may have slept in one of the two beds in the "other chamber," under his picture of *L'École des maris*.

That painting has not survived, but many other paintings of Molière have. A few show him in character, but most do not. What these latter have in common, whether by one of the Mignards, by Coypel, or by Lefèbvre, is that they depict him in a dressing gown. The last one he wore was listed in the inventory, made of striped brocade, lined with blue taffeta, and valued at 25 *livres*. This must be the image Molière himself wanted to survive, this rather plain man, usually bewigged, and holding a book or a notebook and pen. There is little of the actor about him.

Grimarest would have us believe that Molière, who had that "invincible inclination" for the stage, grew to despise his own profession. The anecdote he relates probably does not come from Baron, who was himself an actor, but perhaps from Louis Racine, who despised the theatre, or from someone whose mission was to redeem Molière.[53] According to this unidentified source, Molière's advice was sought by a young man who passionately wanted to go on the stage. He auditioned with several scenes, both tragic and comic, and Molière was surprised by his talent. It seems the young man had, perhaps like Molière himself, acted at school. His father, he admitted, was a rather well-to-do lawyer.

"Well," finally responded Molière, "I advise you to adopt his profession; ours does not suit you. It is the final resource of those who can do no better, or of libertines, who want to avoid work. Moreover, it will strike a dagger in the hearts of your parents, mounting the stage; you know the reasons for that, I have always reproached myself for giving this grief to my family. And I swear to you that if I were to start over, I would never choose this profession . . . You think that it has its charms; you are wrong. It is true that we are apparently sought out by Great Lords, but they subject us to their whims; it is the saddest of situations, to be the slave of their fantasies. The rest of the world regards us as lost souls and despises us. Thus, sir, give up a plan so contrary to your honor and your peace of mind."

The rest of the diatribe sounds more like an actor speaking, if not necessarily like Molière. "Picture the troubles we have. Sick or not, we have to take our marching orders and give pleasure even when we are overcome with grief; we must endure the vulgarity of most of the people with whom we have to live, and charm the public who assume the money they pay us gives them the right to abuse us."[54]

Grimarest includes other anecdotes suggesting that Molière had, in his heart at least, recanted the low business of acting. It was important to him, as to all those biographers of Molière who were engaged in the creation of a great man, to show that their subject had distanced himself

from performance and from the fellowship of the troupe. Yet why would
Molière condemn a profession that had brought him fame, friends, and
fortune? He had worked hard, far harder than the Boileaus, the La
Fontaines, and the Racines, but in recompense he was part of a much
wider world than they. His comic vision embraced everyone: nobles and
peasants, bourgeois and provincials, misanthropes, misers, and hypocrites, boors, bores, and snobs. His wisdom was in his recognition of the
complexity of life, its ironies and its ambiguities, expressed not in Latin
tomes but animated on the stage. He wrote wonderful roles because he
respected the power of the actor to bring a character to full and nuanced
life. No doubt there were times when he was overwhelmed by the mag-
nitude of his responsibilities to the troupe, no doubt he was irritated by
the claims and counterclaims of his colleagues, the intrigues that are
natural to any group of humans working intensely together. Nonetheless, his overriding assumption must have been, as he says in the
preface of *L'Amour médecin*, that plays are made to be acted. He was,
finally, whatever Grimarest would have us think, whatever the portraits
show, not a man of letters but a man of the stage. "He was all actor, from
his feet to his head; it seemed that he had many voices, everyone spoke
in him, and, with a step, a smile, a wink of the eye and a shake of the
head, he conveyed more meaning than the greatest speaker could have
done in an hour."[55] So said Jean Donneau de Visé in the *Mercure galant*
on June 14, four months after Molière's death.

The romantic myth has had it that Molière died on the stage; in fact,
he very nearly did. He performed *Le Malade imaginaire* for the fourth time,
with his cough very troublesome. After the play he was taken home and
he began to hemorrhage. A little later he was dead. The date was
February 17, 1673, exactly a year after the death of Madeleine.

Two contemporary accounts exist of Molière's death, both by
members of the company. The best known is La Grange's entry in his
Registre; the other is Baron's memory of events as recorded by Grimarest.
La Grange writes: "This same day, after the play, about 10 o'clock in the
evening, Monsieur de Molière died in his house, rue de Richelieu,
having played the role of the Imaginary Invalid, very ill of a cold and
fluxion of the chest that caused him to cough heavily, so that with the
great effort he made to spit he broke a vein in his body and lived no more
than a half hour or three quarters after the vein broke."[56]

Baron's recital is more detailed. He remembers that Molière had said
to Armande, earlier in the day, "As long as my life was an equal mixture
of pain and pleasure, I thought I was happy; but today since I am over-

whelmed with troubles without any moments of satisfaction or sweetness, I see that I should give up the game. I can no longer stand these
pains and griefs, that give me not a moment of relief. A man must suffer
before he dies. However, I feel that I am done for."[57] Armande and
Baron knew Molière was ill, of course, but did not expect anything so
despairing. They begged him to rest, to stay away from the theatre, but
he reminded them of all the people – porters, ushers, dressers, musicians
– relying on him for their daily wages. He did insist that the play should
start on time, exactly at 4:00. "Molière performed with great difficulty;
and half the Spectators noticed that in pronouncing 'Juro' in the ceremony he was seized by a convulsion. Realizing that the audience had
noticed it, he made an effort and hid what had happened with a forced
laugh."[58]

Once off-stage, in Baron's dressing room, he confessed to being
deathly cold. Baron touched his hands, that were like ice, put them in a
muff to get warm, and sent for the bearers of his sedan chair to take him
home to the rue de Richelieu. Baron stayed with him, and when they
reached his bedroom, Baron wanted to get him some of the warm soup
that Armande always had ready, but Molière refused it. "My wife's
broths are too strong for me, you know all the ingredients she puts in
them; give me instead a little piece of parmesan cheese." The servant
La Forest brought it and he ate it with a little bread and went to bed.
Then he sent to ask his wife for a pillow stuffed with an herb that she had
promised him to help him sleep. "A minute later he began to cough
extremely hard, and after having spat he asked for a light." The basin
was bloody. Baron was extremely frightened; Molière reassured him, but
asked Baron to find Armande. The hemorrhage grew worse, and by the
time Baron returned with Armande, Molière was dead at the age of 51.[59]

The two accounts support each other, with the small details of Baron's
story adding specificity and color. However, Grimarest adds that, by
some happy chance, two nuns were staying in the house and, somehow,
came upon Molière in his last agony. These convenient nuns, to whom
he was able to show "all the sentiments of a good Christian," were supporting evidence in the struggle to bury Molière, who – unlike
Madeleine – had died without recanting his profession.

Molière was baptized a Catholic, was married in a Catholic church,
and was the godfather of many children, the last of whom he held at the
font at St-Sauveur six days before he died. He was a practicing Christian,
although there is no evidence that he was especially pious. There were
religious paintings in his apartment, a Virgin, a Saint Catherine, and a

Holy Family, but among his several hundred books the only one of a devotional nature was the Bible. No doubt if he had realized he was about to die he would have done what other actors did and recanted, not necessarily because he was truly repentant for a misspent life, but to save his family the kind of trouble they encountered.

If Molière had stayed on the rue St-Thomas-du-Louvre, in the parish where he had been married, the Church would probably not have refused him burial in sacred ground. It was the *curé* of St-Eustache who made the decision. The Hôtel de Bourgogne was around the corner from St-Eustache, and the priests of that parish were particularly aware of actors and things theatrical. It may even be that they had a special awareness of the author of *Tartuffe* and *Don Juan*.

When Armande petitioned the archbishop of Paris for the right to bury her husband, she added to the story of the night of his death. "On Friday last . . . toward nine o'clock in the evening, the late sieur Molière, being ill of the malady of which he would die an hour later, wanted to repent his faults and die a good Christian; . . . to that effect he asked for a priest to receive the sacraments and sent several times his valet and maidservant to St-Eustache, his parish, who addressed themselves to Messieurs Lenfant and Lechat, two priests resident in the said parish, who refused several times to come."[60] Geneviève Béjart's husband, Jean Aubry, then went to St-Eustache himself and found another priest named Paysant, who did come, but arrived too late. Everything possible had been done to get a priest for the dying man.

Armande further argued that those two serendipitous nuns and a gentleman named Couton, in whose arms Molière breathed his last, could testify that he died a good Christian and that his habitual confessor, M. Bernard, had administered the Eucharist to him the previous Easter. For all these reasons, she asks the special grace of the archbishop.

She also went to Versailles to see the king, who told her it was all up to the archbishop. His Majesty, however, made sure the archbishop knew that the king's wish was to avoid scandal.[61] The archbishop, on February 21, ordered the *curé* of St-Eustache to bury Molière in the parish cemetery, but at night, without pomp, and with only two priests in attendance. Nor was there to be any service for him, neither in St-Eustache nor elsewhere within the jurisdiction of the archbishop.

Descriptions of Molière's funeral convoy are inconsistent. Grimarest writes of an incredible crowd of people gathered before his door on the rue de Richelieu, so many people that Armande, unsure of their intentions, was frightened and flung money out of the window to them, begging them to pray for her husband. The funeral procession then moved tranquilly up the street to the light of a hundred torches.[62] Brossette, presumably informed by Boileau, agrees with Grimarest about the convoy; all of Molière's friends went to the cemetery with torches in their hands.[63] A less reliable source speaks of three ecclesiastics, four priests to bear the wooden coffin, a tapestry pall, six children carrying six tapers in six silver candlesticks, lackeys with torches of white wax, the distribution of 1,200 *livres* to the poor.[64] Somehow that rather sounds like what the archbishop did not want. The quiet walk with friends carrying torches rather sounds like what Molière himself might have preferred.

Robinet, the gazetteer who had christened Molière "the god of laughter," broke the news of Molière's death to Paris on February 18. Busy praising "our French Terence" for his incomparable new play, Robinet breaks off his couplets at the sight of someone coming to give him bad news. "Molière . . ." "Well, Molière?" ". . . has completed his destiny. Yesterday, after the play, he suddenly lost his life." Robinet is unable to continue writing: "I have no more heart to rhyme," he says. "The pen falls from my fingers."[65]

Although he had been ill for years, neither Molière himself nor his family nor his colleagues and friends expected him to die when he did. The irony of the "imaginary" invalid, who pretends to be dead on stage, actually dying after four performances struck the fancy of literary Paris, which responded with an outpouring of epigrams and epitaphs.[66] These both denounce and celebrate Molière, but leave no doubt about his importance. Among the nearly ninety epitaphs, in French and Latin, that have survived, the most often recurring theme is that of the *mort imaginaire,* the imaginary corpse. The denunciatory verses refer to atheism and libertinism, of course, and assure the reader that this *singe,* this ape, got what he deserved from the doctors and from the Church. Others stress his irregular life, his commerce with "the mother and the daughter," his special skill at playing the cuckold on stage and in life. The laudatory verses tend to praise him first as an actor, second as a moralist eager to reform manners in "this corrupt century."

Several of Molière's friends wrote for him. La Fontaine's epitaph was solicited by Donneau de Visé for the *Mercure galant.* The *bonhomme* returned to the theme he had expressed in 1661 when he concluded that Molière would bring to the French theatre the good taste and the style of Terence. Now he writes:

Under this tomb lie Plautus and Terence,
And yet only Molière lies there.
His spirit brought them back to life,
Delighting France with their great art.
They are gone! And I have little hope
To see them again, in spite of all our efforts.
For a long time to come, so it appears,
Terence and Plautus and Molière are dead.[67]

This graceful if rather impersonal compliment suggests that La Fontaine and Molière were no longer close. Chapelle, who was still a dear friend, wrote more passionately, even angrily:

Since in Paris one denies
Holy Ground after Death
To those who pass their lives
Acting on the stage,
Why should one not throw
The Impostors into the sewer?
Their situation is the same.[68]

Dassoucy, the wandering musician, composer, libertine, and lover, who had made common cause with the actors so many years before in Provence, was annoyed with Molière. He had complained bitterly – when Molière selected Charpentier instead of himself to replace Lully – that although he loved and revered Molière the great actor did not like him very much at all.[69] Nonetheless, he wrote the simplest and most moving of the epitaphs:

Passerby, if . . . this famous poet
Was dear to you
Give at least a sigh or two
For his enlightened spirit,
And say, approaching his grave,
Farewell laughter . . .[70]

CHAPTER TWELVE

Envoi

On May 3, 1673, two and a half months after Molière's death, the second wife of Jean-Baptiste L'Hermite wrote a letter to her husband's son-in-law, the comte de Modène. "I met no one at Mlle Molière's. I assure you the poor Molière is no longer spoken of as if he had never been and his theatre, that had such a great reputation, so little time ago, is entirely abolished. . . . Thus the expectations of the widow are thwarted."[1] The writer, who signed herself "L'Hermite," was clearly not a well-wisher, but fortunately she was wrong. The troupe did survive and owed its survival, in some measure, to Armande.

Play was resumed on February 24, a week after Molière's death, and continued to the end of the season. At that point four actors left the troupe for the Hôtel de Bourgogne and the king awarded the theatre at the Palais-Royal, now nicely fitted out for spectacle, to Lully for his opera. However, the remaining members of what had been the *comédiens du roi* managed to survive, to buy a new theatre, and eventually to thrive.[2] The money to buy the theatre came from Molière himself, via Armande. He had loaned 11,000 livres to Lully in December 1670. When Lully repaid it, as he was obliged to do upon Molière's death, Armande loaned it again, through a third party, to the troupe to make the down payment on the theatre on the rue Mazarine. Merged with the "better actors" of the Théâtre du Marais, Mlle Molière, Mlle de Brie, La Grange, Du Croisy, Hubert, and the others persevered until 1680, when a final merger with the Hôtel de Bourgogne created the Comédie-Française, the house of Molière.

Molière's legacy encompassed more than his plays. He left behind an acting style developed with his company over many years. Based at least in part on their observations of the Italian actors who shared their theatres, this style was far more realistic, more modern, than the orotund declamation and practiced posturing of the tragedians at the Hôtel de Bourgogne. Because the Italians improvised their dialogue and action, at least while they were developing a new play, they acted with what we now call "concentration," that is, they were alert to each other and to whatever was happening on the stage. They played together in the scene and in the moment. The classical tragic style, that Molière burlesqued in the *Impromptu de Versailles*, was rather more like that of opera as it was performed until relatively recently. Actors, for the most part, delivered arias while other actors waited their turns.

An anonymous writer has left us a detailed account of two actors formed by Molière performing in a play by Molière a few years after his death. On stage were Mlle Molière and the sieur de La Grange in the scene from *Le Malade imaginaire* where Angélique and Cléante, disguised as a music master, improvise their pastoral operetta, making love under the nose of the disgruntled father. The appreciative spectator writes:

Mlle Molière and La Grange . . . have not the world's finest voices. I don't believe they even have a particularly subtle understanding of music, and although they sing acceptably it is not the quality of their voices that wins them such general acclaim. But they know how to touch the spectators' hearts, it is passion that they protray, and their depiction of it is true to life, their technique so skillfully concealed in a natural representation that we can scarcely distinguish reality from mere appearance.

They are already quite striking just to look at. They convey emotion by their very bearing, and their acting style is so natural that everyone appreciates them even in scenes were they have nothing to say. . . . They are never useless on the stage. . . . They never look around them. . . . They know the house is full, but they speak and they act as if they can see no one other than those involved in their part and their action. They are appropriate and magnificent, without appearing affected in any way.[3]

At the end of May 1677, Mlle Molière became Mlle Guérin; she married Isaac-François Guérin, one of the actors who had come from the Marais. They became parents of a single son, Nicolas, born shortly after the marriage. Matters did not go well between Armande, her new family, and her daughter, Esprit-Madeleine Poquelin. In 1691, shortly after she reached the age of twenty-five, then the age of majority, Esprit-Madeleine renounced the community of property between herself and her mother and asked for an accounting of her father's estate and of Madeleine Béjart's. One François Pillon was appointed to look into the matter. After nearly two years he reported his findings, which the warring parties agreed to accept. Esprit-Madeleine was to receive 800 *livres* in cash, an income of 275 *livres* arising from the 11,000 *livres* paid to Molière's estate by Lully, and 500 *livres* in rental income from her grandfather's house in the market, with half of the latter to be paid to her mother during Armande's lifetime.[4]

Armande retired from the Comédie-Française in October 1694 and died on November 30, 1700. Two years later her husband and children agreed to settle her estate, which was far more substantial than the previous settlement with her daughter might lead one to expect. On July 29, 1705, Esprit-Madeleine Poquelin Molière, a few days before her fortieth birthday, signed a contract of marriage with Claude de Rachel de Montalant, a fifty-nine-year-old widower. He brought to the marriage almost nothing, an income of 450 *livres* a year, but he was a gentleman. The bride brought an estate valued at 65,775 *livres* and a yearly income of 3,431 *livres*. Not surprisingly, she insisted that there would be no community of property, and a careful inventory of her possessions was made to "avoid confusion."

Her apartment was rather luxurious. There was a kitchen, a dining room, a salon, a bedroom, a little "cabinet" which served as a dressing room and library, and a storeroom. In the salon she had a set of Flemish tapestries, "very fine," a sofa and chairs upholstered in blue velvet trimmed with tapestry with curtains of taffeta and damask. In the bedroom was her grand bed *à la duchesse*, with its coverlet of white satin lined with pink taffeta. There were family portraits in the dining room and the hall, landscapes and more family portraits in the bedroom, porcelains on the mantelpiece in the salon. On her bedside table was her father's clock, on the salon wall hung her father's painting of *L'École des maris*. In the *petit cabinet* was a bookcase, inlaid with copper marquetry, holding a crèche with a wax Christ Child and sixty books. Next to it stood a dressing table with boxes of powder and flacons of perfume. Esprit-Madeleine's household was feminine and of the eighteenth century.

She died, childless, on May 24, 1723, at the age of fifty-seven; her half-brother Nicolas Guérin preceded her in death by fifteen years. Her stepfather, Isaac-François Guérin, died in January 1728, nine years after a stroke that had paralyzed his right side. Claude de Rachel de Montalant lived on until 1738 when he died at the vast age of ninety-two in Argenteuil, in a house bought by his wife in 1713. The executor of his estate was Pierre Chapuis, the husband of Louise Poquelin, granddaughter of Molière's brother Jean.

Montalant still owned a few of his father and mother-in-law's things: some old tapestries, partly rotted, a clavier (which might have been Armande's), some family portraits, and the painting of *L'École de maris*.

He was evidently himself a collector; he owned seventy-two paintings and a number of prints. For someone who brought to his marriage so little, Montalant ended his life unexpectedly well-to-do. What Molière and Madeleine (and, to be fair, Armande) had worked so hard for ended in a grand house with a private chapel in Argenteuil where an old man kept a hoard of gold – 725 *louis d'or* worth 17,400 *livres* – hidden behind his books. Among those books: *The Works of Molière*.

Molière had no direct descendants, nor did his sister Madeleine Poquelin Boudet, both of whose sons died childless. His nephew and godson Jean-Baptiste Poquelin, whose profession of advocate would have pleased his grandfather, had two daughters, Louise and Marie-Élisabeth. Louise married Pierre Chapuis and had one daughter, Louise-Angélique; Marie-Élisabeth never married. She had inherited income from Esprit-Madeleine's estate, which she left in 1756 to her maidservant; her niece Louise-Angélique was almost certainly then dead without issue. The Poquelin family, so bravely begun in 1621 in the Maison des Singes, ended with the death of a spinster great-granddaughter 135 years later.

The Béjart family also seems to have ended. Armande's son Nicolas Guérin married but died childless in 1708. Geneviève Béjart also had a son, Jean-Baptiste Loménie, who was living when she died in July 1675. Nothing further is known of him. And Louis Béjart, who died in October 1678, may have left an illegitimate son, Dominique, born in 1661, but again nothing further is known.

Molière did not rest in peace. Perhaps he could have, if he had only known what his English predecessor Shakespeare had ordered carved on his tomb (and had had time to order it himself): "Blest be ye man ty spares thes stones, and curst be he ty moves my bones." The story of what happened to Molière's remains is grotesque and complicated. He was originally buried in the cemetery of St-Joseph. This cemetery belonged to the parish of St-Eustache and was next to a subsidiary chapel several blocks northwest of St-Eustache itself. In modern Paris the site probably lies somewhere in the rectangle marked by the rue Montmartre, the rue St-Joseph, the rue du Sentier, and the rue Réamur.

Exactly where in the cemetery he was buried is an issue. According to a supposed eye-witness, who wrote about the event to a priest of the parish, the burial took place at the foot of the cross. Although it seems unlikely that the *curé* of St-Eustache, accepting Molière into his particular Holy Ground under duress, would permit such a dubious corpse to claim center stage in the cemetery, the tomb that Armande had placed over the grave was, according to another witness, still visible "in the middle of St-Joseph's cemetery" in 1732.[5] Titon de Tillet adds, however, that the body of Molière was not actually under the tomb but had been, according to a former chaplain who had assisted at the burial, interred "in a more distant spot near the chaplain's house."[6]

Although the thought seems surreal, perhaps some such unlikely compromise was reached between Armande and the *curé*. The tomb, as suited Molière's celebrity, was raised in the center; the corpse, as suited Molière's status as excommunicate, was lowered into more marginal earth. Grimarest does note that he has not included everything relevant in his discussion of Molière's death, since "I found the matter . . . so delicate and so difficult to treat that I admit frankly I did not dare to undertake it."[7]

In any case, on July 6, 1792, the good revolutionary citizens of the quarter disinterred the bones they believed to be those of Molière from a grave located "near a little house situated at the edge."[8] Five months later they removed, or so they thought, the bones of La Fontaine from a grave at the foot of the cross. Unfortunately, it seems unlikely that they retrieved the actual remains of either, especially of La Fontaine, who had been buried not in St-Joseph but in the cemetery of the Innocents.

The bones were kept for seven years, boxed and labeled, in a basement of the Chapel of St-Joseph, then in an attic above the guardroom of the section. Molière's remains were for a time destined for the Pantheon, La Fontaine's for the Quatre Nations, but in May of 1800 they were taken instead to the garden of the Musée des Monuments Français being established in the Elysée palace. When that museum was suppressed in 1817, the much traveled bones were finally taken to the new Cimetière de l'Est, Père-Lachaise, and reinterred.

At least most of them were. Not the least bizarre aspect of this inglorious odyssey is the passion of various nineteenth-century collectors to own relics of this "great man of France." One "scholar" wore a tooth, said to be Molière's, mounted in a ring. Another kept a vertebra in a fold of paper labeled "J.-B. Molierii sanctae relique."[9] The celebrated cabinet of the baron Dominique-Vivant Denon, long-time director of the Imperial and Royal Museums of France – and the gentleman for whom one of the three wings of the modern Musée du Louvre is named – featured a gothic reliquary, sold after his death in 1826 and resold in 1865 for the modest sum of 300 *francs*. The reliquary contained, among other curiosities, fragments of the bones of Héloise and Abelard, hair from Agnès Sorel, a piece of the mustache of Henri IV, taken when the royal tombs were pillaged in 1793, half of one of Voltaire's teeth, a piece of the bloody shirt Napoleon was wearing when he died, and – of course – bone fragments of La Fontaine and Molière.

Shakespeare knew what he was about. But, at least Molière's spirit has been spared the mortification of his becoming a tourist attraction. There are almost no material remains of Molière. His tomb is raised over unknown bones. No house he lived in, no stage he acted on has survived. Only the chair he sat in to speak his final lines remains in a glass case in the upper lobby of the Comédie-Française, the institution which is his real monument. The house of Molière and the plays of Molière live on, and they are finally what matter.

Notes

I JEAN-BAPTISTE POQUELIN

1 There is no English equivalent for the word *"tapissier."* *Tapissiers* could be many things, artisans and merchants, makers and sellers of all kinds of furnishings. In fact, as the result of a series of mergers, by 1636 the *corps de tapissiers* included men practicing six different *métiers.* The *tapissiers-haute-lissiers* made and repaired tapestries; the *tapissiers-sarrasinois* made carpets; *the tapissiers-notrés* worked in serges and druggets, and made covers of silk, cotton and wool. The *coutiers* made cushions and the *coutrepointiers* made bed furnishings, seats, tents, and flags that the *contrepointiers* sold. René de Lespinasse, *Les Métiers et corporations de la ville de Paris. II. Orfèvrerie, sculpture, mercerie, ouvriers en métaux, bâtiment et ameublement* (Paris: Imprimerie Nationale, 1892), pp. 687–721. Jean Poquelin, like his father-in-law, was a *maître marchand contrepointier.*

2 All descriptions of the interior furnishings of the Pavillon des Singes come from the *Inventaire après décès* de Marie Cressé. This document has disappeared, but it was published in Eudore Soulié, *Recherches sur Molière et sur sa famille* (Paris: Librairie de L. Hachette et Cie., 1863).

3 Georges Bordonove, *Molière génial et familier* (Paris: Robert Laffont, 1967), p. 12n.

4 Only Molière and his grandfather spelled the name without a "c." Madeleine Jurgens and Elizabeth Maxfield-Miller, *Cent Ans de recherches sur Molière* (Paris: S.E.V.P.E.N., 1963), p. 18n.

5 Bordonove, *Molière,* p. 497n. "Ci-devant git un honnête marchand / Et bon bourgeois . . . / De tous aimé, prisé et estimé./ Pocquelin nommé et Martin cognommé." Révérend du Mesnil promoted the notion that the original Poquelin was Scots.

6 Jurgens and Maxfield-Miller, *Cent Ans,* p. 27. Unless otherwise cited, the information about Molière's family tree comes from this source.

7 The sum was, however, to be subtracted from Jean Poquelin the younger's eventual inheritance. *ibid.,* pp. 47–8.

8 Marriage contract between Jean Poquelin and Marie Cressé, Soulié, *Recherches,* pp.127–30.

9 Jurgens and Maxfield-Miller, *Cent Ans,* p. 215.

10 René Pillorget, *Nouvelle Histoire de Paris: Paris sous les premiers Bourbons, 1594–1661* (Paris: Hachette, 1988), pp. 116–17.

11 Roland Mousnier, *Paris. Capitale au temps de Richelieu et de Mazarin* (Paris: Éditions A. Pedone, 1978), p. 179. See also Mousnier, *Recherches sur la stratification sociale à Paris aux XVIIᵉ et XVIIIᵉ siècles* (Paris: Éditions A. Pedone, 1976).

12 Jurgens and Maxfield-Miller, *Cent Ans*, p. 601.

13 Both house and beam are long gone, although the beam, the *poteau cornier*, was salvaged and placed in the court of the Beaux-Arts in the early nineteenth century and later destroyed. The beam is illustrated in Alexandre LeNoir's *Musée des monuments français*. See the articles by J. Romain Boulenger in *Le Moliériste* I (1879–80) which include a reproduction of the engraving made for LeNoir on p. 113.

14 The arrangement of the house is well known, thanks to two descriptions made of it, one when it was bought by Martin Morot in 1578, one when it was assessed for Morot's heirs just before Jean Poquelin leased it. (See Jurgens and Maxfield-Miller, *Cent Ans*, pp. 208–10.)

15 When Louis died is not known, but he was dead by the time his mother's property was inventoried in January 1633.

16 Louis XIII received his culottes and doublet at seven years, eight months according to the journal of the king's doctor Héroard. For an exhaustive study of what children wore see Philippe Ariès, *L'Enfant et la vie familiale sous l'ancien régime*, new edn. (Paris: Editions du Seuil), 1973.

17 Charles Varlet *dit* La Grange and Vivot, *Préface* to Molière, *Les Oeuvres* (Paris, 1682). Reprinted in Molière, *Oeuvres complètes*, ed. Georges Couton (Paris: Gallimard, 1971), I, 996. "Il fit ses humanités au collège de Clermont; . . . Le succès de ses études fut tel qu'on pouvait l'attendre d'un génie aussi heureux que le sien. Sil fut fort bon humaniste, il devint encore plus grand philosophe." For a thorough discussion of the authorship of this preface, see Bert Edward Young and Grace Philputt Young, eds., *Le Registre de La Grange* (Paris: E. Droz, 1947), II, 151–7.

18 Recent studies of seventeenth-century education demonstrate conclusively that there was no average age at which a boy began or ended his secondary education. Records from Clermont later in the century show that a single class, the third, included students aged from ten to twenty, with the largest number ranging from fourteen to seventeen. See Pierre Delattre, S.J., *Les Établissements des Jésuites en France* (Enghien: Institut Supérieur de Théologie, 1955), III, 1150.

19 H. C. Barnard. *The French Tradition in Education* (Cambridge University Press, 1922), p. 44. "Ceans on tient petites écoles. N. qui enseigne à la jeunesse le service, à lire, écrire et former les lettres, la grammaire, l'arithmétique, et le calcul, tant au jet qu'à la plume, et prend des pensionnaires."

20 For a long time it was conventional to believe that Molière's father wanted nothing more for his son than a continuation of his own career. According to Grimarest, Molière's first biographer in 1705, the Poquelin parents were good folk who could not have imagined a destiny for their child more elevated than their own. Indeed, writes Grimarest, Jean-Baptiste was kept

serving in the shop until he was fourteen and then went to Clermont only because his grandfather Cressé insisted on it. Jean Grimarest, *La Vie de M. de Molière*, ed. Georges Mongrédien (Paris: Michel Brient, 1955), p. 37.

21 Pillorget, *Nouvelle Histoire*, p. 67. "Une pédagogie fondée sur le réalisme, le bon sens et la ténacité."

22 Delattre, *Établissements*, III, 1151.

23 Richeome, *Oeuvres*, II, 648. Quoted in François de Dainville, *L'Éducation des Jésuites: XVIᵉ-XVIIᵉ siècles* (Paris: Les Editions de Minuit, 1978), pp. 185–6. "C'est une chose humainement divine et divinement humaine de sçavoir dignement manier d'esprit et de langue un subject, le concevoir en l'âme avec de belles et judicieuses pensées, ranger ces pensées d'une sage ordonnance, les revestir d'un riche langage, et les porter à l'oreille de l'auditeur avec une mémoire ferme, une voix vivement esclattante, et doucement pénétrante, et d'une pareille séance de tout le corps, se faire efficacement entendre; planter de nouvelles opinions et nouveaux désirs ès coeurs et en arracher les vieux; fleschir et plier les volontez roidies; s'adresser et roidir les tortues et lasches: et victorieusement persuader et dissuader ce qu'on veut."

24 See below on the subject of Georges Pinel. Charles Perrault mentions "the master, in whose home [Molière] had lived during the early years of his studies." ("... le Maistre chez qui il l'avoit mis en pension pendant les premieres années de ses Estudes.") *Les Hommes illustres qui ont paru en France* (Geneva: Slatkine Reprints, 1970), I, 79.

25 Georges Mongrédien and Jean Robert, *Les Comédiens français du XVIIᵉ siècle: Dictionnaire biographique* (Paris: editions de CNRS, 1981), p. 118.

26 Abraham du Pradel, *Le Livre commode*, ed. Édouard Fournier (Paris: Paul Daffis, 1878), I, 249.

27 Delattre, *Établissements*, III, 1149–50. Quoted from M.B., *Description nouvelle de ce qu'il y a de plus remarquable dans la Ville de Paris* (The Hague, n.d.), II, 221–48. "Le grand nombre de pensionnaires, qui la plupart sont de qualité, outre la multitude d'écoliers externes, qui monte quelquefois jusqu'au deux ou trois mille, qui étudient tous ensemble dans un ordre et dans une discipline la plus régulière du monde."

28 Even quite recent biographers of Molière still repeat the idea that noble boys were separated from commoners at Clermont by means of a gilded balustrade. That may have been true for the prince de Conti, who was royal, but in general at Clermont social distinctions gave way to academic ones in the classroom. It is true, however, that the noble boys usually had private tutors who helped to speed their often astonishing progress.

29 Information about *émulation* is taken from Delattre, *Établissements*, II, 1163–6.

30 In addition to the testimony of La Grange and Vivot that Molière was a good student, we have the witness of Charles Perrault that Molière "succeeded perfectly" in his studies, *Hommes illustres*, I, 79.

31 Jacques Silvestre de Sacy, *Le Quartier des Halles* (Paris: Le Temps, 1969), pp. 83–100.

32 Ibid., p. 19.

33 Bordonove, *Molière*, p. 27.

34 André Duchesne, *Antiquités des villes et chasteaux de France*. Quoted by François
    Boucher, *Le Pont-Neuf* (Paris: Chez Le Goupy, 1925), I, 125.

35 Robert M. Isherwood, *Farce and Fantasy: Popular Entertainment in Eighteenth-
    Century Paris* (New York & Oxford: Oxford University Press, 1986), p. 15.

36 *Ibid.*, p. 16. "L'Orviétan est bon/ Contre toute sorte de vermin. / Contre
    beste vénimeuse, et chiens enragés / Contre la peste. Contre les vers qui
    nous mange / Contre la petite verole et autre . . ." The anonymous engrav-
    ing is reproduced in Alfred Simon, *Molière, une vie* (Lyon: La Manufacture,
    1988), after p. 224.

37 Jacques Scherer, "Notice," *Théâtre du XVII' siècle* (Paris: Gallimard, 1975), pp.
    1199–203.

38 Grimarest, *Vie de Molière*, p. 37n.

39 *État général des officiers de la maison du roi* for 1637. "Jean Poquelin a succedé à
    Jean Poquelin, son pere." The documents attesting to this transfer were
    among the papers described in Molière's *Inventaire après décès*. See Jurgens
    and Maxfield-Miller, *Cent Ans*, p. 217n, p. 580.

40 Lespinasse, *Métiers*, I, 90.

41 "Corps des métiers" in François Bluche, ed., *Dictionnaire du grand siècle* (Paris:
    Fayard, 1990), pp. 412–14.

42 After 1637, in successive *États généraux des officiers de la maison du roi*, the name
    Jean Poquelin, which had been listed second from the last in the list of *tapis-
    siers du roi*, was always last. Jurgens and Maxfield-Miller, *Cent Ans*, 217n.

43 Pierre Chevallier, *Louis XIII, roi cornelian* (Paris: Fayard, 1979), p. 582.

44 Bluche, *Dictionnaire*, p. 644.

45 Bordenove, *Molière*, p. 54.

46 Somewhat later, after Descartes published his *Principes de la philosophie*, young
    Jesuit teachers began to include Descartes in their discourse, to the point
    that their alarmed superiors had to forbid it. Nicolas Grimaldi, "Descartes,"
    in Bluche, *Dictionnaire*, p. 458.

47 La Grange and Vivot, *Préface*, 997; Le Boulanger de Chalussay, *Élomire hypo-
    condre*, in Moliére, *Oeuvres complètes*, ed. Georges Couton (Paris: Gallimard,
    1971), II, 1268; Grimarest, *Vie de Molière*, p. 128.

48 Jules Loiseleur. *L'Université d'Orléans pendant sa période de décadence* (Orléans: H.
    Herluison, 1886), pp. 32–3.

49 L. W. B. Brockliss, *French Higher Education in the Seventeenth and Eighteenth
    Centuries* (Oxford: The Clarendon Press, 1987), p. 77.

50 *Ibid.*, p. 64n.

51 La Grange and Vivot, *Préface*, 997. ". . . il choisit la profession de comédien
    par l'invincible penchant qu'il se sentait pour la comédie."

2 MADELEINE

1 The word is "*galante*," which has many meanings and is probably being used
   equivocally here. It means "elegant," "having the social graces," but it also
   suggests a courtesan, someone who is part of *la galanterie*, a world of sexual

intrigues. The author does not use the term "*femme galante*," which would not
be ambiguous at all. He rather suggests that his subject was both elegant,
charming, and not precisely chaste.

2 Georges [Madeleine?] de Scudéry, *Almahide* (Paris: 1661), V, 1536–7. "Elle
était belle, elle était galante, elle avait beaucoup d'esprit, elle chantait
bien; elle dansait bien; elle jouait de toutes sortes d'instruments; elle
écrivait fort joliment en vers et en prose et sa conversation était fort divertissante. Elle était de plus une des meilleures actrices de son siècle et son
récit avait tant de charmes qu'elle inspirait véritablement toutes les feintes
passions qu'on lui voyait représenter sur le Théâtre. Cette aimable comédienne s'appelait Jebar et, comme Abindarrays cherchait à se divertir pour
effacer de sa mémoire le souvenir de ses aventures passées, il s'en alla à la
comédie où il lui vit jouer le rôle de Sophonisbe d'une manière si tou-
chante et si passionnée qu'après lui avoir donné de l'admiration, elle lui
donna de l'amour, qu'après lui avoir attendri le coeur par la pitié, elle le
lui déroba."

3 Jurgens and Maxfield-Miller, *Cent Ans*, p. 85.

4 Madeleine Jurgens, "L'Aventure de l'Illustre Théâtre," *Revue d'Histoire
Littéraire de la France* 72 (1972), 978.

5 Jurgens and Maxfield-Miller, *Cent Ans*, pp. 74–7.

6 Molière, *Tartuffe* in *Oeuvres complètes*, ed. Couton (Paris: Gallimard, 1971), I,
922. "Lui dire qu'un coeur n'aime point pour autrui, / Que vous vous
mariez pour vous, non pas pour lui, / Qu'étant celle pour qui se fait toute
l'affaire, / C'est à vous, non à lui, que le mari doit plaire, / Et que si son
Tartuffe est pour lui si charmant, / Il le peut épouser sans nul empêche-
ment." All quotations from the works of Molière are taken from this edition
unless otherwise cited.

7 Jurgens and Maxfield-Miller, *Cent Ans*, p. 80.

8 N.-M. Bernardin, *Un Précurseur de Racine, Tristan L'Hermite, sieur de Soliers
(1601–1655), sa famille, sa vie, ses oeuvres* (Paris: A. Picard et fils, 1895), p. 186.
"Elégants, galants, beaux danseurs, passionnés pour le jeu, amis des lettres,
de la comédie et des comédiennes."

9 Gédéon Tallemant des Réaux, *Historiettes*, ed. Antoine Adam (Paris:
Gallimard, 1961), II, 368.

10 Jurgens and Maxfield-Miller, *Cent Ans*, p. 83.

11 *Ibid.*, p. 639.

12 *Ibid.*

13 *Ibid.*

14 *Ibid.*, p. 366.

15 *Ibid.*, p. 81n.

16 Madeleine Jurgens suggests that Madeleine Béjart may also have been connected to the theatre through the Bedeau family. One Simon Bedeau is
named as a guardian of the minor Béjart children after their father's death.
Nothing specific, however, connects him to François and Julien Bedeau who
acted as Jodelet and L'Espy at the Marais and the Hôtel de Bourgogne and

who joined Molière and the others in the troupe of Monsieur in 1659. "L'Aventure," 980.

17 Georges Mongrédien, *Recueil des textes et des documents du XVIIe siècle relatifs à Molière* (Paris: Éditions du Centre National de la Recherche Scientifique, 1965), I, 59. "Ton Hercule mourant te va rendre immortel; / Au Ciel comme en la terre, il publiera ta gloire, / Et, laissant ici-bas un temple à ta Mémoire, / Son bûcher servira pour te faire un autel."

18 See Jurgens and Maxfield-Miller, *Cent Ans*, pp. 639–42. In fall 1639, Madeleine rented her house in Bagnolet; in November 1639 she was godmother to her sister Bénigne-Madeleine and in June 1640 to a child of Robert La Voypierre; in September 1641 she sold the house in Bagnolet; in December of that same year she signed a receipt for a payment due on the house; in March 1642 she signed another receipt. No extant documents generated between March 1642 and March 1643 attest to her presence in Paris, or anywhere else.

19 Tallemant des Réaux, *Historiettes*, II, 775. ". . . et dans peu sa troupe valut encore mieux que l'autre; car luy seul valoit mieux que tout le reste."

20 *Ibid.*, II, 778. "Il faut finir par la Béjard. Je ne l'ay jamais veûe joüer; mais on dit que c'est la meilleure actrice de toutes. Elle est dans une troupe de campagne; elle a joüé à Paris, mais ç'a esté dans une troisieme troupe qui ne fut que quelque temps. Son chef-d'oeuvre, c'estoit le personnage d'Epicharis."

21 Ferdinando Taviani, "La Fleur et le guerrier: les actrices de la *commedia dell'arte*," *Buffoneries*, 15/16.

22 See Lynne Lawner, *Lives of the Courtesans: Portraits of the Renaissance* (New York: Rizzoli, 1987), chap. 1 for a discussion of the Roman courtesans before and after the council of Trent.

23 Winifred Smith, *Italian Actors of the Renaissance* (New York: Coward McCann, 1939), p. 53.

24 Jurgens and Maxfield-Miller, *Cent Ans*, pp. 640–1.

25 From the Act of Parlement ordering the trial *in memoria* of the comte de Soissons. See *ibid.*, p. 641.

26 Bernardin, *Précurseur de Racine*, p. 218.

27 *Ibid.*

28 Jurgens and Maxfield-Miller, *Cent Ans*, p. 87. According to Modène's brother Charles, in a deposition given many years later, there was no possible doubt that Marie Courtin was Esprit de Rémond's mistress in 1643–4.

29 *Ibid.*, p. 643.

30 Although she is usually referred to as Armande Béjart, various documents indicate that she may actually have used "Grésinde." See, for instance, the marriage contract of her sister Geneviève and Léonard de Loménie (*ibid.*, pp. 397–8). Since, however, a change to "Grésinde" would create confusion for those readers already familiar with Molière, I shall retain "Armande."

31 Georges Mongrédien, *La Vie priveé de Molière* (Paris: Hachette, 1950), p. 88.

32 Gustave Larroumet, "Une Comédienne au XVIIe siècle, Madeleine Béjart," *Revue des Deux Mondes*, May 1, 1885, pp. 123–57.

33 A child's names are a clue to its baptism; its names often come from its godparents, as "Esprit" and "Madeleine." Thus we can ask where the names "Armande" and "Grésinde" are likely to have come from and whether they offer any clues to Armande's provenance. "Grésinde" was apparently one of Madeleine's names. It appears in an act of baptism of November 20, 1661 when Jeanne-Madeleine-Grisinde Prévost had, as godmother, "Magdelaine-Gresaindre" Béjart (Jurgens and Maxfield-Miller, *Cent Ans*, p. 365). The name "Armande" should refer to the godfather, but no obvious candidate presents himself. One not so obvious candidate is Armand, prince de Conti. However, this choice proposes a formal baptism delayed until the child was eleven or twelve. One imaginable if unlikely narrative is that the child, having received the sacrament of baptism without the formal ceremony (that is, having been "*ondoyée*") and having been called "Grésinde" for a number of years, was finally "named" in a ceremony held in Languedoc in 1653 or 54 with the prince de Conti as her godfather and her mother/sister Madeleine-Grésinde as her godmother.

34 See *ibid.*, esp. pp. 636–45. The relationship of Marie Hervé to the property located on the rue de Thorigny/rue de Perle is almost impossible to determine, although it seems she must have sold it more than once.

35 Henri Chardon, *M. de Modène, ses deux femmes et Madeleine Béjart* (Paris: A. Picard, 1886), p. 138.

36 *Ibid.*, p. 124. "Le roi étoit à Montfrin, oú il prenoit les eaux. . . . Mme de Rohan étoit là chez laquelle il y avoit tous les jours bal et Comédie."

37 Grimarest, *Vie de Molière*, p. 40. "Quand Molière eut achevé ses études, il fut obligé . . . d'exercer sa Charge pendant quelque tems; et meme il fit le voyage de Narbonne à la suite de Louis XIII."

3 THE *ILLUSTRE THÉÂTRE*

1 Jurgens and Maxfield-Miller, *Cent Ans*, p. 220. *Inventoire après décès* of Louis de Cressé.

2 Grimarest, *Vie de Molière*, p. 42. "Molière en formant sa troupe, lia une forte amitié avec la Béjart . . ."

3 *Mémoires de Brossette sur Boileau* in *Correspondance entre Boileau Despréaux et Brossette*, ed. August Laverdet (Paris: J. Techner, 1858), p. 517. Cited hereafter as "Brossette."

4 Tallemant des Réaux, *Historiettes*, II, 778. "Un garçon, nommé Moliere, quitta les bancs de Sorbonne pour la suivre; il en fut longtemps amoureux . . . et enfin s'en mit et l'espousa."

5 Jurgens and Maxfield-Miller, *Cent Ans*, p. 223.

6 Le Boulanger de Chalussay. "ᴀɴɢ: Mais, de grâce, admirez l'étrange ingratitude!/ Au lieu de se donner tout à fait à l'étude, / Pour plaire à ce bon père, et plaider doctement, / Il ne fut au Palais qu'une fois seulement. /

Cependant savez-vous ce que faisait le drôle? / Chez deux grands charlatans, il apprenait un rôle, / Chez ces originaux, l'Orviétan et Bary, / Dont
le fat se croyait déjà le favori. / ÉLO: / Pour l'Orviétan, d'accord, mais pour
Bary je nie / D'avoir jamais brigué place en sa compagnie. / ANG:/ Tu
briguas chez Bary le quatrième emploi: / Bary t'en refusa; tu t'en plaignis
à moi, / Et je me souviens bien qu'en ce temps-là mes frères / T'en gaus-
saient, t'appelant le mangeur de vipères. / Car tu fus si privé de sens et de
raison, / Et si persuadé de son contrepoison, / Que tu t'offris à lui pour faire
ses épreuves, / Quoi qu'en notre quartier nous connussions les veuves / De
six fameux bouffons crevés dans cet emploi," *Oeuvres complètes*, II, 1272–3.

7 *Ibid.*, p. 1235.

8 *French Theatre in the Neo-Classical Era, 1550–1789*, ed. William D. Howarth
(Cambridge University Press, 1997), pp. 104–5.

9 Pierre Corneille, *L'Illusion comique* in *Oeuvres complètes*, ed. Georges Couton
(Paris: Gallimard, 1980), I, 687. "Cessez de vous en plaindre: à présent le
Théâtre / Est en un point si haut qu'un chacun l'idolâtre, / Et ce que votre
temps voyait avec mépris / Est aujourd'hui l'amour de tous les bons esprits,
. . . / Même notre grand Roi, ce foudre de la guerre / Dont le nom se fait
craindre aux deux bouts de la terre, / Le front ceint de lauriers daigne bien
quelquefois / Prêter l'oeil et l'oreille au Théâtre François."

10 Jurgens and Maxfield-Miller, "Contrat de société entre les comédiens de
l'Illustre Théatre," *Cent Ans*, pp. 224–6. ". . . se lient ensemble pour l'exercice de la comedie affin de conservation de leur trouppe soubz le tiltre de
l'Illustre Theatre."

11 *Ibid.* As is the case with so many of the documents relevant to Molière, this
one is no longer to be found. An "exact copy" was made in 1876 by a notary
in whose office the contract was then on file and published in *Le Français* of
January 16, 1876.

12 Grimarest, *Vie de Molière*, p. 40.

13 Molière, *Oeuvres complètes*, I, 997.

14 Jurgens and Maxfield-Miller, *Cent Ans*, p. 228. ". . à commancer du jour que
lesdicts preneurs auront commancé de faire porter du bois audict jeu pour
faire faire leur theatre, galleries et loges."

15 *Ibid.*, "Bail du jeu de paume des Mestayers," pp. 227–31.

16 *Ibid.*, pp. 232–4.

17 *Ibid.*, pp. 239–40.

18 François and Claude Parfaict, *L'Histoire du théâtre françois* (Amsterdam: Le
Mercier, 1746), VI, 173–5. "Tout le monde paroît content, excepté les
Spectateurs, qui ont dû . . . avoir été furieusement ennuyés des longs plai-
doyers des Amans d'Alcidiane."

19 Le Boulanger de Chalussay in Molière, *Oeuvres complètes*, II, 1269.

20 Grimarest, *Vie de Molière*, p. 40. "Molière . . . qui avoit le discernement et les
vues beaucoup plus justes, que des gens qui n'avoient pas été cultivez avec
autant de soin que lui."

21 Antoine Adam, *Histoire de la littérature française au XVIIᵉ siècle* (Paris: Domat,
Montchrestian, 1948–56), II, 1, 319n.

22 *Ibid.*, 322–3.

23 Jurgens and Maxfield-Miller, *Cent Ans*, pp. 644–5.

24 Tallemant des Réaux, *Historiettes*, II, 778.

25 Grimarest, *Vie de Molière*, pp. 99–100. "Dans les commencemens . . . il parois-
soit mauvais Comédien à bien des gens; peut-être à cause d'un hoquet ou
tic de gorge qu'il avoit, et qui rendoit d'abord son jeu desagreable . . . Dans
les commencemens qu'il monta sur le theâtre, il reconnut qu'il avoit une vol-
ubilité de langue, dont il n'étoit pas le maître et qui rendoit son jeu desagreable. Et des efforts qu'il se fesoit pour se retenir dans la prononciation, il s'en
forma un hoquet, qui lui demeura jusques à la fin . . . Il est vrai que Molière
n'étoit bon que pour representer le Comique; il ne pouvoit entrer dans le
serieux, et plusieurs personnes assurent qu'aïant voulu le tenter, il réussit si
mal la première fois qu'il parut sur le theâtre, qu'on ne le laissa pas achever."

26 Quoted in Mongrédien, *Vie privée*, pp.166–7. "il vient, le nez au vent, / Les
pieds en parenthèse et l'épaule en avant, / Sa perruque, qui suit le côté qu'il
avance, / Plus pleine de lauriers qu'un jambon de Mayence, / Les mains
sur les côtés, d'un air peu négligé, / La tête sur le dos comme un mulet
chargé, / Les yeux fort égarés; puis, débitant ses roles, / D'un hoquet éternel
sépare ses paroles."

27 *Lettres au Mercure sur Molière, sa vie, ses oeuvres et les comédiens de son temps*, ed.
Georges Monval (Geneva: Slatkine Reprints, 1969), pp. 54–5. "Moliere
n'étoit ni trop gras ni trop maigre; il avoit la taille plus grande que petite, le
port noble, la jambe belle; il marchoit gravement, avoit l'air très-sérieux, le
nez gros, la bouche grande, les lèvres épaisses, le teint brun, les sourcils noirs
et forts, et les divers mouvemens qu'il leur donnoit lui rendoient la physio-
nomie extrémement comique. . . . La nature . . . lui avoit refusé ces dons
exterieurs, si nécessaires au théatre, surtout pour les rôles tragiques."

28 Jurgens and Maxfield-Miller, *Cent Ans*, pp. 241–2.

29 *Ibid.*, pp. 244–6.

30 Bernardin, *Précurseur de Racine*, pp. 238–40.

31 For the accord and contracts of December 17, 1644, see Jurgens and
Maxfield-Miller, *Cent Ans*, pp. 247–55.

32 *Ibid.*, pp. 265–6.

33 The claims and counterclaims are more complicated than this and change
from document to document, but finally everyone seemed to agree that the
actors still owed Baulot 200 *livres*, which means that 400 had been paid
between December and April. Pommier insisted throughout that the actors
still owed him the entire 2000. See Jurgens and Maxfield-Miller, *ibid.*
Documents XLIII–XLIX, pp. 266–75.

34 They agreed they still owed Baulot 200 *livres* of the 1,100 they had borrowed
from him in September, but they were unaware that Pommier had, as it
were, sold their loan contract to Baulot.

35 Jurgens, "L'Aventure," 1001.

36 Jurgens and Maxfield-Miller, *Cent Ans*, p. 456. From Jean Poquelin's *Inventaire
après décès*.

37 In the 1630s, plays often had women in title roles. There was Sophonisbe,

of course, which gave rebirth to tragedy in France, and Mariane, the heroine of Tristan's model tragedy. But there were also some Lucrèces and Cléopatres and Didons. Even Corneille wrote his first tragedy about a woman, Medée. The change in repertory may have been a response to the war which broke out in 1635 and lasted into the mid-1640s.

4 EXILE

1 At least one member of the troupe was in Paris in March 1646. Pierre Réveillon paid back his brother-in-law some of the money he had borrowed from him. (Jurgens and Maxfield-Miller, *Cent Ans*, pp. 690–1.) Probably most of the troupe was there during the Easter break, as would be the custom, seeing old friends and signing on new actors.

2 Mongrédien, *Recueil*, I, 77.

3 An interesting note is that Pierre Réveillon's father, a master tinsmith, was a member of the Confrérie de la Passion, owners of the Hôtel de Bourgogne, and dean of that society in 1627. Jurgens and Maxfield-Miller, *Cent Ans*, p. 690.

4 *Ibid.*, p. 292. Marie Hervé, Joseph and Geneviève Béjart signed a power of attorney giving their lawyer André de Lamarre the right to act for them and for the absent Madeleine and Molière in the matter of Antoinette Simony.

5 Mongrédien, *Recueil*, I, 78. "Cette protection et ce secours . . . que vous avez donnés à la plus malheureuse et à l'une des mieux méritantes comédiennes de France, n'est pas la moindre action de votre vie. . . . Vous avez tiré cette infortunée d'un précipice où son mérite l'avait jetée, et vous avez remis sur the théâtre un des beaux personnages qu'il ait jamais portés. Elle n'y est remontée, Monseigneur, qu'avec cette belle espérance de jouer un jour dignement son rôle dans cette illustre pièce, où, sous des noms empruntés, on va représenter une partie de votre vie."

6 "Inventaire après décès" of Pierre Réveillon. Jurgens and Maxfield-Miller, *Cent Ans*, pp. 693–5.

7 Paul Scarron, *Le Roman comique*, ed. Yves Giraud (Paris: GF-Flammarion, 1981), pp. 65–7. ". . . il était entre cinq et six quand une charrette entra dans les halles du Mans. Cette charrette était attelée de quatre boeufs fort maigres, conduits par une jument poulinière dont le poulain allait et venait à l'entour de la charrette comme un pitit fou qu'il était. La charette était pleine de coffres, de malles et de gros paquets de toiles peintes qui faisaient comme une pyramide au haut de laquelle paraissait une demoiselle habillée moitié ville, moitié campagne. Un jeune homme, aussi pauvre d'habits que riche de mine, marchait à coté de la charrette . . . Un vieillard vêtu plus régulièrement, quoique très mal, marchait à côté de lui. Il portait sur ses épaules une basse de viole et, parce qu'il se courbait un peu en marchant, on l'eût pris de loin pour une grosse tortue qui marchait sur les jambes de derrière . . . Un lieutenant de prévôt . . . nommé La Rappinière, les vint accoster et leur demanda avec un autorité de magistrat quelles gens ils

étaient. Le jeune homme . . . lui dit qu'ils étaient Français de naissance, comédiens de profession; que son nom de théâtre était Le Destin, celui de son vieil camarade, La Rancune, et celui de la demoiselle qui était juchée comme une poule au haut de leur bagage, La Caverne. Ce nom bizarre fit rire quelques-uns de la compagnie; sur quoi le jeune comédien ajouta que le nom de Caverne ne devait pas sembler plus étrange à des hommes d'esprit que ceux de La Montagne, La Vallée, La Rose ou L'Épine. La conversation finit par quelques coups de poing et jurements de Dieu que l'on entendit au devant de la charrette. C'était le valet du tripot qui avait battu le charretier sans dire gare, parce que ses boeufs et sa jument usaient trop librement d'un amas de foin qui était devant la porte. . . . et la maîtresse du tripot, qui aimait la comédie plus que sermon ni vêpres, par une générosité inouïe en une maîtresse de tripot, permit au charretier de faire manger ses bêtes tout leur soûl."

8 Jurgens and Maxfield-Miller, *Cent Ans*, p. 294. "Messieurs, Estant arrivé en ceste ville j'ay trouvé la troupe des comediens de Monsieur le duc d'Espernon qui m'ont dit que vostre ville les avoit mandez pour donner la comedye pendant que Monsieur le comte d'Aubijoux y a demeuré, ce qu'ilz on faict, sans qu'on leur ayt tenu la promesse qu'on leur avoir faicte qui est qu'on leur avoit promis une somme de six cens livres et le port et conduite de tout leur bagage. Ceste troupe est remplie de fort honnestes gens et de très bons acteurs qui meritent estre recompensez de leurs peines."

9 *Ibid.*, p. 304. "Monsieur le maire a proposé qu'il a receu une lettre du sieur Morliere, comedien, qui demande permition de venir en ville avecq ses compagnons pour y passer ung couple de mois, qu'il n'a voullu faire response sans en conferer. A esté arresté que Monsieur le maire verra avecq Monsieur le lieutenant general pour empescher que lesdicts comediens viennent en ville, attandu la misere du temps et chereté des bledz."

10 *Ibid.*, pp. 217–18 and p. 218 n. After 1648 there is a hiatus of nine years. In 1657 is found "Jean Poquelin et Jean [the second Jean] son fils en survivance."

11 Mongrédien, *Recueil*, I, 82. "Il ne l'anathématisait pas, à l'exemple de quelques-uns qui affectaient une sotte et insolente sévérité . . . Il faisait même asseoir à sa table cet homme éminent dans son art. Il lui donnait de somptueux repas. Il ne le mettait pas, comme un excommunié, au nombre des impies et des scélérats . . ."

12 Jurgens and Maxfield-Miller, *Cent Ans*, p. 306.

13 Claude Alberge, *Le Voyage de Molière en Languedoc: 1647–1657* (Montpellier: Les Presses de Languedoc, 1988), p. 107. The quotation is from a definition given by the president of the États in 1651: Languedoc should be "distingué de la plupart des autres provinces du royaume conquises par la force des armes, sur lesquelles le prince a le pouvoir de faire cette levée des deniers et impositions que bon lui semble, sans demander leur consentement."

14 Elie Brackenhoffer, *Voyage de Paris en Italie: 1644–1646* (Paris: Berger-Levrault, 1925), pp. 131–2. "Bon chemin, temps agréable, jolie campagne, pleine

d'oliviers . . . C'est un des plus beaux lieux de tout le Languedoc; . . . elle est presque carrée, close de murailles et de portes; elle a de belles rues et un assez grand nombre de somptueuses et de jolies maisons, qui sont merveilleuses à voir. Çà et là, il y a de belles *fontaines* et d'assez grandes places, où les habitants se divertissent et se promènent. L'hôtel de ville, aussi, est *magnifique* . . . Les gens du pays sont aimables et respectent les étrangers; les femmes sont d'une très remarquable beauté; elles ont un costume provocant, elles vont presque à demi nues, de telle sorte qu'on voit à peu près complètement leurs épaules et leur poitrine nues, ce que je n'ai encore observé en aucun lieu de France qu'ici."

15 Jurgens and Maxfield-Miller, *Cent Ans*, pp. 306–7. Roger Duchêne, in his recent book *Molière* (Paris: Fayard, 1998), states that the "best experts" consider this document to be false and, in any case, the sum seems excessive (p. 114). Duchêne ignores, however, other evidence that absolutely confirms the sum. See Jurgens and Maxfield-Miller, *ibid.*, p. 307n3.

16 Mongrédien and Robert, *Comédiens français*, p. 272. Madeleine Béjart was in Montpellier on January 6, 1651.

17 Alberge, *Voyage de Molière*, p. 120. "Ces Messieurs plus jaloux de leur divertissement que du soulagement du peuple, dans une comédie continuelle stipendiée et salariée du sang de la veuve et de l'orphelin et de la substance des pauvres, excitaient des larmes et arrachaient des soupirs des coeurs de toute la province . . . Les charges de la province diminueraient de moitié si celles qui ne sont que pour l'avantage du particulier en étaient retranchées."

18 Jurgens and Maxfield-Miller, *Cent Ans*, p. 309. "Ledict sieur Berthellot . . . a faict . . . ce promet de l'habiller et enjoaller de bons habiz, bagues et joyaux suivant sa quallité."

19 The title page is reproduced in Suzanne Dulait, *Inventaire raisonné des autographes de Molière* (Geneva: Librairie Droz, 1967), plate 73.

20 Corneille, *Oeuvres complètes*, II, 448. ". . . mon principal but ici a été de satisfaire la vue par l'éclat et la diversité du spectacle."

21 Alberge, *Voyage de Molière*, pp. 149–50.

22 Daniel de Cosnac, *Mémoires* (Paris: Jules Renouard, 1852), I, 126–8. "Aussitôt qu'elle fut logée dans La Grange, elle proposa d'envoyer chercher des comédiens. Comme j'avois l'argent des menus plaisirs de ce prince, il me donna ce soin. J'appris que la troupe de Molière et de La Béjart étoit en Languedoc; je leur mandai qu'ils vinssent à La Grange. Pendant que cette troupe se disposoit à venir sur mes ordres, il en arriva une autre à Pézenas qui étoit celle de Cormier. L'impatience naturelle de M. le prince de Conti, et les présents que fit cette dernière troupe à Mme de Calvimont, engagèrent à les retenir. Lorsque je voulus représenter à M. le prince de Conti que je m'étois engagé à Molière sur ses ordres, il me répondit qu'il s'étoit depuis lui-même engagé à la troupe de Cormier, et qu'il étoit plus juste que je manquasse à ma parole que lui à la sienne. Cependant Molière arriva et, ayant demandé qu'on lui payât au moins les frais qu'on lui avoit fait faire pour venir, je ne pus jamais l'obtenir, quoiqu'il y eût beaucoup de

justice; mais M. le prince de Conti avoit trouvé bon de s'opiniâtrer à cette bagatelle. Ce mauvais procédé me touchant de dépit, je résolus de les faire monter sur le théâtre à Pézenas, et de leur donner mille écus de mon argent, plutôt que de leur manquer de parole. Comme ils étoient prêts de jouer à la ville, M. le prince de Conti, un peu piqué d'honneur par ma manière d'agir, et pressé par Sarrasin [Sarasin in modern spelling] que j'avois intéressé à me servir, accorda qu'ils viendroient jouer une fois sur le théâtre de La Grange. Cette troupe ne réussit pas dans sa première représentation au gré de Mme de Calvimont, ni par conséquent au gré de M. le prince de Conti, quoique, au jugement de tout le reste des auditeurs, elle surpassât infiniment la troupe de Cormier, soit par la bonté des acteurs, soit par la magnificence des habits. Peu de jours après, ils représentèrent encore, et Sarrasin, à force de prôner leurs louanges, fit avouer à M. le prince de Conti qu'il falloit retenir la troupe de Molière, à l'exclusion de celle de Cormier. Il les avoit suivis et soutenus dans le commencement à cause de moi; mais alors, étant devenu amoureux de la Du Parc, il songea à se servir lui-même. Il gagna Mme de Calvimont, et non-seulement il fit congédier la troupe de Cormier, mais il fit donner pension à celle de Molière."

23 Molière, *Oeuvres complètes*, I, 996. ". . . et, comme il eut l'avantage de suivre feu Monsieur le prince de Conty dans toutes ses classes, la vivacité d'esprit qui le distinguait de tous les autres lui fit acquérir l'estime et les bonnes grâces de ce prince, qui l'a toujours honoré de sa bienveillance et de sa protection."

24 Abbé de Voisin, *Défense du traité du prince de Conti* (Paris: J.-B. Coignard, 1671), p. 419.

25 Cosnac, *Mémoires*, I, 137.

26 Mongrédien, *Recueil*, I, 89.

27 Molière, *Oeuvres complètes*, I, 1371n.

28 *Ibid.*, 990. "Philosophes fameux, qui d'une ardeur si pure / De ce vaste univers recherchez les secrets, / Demeurez tous d'accord qu'avec notre peinture, / Nos vers ingénieux et nos divins creusets, / S'il est du vuide en la nature, / Il faut qu'il soit en nos goussets." The verse ends with the word "goussets," which can mean "purses" but more usually means "armpits." Perhaps it is this sort of pun that led Despois to doubt Molière's authorship.

29 *Ibid.*, 993. "Je fais d'aussi beaux vers que ceux que je récite, / Et souvent leur style m'excite / À donner à ma muse un glorieux emploi. / Mon esprit de mes pas ne suit pas la cadence: / Loin d'etre incompatible avec cette Éloquence, / Tout ce qui n'en a pas l'est toujours avec moi."

30 The sentence in La Grange and Vivot's preface is somewhat ambiguous. "Il vint à Lyon en 1653, et ce fut là qu'il exposa au public sa première comédie." Couton reads this: "He came to Lyon in 1653 [for the first time], and it was there [but not necessarily in 1653] that he showed his first play to the public." Molière, *Oeuvres Complètes*, I, 47n.

31 John Palmer, *Molière* (New York: Benjamin Blom Reprint, 1970), p. 111.

32 Molière, *Oeuvres complètes*, I, 678. "Vous deviez faire une comédie où vous auriez joué tout seul."

33 Molière met the Mignard brothers, Nicolas and Pierre, in Lyon in the mid-1650s. Both did portraits of him in life as well as in character. Nicolas Mignard painted him as Caesar in Corneille's *La Mort de Pompée* and his more celebrated brother used Molière and Madeleine as models for his *Mars et Venus*. A third portrait attributed to Sébastien Bourdon shows Molière in *habit à romaine*, but the character is not identified.

34 Mongrédien, *Recueil*, I, 89–90.

35 *Ibid.*, 93. According to Alberge, *Voyage de Molière*, p. 194, there exists a long history of this subvention.

36 Jurgens and Maxfield-Miller, *Cent Ans*, pp. 314–15.

37 Charles Coypeau Dassoucy, *Aventures burlesques* (Paris: Audinet, 1677), p. 96.

38 *Ibid.*, pp. 101–2. ". . . ayant Molière . . . et toute la maison des Béjarts pour amis . . . je me vis plus riche et plus content que jamais. Car ces généreuses personnes ne se contentèrent pas de m'assister comme ami, ils me voulurent traiter comme parent . . . On dit que le meilleur frere est las au bout d'un mois de donner à manger à son frere, mais ceux-cy, plus genereux que tous les freres qu'on puisse avoir, ne se lasserent point de me voir à leur table tout un hyver, et je puis dire: Qu'en cette douce compagnie / Que je repaissais d'harmonie, / Au milieu de sept ou huit plats, / Exempt de soin et d'embarras, / Je passois doucement la vie."

39 *Ibid.* ". . . ces gens-là, bien dignes de représenter dans le monde les personnages des princes qu'ils représentent tous les jours sur le théâtre."

40 Jurgens and Maxfield-Miller, *Cent Ans*, pp. 382, 544, 690–3.

41 Alberge, *Voyage de Molière*, pp. 193–4.

42 Mongrédien, *Recueil*, I, 96.

43 Couton, "Introduction," in Molière, *Oeuvres complètes*, I, xxvn.

44 Jurgens and Maxfield-Miller, *Cent Ans*, p. 320.

45 Alberge, *Voyage de Molière*, p. 211.

46 Mongrédien, *Recueil*, I, 97–8.

47 Jurgens and Maxfield-Miller, *Cent Ans*, p. 326.

48 Mongrédien. *Recueil*, I, 95. "Le noble amusement des honnêtes gens, la digne débauche du beau monde et des bons esprits, la comédie, pour n'être pas fixe comme à Paris, ne laisse pas de se jouer ici à toutes les saisons qui la demandent, et par une troupe ordinairement qui, tout ambulatoire qu'elle est, vaut bien celle de l'hôtel qui demeure en place."

49 *Ibid.*, 100. "Nous attendons ici les deux beautés que vous croyez devoir disputer cet hiver d'éclat avec la sienne [Mlle Baron]. Au moins ai-je remarqué en Mlle Béjart grande envie de jouer à Paris, et je ne doute point qu'au sortie d'ici, cette troupe n'y aille passer le reste de l'année. Je voudrais qu'elle voulût faire alliance avec le Marais, cela en pourrait changer la destinée."

50 Jurgens and Maxfield-Miller, *Cent Ans*, pp. 327–8.

51 La Grange and Vivot in Molière, *Oeuvres complètes*, I, 997. "En 1658, ses amis lui conseillèrent de s'approcher de Paris en faisant venir sa troupe dans une

ville voisine: c'était le moyen de profiter du crédit que son mérite lui avait acquis auprès de plusieurs personnes de considération, qui, s'intéressant à sa gloire, lui avaient promis de l'introduire à la Cour. Il avait passé le carnaval à Grenoble, d'où il partit après Pâques, et vint s'etablir à Rouen Il y séjourna pendant l'été; et après quelques voyages qu'il fit à Paris secrètement, il eut l'avantage de faire agréer ses services et ceux de ses camarades à MONSIEUR, frère unique de Sa Majesté, qui, lui ayant accordé sa protection et le titre de sa troupe, le présenta en cette qualité au Roi et à la Reine mère."

5 RETURN TO PARIS

1 François Bluche, *Louis XIV* (Paris: Hachette, 1986), pp. 126–8. "La taille de ce monarque est autant par-dessus celle des autres que sa naissance aussi bien que sa mine. Il a l'air haut, relevé, hardi, fier et agréable, quelque chose de fort doux et de majestueux dans le visage, les plus beaux cheveux du monde en leur coleur et en la manière dont ils sont frisés. Les jambes belles, le port beau et bien planté; enfin, à tout prendre, c'est le plus bel homme et le mieux fait de son royaume . . . Son abord est froid, il parle peu; mais aux personnes avec qui il est familier il parle bien, juste et ne dit rien que de très à propos, raille fort agréablement, a le goût bon; discerne et juge le mieux du monde, a de la bonté naturelle, est charitable, libéral, joue en roi et ne fait nulle action qui n'en soit . . . Il a fort bon sens pour les affaires, parle bien dans ses conseils, et en public quand il est nécessaire. . . . Il est fort propre à être galant."

2 Alfred Simon, *Molière par lui-même* (Paris: Éditions du Seuil, 1967), p. 31.

3 La Grange and Vivot in Molière, *Oeuvres complètes*, I, 999.

4 Donneau de Visé, *Zélinde* in *ibid.*, 1032. "Madame, je suis au désespoir de n'avoir pu vous satisfaire; depuis que je suis descendu, Élomire n'a pas dit une seule parole. Je l'ai trouvé appuyé sur ma boutique, dans la posture d'un homme qui rêve. Il avait les yeux collés sur trois ou quatre personnes de qualité qui marchandaient des dentelles, il paraissait attentif à leurs discours, et il semblait, par le mouvement de ses yeux, qu'il regardait jusques au fond de leurs âmes pour y voir ce qu'elles ne disaient pas; je crois même qu'il avait des tablettes, et qu'à la faveur de son manteau, il a écrit, sans être aperçu, ce qu'elles ont dit de plus remarquable."

5 For a full study of this troupe during its long tenure in Paris, see Virginia Scott, *The Commedia dell'arte in Paris* (Charlottesville, VA: University Press of Virginia, 1990.

6 Information about the Salle des Caryatides comes from Christiane Aulanier, *Histoire du Palais et du Musée du Louvre* (Paris: Éditions des Musées Nationaux, s.d.),VI, 7–76.

7 Henri Sauval, *Histoire et recherches des antiquités de la Ville de Paris* (Geneva: Minkoff Reprints, 1973), II, 33. ". . . le grand tribunal du Louvre, & qui sert maintenant de salle des Gardes à l'appartement de la Reine Regente." The

caryatides ". . . sont à present cachés derriere un Theâtre bâti nouvellement dans cette salle."

8   La Grange and Vivot seem to be using "*petites comédies*" as a code word for farce, which is what these little comedies were.

9   La Grange and Vivot in Molière, *Oeuvres complètes*, I, 997–8. ". . . le 24ᶜ octobre 1658, cette troupe commença de paraîtra devant Leurs Majestés et toute la Cour, sur un théâtre que le Roi avait fait dresser dans la salle des Gardes du vieux Louvre. *Nicomède*, tragédie de Monsieur de Corneille l'ainé, fut la pièce qu'elle choisit pour cet éclatant début. Ces nouveaux acteurs ne déplurent point, et on fut surtout fort satisfait de l'agrément et du jeu des femmes. Les fameux comédiens qui faisaient alors si bien valoir l'Hôtel de Bourgogne étaient présents à cette représentation. La pièce étant achevée, Monsieur de Molière vint sur le théâtre; et, après avoir remercié Sa Majesté en des termes très modestes de la bonté qu'Elle avait eue d'excuser ses défauts et ceux de toute sa troupe, qui n'avait paru qu'en tremblant devant une assemblée si auguste, il lui dit que l'envie qu'ils avaient eue d'avoir l'honneur de divertir le plus grand Roi du monde, leur avait fait oublier que Sa Majesté avait à son service d'excellents originaux, dont ils n'étaient que de très faibles copies; mais que puisqu'Elle avait bien voulu souffrir leurs manières de campagne, il la suppliait très humblement d'avoir agréable qu'il lui donnât un de ces petits divertissements qui lui avaient acquis quelque réputation, et dont il régalait les provinces."

"Ce compliment, dont on ne rapporte que la substance, fut si agréablement tourné et si favorablement reçu, que toute la Cour y applaudit, et encore plus à la petite comédie, qui fut celle du *Docteur amoureux*. Cette comédie, qui ne contenait qu'un acte, et quelques autres de cette nature, n'ont point été imprimées: il les avait faites sur quelques idées plaisantes sans y avoir mis la dernière main; et il trouva à propos de les supprimer, lorsqu'il se fut proposé pour but dans toutes ses pièces d'obliger les hommes à se corriger de leur défauts. Comme il y avait longtemps qu'on ne parlait plus des petites comédies, l'invention en parut nouvelle, et celle qui fut représentée ce jour-là divertit autant qu'elle surprit tout le monde. Monsieur de Molière faisait le Docteur; et la manière dont il s'acquitta de ce personnage le mit dans une si grande estime, que Sa Majesté donna ses ordres pour établir sa troupe à Paris. La salle du Petit-Bourbon lui fut accordée pour y représenter la comédie alternativement avec les comédiens italiens. Cette troupe dont Monsieur de Molière était le chef, et qui, comme je l'ai déjà dit, prit le titre de la troupe de MONSIEUR, commença à représenter en public le 3ᶜ [*sic*; actually the 2nd] novembre 1658 et donna pour nouveautés *L'Étourdi* et le *Dépit amoureux*, qui n'avaient jamais été joués à Paris."

10 La Grange adds a marginal note to his *Registre*, I, 5 (May 11, 1659). "Mr Bejard tomba malade et acheva son rosle de L'Estourdy avec peyne." Lélie is certainly the *étourdi*, the bungling lover. As for *Le Dépit amoureux*, Le Boulanger de Chalussay has Élomire refer to Éraste as "mon bégue," and Joseph Béjart was the actor who stammered.

11 Le Boulanger de Chalussay *Elomire hypocondre*, in Molière, *Oeuvres complètes*, II, 1270. "Nous y revînmes donc, sûrs d'y faire merveille, / Après avoir appris l'un et l'autre Corneille: / Et tel était déjà le bruit de mon renom / Qu'on nous donna d'abord la salle de Bourbon. / Là, par *Héraclius*, nous ouvrons un théâtre, / Où je crois tout charmer et tout rendre idolâtre; / Mais, hélas! qui l'eût cru, par un contraire effet, / Loin que tout fût charmé, tout fut mal satisfait; / Et par ce coup d'essai, que je croyais de maître, / Je me vis en état de n'oser plus paraître. / Je prends coeur, toutefois, et d'un air glorieux, / J'affiche, je harangue, et fais tout de mon mieux, / Mais inutilement je tentai la fortune: / Apres *Héraclius*, on siffla *Rodogune*, / *Cinna* le fut de même, et *le Cid* tout charmant / Reçut avec *Pompée* un pareil traitement. / Dans ce sensible affront, ne sachant où m'en prendre, / Je me vis mille fois sur le point de me pendre."

12 *Ibid.*, 1271.

13 La Grange, *Registre*, I, 2–3. "L'Estourdy comedie du Sr. Moliere, passa pour nouvelle a Paris eust un grand succez et produisit de part pour chaque acteur soixante et dix pistolles." A *pistole* was worth 11 *livres*, so 770 *livres*.

14 Samuel Chappuzeau, *Le Théâtre François* (Paris: Éditions d'Aujourd'hui, s.d), p. 60.

15 Jean Loret, *La Muze historique*, eds. J. Ravenal and V. de La Pelouze (Paris: Jamet, 1859–78), III, 22.

16 La Grange, *Registre*, I,1.

17 *Ibid.*, 5.

18 Jurgens and Maxfield-Miller, *Cent Ans*, pp. 647–9.

19 Soulié, *Recherches*, p. 234.

20 Georges Mongrédien, *Daily Life in the French Theatre at the Time of Molière*, trans. Claire Eliane Engel (London: George Allen and Unwin, Ltd., 1969), p. 68.

21 Molière, *Oeuvres complètes*, II, 1183–4. "D'une brillante grâce / Vos traits sont embellis, / Et votre teint efface / Les roses et les lys / De nos jeunes Philis; / L'esprit, l'air agréable, / Et la taille admirable / En vous se trouvent joints . . ."

22 Grimarest, *Vie de Molière*, pp. 109–10. ". . . la de *** l'amusoit quand il ne travailloit pas. Un de ses amis, qui étoit surpris qu'un homme aussi délicat que Molière eût si mal placé son inclination, voulut le dégouter de cette Comédienne. 'Est-ce la vertu, la beauté ou l'esprit,' lui-dit-il, 'que vous font aimer cette femme-là? Vous savez que la Barre, et Florimont sont de ses amis; qu'elle n'est point belle, que c'est un vrai squelette; et qu'elle n'a pas le sens commun.' 'Je sais tout cela, Monsieur,' lui répondit Molière; 'mais je suis acoutumé à ses deffauts; et il faudroit que je prisse trop sur moi, pour m'acommoder aux imperfections d'une autre; je n'en ai ni le tems, ni la patience.'"

23 *Oeuvres de Chapelle et de Bachaumont* (Paris: P. Jannet, 1854), p. 202. "Jeune et faible, rampe par bas / Dans le fond des prés, et n'a pas / Encor la vigueur et la force / De pénétrer la tendre écorce / Du saule qui lui tend les bras. / La branche, amoureuse et fleurie, / Pleurant pour ses naissants appas, /

Toute en sève et larmes, l'en prie, / Et, jalouse de la prairie, / Dans cinq ou six jours se promet / De l'attirer à son sommet."

24 *Ibid.* "Vous montrerez ces beaux vers à mademoiselle Menou seulement; aussi bien sont-ils la figure d'elle et de vous." The only other mention of "Menou" known to us is in the cast list of *Andromède* from Lyon where Menou is assigned to play the role of the nymph Éphire. Éphire was one of two little nymphs, apparently played by two young girls, children of actors then in the troupe: the seventeen-year-old Madeleine L'Hermite – Madlon – and the ten-year-old Armande Béjart – Menou.

25 Ibid., p. 204. "Pour les autres, vous verrez bien qu'il est à propos surtout que vos femmes ne les voient pas, et pour ce qu'ils contiennent, et, parce qu'ils sont . . . tous des plus méchants. Je les ai faits pour répondre à cet endroit de votre lettre où vous particularisez le déplaisir que vous donnent les partialités de vos trois grandes actrices pour la distribution de vos rôles. Il faut être à Paris pour en résoudre ensemble, et tâchant de faire réussir l'application de vos rôles à leur caractère, remédier à ce démêlé qui vous donne tant de peine. En vérité, grand homme, vous avez besoin de toute votre tête en conduisant les leurs, et je vous compare à Jupiter pendant la guerre de Troie. La comparaison n'est pas odieuse, et la fantaisie me prit de la suivre quand elle me vint. Qu'il vous souvienne donc de l'embarras où ce maître des dieux se trouva pendant cette guerre . . . pour réduire les trois déesses à ses volontés: . . . Voilà l'histoire. Que t'en semble? / Crois-tu pas qu'un homme avisé / Voit par là qu'il n'est pas aisé / D'accorder trois femmes ensemble. / Fais-en donc ton profit; surtout, / Tiens-toi neutre, et tout plein d'Homère, / Dis-toi bien qu'en vain l'homme espère / Pouvoir jamais venir à bout / De ce qu'un grand Dieu n'a su faire."

26 Couton, "Notice," in Molière, *Oeuvres complètes*, I, 255. "Tout le monde dit qu'ils ont joué détestablement sa pièce; et le grand monde qu'ils ont eu à leur farce des *Précieuses*, après l'avoir quittée, fait bien connaître qu'ils ne sont propres qu'à soutenir de semblables bagatelles, et que la plus forte pièce tomberait entre leurs mains."

27 *Ibid.*, pp. 254–5.

28 The doubling of the price in the *parterre* appears to have continued until the last performance during carnival on February 22. This, like all information on repertory and receipts, unless specifically cited to another source, can be found in the *Registre* of La Grange.

29 See *Le Songe de reveur* in *Collection Moliéresque* (Geneva: Slatkine Reprints, 1969), p. 8. The author may have been Quinault.

30 The machinations of Somaize are revealed at length by Georges Couton in his "Notice," Molière, *Oeuvres complètes*, I, 249–62, and in Georges Mongrédien, *Comédies et pamphlets sur Molière* (Paris: A.-G. Nizet, 1986), pp. 11–25. The latter publication also includes a complete text of *Les Véritables Prétieuses.*

31 Mongrédien, *Comédies et pamphlets*, p. 36. ". . . il a copié les Pretieuses de Monsieur l'abbé de Pure, joüées par l'Italiens, mais encore qu'il a imité par

une singerie, dont il est seul capable, le Medecin volant, et plusieurs autres pieces des mesmes Italiens qu'il n'imite pas seulement en ce qu'ils ont joüé sur leur theatre, mais encor en leurs postures, contrefaisant sans cesse sur le sien et Trivelin et Scaramouche, mais qu'attendre d'un homme qui tire toute sa gloire de Memoires Gillot-Gorgeu [Guillot-Gorju], qu'il a achetez de la veufve, et dont il s'adopte tous les ouvrages?"

32 *La Muse royale,* May 3, 1660, in Mongrédien, *Recueil,* I, 124–5.

33 Couton, "Notice," in Molière, *Oeuvres complètes,* I, 250. "Le livre propose d'autre part une étude psychologique voire sociologique de la précieuse, de ses diverses variétés, de ses conditions de vie."

34 Mongrédien, *Recueil,* I, 123. "C'est toujours quelque chose d'excellent en quelque métier que ce soit et, pour parler selon le vulgaire, il vaut mieux être le premier d'un village que le dernier d'une ville, bon *farceur* que méchant comédien."

35 Molière, *Oeuvres complètes,* I, 264.

36 Mongrédien, *Recueil,* I, 112. "J'étais à la première représentation des *Précieuses ridicules* de Molière, au Petit-Bourbon. Mlle de Rambouillet y était, Mme de Grignan, tout le cabinet de l'Hôtel de Rambouillet, M. Chapelain et plusieurs autres de ma connaissance. La pièce fut jouée avec un applaudissement général, et j'en fus si satisfait en mon particulier, que je vis dès lors l'effet qu'elle allait produire. Au sortir de la comédie, prenant M. Chapelain par la main: 'Monsieur, lui dis-je, nous approuvions vous et moi toutes les sottises qui viennent d'être critiquées si finement et avec tant de bon sens; mais, croyez-moi, pour me servir de ce que Saint-Remy dit à Clovis, il nous faudra brûler ce que nous avons adoré et adorer ce que nous avons brûler.'"

37 Molière, *Oeuvres complètes,* I, 264.

38 *Oeuvres de Chapelle et de Bachaumont,* pp. 81–2.

39 Molière, *Oeuvres complètes,* I, 266. "J'ai un certain valet . . . qui passe, au sentiment de beaucoup de gens, pour une manière de bel esprit; car il n'y a rien à meilleur marché que le bel esprit maintenant. C'est un extravagant, qui s'est mis dans la tête de vouloir faire l'homme de condition."

40 This odd description of the play circulated in manuscript and was later printed. Mlle Desjardins claims to not have seen the play herself, but only to have heard about it from a spectator. Nonetheless, her delightful description of Mascarille deserves to be read.

41 In Molière, *Oeuvres complètes,* I, 1008. "Imaginez-vous donc, Madame, que sa perruque était si grande qu'elle balayait la place à chaque fois qu'il faisait la révérence, et son chapeau si petit qu'il était aisé de juger que le marquis le portait bien plus souvent dans la main que sur la tête; son rabat se pouvait appeler un honnête peignoir, et ses canons semblaient n'être faits que pour servir de caches aux enfants qui jouent à la clinemusette; . . . Un brandon de galants lui sortait de sa poche comme une corne d'abondance, et ses souliers étaient si couverts de rubans qu'il ne m'est pas possible de vous dire s'ils étaient de roussi, de vache d'Angleterre ou de maroquin; de moins sais-je bien qu'ils avaient un demi-pied de haut, et que j'étais fort en peine de savoir

comment des talons si hauts et si délicats pouvaient porter le corps du marquis, ses rubans, ses canons et la poudre."

6 HUSBANDS AND WIVES

1 Jurgens and Maxfield-Miller, *Cent Ans*, p. 344. ". . . pour lui donner moien de supporter les frais et despences qui lui convient faire en ceste ville de Paris où il est venu par son commandement pour le plaisir et recreation de Sadite Majesté, et ce pour les six premiers moys de ladict année."

2 Mongrédien, *Recueil*, I, 128. The author's name in the *Registre* of privileges is La Neufvillaine; in the printed edition it is La Neufvillenaine. Both names are susceptible to interpretation.

3 *Ibid.*, 129–30.

4 Jurgens and Maxfield-Miller, *Cent Ans*, pp. 345–51.

5 La Grange, *Registre*, I, 25–6. "Le Lundy 11me Octob. le Theastre du petit-Bourbon commancea à estre desmoly par Monsr de Ratabon sur Intendant des bastimens du Roy sans en avertir La Troupe qui se trouva fort surprise de demeurer sans Theastre, on alla se plaindre au Roy, a qui Monsr de Ratabon dit que la place de la salle estoit necessaire pour le bastiment du Louvre, et que les dedans de la salle qui avoient esté faits pour les ballets du Roy appartenans a S. Mté il n'avoit pas cru qu'il fallut entrer en considera-tion de la Comedie pour avancer le dessein du Louvre. La meschante inten-tion de Mr de Ratabon estoit apparente." This is a curious tale. Historians of the Louvre do not report any construction or plans for construction between the death of Lemercier, who had extended the south wing of the Cour Carré and built the western half of the north wing, in 1654 and the appointment of Colbert as Surintendant des Bâtiments in 1664. (See Paul Fréart de Chantelou, *Diary of the Cavaliere Bernini's Visit to France*, ed. with introduction and notes by Anthony Blunt [Princeton, NJ: Princeton University Press, 1985], Appendix A, "The Louvre," p. 337.) On the other hand, the gazetteer Loret reported a plan to demolish the Petit-Bourbon in July 1659. (See Léon Chancerel, "Antoine de Ratabon et la démolition du Théâtre du Petit-Bourbon," *Revue d'Histoire du Théâtre* 2 [1950] 195–7.) If he was right and the actors were paying attention, then there was no reason for their astonishment on October 10, 1660. It seems a little unreasonable to suppose, as some have done, that Molière's enemies at court were so pow-erful they could have had his theatre pulled down.

6 Sauval, *Histoire et recherches*, I, 163.

7 La Grange says L'Espy was in charge, but the contracts were made by Du Croisy. Jurgens and Maxfield-Miller, *Cent Ans*, pp.351–5.

8 According to the *Registre*, I, 42, the troupe had paid out 2,114 *livres* at the time it moved into the new theatre, and continued to make payments through the end of the season. However, La Grange is not specific about the amounts of all these payments. The 4,000-*livre* figure is based on the amount paid by

the Italians when they returned to Paris in January 1662 and began to play the *jours extraordinaire* at the Palais-Royal. They paid the Troupe de Monsieur 2,000 *livres* or half of the cost of establishing the theatre.

9 La Grange, *Registre*, I, 27. "Mais toutte la Troupe de MONSIEUR demeura stable, tous les acteurs aymoient le Sr de Molière leur chef qui joignoit a un merite et une capacité extraordinaire une honnesteté et une maniere engageante qui les obligea tous a luy protester qu'ils vouloient courir sa fortune et qu'ils ne le quitteroient jamais quelque proposition qu'on leur fist et quelque avantage qu'ils pussent trouver ailleurs."

10 This comparison is made by Georges Couton in the "Notice" for *Dom Garcie*. Molière, *Oeuvres complètes*, I, 338–9.

11 *Ibid.*, 349. "Et que vous bannirez enfin ce monstre affreux / Que de son noir venin empoisonne vos feux."

12 *Ibid.*, 394. ". . . Les moyens glorieux de sortir de la vie, / Faire par un grand coup, qui signale ma foi, / Qu'en expirant pour elle, elle ait regret à moi, / Et qu'elle puisse dire, en se voyant vengée: / 'C'est par son trop d'amour qu'il m'avait outragée.'"

13 *Ibid.*, 1020.

14 Bordonove, *Molière*, p. 136. A reference in Donneau de Visé's *La Vengeance des marquis*, written during the quarrel of *L'École des femmes*, seems to show conclusively that Madeleine played Done Elvire. In Molière, *Oeuvres complètes*, I, 1104.

15 La Grange, *Registre*, I, 33.

16 Molière, *Oeuvres complètes*, I, 425. "Et l'école du monde . . . / Instruit mieux, à mon gré, que ne fait aucun livre."

17 *Ibid.*, I, 426–7. "SGAN: Quoi? si vous l'épousez, elle pourra prétendre / Les mêmes libertés que fille on lui voit prendre? / ARIS: Pourquoi non? SGAN: Vos désirs lui seront complaisants, / Jusques à lui laisser et mouches et rubans? / ARIS: Sans doute. SGAN: À lui souffrir, en cervelle troublée, / De courir tous les bals et les lieux d'assemblée? / ARIS: Oui, vraiment. SGAN: Et chez vous iront les damoiseaux? / ARIS: Et quoi donc? SGAN: Qui joueront et donneront cadeaux? / ARIS: D'accord. SGAN: Et votre femme entendra les fleurettes? / ARIS: Fort bien. SGAN: Et vous verrez ces visites muguettes / D'un oeil à témoigner de n'en être point soûl? / ARIS: Cela s'entend. SGAN: Allez, vous êtes un vieux fou."

18 *Ibid.*, 471. "Cette déloyauté confond mon jugement; / Et je ne pense pas que Satan en personne / Puisse être si méchant qu'une telle friponne. / J'aurais pour elle au feu mis la main que voilà: / Malheureux qui se fie à femme après cela! / La meilleure est toujours en malice féconde; / C'est un sexe engendré pour damner tout le monde. / J'y renonce à jamais, à ce sexe trompeur, / Et je le donne tout au diable de bon coeur."

19 *Ibid.*, 425. "Un ordre paternel l'oblige à m'épouser; / Mais mon dessein n'est pas de la tyranniser. / Je sais bien que nos ans ne se rapportent guère, / Et je laisse à son choix liberté tout entière./ Si quatre mille écus de rente bien

venants, / Une grande tendresse et des soins complaisants / Peuvent, à son avis, pour un tel mariage, / Réparer entre nous l'inégalité d'âge, / Elle peut m'épouser; sinon, choisir ailleurs."

20 See Couton, "Chronologie de la querelle de *L'École des femme*," in Molière, *Oeuvres complètes*, I, 1013.

21 Frontispieces by François Chauveau, *Oeuvres de Monsieur de Molière*, Paris, 1666. Vol. 1, Sganarelle; Vol. 2, Arnolphe. Frontispieces by Brissart, *Les Oeuvres*, 1682. *Le Cocu imaginaire*, *L'École des maris*, *L'École des femmes*.

22 Molière, *Oeuvres complètes*, I, 548. "Mais une femme habile est un mauvais présage."

23 *Ibid.*, 572–4. "Il jurait qu'il m'aimait d'une amour sans seconde, / Et me disait des mots les plus gentils du monde, / Des choses que jamais rien ne peut égaler, / Et dont, toutes les fois que je l'entends parler, / La douceur me chatouille et là-dedans remue / Certain je ne sais quoi dont je suis toute émue."

24 *Ibid.*, 580. "Bien qu'on soit deux moitiés de la société, / Ces deux moitiés pourtant n'ont point d'égalité."

25 *Ibid.*, 613. "Mais, à vous parler franchement entre nous, / Il est plus pour cela selon mon goût que vous. / Chez vous le mariage est fâcheux et pénible, / Et vos discours en font une image terrible; / Mais, las! il le fait, lui, si rempli de plaisirs, / Que de se marier il donne des désirs."

26 *Ibid.*, 616–17. "ARN: Hé bien! faisons la paix. Va, petite traitresse, / Je te pardonne tout et te rends ma tendresse. / Considère par-là l'amour que j'ai pour toi, / Et me voyant si bon, en revanche aime-moi. AGN: Du meilleur de mon coeur je voudrais vous complaire: / Que me coûterait-il, si je le pouvais faire? / ARN: Mon pauvre petit bec, tu le peux, si tu veux. / Écoute seulement ce soupir amoureux, / Vois ce regard mourant, contemple ma personne, / Et quitte ce morveux et l'amour qu'il te donne. / C'est quelque sort qu'il faut qu'il ait jeté sur toi, / Et tu seras cent fois plus heureuse avec moi. / Ta forte passion est d'être brave et leste: / Tu le seras toujours, va, je te le proteste, / Sans cesse, nuit et jour, je te caresserai, / Je te bouchonnerai, baiserai, mangerai . . ."

27 *Ibid.*, 551. "Je sais un paysan qu'on appelait Gros-Pierre, / Qui n'ayant pour tout bien qu'un seul quartier de terre, / Y fit tout à l'entour faire un fossé bourbeux, / Et de Monsieur de l'Isle en prit le nom pompeux."

28 "Au Lecteur," *Le Portrait du Peintre* in Molière, *Oeuvres complètes*, I, 1050. ". . . la gloire outragée des plus honnêtes gens de notre siècle."

29 In Molière, *Oeuvres complètes*, I, 1009–142. See also Georges Mongrédien, *La Querelle de* L'École des femmes (Paris: Marcel Didier, 1971).

30 Donneau de Visé, *Nouvelles nouvelles*, in Molière, *Oeuvres complètes*, I, 1021.

31 Molière, I, 644. ". . . ramassées parmi les boues des halles et de la place Maubert."

32 *Ibid.*, 566.

33 *Ibid.*, 649–50. "CLIM: Ah! ruban tant qu'il vous plaira; mais ce *le*, où elle s'arrête, n'est pas mis pour des prunes. Il vient sur ce *le* d'étranges pensées. Ce

le scandalise furieusement; et, quoi que vous puissiez dire, vous ne sauriez défendre l'insolence de ce *le*. ÉLISE: Il est vrai, ma cousine, je suis pour Madame contre ce *le*. Ce *le* est insolent au dernier point, et vous avez tort de défendre ce *le*. CLIM: Il a une obscénité qui n'est pas supportable. ÉLISE: Comment dites-vous ce mot-là, Madame? CLIM: Obscénité, Madame. ÉLISE: Ah! mon Dieu! obscénité. Je ne sais ce que ce mot veut dire; mais je le trouve le plus joli du monde."

34 *Ibid.*, 662–3. "Il semble, à vous ouïr parler, que ces règles de l'art soient les plus grands mystères du monde; et cependant ce ne sont que quelques observations aisées, que le bon sens a faites sur ce qui peut ôter le plaisir que l'on prend à ces sortes de poèmes; et le même bon sens qui a fait autrefois ces observations les fait aisément tous les jours sans le secors d'Horace et d'Aristote. Je voudrais bien savoir si la grande règle de toutes les règles n'est pas de plaire, et si une pièce de théâtre qui a attrapé son but n'a pas suivi un bon chemin."

35 *Ibid.*, 663. "J'ai remarqué une chose de ces messieurs-là: c'est que ceux qui parlent le plus des règles, et qui les savent mieux que les autres, font des comédies que personne ne trouve belles."

36 *Ibid*, 1287–9 and 1289n.

37 *Ibid*, 1290n. Taken from a "vie de Molière" that precedes an *Oeuvres* published in The Hague in 1725. The anecdote is supported by Donneau de Visé's allusion in *Zélinde* to "l'avanture de Tarte à la crème arrivée depuis peu à Élomire." In Molière, *Oeuvres complètes*, I, 1039.

38 In *ibid.*, 1022. ". . . si vous voulez savoir pourquoi presque dans toutes ses pièces il raille tant les cocus, et dépeint si naturellement les jaloux, c'est qu'il est du nombre de ces derniers . . . Pour lui rendre justice, qu'il ne témoigne pas sa jalousie hors du théâtre, il a trop de prudence . . ."

39 In *ibid.*, 1055.

40 Donneau de Visé, *La Vengeance des marquis* in *ibid.*, 1106.

41 Brossette, *Correspondance*, p. 533.

42 Molière, *Oeuvres complètes*, I, 694–6. "Vous voudriez que je prisse feu d'abord contre eux, et qu'à leur exemple j'allasse éclater promptement en invectives et en injures . . . Ne se sont-ils pas préparés de bonne volonté à ces sortes de choses? Et lorsqu'ils ont délibéré s'ils joueraient *Le Portrait du peintre* sur la crainte d'une riposte, quelques-uns d'entre eux n'ont-ils pas répondu: 'Qu'il nous rende toutes les injures qu'il voudra, pourvu que nous gagnions de l'argent.' N'est-ce pas là la marque d'une âme fort sensible à la honte? et ne me vengerais-je pas bien d'eux en leur donnant ce qu'ils veulent bien recevoir? . . . Allez, allez, ce n'est pas cela. Le plus grand mal que je leur aie fait, c'est que j'ai eu le bonheur de plaire un peu plus qu'ils n'auraient voulu; . . . Mais laissons-les faire tant qu'ils voudront; toutes leur entreprises ne doivent point m'inquiéter. Ils critiquent mes pièces; tant mieux; et Dieu me garde d'en faire jamais qui leur plaise! Ce serait une mauvaise affaire pour moi . . . les comédiens ne me l'ont déchaîné que pour m'engager à une sotte guerre, et me détourner, par cet artifice, des autres ouvrages que j'ai à faire; . . . Mais

enfin j'en ferai ma déclaration publiquement. Je ne prétends faire aucune réponse à toutes leurs critiques et leurs contre-critiques. Qu'ils disent tous les maux du monde de mes pièces, j'en suis d'accord. Qu'ils s'en saisissent après nous, qu'ils les retournent comme un habit pour le mettre sur leur théâtre, et tâchent à profiter de quelque agrément qu'on y trouve, et d'un peu de bonheur que j'ai, j'y consens: ils en ont besoin, et je serai bien aise de contribuer à les faire subsister, pourvu qu'ils se contentent de ce que je puis leur accorder avec bienséance. La courtoisie doit avoir des bornes; et il y a des choses qui ne font rire ni les spectateurs, ni celui dont on parle. Je leur abandonne de bon coeur mes ouvrages, ma figure, mes gestes, mes paroles, mon ton de voix, et my façon de réciter, pour en faire et dire tout ce qu'il leur plaira, s'ils en peuvent tirer quelque avantage: ... Mais, en leur abandonnant tout cela, ils me doivent faire la grâce de me laisser le reste et de ne point toucher à des matières de la nature de celles sur lesquelles on m'a dit qu'ils m'attaquaient dans leurs comédies. C'est de quoi je prierai civilement cet honnête Monsieur qui se mêle d'écrire pour eux, et voilà toute la réponse qu'ils auront de moi."

43 In *ibid.*, 1100.

44 Jean Racine, "Correspondance" in *Oeuvres complètes*, ed. Raymond Picard (Paris: Gallimard, 1950–2), II, 459. "Montfleury a fait une requête contre Molière, et l'a donnée au Roi. Il l'accuse d'avoir épousé la fille, et d'avoir autrefois couché avec la mère. Mais Montfleury n'est point écouté à la cour." All quotations from Racine are taken from this edition unless otherwise cited.

7 THE COURTIER

1 Jean de La Fontaine, *Oeuvres complètes. II. Oeuvres diverses*, ed. Pierre Clarac (Paris: Gallimard, 1958), p. 523. All quotations from La Fontaine are taken from this edition, unless otherwise cited.

2 *Ibid.*, p. 522.

3 Anatole France, *Vaux le Vicomte* (Etrépilly: Les Presses du Village, 1987), p. 64. "Il y avait longtemps que le Roi avait dit qu'il voulait aller à Vaux, maison superbe de ce surintendant; et, quoique la prudence dût l'empêcher de faire voir au Roi une chose que marquait si fort le mauvais usage des finances, et qu'aussi la bonté du Roi dût le retenir d'aller chez un homme qu'il allait perdre, néanmoins ni l'un ni l'autre n'y firent réflexion."

4 *Ibid.*, pp. 100–1.

5 La Fontaine, *Oeuvres diverses*, p. 525. In a variant version of the letter, La Fontaine writes "notre homme."

6 Molière, *Oeuvres complètes*, I, 483. "C'est une chose, je crois, toute nouvelle qu'une comédie ait été conçue, faite, apprise et représentée en quinze jours."

7 Roger Herzel, *The Original Casting of Molière's Plays* (Ann Arbor, MI: UMI Research Press, 1981), pp. 43–5. Herzel believes Molière played only four

roles in the original production, but the gazetteer Robinet indicates that the author played seven roles in a 1668 revival.

8 In La Fontaine, *Oeuvres diverses*, p. 525.

9 Molière, *Oeuvres complètes*, I, 484. "Il ne sera pas hors de propos de dire deux paroles des ornements qu'on a mêlés avec la comédie. Le dessein était de donner un ballet aussi; et, comme il n'y avait qu'un petit nombre choisi de danseurs excellents, on fut contraint de séparer les entrées de ce ballet, et l'avis fut de les jeter dans les entractes de la comédie, afin que ces intervalles donnassent temps aux mêmes baladins de revenir sous d'autres habits. De sorte que, pour ne point rompre aussi le fil de la pièce par ces manières d'intermèdes, on s'avisa de les coudre au sujet du mieux que l'on put, et de ne faire qu'une seule chose du ballet et de la comédie."

10 *Ibid.*, 1253–4 and 1254n. Molière definitely played this role. Among the costumes for *Les Fâcheux* described in his inventory were "le justeaucorps de chasse, sabre et le sangle."

11 *Ibid.*, 481–2. ". . . et je conçois par-là ce que je serais capable d'exécuter pour une comédie entière, si j'étais inspiré par de pareils commandements. Ceux qui sont nés en un rang élevé peuvent se proposer l'honneur de servir Votre Majesté dans les grands emplois, mais, pour moi, toute la gloire où je puis aspirer, c'est de la réjouir. Je borne là l'ambition de mes souhaits; et je crois qu'en quelque façon ce n'est pas être inutile à la France que de contribuer quelque chose au divertissement de son roi."

12 La Grange and Vivot in Molière, *Oeuvres complètes*, I, 999. "L'estime dont Sa Majesté l'honorait augumentait de jour en jour, aussi bien que celle des courtisans les plus éclairés . . . Son éxercice de la comédie ne l'empêchait pas de servir le Roi dans sa charge de valet de chambre, oú il se rendait très assidu. Ainsi il se fit remarquer à la Cour pour un homme civil et honnête . . . s'accommodant à l'humeur de ceux avec qui il était obligé de vivre."

13 Pierre Bonvallet, *Molière de tous les jours: Echos, potins et anecdotes* (Paris: Le Pré aux Clercs, 1985), 79–80. "Voici un trait que j'ai appris de feu Bellocq, valet de chambre du roi, homme de beaucoup d'esprit et qui faisoit de trés jolis vers. Un jour que Molière se présenta pour faire le lit du Roi, R . . ., aussi valet de chambre de Sa Majesté, qui devoit faire le lit avec lui, se retira brusquement en disant qu'il ne le feroit pas avec un comédien; Bellocq s'approcha dans le moment et dit: 'Monsieur de Molière, vous voulez bien que j'ai l'honneur de faire le lit du Roi avec vous?'" According to the *État général des officiers de la maison du Roi*, the names of Poquelin and Bellocq coincide in 1662.

14 Bonvallet, *Tous les jours*, 110–11.

15 *Ibid.* "Un vieux médecin ordinaire de Louis XIV, qui existait encore lors du mariage de Louis XV, raconta au père de M. Campan une anecdote trop marquante pour qu'elle soit restée inconnue. Cependant ce vieux médecin, nommé M. Lafosse, était un homme d'esprit, d'honneur, et incapable d'inventer cette histoire. Il disait que Louis XIV, ayant su que les officiers de sa chambre témoignaient, par des dédains offensants, combien ils étaient

blessés de manger à la table du contrôleur de la bouche avec Molière, valet de chambre du roi, parce qu'il avait joué la comédie, cet homme célèbre s'abstenait de se présenter à cette table.

Louis XIV, voulant fair cesser des outrages qui ne devaient pas s'adresser à un des plus grands génies de son siècle, dit un matin à Molière à l'heure de son petit lever:

'On dit que vous faites maigre chère ici, Molière, et que les officiers de ma chambre ne vous trouvent pas fait pour manger avec eux. Vous avez peut-être faim; moi-même je m'éveille avec un très bon appétit: mettez-vous à cette table, et que l'on me serve mon en-cas de nuit.'

Alors le roi, coupant sa volaille et ayant ordonné à Molière de s'asseoir, lui sert une aile, en prend en même temps une pour lui, et ordonne que l'on introduise les entrées familières, qui se composaient des personnes les plus marquantes et les plus favorisées de la cour.

'Vous me voyez, leur dit le roi, occupé de faire manger Moliére, que mes valets de chambre ne trouvent pas assez bonne compagnie pour eux.'

De ce moment, Molière n'eut plus besoin de se présenter à cette table de service; toute la cour s'empressa de lui faire des invitations."

16 Louis XIV, *Mémoires pour l'instruction du Dauphin*, ed. Pierre Goubert (Paris: Imprimerie Nationale, 1992), p. 134. ". . . ces divertissements publics, qui ne sont pas tant les nôtres que ceux de notre cour et de tous nos peuples." These *Mémoires* were partly the work of Louis himself, partly the work of a series of collaborators, including Colbert. The final collaborator was Pellisson, Fouquet's former secretary. Louis thus added Fouquet's panegyrist to the list of those employed by him who had formerly worked for the Intendant.

17 *Ibid.*, pp. 136–7. "Je crus que, sans s'arrêter à quelque chose de particulier et de moindre, elle devait représenter en quelque sorte les devoirs d'un prince, et m'exciter éternellement moi-même à les remplir."

18 Mnouchkine, of course, has an agenda; she proposes to show the unhappy effects of court patronage and commercial success.

19 Jurgens and Maxfield-Miller, *Cent Ans*, p. 570. "*Item*, un juste à corps, un haulte de chausse de petite estoffe avecq une veste de satin doublé de ouate et un bas de soye, prisé quinze *livres*; *Item*, un juste au corps et chausse de drap d'Hollande noir, une paire de bas de soye, prisé dix *livres*; *Item*, un juste à corps et chausse de droguet brun, un juste au corps doublé de taffetas noir, une paire de bas de laine et une d'estame, prisé quinze *livres*; *Item*, un juste à corps et reingrave de drap d'Holland musque avec une veste de satin de la Chine blanc, les jaretieres et bas de soye avecq une garnitture de satin, prisé vingt cinq *livres*; *Item*, une robbe de chambre de brocard rayé, doublé de taffetas bleu, prisé vingt cinq *livres*."

20 *Ibid.*, p. 709.

21 Couton, "Notice," in Molière, *Oeuvres complètes*, I, 629.

22 Mongrédien, *Recueil*, I, 183. "Avez-vous le Remerciement qu'il a fait sur sa pension de bel esprit? Rien n'a été trouvé si galant ni si joli."

23 Molière, *Oeuvres complètes*, I,633. "Mais les grands princes n'aiment guère / Que les compliments qui sont courts; / Et le nôtre surtout a bien d'autres affaires / Que d'écouter tous vos discours. / La louange et l'encens n'est pas ce qui le touche; / Dès que vous ouvrirez la bouche / Pour lui parler de grâce et de bienfait, / Il comprendra d'abord ce que vous voudrez dire, / Et se mettant doucement à sourire / D'un air qui sur les coeurs fait un charmant effet, / Il passera comme un trait, / Et cela vous doit suffire: / Voilà votre compliment fait."

24 A figure based on La Grange's *Registre* that is probably not accurate. For instance, La Grange makes no mention of any payment for the visit the troupe made to Fontainebleau in August 1661, while court records include a sum of 15,428 *livres* spent on that occasion for decorations, dancers, and "*nourriture et récompense des comédiens.*" (Mongrédien, *Recueil*, I, 152, citing BN Ms. Mélanges Colbert, 264, fol. 11.) Another entry in court records, however, assigns this payment to 1662. Other inconsistencies exist as well. La Grange's figures are interesting, however, because of the average of about 6,000 *livres* a year. This was the amount of the subsidy granted the troupe when the king took over its patronage.

25 Molière, *Oeuvres complètes*, I, 677–8. ". . . les rois n'aiment rien tant qu'une prompte obéissance, et ne se plaisent point du tout à trouver des obstacles . . . Ils veulent des plaisirs qui ne se fassent point attendre; et les moins préparés leur sont toujours les plus agréables. Nous ne devons jamais nous regarder dans ce qu'ils désirent de nous; nous ne sommes que pour leur plaire; et lorsqu'ils nous ordonnent quelque chose, c'est à nous à profiter vite de l'envie où ils sont. Il vaut mieux s'acquitter mal de ce qu'ils nous demandent que de ne s'en acquitter pas assez tôt; et si l'on a la honte de n'avoir pas bien réussi, on a toujours la gloire d'avoir obéi vite à leur commandements."

26 *Ibid.*, 679–80. "Qui? Ce jeune homme bien fait? Vous moquez-vous? Il faut un roi qui soit gros et gras comme quatre, un roi, morbleu! qui soit entripaillé comme il faut, un roi d'une vaste circonférence, et qui puisse remplir un trône de la belle manière. La belle chose qu'un roi d'une taille galante!"

27 Couton, "Notice," in Molière, *Oeuvres complètes*, I, 741. ". . . comme un abcès, purulent, nauséeux, dans le décor splendide . . ."

28 I have drawn largely from the official description: *Les Plaisirs de l'Île enchantée, Course de bague, collation ornée de machines, comédie mêlée de danse et de musique, Ballet du Palais d'Alcine, Feu d'artifice et autres fêtes galantes et magnifiques, faites par le Roi à Versailles, le 7 mai 1664 et continuées plusieurs autres jours* (Paris: Robert Ballard, 1664). This is reprinted in Molière, *Oeuvres complètes*, I, 748–829. It includes the text of *La Princesse d'Élide*.

29 Molière, *Oeuvres*, I, 788. "Ah, Monsieur l'ours, je suis votre serviteur de tout mon coeur. De grâce, épargnez-moi. Je vous assure que je ne vaux rien du tout à manger, je n'ai que la peau et les os, et je vois de certaines gens là-bas qui seraient bien mieux votre affaire. Eh! eh! eh! Monseigneur, tout doux, s'il vous plaît. La! la! la! la! Ah! Monseigneur, que Votre Altesse est jolie et

bien faite! Elle a tout à fait l'air galant et la taille la plus mignonne du monde. Ah! beau poil, belle tête, beaux yeux brillants et bien fendus! Ah! beau petit nez! belle petite bouche! petites quenottes jolies! Ah! belle gorge! belles petites menottes! petits ongles bien faits! A l'aide! au secours! . . ."

30 *Ibid.*, 777. "Je crois que d'un prince on peut tout présumer, / Dès qu'on voit que son âme est capable d'aimer. / . . . Aux nobles actions elle pousse les coeurs, / Et tous les grands héros ont senti ses ardeurs. / Devant mes yeux, Seigneur, a passé votre enfance, / Et j'ai de vos vertus vu fleurir l'esperance; / Mes regards observaient en vous des qualités / Où je reconnaissais le sang dont vous sortez; / J'y découvrais un fonds d'esprit et de lumière; / Je vous trouvais bien fait, l'air grand, et l'âme fière; / . . . Mais je m'inquiétais de ne voir point d'amour."

31 Couton, "Notice," in Molière, *Oeuvres complètes*, I, 743–4.

32 Molière, *Oeuvres complètes*, I, 641. ". . . qui prouve se bien que la véritable dévotion n'est point contraire aux honnêtes divertissements; qui . . . ne dédaigne pas de rire de cette même bouche dont Elle prie si bien Dieu."

33 Couton, "Notice," in *ibid.*, I, 838.

34 A stage direction indicates that Molière also sang in the role of Sosie in *Amphitryon*.

35 Molière, *Oeuvres complètes*, II, 295.

36 *Ibid.*, 503. ". . . lorsqu'on a, comme moi, épousé une méchante femme, le meilleur parti qu'on puisse prendre, c'est de s'aller jeter dans l'eau la tête la première."

37 *Ibid.*, 440. "Et c'est assez, je crois, pour remettre ton coeur / Dans l'état auquel il doit être, / Et rétablir chez toi la paix et la douceur. / Mon nom, qu'incessamment toute la terre adore, / Étouffe ici les bruits qui pouvaient éclater. / Un partage avec Jupiter / N'a rien du tout qui déshonore; / Et sans doute il ne peut être que glorieux / De se voir le rival du souverain des dieux."

38 *Ibid.*, 439–40. "Et les coups de bâton d'un dieu / Font honneur à qui les endure." . . . "Et je ne vis de ma vie / Un dieu plus diable que toi."

39 *Ibid.*, 441. "Chez toi doit naître un fils qui . . . / Remplira de ses faits tout le vaste univers."

40 Couton, "Notice," in *ibid.*, II, 355.

41 Molière, *Oeuvres complètes*, II, 482–3. ". . . mon dessein n'est pas de renoncer au monde, et de m'enterrer toute vive dans un mari. Comment? parce qu'un homme s'avise de nous épouser, il faut d'abord que toutes choses soient finies pour nous, et que nous rompions tout commerce avec les vivants . . . Je me moque de cela, et ne veux point mourir si jeune . . . je veux jouir . . . de quelque nombre de beaux jours que m'offre la jeunesse, prendre les douces libertés que l'âge me permet, voir un peu le beau monde, et goûter le plaisir de m'ouïr dire des douceurs."

42 An interesting comparison could be made between the scene in *L'École des femmes* when Horace reveals his love of Agnès to Arnolphe and the scene in *George Dandin* when Lubin reveals his master's plot to Dandin.

8 ENEMIES

1 *Troisième placet présenté au Roi*, Molière, *Oeuvres complètes*, I, 893. "Un fort honnête médecin, dont j'ai l'honneur d'être le malade, me promet et veut s'obliger par-devant notaires de me faire vivre encore trente années, si je puis lui obtenir une grâce de Votre Majesté. Je lui ai dit, sur sa promesse, que je ne lui demandais pas tant, et que je serais satisfait de lui pourvu qu'il s'obligeât de ne me point tuer. Cette grâce, Sire, est un canonicat de votre chapelle royale de Vincennes . . . Oserais-je demander encore cette grâce à Votre Majesté le propre jour de la grande résurrection de *Tartuffe*, ressuscité par vos bontés? Je suis, par cette première faveur, réconcilié avec les dévots; et je le serais par cette seconde, avec les médecins. C'est pour moi, sans doute, trop de grâce à la fois; mais peut-être n'en est-ce pas trop pour Votre Majesté . . ."

2 Letter of Elie Richard to Elie Bouhéreau, Mongrédien, *Recueil*, I, 257.

3 Robinet, *Lettres en vers*, February 21, 1666, in *Les Continuateurs de Loret*, ed. James de Rothschild (Paris: Margand et Fatou, 1881–2), I, 712. It was Robinet who christened Molière "le Dieu du ris."

4 *Ibid.*, II, 810.

5 September 16–October 9, 1662; August 17–21, 1663; March 18–21, 1664; May 30–June 1, 1664. La Grange gives no reason for any of these "interruptions."

6 This is according to Brossette. Another may have taken place at the salon of Ninon de Lenclos. Molière, *Oeuvres complètes*, I, 833n.

7 Voyer d'Argenson, *Annales de la Compagnie du Saint-Sacrement* in Mongrédien, *Recueil*, I, 214.

8 Mongrédien, *Recueil.*, I, 216. ". . . ses défenses de représenter une pièce de théâtre intitulée *l'Hypocrite*, que Sa Majesté, pleinement éclairée en toutes choses, jugea absolument injurieuse à la religion et capable de produire de très dangereux effets."

9 *Ibid.*, 215. "Sa majesté fit jouer une comédie nommée *Tartuffe*, que le sieur de Molière avait faite contre les hypocrites; mais quoiqu'elle eût été trouvée fort divertissante, le Roi connut tant de conformité entre ceux qu'une véritable dévotion met dans le chemin du Ciel et ceux qu'une vaine ostentation des bonnes oeuvres n'empêche pas d'en commettre de mauvaises, que son extrême délicatesse pour les choses de la religion ne put souffrir cette ressemblance du vice avec la vertu, qui pouvaient être prises l'une pour l'autre et quoi qu'on ne doutât point des bonnes intentions de l'auteur, il la défendit pourtant en public, et se priva soi-même de ce plaisir, pour n'en pas laisser abuser à d'autres, moins capable d'en faire un juste discernement."

10 Couton, "Notice," in Molière, *Oeuvres complètes*, I, 839.

11 John B. Wolf, *Louis XIV* (New York: W. W. Norton and Co., 1968), p. 294.

12 Molière, *Préface* to *Tartuffe*, *Oeuvres complètes*, I, 888. "Huit jours après qu'elle eut été défendue, on représenta devant la Cour une pièce intitulée *Scaramouche ermite*; et le roi, en sortant, dit au grand prince que je veux dire:

'Je voudrais bien savoir pourquoi les gens que se scandalisent si fort de la comédie de Molière ne disent mot de celle de *Scaramouche*'; à quoi le prince répondit: 'La raison de cela, c'est que la comédie de *Scaramouche* joue le ciel et la religion, dont ces messieurs-là ne se soucient point; mais celle de Molière les joue eux-mêmes; c'est ce qu'ils ne peuvent souffrir.'"

13 Raoul Allier, *La Cabale des dévots: 1620–1666* (Geneva: Slatkine Reprints, 1970), pp. 335–6.

14 *Ibid.*, pp. 347ff.

15 Couton, "Notice," in Molière, *Oeuvres complètes*, I, 868.

16 Mongrédien, *Recueil*, I, 220. "Un homme, ou plutôt un Démon vêtu de chair et habillé en homme et le plus signalé impie et libertin qui fût jamais dans les siècles passés, avait eu assez d'impiété et d'abomination pour faire sortir de son esprit diabolique une pièce toute prête d'être rendue publique en la faisant monter sur le théâtre à la dérision de toute l'Église et au mépris du caractère le plus sacré et de la fonction la plus divine, et au mépris de ce qu'il y a de plus saint dans l'Église, ordonné du Sauveur pour la sanctification des âmes, à dessein d'en rendre l'usage ridicule, contemptible, odieux."

17 *Ibid.*, 221.

18 *Ibid.*, 220.

19 Molière, *Oeuvres complètes*, I, 890.

20 *Ibid.*, 1330n.

21 *Ibid.*, 890. "Les tartuffes, sous main, ont eu l'adresse de trouver grâce auprès de Votre Majesté; et les originaux enfin ont fait supprimer la copie."

22 Couton, "Notice," in Molière, *Oeuvres complètes*, I, 839. "Il défendit cette comédie jusqu'à ce qu'elle fût entièrement achevée et examinée par des gens capable d'en juger."

23 Molière, I, 890. *Premier Placet présenté au Roi*. ". . . j'ai cru, Sire, qu'elle m'ôtait tout lieu de me plaindre."

24 La Grange, *Registre*, I, 69.

25 Loret, *Muze historique*. IV, 251.

26 La Grange, *Registre*, I, 71.

27 Archives de Chantilly. Reprinted in Mongrédien, *Recueil*, I, 249–50.

28 Loret, *Muze historique*, IV, 312. "L'effroyable *Festin de Pierre* / Si fameux par toute la Terre, / Et qui réussissoit si bien / Sur le Théâtre Italien, / Va commencer, l'autre semaine, / À paraître sur nôtre Scène, / . . . Car le rare Esprit de Moliére / L'a traité de telle maniére / Que les gens qui sont curieux / Du solide et beaux serieux, /. . . Sans doute y trouveront leur compte; / . . . Les Actrices et les Acteurs . . . Y feront, dit on, des merveilles. / C'est ce que nous viennent conter / Ceux qui les ont vû répéter. / Pour les changements de Théatre, / Dont le Bourgeois est idolâtre, / Selon le discours qu'on en fait, / Feront un surprenant effet."

29 Jurgens and Maxfield Miller, *Cent Ans*, 399–401.

30 Molière, *Oeuvres complètes*, II, 1540–1 and 154n.

31 For a history of these texts see Couton, "Notice," in *ibid.*, 3–8.

32 Molière, II, 59–60. "DOM J: Voilà qui est étrange, et tu es bien mal reconnu

de tes soins. Ah! Ah! je m'en vais te donner un louis d'or tout à l'heure, pourvu que tu veuilles jurer. LE P: Ah! Monsieur, voudriez-vous que je commisse un tel péché? DOM J: Tu n'as qu'à voir si tu veux gagner un louis d'or ou non. En voici un que je te donne, si tu jures; tiens, il faut jurer. LE P: Monsieur! DOM J.: À moins de cela, tu ne l'auras pas. SGAN: Va, va, jure un peu, il n'y a pas de mal. DOM J.: Prends, le voilà; prends, te dis-je, mais jure donc. LE P: Non, Monsieur, j'aime mieux mourir de faim. DOM J.: Va, va, . . ."

33 *Ibid.*, 79.

34 *Ibid.*, 80–1. "Il y en a tant d'autres comme moi, qui se mêlent de ce métier, et qui se servent du même masque pour abuser le monde . . . Il n'y a plus de honte maintenant à cela: l'hypocrisie est un vice à la mode, et tous les vices à la mode passent pour vertus. Le personnage d'homme de bien est le meilleur de tous les personnages qu'on puisse jouer aujourd'hui, et la profession d'hypocrite a de merveilleux avantages. C'est un art de qui l'imposture est toujours respectée; et quoiqu'on la découvre, on n'ose rien dire contre elle. Tous les autres vices des homme sont exposés à la censure, et chacun a la liberté de les attaquer hautement; mais l'hypocrisie est un vice privilégié, qui, de sa main, ferme la bouche à tout le monde, et jouit en repos d'une impunité souveraine."

35 *Ibid.*, 81. ". . . c'est là le vrai moyen de faire impunément tout ce que je voudrai. Je m'érigerai en censeur des actions d'autrui, jugerai mal de tout le monde, et n'aurai bonne opinion que de moi. Dès qu'une fois on m'aura choqué tant soit peu, je ne pardonnerai jamais et garderai tout doucement une haine irréconciliable. Je ferai le vengeur des intérêts du Ciel, et, sous ce prétexte commode, je pousserai mes ennemis, je les accuserai d'impiété, et saurai déchaîner contre eux des zélés indiscrets, qui, sans connaissance de cause, crieront en public contre eux, qui les accableront d'injures, et les damneront hautement de leur autorité privée. C'est ainsi qu'il faut profiter des faiblesses des hommes, et qu'un sage esprit s'accommode aux vices de son siècle."

36 *Ibid*, 57–8. ". . . je n'ai point étudié comme vous. Dieu merci, et personne ne saurait se vanter de m'avoir jamais rien appris; mais avec mon petit sens, mon petit jugement, je vois les choses mieux que tous les livres, et je comprends fort bien que ce monde que nous voyons n'est pas un champignon, qui soit venu tout seul en une nuit. Je voudrais bien vous demander qui a fait ces arbres-là, ces rochers, cette terre, et ce ciel que voilà là-haut, et si tout cela s'est bâti de lui-même. Vous voilà vous, par exemple, vous êtes là: est-ce que vous vous êtes fait tout seul, et n'a-t-il pas fallu que votre père ait engrossé votre mère pour vous faire? Pouvez-vous voir toutes ces inventions dont la machine de l'homme est composée sans admirer de quelle façon cela est agencé l'un dans l'autre: ces nerfs, ces os, ces veines, ces artères, ces . . . ce poumon, ce coeur, ce foie, et tous ces autres ingrédients qui sont là, et qui . . . . Oh! dame, interrompez-moi donc si vous voulez: je ne saurais disputer si l'on ne m'interrompt . . ."

37 *Ibid.*, 58 ". . . il y a quelque chose d'admirable dans l'homme, quoi que vous puissiez dire, que tous les savants ne sauraient expliquer. Cela n'est-il pas merveilleux que me voilà ici, et que j'aie quelque chose dans la tête qui pense cent choses différentes en un moment, et fait de mon corps tout ce qu'elle veut? Je veux frapper des mains, hausser le bras, lever les yeux au ciel, baisser la tête, remuer les pieds, aller à droit, à gauche, en avant, en arrière, tourner . . . DOM J: Bon! voilà ton raisonnement qui a le nez cassé."

38 La Grange, *Registre*, I, 78. "Vendredy 14th Aoust La Troupe alla a Saint Germain en Laye, le Roy dit au Sr de Moliere qu'il vouloit que la Troupe doresnavant luy appartinst et la demanda a MONSIEUR, S. Mte donna en mesme tems six mil *livres* de Pension a la Troupe qui prist congé de MONSIEUR luy demanda la continuation de sa protection, et prist ce tiltre: LA TROUPE DU ROY, au pallais Royal." Some evidence exists that the pension was for 6,000, some that it was for 7,000. See Jurgens and Maxfield-Miller, *Cent Ans*, pp. 409, 427, 446, 469, 493. Most of the evidence suggests 6000 is the right figure until 1671, when it was increased to 7,000.

39 Molière, *Oeuvres complètes*, II, 56–7. "SGAN: Il y avait un homme qui, depuis six jours, était à l'agonie; on ne savait plus que lui ordonner, et tous les remèdes ne faisaient rien; on s'avisa à la fin de lui donner de l'émétique. DOM J: Il réchappa, n'est-ce pas? SGAN: Non, il mourut. DOM J: L'effet est admirable. SGAN: Comment? il y avait six jours entiers qu'il ne pouvait mourir, et cela le fit mourir tout d'un coup. Voulez-vous rien de plus efficace?"

40 *Ibid.*, 95.

41 *Ibid.*, 112–13. "Puisque le Ciel nous fait la grâce que . . . on demeure infatué de nous, ne désabusons point les hommes . . . et profitons de leur sottise. . . . Nous ne sommes pas les seuls . . . qui tâchons à nous prévaloir de la faiblesse humaine. . . . Mais le plus grand faible des hommes, c'est l'amour qu'ils ont pour la vie; et nous en profitons, nous autres, par notre pompeux galimatias, et savons prendre nos avantages de cette vénération que la peur de mourir leur donne pour notre métier."

42 Two separate pieces of evidence testify to this. *Ibid.*, 132on.

43 Mongrédien, *Recueil*, I, 245–6.

44 Molière's own experiences with doctors may have motivated some later changes to the text of *L'Amour médecin*. Although it was originally written before he became seriously ill, the version we have may include revisions he made between its first performance in September 1665 and its reprise in February 1666. According to Le Boulanger de Chalussay in *Élomire hypocondre*, Molière touched up the doctors as a result of "confronting the originals."

45 Roger Duchêne (*Molière*, p. 439) suggests that Molière was also influenced by the treatment given beginning in August to the queen mother, whose cancer was reaching a desperate stage. The doctor who "mortified her flesh" and "cut slits in it with a razor" was Alliot, not one of the doctors specifically satirized by Molière, but Guénaut (ridiculed as Macrotan) was involved in the queen mother's treatment. See Mme de Motteville, *Memoires*

pour servir á l'histoire d'Anne d'Autriche (Amsterdam: François Changuion, 1750), VI, 254.

46 Le Boulanger de Chalussay in Molière, *Oeuvres complètes*, II, 1239–40. See also Grimarest, *Vie de Molière*, pp. 61–2, for a version that makes Armande the real trouble-maker. Might a vein of anti-semitism be running through this story? Daquin was the son of Philippe Daquin or D'Aquin, also known as Rabbi Mardocaï, originally of Avignon. See Jurgens and Maxfield-Miller, *Cent Ans*, p. 361n. The father's alias and place of birth in the Comtat Venaissin where Jews were protected suggest the possibility that Daquin was a Jew.

47 Mongrédien, *Recueil*, I, 244.

48 *Ibid.*

49 *Ibid.*, 247.

50 Robinet in Rothschild, *Continuateurs*, II, 181–2.

51 Molière, *Oeuvres complètes*, II, 246. "Or ces vapeurs dont je vous parle venant à passer, du coté gauche, où est le foie, au coté droit, où est le coeur, il se trouve que le poumon, que nous appelons en latin *armyan*, ayant communication avec le cerveau, que nous nommons en grec *nasmus*, par le moyen de la veine cave, que nous appelons en hébreu *cubile*, rencontre en son chemin lesdites vapeurs, qui remplissent les ventricules de l'omoplate; et parce que lesdites vapeurs . . . comprenez bien ce raisonnement, je vous prie; et parce que lesdites vapeurs ont une certaine malignité . . . Écoutez bien ceci, je vous conjure . . . Ont une certaine malignité, qui est causée . . . Soyez attentif, s'il vous plaît . . . Qui est causée par l'âcreté des humeurs engendrées dans la concavité du diaphragme, il arrive que ces vapeurs . . . *Ossabandus, nequeys, nequer, potarinum, quipsa milus.* Voila justement ce qui fait que votre fille est muette."

52 Selman A. Waksman, *The Conquest of Tuberculosis* (Berkeley, CA: University of California Press, 1966), p. 9.

53 *Ibid.*, p. 49.

54 Jurgens and Maxfield-Miller, *Cent Ans*, p. 426.

55 *Ibid.*, pp. 411, 414, 531.

56 Molière, *Second placet présenté au roi, Oeuvres complètes*, I, 891. "En vain je l'ai produite sous le titre de *L'Imposteur*, et déguisé le personnage sous l'ajustement d'un homme du monde; j'ai eu beau lui donner un petit chapeau, de grands cheveux, un grand collet, une épée, et des dentelles sur tout l'habit."

57 *Ibid.*, 892. ". . . et retrancher avec soin tout ce que j'ai jugé capable de fournir l'ombre d'un prétexte aux célèbres originaux du portrait que je voulais faire."

58 La Grange, *Registre*, I, 91. ". . . nous fusmes tres bien receus. MONSIEUR nous protegea a son ordre et Sa Mte nous fist dire qu'a son retour à Paris il feroit examiner la piece de Tartuffe et que nous la jouerions."

59 This and what follows were told to Brossette by Boileau. Brosette, *Correspondance*, pp. 563–5.

60 *Ibid.*, p. 565. "Molière expliqua le sujet de sa visite. Monsieur le premier président lui répondit en ces termes: Monsieur, je fais beaucoup de cas de votre mérite; je say que vous êtes non seulement un acteur excellent, mais encore un très habile homme qui faites honneur à votre profession, et à la France, votre pays; cependant avec toute la bonne volonté que j'ay pour vous, je ne saurois vous permettre de jouer votre comédie. Je suis persuadé qu'elle est fort belle et fort instructive, mais il ne convient pas à des comédiens d'instruire les hommes sur les matières de la morale chrétienne et de la religion; ce n'est pas au théâtre à se mêler de prêcher l'Evangile. Quand le Roi sera de retour, il vous permettra, s'il le trouve à propos, de représenter le *Tartuffe*, mais, pour moy, je croirois abuser de l'autorité que le Roy m'a fait l'honneur de me confier pendant son absence, si je vous accordois la permission que vous me demandez."

61 Mongrédien, *Recueil*, I, 292. ". . . à toutes personnes de notre diocèse de représenter, lire ou entendre réciter la susdite comédie, soit publiquement, soit en particulier, sous quelque nom et quelque prétexte que ce soit, et ce sous peine d'excommunication."

62 In Molière, *Oeuvres complètes*, I, 1149–80. One surviving copy of the *Lettre* is signed "C," which might indicate Molière's good friend Chapelle. The text of *L'Imposteur* has not survived, but the *Lettre*, which includes a careful plot summary with occasional lines of dialogue, permits the conclusion that *l'Imposteur* was in most important ways the same as the five-act *Tartuffe*. See Couton, "Notice" in *ibid.*, 1405–6, for differences that this editor has perceived.

63 *Lettre* in *ibid.*, 1169. ". . . l'étrange disposition d'esprit . . . de certaines gens qui . . . la condamnent toutefois en général, à cause seulement qu'il y est parlé de la religion, et que le théâtre . . . n'est pas un lieu où il la faille enseigner."

64 *Ibid.*, 1172. ". . . les païens, qui n'avaient pas moins de respect pour leur religion que nous en avons pour la nôtre, n'ont pas craint de la produire sur leurs théâtres . . . ils ont cru sagement ne pouvoir mieux lui en persuader la vérité que par les spectacles, qui lui sont si agréables. C'est pour cela que leurs dieux paraissent si souvent sur la scène, que les dénoûments, qui sont les endroits les plus importants du poème, ne se faisaient presque jamais de leur temps que par quelque divinité, et qu'il n'y avait point de pièce qui ne fût . . . une preuve exemplaire de la clémence ou de la justice du Ciel envers les hommes."

65 Molière, *Second Placet, Oeuvres complètes*, I, 892–3. "J'attends avec respect l'arrêt que Votre Majesté daignera prononcer sur cette matière; mais il est très assuré, Sire, qu'il ne faut plus que je songe à faire des comédies, si les tartuffes on l'avantage . . ."

66 Robinet in Rothschild, *Continuateurs*, II, 1044. "Molière reprenant courage, / Malgré la Bourrasque et l'Orage, / Sur la Scène se fait revoir."

67 I am assuming that by 1665 Molière had given up acting in tragedy. He might have acted in comedies other than his own, but we know in at least

several instances that he did not. Thus, I propose that by 1664–5 if no play by Molière was on stage, neither was Molière.

68 Mongrédien, *Recueil*, I, 336. "Ce Molière, par son pinceau, / En a fait le parlant tableau, / Avec tant d'art, tant de justesse, / Et, bref, tant de délicatesse, / Qu'il charme tous les vrais dévots / Comme il fait enrager les faux; / Et les caractères, au reste, / C'est chose manifeste, / Sont tous si bien distribués / Et naturellement joués / Que jamais nulle comédie / Ne fut aussi tant applaudie."

69 Molière, *Oeuvres complètes*, I, 883. ". . . pleine d'abominations, et l'on n'y trouve rien qui ne mérite le feu. Toutes les syllabes en sont impies; les gestes même y sont criminels; et le moindre coup d'oeil, le moindre branlement de tête, le moindre pas à droite ou à gauche y cache des mystères qu'ils trouvent moyen d'expliquer à mon désavantage."

70 *Ibid.*, 983. "Nous vivons sous un Prince ennemi de la fraude, / Un Prince dont les yeux se font jour dans les coeurs, / Et que ne peut tromper tout l'art des imposteurs."

9 FRIENDS

1 A number of articles have questioned this identification. Probably the one most often referred to is Jean Demeures, "Les quatre amis de *Psyché*," *Mercure de France* (June 15, 1928), pp. 331–5. This author follows Gustave Michaut who argues that the four friends represent not real people but diverse tastes. See also Jean Rousset, "*Psyché*, ou le plaisir des larmes," *Nouvelle Revue Française* (April 1966), pp. 1058–66. Rousset suggests that the friends represent the different genres: Gélaste comedy, Ariste tragedy, Acante (who loves gardens and trees) the pastoral, and Polyphile (lover of all) the synthesis of the genres as represented by his *Psyché*. While this reading makes sense, it does not preclude La Fontaine's also drawing on his personal experience of his friends.

2 La Fontaine, *Les Amours de Psyché et Cupidon, Oeuvres diverses*, p. 127. ". . . si le hasard les faisait tomber sur quelque point de science ou de belles-lettres, ils profitaient de l'occasion: c'était toutefois sans s'arrêter trop longtemps à une même matière, voltigeant de propos en autre, comme des abeilles qui rencontreraient en leur chemin diverses sortes de fleurs."

3 Louis Racine, *Mémoires sur la vie et les ouvrages de Jean Racine* in Racine, *Oeuvres complètes*, I, 28.

4 La Fontaine, *Amours, Oeuvres diverses*, p. 174. "Dispensez-moi de vous raconter le reste: vous seriez touchés de trop de pitié au récit que je vous ferais . . . Ce n'est pas mon talent d'achever une histoire qui se termine ainsi."

5 *Ibid.*, p. 175. "La compassion a aussi ses charmes, qui ne sont pas moindres que ceux du rire. Je tiens même qu'ils sont plus grands, et crois qu'Ariste est de mon avis. Soyez si tendre et si émouvant que vous voudrez, nous ne vous en écouterons tous deux que plus volontiers."

6 *Ibid.* "J'aime beaucoup mieux qu'on me fasse rire quand je dois pleurer, que si l'on me faisait pleurer lorsque je dois rire." This makes an interesting contrast to Bossuet's warning that Molière, after his death, faced the judgment of one who said: "Unhappy are you who laugh, for you shall weep."

7 This suggestion that Gélaste is a womanizer was a reason for nineteenth-century Moliéristes to deny that Molière could possibly have been a model for the character. Moland wrote in 1863 that any such indentification was an insult to the author of *Le Misanthrope*. See Demeures, "Quatre amis," p. 334.

8 La Fontaine, *Oeuvres diverses*, pp. 175–85. ". . . la pitié est celui des mouvements du discours que nous tenons le plus noble, le plus excellent si vous voulez; je passe encore outre et le maintiens le plus agréable: voyez la hardiesse de ce paradoxe!" "O dieux immortels! y a-t-il gens assez fous au monde pour soutenir une opinion si extravagante? Je ne dis pas que Sophocle et Euripide ne me divertissent davantage que quantité de faiseurs de comédies; mais mettez les choses en pareil degré d'excellence, quitterez-vous le plaisir de voir attraper deux vieillards pour un drôle comme Phormion, pour aller pleurer avec la famille du roi Priam?" ". . . la plus saine partie du monde préféra toujours la comédie à la tragédie. . . . Hé! mon ami, ne voyez-vous pas qu'on ne se lasse jamais de rire? On peut se lasser du jeu, de la bonne chère, des dames; mais de rire, point. Avez-vous entendu dire à qui que se soit: 'Il y a huit jours entiers que nous rions; je vous prie, pleurons aujourd'hui?'" ". . . lorsque Achille . . . s'est rassasié de ce beau plaisir de verser des larmes, il dit à Priam: 'Vieillard, tu es misérable: telle est la condition des mortels, ils passent leur vie dans les pleurs. Les dieux seuls sont exempts de mal, et vivent là-haut à leur aise, sans rien souffrir.' Que répondrez-vous à cela?" "Je répondrai . . . que les mortels sont mortels quand ils pleurent de leurs douleurs; mais, quand ils pleurent des douleurs d'autrui, ce sont proprement des dieux." "Les dieux ne pleurent ni d'une façon ni d'une autre; pour le rire, c'est leur partage . . . la béatitude consiste au rire."

9 Raymond Picard, *La Carrière de Jean Racine* (Paris: Gallimard, 1961), p. 23n.

10 Racine, *Oeuvres complètes*, II, 403. "Toutes les femmes y sont éclatantes, et s'y ajustent d'une façon qui leur est la plus naturelle du monde; et pour ce qui est de leur personne, *Color verus, corpus solidum et succi plenum.* Mais comme c'est la première chose dont on m'a dit de me donner de garde, je ne veux pas en parler davantage: . . . On m'a dit 'soyez aveugle.' Si je ne le puis être tout à fait, il faut du moins que je sois muet; car, voyez-vous? il faut être régulier avec les réguliers, comme j'ai été loup avec vous et les autres loups vos compères."

11 Tallemant des Réaux, *Historiettes*, I, 392. "On luy dit: 'Mais un tel cajolle vostre femme.' – 'Ma foy!' respond-il, 'qu'il face ce qu'il pourra; je ne m'en soucie point. Il s'en lassera comme j'ay fait.'"

12 Louis Racine in Racine, *Oeuvres complètes*, I, 43. "Ne nous moquons pas du bonhomme; il vivra peut-être plus que nous tous." The other version is found in the abbé d'Olivet's *Histoire de l'Académie françoise* (1729), XI, 309.

13 After 1661, any false claims to nobility were punished by fines. Agnes Ethel Mackey, *La Fontaine and His Friends* (London: Garnstone Press, 1972), p. 101.

14 La Fontaine, *Oeuvres diverses*, p. 570. "Mais le moins fier, mais le moins vain des hommes, / Qui n'a jamais prétendu s'appuyer/ Du vain honneur de ce mot d'ecuyer . . . J'étais lors en Champagne/ Dormant, rêvant, allant par la campagne."

15 Boileau, *Oeuvres complètes*, ed. Françoise Escal (Paris: Gallimard, 1966), p. 73. ". . . cette Sçavante . . . D'où vient qu'elle a l'oeil trouble, et le teint si terni? / . . . Un astrolabe en main, elle a dans sa goûtiere / A suivre Jupiter passé la nuit entière." All quotations from Boileau are taken from this edition unless otherwise indicated.

16 La Fontaine, *Oeuvres diverses*, p. 644. "Désormais que ma Muse, aussi bien que mes jours, / Touche de son déclin l'inévitable cours, / Et que de ma raison le flambeau va s'éteindre, / Irai-je en consumer les restes à me plaindre, / Et prodigue d'un temps par la Parque attendu, / Le perdre à regretter celui que j'ai perdu? / Si le Ciel me réserve encor quelque étincelle / Du feu dont je brillais en ma saison nouvelle, / Je la dois employer, suffisamment instruit /Que le plus beau couchant est voisin de la nuit."

17 Boileau, *Oeuvres complètes*, p. 880.

18 *Ibid.*, p. 246. "Laisse gronder tes Envieux, / Ils ont beau crier en tous lieux, / Qu'en vain tu charmes le Vulgaire, / Que tes vers n'ont rien de plaisant; / Si tu sçavois un peu moins plaire, / Tu ne leur déplairois pas tant."

19 Brossette, *Correspondance*, pp. 515–16.

20 *Ibid.*, p. 516. "Il m'a dit qu'il auroit été bien facile à M. Molière de mettre un dénouement heureux et naturel dans le *Tartuffe*. Car au lieu d'aller chercher de loin le secours de la cassette où il y a des papiers contre l'État, que sans introduire un exempt et sans employer l'autorité du Roy, il pouvoit, après la découverte de l'imposture de Tartuffe, faire délibérer sur le théâtre, par tous les personnages de la comédie, quelle peine on feroit souffrir à ce coquin."

21 One legend is that he was injured as a child by an angry turkey. But the comment of Louis Racine, that the operation for the stone was badly done and left him impotent, seems less improbable. See Boileau, *Oeuvres complètes*, ed. Ch. Gidel (Paris: Garnier frères, 1870), I, xx.

22 Louis Racine in Racine, *Oeuvres complètes*, I, 19.

23 Charles Nuitter and Ernest Thoinan, *Les Origines de l'opéra français* (Paris: Librairie Plon, 1886), p. 74.

24 Tallemant des Réaux, *Historiettes*, II, 333.

25 Boileau, *Oeuvres complètes*, p. 38. "Un éloge ennuyeux, un froid panégyrique, / Peut pourrir à son ayse au fond d'une boutique, / . . . Et n'a pour ennemis que la poudre et les vers . . ."

26 There exists some confusion about the taverns frequented by groups of libertine writers. According to Boileau's friend Le Verrier, the writer was introduced into the libertine circle after he wrote his satire against the pensioners by one "Du Tot," probably Fauvelet du Toc, a "man of great wit but very

debauched." Fauvelet du Toc presumably introduced him to Molière's great friend Chapelle, who took him for the first time to La Croix-Blanche, where he read his satire to the applause of the *débauchez*. Adam, *Histoire*, III, 75–6). Adam, however, confuses this band of *débauchez* with the drinkers at the Croix-de-Lorraine identified by Chapelle in his verses addressed to the marquis de Jonzac (See Chapelle, *Oeuvres*, pp. 206–10). This group includes Fauvelet du Toc, Des Barreaux, the abbé La Mothe Le Vayer, the abbé de Broussin and his brother, and Molière, who "buvoit assez / Pour, vers le soir, être en goguettes" (p. 208). The Croix-Blanche was on the rue de Bercy-au-Marais near the church of St-Gervais (See Pradel, *Livre commode*, and Félix Lazare, *Dictionnaire administrative et historique des rues de Paris* [Paris: Félix Lazare, 1844]). Chapelle clearly identifies the gathering place of his happy band as not in the Marais. ("Du Toc, d'entre nous le plus sage, / Ravi de voir les beaux esprits / Quitter Marais et marécage / Pour venir dans son voisinage / Boire à l'autre bout de Paris.")

27 Adam, *Histoire*, III, 79–80.

28 *Ibid.*, 82. ". . . se hâta de désavouer cette pièce indécente et charitablement fit connaître à Chapelain que son frère Despréaux en était l'auteur."

29 *Ibid.*, 102–3.

30 *Ibid.*, 153.

31 Boileau, *Oeuvres complètes*, p. 178. "Si moins ami du peuple en ses doctes peintures, / Il n'eust point fait souvent grimacer ses figures, / Quitte, pour le bouffon, l'agreable et le fin, / Et sans honte à Terence allié Tabarin./ Dans ce sac ridicule ou Scapin s'enveloppe, / Je ne reconnois plus l'Auteur du Misanthrope."

32 *Défense du poème héroique*, quoted in Mongrédien, *Recueil*, II, 496. "Coeur lâche qui poursuit les vivants et les morts, / Tu m'adorais vivant; maintenant quand je dors / . . . Du titre de bouffon tu noircis mon génie . . ."

33 Mongrédien, *Recueil*, II, 498. "On a cru que Boileau s'est servi de cette politique envers Molière à qui il a donné l'encens avec profusion dans une de ses satires; et . . . depuis la mort de Molière, Boileau a publié fort hardiment ce qu'il trouvait à reprendre dans ses comédies."

34 Louis Racine in Racine, *Oeuvres complètes*, I, 43. "Dans la suite, Boileau lui conseilla de quitter le théâtre, du moins comme acteur: 'Votre santé, lui dit-il, dépérit, parce que le métier du comédien vous épuise: que n'y renoncez-vous? – Hélas! lui répondit Molière en soupirant, c'est le point d'honneur qui me retient. – Eh quel point d'honneur? repondit Boileau. Quoi! Vous barbouiller le visage d'une moustache de Sganarelle, pour venir sur un théâtre recevoir des coups de bâton? Voila un beau point d'honneur pour un philosophe comme vous!'" Palmer reports in his *Molière* (p. 443) that Louis Racine extended this anecdote and recorded that the Académie Française, prompted by Boileau, offered to receive Molière if he abandoned the stage. I am unable to find this in Louis Racine's *Mémoires*, but in any case, the idea is not tenable. Boileau, himself, was not inducted into the Académie Française until 1684, eleven years after Molière's death. During Molière's

life, the Académie was still dominated by Boileau's enemies, and it is hard to imagine Cotin, for instance, or Ménage agreeing to Molière's reception after he had caricatured them in *Les Femmes savantes*. The source of this notion seems to be a publication of 1765 by Cizeron-Rival. See Mongrédien, *Recueil*, II, 797–8.

35 Boileau, *Oeuvres complètes*, p. 642.

36 Louis Racine in Racine, *Oeuvres complètes*, I, 22. "J'ai résolu de m'en corriger; je sens la vérité de vos raisons; pour achever de me persuader, entrons ici; vous me parlerez plus à votre aise."

37 Raymond Picard, *Carrière*, p. 43.

38 *Ibid.*, p. 46. "L'ode est fort belle, fort poétique, et il y a beaucoup de stances qui ne se peuvent mieux. Si l'on repasse ce peu d'endroits marqués, on en fera une fort belle pièce."

39 Racine, *Oeuvres complètes*, II, 382. ". . . les comédiens n'aiment à présent que le galamatias, pourvu qu'il vienne d'un grand auteur."

40 Picard, *Carrière*, p. 68.

41 Racine, *Oeuvres complètes*, II, 457. "Le 4e était fait dès samedi; mais malheu-reusement je ne goûtais point, ni les autres non plus, toutes les épées tirées." ". . . j'y ai trouvé Molière, à qui le Roi a donné assez de louanges, et j'en ai été bien aise pour lui; il a été bien aise aussi que j'y fusse présent."

42 Brossette, *Correspondance*, p. 519.

43 Racine, *Oeuvres complètes*, II, 459

44 La Grange, *Registre*, I, 63.

45 Racine, *Oeuvres complètes*, II, 457.

46 La Grange, *Registre*, I, 81. "Ce mesme jour La Troupe fust surprise que la mesme piece d'Allexandre fust jouée sur le Theastre de l'Hostel de Bourgogne. Comme la chose s'estoit faite de complot avec M^r. Racine, La Trouppe ne crust pas devoir les parts d'autheur audt M^r. Racine qui en usoit si mal que d'avoir donné et faict aprendre la piece aux autres Comediens. Lesdtes partz d'autheur furent repartagées et chacun des douze acteurs eust pour sa part 47 *livres*."

47 Brossette, *Correspondance*, p. 521.

48 Pierre Mélèse, *Le Théâtre et le public à Paris sous Louis XIV* (Geneva: Slatkine Reprints, 1976), p. 232.

49 Louis Racine in Racine, *Oeuvres complètes*, I, 40–41. "Cette femme n'était point née actrice. La nature ne lui avait donné que la beauté, la voix et la mémoire: du reste, elle avait si peu d'esprit, qu'il fallait lui faire entendre les vers qu'elle avait à dire, et lui en donner le ton. Tout le monde sait le talent que mon père avait pour la déclamation, dont il donna le vrai goût aux comédiens capables de le prendre . . . il avait formé la Champmeslé, mais avec beaucoup de peine. Il lui faisait d'abord comprendre les vers qu'elle avait à dire, lui montrait les gestes, et lui dictait les tons, que même il notait. L'écolière, fidèle à ses leçons, quoique actrice par art, sur le théâtre parais-sait inspirée par la nature."

50 *Ibid.*, 24–5.

51 *Ibid.*, I, 22.

52 Grimarest, *Vie de Molière*, pp. 116–7. "Bien des gens s'imaginent que Molière a eu un commerce particulier avec Mr R***. Je n'ai point trouvé que cela fût vrai, dans la recherche que j'en ai faite; au contraire l'âge, le travail, et le caractère de ces Messieurs étoient si differens que je ne crois pas qu'ils deussent se chercher; et je ne pense pas même que Molière estimât R***."

53 Louis Racine in Racine, *Oeuvres complètes*, I, 34. "Avouez-moi en ami, lui dit-it, votre sentiment. Que pensez-vous de *Bérénice*? – Ce que j'en pense? répondit Chapelle: Marion pleure, Marion crie, Marion veut qu'on la marie."

54 *Ibid.*, 46. "J'arrive enfin à l'heureux moment où les grands sentiments de religion dont mon père avait été rempli dans son enfance, et qui avaient été longtemps comme assoupis dans son coeur . . . se réveillèrent tout à coup."

55 *Ibid.* ". . . [N]i l'amour ni l'intérêt n'eurent aucune part à son choix: il ne consulta que la raison pour une affaire si sérieuse."

56 *Ibid.*, 1047n.

57 *Ibid.*, 43.

58 Grimarest, *Vie de Molière*, pp. 83–6. "Je suis un grand fou de venir m'enyvrer ici tous les jours, pour faire honneur à Molière; je suis bien las de ce train-là: et ce qui me fâche c'ést qu'il croit que j'y suis obligé." – "Que notre vie est peu de chose! Qu'elle est remplie de traverses! Nous sommes à l'affût pendant trente ou quarante années pour jouir d'un moment de plaisir, que nous ne trouvons jamais! Notre jeunesse est harcellée par de maudits parens, qui veulent que nous nous metions un fatras de fariboles dans la tête." . . . "Toutes ces femmes . . . sont des animaux qui sont ennemis jurés de notre repos. Oui morbleu, chagrins, injustice, malheurs de tous côtés dans cette vie-ci." . . . "Quitons-là. . . . Allons nous noyer de compagnie; la rivière est à notre portée." . . . "Écoute, mon cher Molière, tu as de l'esprit, voi si nous avons tort. Fatigués des peines de ce monde-ci, nous avons fait dessein de passer en l'autre pour être mieux: la rivière nous a paru le plus court chemin pour nous y rendre." . . . "Comment! Messieurs, que vous ai-je fait pour former un si beau projet sans m'en faire part? Quoi, vous voulez vous noyer sans moi? Je vous croyois plus de mes amis." . . . "Il a parbleu raison, voila une injustice que nous lui faisions. Vien donc te noyer avec nous." . . . "Oh! doucement, ce n'est point ici une affaire à entreprendre mal à propos: c'est la derniere action de notre vie, il n'en faut pas manquer le mérite. On seroit assez malin pour lui donner un mauvais jour, si nous nous noyons à l'heure qu'il est: on diroit à coup seur que nous l'aurions fait la nuit, comme des desespéres, ou comme les gens yvres. Saisissons le moment qui nous fasse le plus d'honneur, et qui réponde à notre conduite. Demain, sur les huit à neuf heures du matin, bien à jeun et devant tout le monde nous irons nous jeter la tête devant dans la rivière." . . . "Molière a toujours cent fois plus d'esprit que nous . . . allons nous coucher, car je m'endors."

59 *Ibid.*, p. 88. "Chapelle est mon ami, mais ce malheureux panchant m'ôte tous les agrémens de son amitié."

60 Jurgens and Maxfield-Miller, *Cent Ans*, pp. 144–5.

61 Molière, *Oeuvres complètes*, II, 1525n. ". . . Le Brun . . . qui, ayant . . . la confidence de Colbert, faisait régner sur les arts une authorité despotique."

62 *Ibid.*, 1195. "Les grands hommes, Colbert, sont mauvais courtisans, / Peu faits à s'aquitter des devoirs complaisant; / À leurs réflexions tout entiers ils se donnent; / Et ce n'est que par-là qu'ils se perfectionnent. / . . . Qui se donne à la cour se dérobe à son art. / Un esprit partagé rarement s'y consomme, / Et les emplois de feu demandent tout un homme. / Ils ne sauraient quitter les soins de leur métier / Pour aller chaque jour fatiguer ton porter."

63 *Ibid.*, I, 1288–9.

64 According to Mme de Sévigné, Molière was to read his "Tricotin" to cardinal de Retz on Saturday. Letter of March 9, 1672. Mongrédien, *Recueil*, II, 407.

65 *Ibid.*, 408–9. "Aristophane ne détruisit pas la réputation de Socrate, en le jouant dans une de ses farces . . ."

66 Molière, *Oeuvres complètes*, II, 1037–8. "Allez, rimeur de balle, opprobre du métier." – "Allez, fripier d'écrits, impudent plagiaire." – "Souviens-toi de ton livre et de son peu de bruit?" – "Et toi, de ton libraire à l'hôpital réduit." – "Ma gloire est établie: en vain tu la déchires." – "Oui, oui, je te renvoie à l'auteur des *Satires*."

67 Grimarest, *Vie de Molière*, p. 115. "Que m'importe," s'écrioit M. le Marquis ***, "de voir le ridicule d'un Pedant? Est-ce un caractère à m'ocuper?" . . . "Où a-t-il été déterrer," ajoutoit M. le Comte de ***, "ces sottes femmes, sur lesquelles il a travaillé aussi sérieusement que sur un bon sujet? Il n'y a pas le mot pour rire à tout cela pour l'homme de Cour, et pour le Peuple."

68 Louis Racine in Racine, *Oeuvres complètes*, I, 43.

10 MARRIAGE (AND LOVE)

1 Auteuil is in the Sixteenth Arrondissement of modern Paris, on the right bank of the Seine a mile or so below the Palais de Chaillot. Travel to and from Auteuil was by *coche d'eau* or *bateau mouche*.

2 Molière is mentioned in a complaint filed by his landlord against the gardener on August 21–2, 1667. Jurgens and Maxfield-Miller, *Cent Ans*, pp. 424–6.

3 Anon., *La Fameuse Comedienne, ou Histoire de la Guerin auparavant femme et veuve de Molière* (Geneva: Slatkine Reprints, 1968), p. 11. ". . . un homme qui comptoit pour peu de bonne fortune le bonheur d'estre aimé des dames." This text has been recently reedited by Cesare Garboli (Milan: Adelphi, 1997), whose preface has also appeared, translated and slightly truncated, along with the text itself in *Comédie-Française: Les Cahiers* 31 (1999), 8–63.

4 Nancy Nichols Barker, *Brother to the Sun King* (Baltimore, MD: The Johns Hopkins University Press, 1989), pp. 61–4.

5 Anon., *Fameuse Comédienne*, p. 12. "irritée par des froideurs du comte de Guiche, se jetta entre les bras du comte de Lauzun."

6 Grimarest, *Vie de Molière*, pp. 65–9.

7 The spinet had three keyboards, one of which appeared to play by itself. It was actually played from inside by Raisin's youngest, a boy of five. See H. C. Lancaster, "Jean Baptiste Raisin, le petit Raisin," *Modern Philology* 38 (1941), 335–49.

8 Robinet in Rothschild, *Continuateurs*, I, 712.

9 Grimarest, *Vie de Molière*, p. 68. "D'être avec vous le reste de mes jours." "Eh! bien, c'est une chose fait."

10 *Ibid.*, p. 71. ". . . elle ne pouvoit souffrir qu'il eût de la bonté pour cet enfant, qui . . . n'avoit pas toute la prudence necessaire, pour se gouverner avec une femme, pour qui il devoit avoir des égards."

11 *Ibid.*, pp. 71–2. "Il se voyoit aimé du mari; necessaire même à ses spectacles, caressé de toute la Cour, il s'embarrassoit fort peu de plaire, ou non à la Molière: elle ne le négligeoit pas moins; elle s'échapa même un jour de lui donner un soufflet sur un sujet assez léger."

12 *Ibid.*, p. 72. "Est-il possible que vous ayez eu l'imprudence de frapper un enfant aussi sensible que vous connoissez celui-là; et encore dans un tems où il est chargé d'un rolle de six cens vers dans la piece que nous devons representer incessamment devant le Roi?"

13 La Grange and Vivot in Molière, *Oeuvres complètes*, II, 316. "Cette comédie n'a point été achevée; il n'y avait que ces deux actes de faits lorsque le roi la demanda. Sa Majesté en ayant été satisfaite pour la fête où elle fut représentée, le sieur de Molière ne l'a point finie."

14 La Grange, *Registre*, I, 87. The entry is curious. "Le Mercredy 1er Decembre nous sommes partis pour Saint Germain en Laye par ordre du Roy. Le lendemain on commença le ballet des Muses ou la Troupe estoit employée dans une Pastoralle intitulée Coridon." La Grange later inserted "Melicerte puis celle de." Perhaps the insertion was made when La Grange decided to include the incomplete *Melicerte* in the *Oeuvres* of 1682.

15 Molière, *Oeuvres complètes*, II, 298–9.

16 *Ibid.*, 302. "LYC: Et savez-vous, morveux, ce que c'est que d'aimer? MYR: Sans savoir ce que c'est, mon coeur a su le faire."

17 That the women are nymphs may be suggestive. Young homosexuals at the court were known as *nymphes*. Barker, *Brother*, p. 61.

18 Molière, *Oeuvres complètes*, II, 300. "Innocente petite bête, / . . . / De votre liberté ne plaignez pointe la perte: / Votre destin est glorieux, / Je vous ai pris pour Mélicerte. / Elle vous baisera, vous prenant dans sa main, / Et de vous mettre en son sein / . . . Et qui des rois, hélas! heureux petit moineau, / Ne voudrait être en votre place?"

19 *Ibid.*, II, 311–12. "Le jour est un présent que j'ai reçu de vous; . . . Et si vous me l'ôtez, vous m'arracher la vie."

20 *Ibid.*, II, 312. "Qui l'aurait jamais cru de ce petit pendard? / Quel amour! quel transports! quels discours pour son âge."

21 Anon., *Fameuse Comédienne*, p. 23. "Il s'alla mettre en teste de s'attacher au jeune Baron, dans l'esperance de trouver plus de solidité dans l'esprit des homme que dans celui des femmes."

22 *Ibid.*, p. 24. "Il estoit escrit dans le ciel qu'il seroit cocu de toutes les manieres."

23 Yves, Giraud "La Fameuse Comédienne (1688): problèmes et perspectives d'une édition critique," *Biblio 17: Studien zur Französischen Literatur des 17. Jahrhunderts* (Paris-Seattle-Tubingen, 1994), p. 190.

24 Molière, *Oeuvres complètes*, II, 298. ". . . de lui remplir l'esprit de sa philosophie."

25 Grimarest, *Vie de Molière*, p. 83. Lully's intervention can perhaps be read as a clue to the relationship of Molière and Baron. Lully himself was involved in several important scandals involving male-male relationships, including the affair Chausson. Chausson was a long-time friend of Lully who began an affair with a boy from a noble family. He was denounced and discovered at night with the boy, who was taken to St-Lazare and whipped. Chausson was burned to death on the Grève in Paris. Many libelous ballads circulated naming Lully, for example: "Imitons Baptiste et Chausson, / N'aimons pas que de garçons." See Henry Prunières, *La Vie illustre et libertine de Jean-Baptiste Lully*. Paris: Librairie Plon, 1929.

26 Bryant T. Ragan, Jr. "The Enlightenment Confronts Homosexuality," in *Homosexuality in Modern France*, eds. Jeffrey M. Merrick and Bryant T. Ragan (New York and Oxford: Oxford University Press, 1996), pp. 8–29.

27 Bert Edward Young, *Michel Baron, Acteur et Auteur Dramatique* (Paris: Albert Fontemoing, Editeur, 1905), pp. 155–6.

28 Anon., *Fameuse Comédienne*, pp. 17–23. This section of the *libelle* is what has given some scholars the idea that the pamphlet was the work of Molière's old friend La Fontaine. Its style is much more subtle than the style of most of the work, and its author either knew Molière well or had a genuine ability to imagine character and situation.

29 *Ibid.*, p. 17. ". . . il estoit alors dans une de ces plenitudes de coeur si connues par les gens qui ont aimé . . ."

30 *Ibid.*, p. 18. "Chapelle, qui le croyoit estre au-dussus des ces sortes de choses, se railla de ce qu'un homme comme lui, qui sçavoit si bien peindre le foible des autres hommes, tomboit dans celui qu'il blasmoit tous les jours, et lui fit voir que le plus ridicule de tous estoit d'aimer une personne qui ne respond pas à la tendresse qu'on a pour elle. 'Pour moi,' lui dit-il, 'je vous avoüe que si j'estois assez malheureux pour me trouver en pareil état, et que je fusse fortement persuadé que la personne que j'aimerois accordast des faveurs à d'autres, j'aurois tant de mépris pour elle, qu'il me gueriroit infailliblement de ma passion.'"

31 *Ibid.*, p. 18. "Ce sera mesme un moyen assuré de vous mettre l'esprit en repos." It was possible in this period for a husband to get a *lettre de cachet* for a wife who was out of his control and have her incarcerated in an institution for wayward women. The old Italian actor Tiberio Fiorilli did just that with his much younger second wife.

32 *Ibid.*, p. 19. "Je vois bien que vous n'avez encore rien aimé, et vous avez pris la figure de l'amour pour l'amour mesme."

33 *Ibid.*, pp. 19–20. "... je suis né avec la derniere disposition à la tendresse, et, comme tous mes efforts n'ont pu vaincre les penchans que j'avois à l'amour, j'ai cherché à me rendre heureux, c'est-à-dire autant qu'on peut l'estre avec un coeur sensible." The French word *tendresse* is difficult to translate. Although it clearly means much the same as the English "tenderness," it also can have strong sexual implications. For Mlle de Scudéry, the inventor of the *carte de tendre* and much of the vocabulary of preciosity, *tendresse* refers to a "friendship that preserves the appearance of love and borrows from it its ceremonial and vocabulary." Others used her vocabulary to indicate intentions that were "very different and much less virtuous." Tristan L'Hermite, for instance, replaced the *carte de tendre* with the *carte du royaume d'amour*. On the first map, the various routes led to three cities of *amitié*, friendship, while on Tristan's map, all roads led to *Jouissance* and *Satiété*. See Jean-Michel Pelous, *Amour précieux, amour galant; essai sur la représentation de l'amour dans la littérature et la société mondaine* (Paris: Librairie Klincksieck, 1980), pp. 18–23. He concludes that a French person in the time of Louis XIV learned from the beginning the words they should use to speak of love, the *code amoureux*. *Tendresse* is clearly an important code word, one that Molière himself sometimes uses to mean sexual sensation, the physical aspects of love, and I take that to be the meaning implied by the anonymous *libelliste* here.

34 Anon., *Fameuse Comédienne*, pp. 20–3. "Comme elle estoit encore fort jeune quand je l'espousai, je ne m'aperçeus pas de ses méchantes inclinations, et je me crus un peu moins malheureux que la plupart de ceux qui prennent de pareils engagemens; aussi, le mariage ne rallentit point mes empressemens, mais je lui trouvai dans la suite tant d'indifference, que je commençai à m'appercevoir que toutes mes precautions avoient esté inutiles, et que ce qu'elle sentoit pour moi estoit bien eloigné de ce que j'aurois souhaitté pour estre heureux . . . j'attribuai à son humeur ce qui estoit un effet de son peu de tendresse pour moi . . . Mais j'eus le chagrin de voir qu'une personne sans grande beauté, qui doit le peu d'esprit qu'on lui trouve à l'education que je lui ai donné, detruisoit en un instant toute ma philosophie; sa presence me fit oublier mes resolutions, et les premieres parolles qu'elle me dit pour sa deffense, me laisserent si convaincu que mes soupçons estoient mal fondés, que je lui demandai pardon d'avoir esté si credule. Mes bontés ne l'ont point changée. Je me suis donc determiné à vivre avec elle, comme si elle n'estoit pas ma femme. Mais si vous sçaviez ce que je souffre, vous auriez pitié de moi; ma passion est venue à un tel point, quelle va jusqu'à entrer avec compassion dans ses interests, et quand je considere combien il m'est impossible de vaincre ce que je sens pour elle, je me dis en mesme temps qu'elle a peut-estre la mesme difficulté à detruire le penchant qu'elle a d'estre coquette, et je me trouve plus de disposition à la plaindre qu'à la blasmer. Vous me direz sans doute qu'il faut estre poëte pour aimer de cette manière? Mais, pour moi, je crois qu'il n'y a qu'une sorte d'amour, et que les gens qui n'ont pas senti de semblables delicatesses n'ont jamais aimé veritablement: toutes les choses du monde ont du rapport avec elle dans ma

coeur; mon idée en est si fort occupée, que je ne sçai rien en son absence qui me puisse divertir; quand je la vois, une emotion et des transports qu'on peut sentir, mais qu'on ne sçauroit exprimer, m'ostent l'usage de la reflexion; je n'ai plus d'yeux pour ses deffauts, il m'en reste seulement pour tout ce qu'elle a d'aimable. N'est-ce-pas le dernier point de folie? et n'admirez pas que tout ce que j'ai de raison ne serve qu'à me faire connoistre ma foiblesse, sans en pouvoir triompher."

35 Grimarest, *Vie de Molière*, pp. 81–2. ". . . je suis le plus malheureux de tous les hommes, et je n'ai que ce que je mérite. Je n'ais pas pensé que j'étois trop austère, pour une societé domestique. J'ai cru que ma femme devoit assujetir ses manières à sa vertu, et à mes intentions; et je sens bien que dans la situation où elle est, elle eût été encore plus malheureuse que je ne le suis, si elle l'avoit fait. Elle a de l'enjouement, de l'esprit; elle est sensible au plaisir de le faire valoir; tout cela m'ombrage malgré moi. J'y trouve à redire, je m'en plains. Cette femme cent fois plus raisonnable que je ne le suis, veut jouir agráblement de la vie; elle va son chemin: et assurée par son innocence, elle dédaigne de s'assujetir aux précautions que je lui demande. Je prens cette négligence pour du mépris; je voudrois des marques d'amitié pour croire que l'on en a pour moi, et que l'on eût plus de justesse dans la conduite pour que j'eusse l'esprit tranquille. Mais ma femme, toujours égale, et libre dans la sienne, qui seroit exempte de tout soupçon pour tout autre homme moins inquiet que je ne le suis, me laisse impitoyablement dans mes peines; et ocupée seulement du désir de plaire en général, comme toutes les femmes, sans avoir de dessein particulier, elle rit de ma foiblesse."

36 Molière, *Oeuvres complètes*, II, 123n.

37 *Ibid.*, 197. "Avez-vous, dites-moi, perdu le jugement?"

38 *Ibid.*, 199. "Tout ce que vous croirez m'est de peu d'importance."

39 *Ibid.*, 200. "Ciel! rien de plus cruel peut-il être inventé? / Et jamais coeur fut-il de la sorte traité? / Quoi? d'un juste courroux je suis ému contre elle, / C'est moi qui me viens plaindre, et c'est moi qu'on querelle! / On pousse ma douleur et mes soupçons à bout, / On me laisse tout croire, on fait gloire de tout; / Et cependant mon coeur est encor assez lâche / Pour ne pouvoir briser la chaîne qui l'attache, / Et pour ne pas s'armer d'un généreux mépris / Contre l'ingrat objet dont it est trop épris! / Ah! que vous savez bien ici, contre moi-même, / Perfide, vous servir de ma faiblesse extrême, / Et ménager pour vous l'excès prodigieux / De ce fatal amour né de vos traîtres yeux! / Défendez-vous au moins d'un crime qui m'accable, / Et cessez d'affecter d'être envers moi coupable; / Rendez-moi, s'il se peut, ce billet innocent: / À vous prêter les mains ma tendresse consent; / Efforcez-vous ici de paraître fidèle, / Et je m'efforcerai, moi, de vous croire telle."

40 *Ibid.*, 20. "Non, vous ne m'aimez point comme il faut que l'on aime."

41 *Ibid.*, *Oeuvres complètes*, I, 349. "Quand vous saurez m'aimer comme il faut que l'on aime."

42 See n33 above.

43 Molière, *Oeuvres complètes*, II, 200–1. "Et puisque notre coeur fait un effort

extrême / Lorsqu'il peut se résoudre à confesser qu'il aime, / Puisque l'honneur du sexe, ennemi de nos feux, / S'oppose fortement à de pareils aveux."

44 Louis Racine in Racine, *Oeuvres complètes*, I, 41. "Je ne prétends pas soutenir qu'il ait toujours été exempt de faiblesse, quoique je n'en ai entendu raconter aucune; mais (et ma piété pour lui ne me permet pas d'être infidèle à la vérité) j'ose soutenir qu'il n'a jamais connu par expérience ces troubles et ces transports qu'ils a si bien dépeints. . . . mais suivant la maxime qu'il fait dire à Burrhus, 'on n'aime point, si l'on ne veut aimer.'" Less respectful biographers believe that Racine was in love with at least two actresses, Mlle Du Parc and Mlle Champsmelé, and deeply upset by the death of the former.

45 Molière, *Oeuvres complètes*, II, 384. "Vous voyez un mari, vous voyez un amant, / Mais l'amant seul me touche, à parler franchement, / Et je sens, près de vous, que le mari le gêne. / Cet amant, de vos voeux jaloux au dernier point, / Souhaite qu'à lui seul votre coeur s'abandonne."

46 *Ibid.*, 402. "On servit. Tête à tête ensemble nous soupâmes; / Et le souper fini, nous nous fûmes coucher."

47 *Ibid.*, 386. "Quinze ans de mariage épuisent les paroles."

48 Herzel, *Original casting*, pp. 63–6.

49 This is generally assumed on the basis of the similarity of the role to others played by Molière and from the description of the costume in his inventory after death. Couton thinks the costume may have been "too sumptuous" for a valet (Molière, *Oeuvres complètes*, II, 1361n), which suggests the remote possibility that Molière may have played Mercure.

50 *Ibid.*, 407. "Je te sus exprimer des tendresses de coeur; / Mais à tous mes discours tu fus comme une souche; / Et jamais un mot de douceur / Ne te put sortir de la bouche."

51 *Ibid.*, 748. "Je fais voir pour une personne toute l'ardeur et toute la tendresse qu'on peut imaginer; je n'aime rien au monde qu'elle, et je n'ai qu'elle dans l'esprit; elle fait tous mes soins, tous mes désirs, toute ma joie; je ne parle que d'elle, je ne pense qu'à elle, je ne fait des songes que d'elle, je ne respire que par elle, mon coeur vit tout en elle; et voilà de tant d'amitié la digne récompense. Je suis deux jours sans la voir, qui sont pour moi deux siècles effroyables: je la rencontre par hasard; mon coeur, à cette vue, se sent tout transporté, ma joie éclate sur mon visage, je vole avec ravissement vers elle; et l'infidèle détourne de moi ses regards, et passe brusquement, comme si de sa vie elle ne m'avait vu!"

52 *Ibid.*, 749–50. "cov: . . . Premièrement, elle a les yeux petits. clé: Cela est vrai, elle a les yeux petits; mais elle les a plein de feux, les plus brilliant, les plus perçants du monde, les plus touchants qu'on puisse voir. cov: Elle a la bouche grande. clé: Out, mais on y voit des grâces qu'on ne voit point aux autres bouches; et cette bouche, en la voyant, inspire des désirs, est la plus attrayante, la plus amoureuse du monde. cov: Par sa taille, elle n'est pas grande. clé: Non; mais elle est aisée et bien prise. cov: Elle affecte une nonchalance dans son parler, et dans ses actions. clé: Il est vrai; mais elle a grâce

à tout cela, et ses manières sont engageantes, ont je ne sais quel charme a s'insinuer dans les coeurs. cov: Pour de l'esprit . . . clé: Ah! elle en a, Covielle, du plus fin, du plus délicat. cov: Sa conversation . . . clé: Sa conversation est charmante. cov: Elle est toujours sérieuse. clé: Veux-tu de ces enjouments épanouis, de ces joies toujours ouvertes? et vois-tu rien de plus impertinent que des femmes qui rient à tout propos. cov: Mais enfin elle est capricieuse autant que personne du monde. clé: Oui, elle est capricieuse, j'en demeure d'accord; mais tout sied bien aux belles, on souffre tout des belles. cov: Puisque cela va comme cela, je vois bien que vous avez envie de l'aimer toujours. clé: Moi, j'aimerais mieux mourir; et je vais la haïr autant que je l'ai aimée. cov: Le moyen, si vous la trouvez si parfaite? clé: C'est en quoi ma vengeance sera plus éclatante, en quoi je veux faire mieux voir la force de mon coeur, à la haïr, à la quitter, toute belle, toute pleine d'attraits, toute aimable que je la trouve."

53 Roger Herzel proposes that Éliante in the *Misanthrope* was one of Mlle Du Parc's roles. This is based on the *Répertoire* of the Comédie-Française in 1685, showing that Mlle de Brie was then playing Arsinoë. The assumption is that since actors usually kept their roles, whoever "owned" a role in 1685 must have originated it. This is a stronger argument if all the original actors have remained in the troupe, but Mlle Du Parc left the Palais-Royal less than a year after the première of *Misanthrope*; the play remained in the repertory, so someone else must have taken her role of Éliante. The only options are Madeleine Béjart, who seems an unlikely choice for the ward of Célimène, who is herself only twenty, or Mlle Hervé, Geneviève Béjart, who never played a role of more than a few lines. I should like to propose that Mlle Du Parc did not, in fact, play Éliante in 1665 and that the role was played by Mlle de Brie, who specialized in young roles. Arsinoë could very well have been played by Madeleine Béjart, since Célimène makes it only too clear that the lady is no longer young. If Madeleine played Arsinoë, we can understand why the troupe found it unnecessary to replace Marquise Du Parc, since most of her earlier roles, in plays still in the repertory, could have been played by Armande.

54 According to Boileau. See Picard, *Carrière*, p. 268n.
55 Robinet, *Lettres en vers à Madâme*, December 13, 1668.
56 Picard, *Carrière*, p. 329.
57 Jurgens and Maxfield-Miller, *Cent Ans*, pp. 614–5.
58 *Ibid.*, pp. 615–16.
59 *Ibid.*, pp. 617–18.
60 *Ibid.*, p. 166.
61 *Ibid.*, p. 578.
62 *Ibid.*, p. 621.
63 Jean Poquelin signed two loan contracts with Molière's close friend Jacques Rohault, who signed two further agreements specifying that the money in question belonged to Molière, *ibid.*, pp. 431–5, 438.
64 Soulié, *Recherches*, pp. 221–3.

65 Roger Duchêne (*Molière*, pp. 518–19) argues that Jean Poquelin was complicit in this arrangement, which guaranteed that the best part of his estate would pass to his son without possible contestation by the other heirs.

66 Jurgens and Maxfield-Miller, *Cent Ans*, pp. 624–6. The half was comprised of her original third, inherited from her father, and another sixth, inherited from her cousin André Boudet.

67 An item in La Grange's accounts suggests, however, that Molière was not taking author's shares of the royal bounty. The summer visit to Fontainebleau included four performances of *La Princesse d'Élide* and one of *La Thébaïde* by Racine. The troupe received 3,000 *livres*, divided partly into fourteen shares and partly into sixteen. Racine's play was still in its first run and he apparently expected to profit. La Grange, *Registre*, I, 68.

68 La Grange notes, for example, that the king "gratified" the troupe with 12,000 *livres* on January 30, 1670, for trips to Chambord and St-Germain. This was divided into twelve shares, with one share for the author.

69 Among the papers found after his death was a contract for a loan of 11,000 *livres* made to Jean-Baptiste Lully and his wife in 1670 at the usual rate of 5 percent. Also there were the two agreements with Jacques Rohault, specifying that the interest owing him on loans made to Jean Poquelin actually belonged to Molière. The loans, made in late 1668, totaled 10,000 *livres*. There was an obligation for a small loan to an officer of the household of the prince de Condé, a neighbor in Auteuil, another to Jacques Crosnier, a former *gagiste* in the company, a third to someone named Fontraelles, a fourth to brother-in-law André Boudet, a fifth to his former publisher Jean Ribou, a sixth to his comrade de Brie, and others made less formally to Baron, to Mlle Beauval, and to Mme Raviguotte, the gardener of the Auteuil house. The small loans were payable *a volonté*, and were not interest bearing. Molière was both rich and, apparently, a soft touch. Jurgens and Maxfield-Miller, *Cent Ans*, pp. 580–3.

11 LAST ACT

1 In Molière, *Oeuvres complètes*, II, 451. "Du Prince des Français rien ne borne la gloire, / À tout elle s'étend, et chez les nations / Les vérités de son histoire / Vont passer des vieux temps toutes les fictions."

2 *Ibid.*, 1185–6. "Et tu mets moins de temps à fair tes conquêtes / Qu'il n'en faut pour les bien louer."

3 Mongrédien, *Recueil*, I, 380.

4 Although La Grange does not specify the amount of extraordinary expenses, they can be easily inferred. The troupe opened two plays at the same time and played them in turn, a week each. For two performances with the same gross revenue, the actor's share was 54 *livres* for *Bourgeois gentilhomme* and 78 *livres* 14 *sous* for Corneille's *Bérénice*. Multiplying the difference by the number of shares, we can estimate expenses of 300 *livres* per performance for *Bourgeois gentilhomme*. Ordinary expenses in the period were 88 *livres*. (La Grange, *Registre*, p. 124.)

5 See Ludovic Celler [Leclerc], *Les Décors, les costumes et la mise en scène au XVIIe siècle* (Paris: Liepmannsohn and Dufour, 1869), pp. 75–6.

6 Molière wrote the prose text and versified Act I, Act II, scene i, and Act III, scene i. Corneille versified the rest, and Quinault wrote the lyrics for the songs and interludes.

7 Jurgens and Maxfield-Miller, *Cent Ans*, pp. 496–502.

8 Saint-Maurice, *Lettres sur la cour de Louis XIV,* in Mongrédien, *Recueil*, I, 386–7. "... je n'ai encore rien vu ici de mieux exécuté ni de plus magnifique et ce sont des choses qui ne se peuvent pas faire ailleurs à cause de la quantité de maîtres à danser, y en ayant soixante-dix qui dansent ensemble en la dernière entrée. Ce qui est aussi merveilleux est la quantité des violons, des joueurs d'instrument et des musiciens, qui sont plus de trois cents, tous magnifiquement habillés. La salle est superbe ...; le théâtre spacieux, merveilleusement bien décoré; les machines et changements de scène magnifiques et qui ont bien joué ...; mais pour la dernière scène, c'est bien la chose la plus étonnante qui se puisse voir, car l'on voit tout en un instant paraître plus de trois cents personnes suspendues ou dans les nuages ou dans une gloire, et cela fait la plus belle symphonie du monde en violons, théorbes, luths, clavecins, hautbois, flûtes, trompettes et cymbales. L'on voit bien qu'il a fallu qu'ils se soient réduits maintenant à suivre en ces sortes de choses les sentiments des Italiens."

9 The story of Perrin and the others is admirably told by Charles Nuitter and Ernest Thoinan, *Origines*.

10 La Grange, *Registre*, I, 134–26. For a complete description of the various repairs and reconstructions made at Palais-Royal during the tenancy of Molière see my *Commedia dell'Arte in Paris,* pp. 89–95 and 161–2.

11 "Lettre de Clément Marat à M. de S***" (Cologne: Pierre Marteau, 1688), in Nuitter and Thoinon, *Origines*, pp. 229–30.

12 Nuitter and Thoinon, *Origines*, pp. 229–30. "Comme j'avois besoin d'un musicien pour exécuter ce projet, je jetai les yeux sur Lulli et lui communiquai ma pensée, persuadé que j'étois que la liaison que nous avions depuis longtemps en concourant ensemble aux plaisirs du Roi, et le succès merveilleux qu'avoit eu ... le charmant spectacle de *Psyché* ... m'estoient des garants infaillibles de notre future intelligence. Je m'en ouvris donc à luy, il applaudit à mon dessein, il me promit un fidélité et même une subordination inviolable. Nous fîmes nos conventions, nous réglâmes nos emplois et nos partages, et nous prîmes jour pour aller ensemble ... demander au Roy le privilège de la représentation des opéras. Voilà ma faute, Madame! ... Je dormois tranquillement sur la bonne foi de ce traité quand Lulli, plus éveillé que moi, partit de la main deux jours avant celui dont nous étions convenus; il alla au Roi demander le privilège pour lui seul ..."

13 Molière, *Oeuvres complètes*, I, 1316n.

14 La Grange, *Registre* (1876), p. 139.

15 Nuitter and Thoinon, *Origines*, p. 239. "... et pour le dédommager des grand frais qu'il conviendra faire pour les ... théâtres, machines, décorations, habits, qu'autres choses nécessaires, Nous luy permettons de donner au

public toutes les pièces qu'il aura composées, mesme celles qui auront esté représentées devant Nous. . . ."

16 Molière, *Oeuvres complètes*, II, 609. ". . . ces yeux rouges et hagard, cette grande barbe, cette habitude du corps, menue, grêle, noire et velue." The only thing in this description that suggests illness is the word "*menue*" which does mean "thin," but also has the connotation of "common" or "mean."

17 Le Boulanger de Chalussay in *Ibid.*, 1234. "ÉLO: Lazarile, ai-je pas le teint blême? LAZ: Oui, Monsieur. ÉLO: Le miroir me l'a dit tout de même; / Et ces bras qui naguère étaient de vrais gigots, / Comment les trouves-tu? LAZ: Ce ne sont que des os, / Et je crois que bientôt, plus secs que vieux sque-lettes, / On s'en pourra servir au lieu de castagnettes. ISA: Lazarile. LAZ: Madame? ISA: Apprenez qu'un valet / Qui se moque d'un maître, a souvent du balet; . . . Quoy! / Votre maître est maigre, et pâle, dites-vous? / LAZ: S'il n'est tel à mes yeux, qu'on m'assomme de coups. / ISA: Est-il tel à vos yeux, s'il est autre à ma vue? / ÉLO: Mais, ma femme, peut-être avez-vous la berlue? / Car enfin, Lazarile . . . ISA: Et Lazarile et vous, / Si vous vous croyez maigre et pâle, êtes deux fous; / Vous dormez comme un porc, vous mangez tout de même; / Qui diantre donc pourrait vous rendre maigre et blême? / ÉLO: J'auray donc la couleur telle que tu voudras; / Et même, si tu veux, je serai gros et gras:/ Mais que m'importe-t-il? je me crois bien malade, / Et qui croit l'être, l'est. ISA: Mais qui se persuade / D'être malade alors qu'il est sain comme vous, / Est dans le grand chemin de l'hôpital des foux."

18 *Ibid.*, 1241 ". . . ces yeux enfoncés, en ce visage blême; / En ce corps qui n'a plus presque rien de vivant, / Et qui n'est presque plus qu'un squelette mouvant."

19 *Ibid.*, 1154. ". . . presque tous les hommes meurent de leurs remèdes et non pas de leurs maladies."

20 Grimarest, *Vie de Molière*, p. 63. "Voila donc votre Médecin? Que vous fait-il?" "Sire, nous raisonnons ensemble; il m'ordonne des remèdes; je ne les fais point, et je gueris."

21 Adam, *Histoire*, III, 341.

22 Donneau de Visé, "Oraison funebre de Molière," *Mercure galant,* June 14, 1673, in *Collection Moliéresque* (Geneva: Slatkine Reprints, 1969), pp. 23–4. "S'il avoit eu le temps d'estre malade, il ne seroit pas mort sans medecin. Il n'estoit pas convaincu luy-mesme de tout qu'il disoit contre les medecins. . . . Il est constant qu'il y a des remedes; les bestes en trouvant et se guéris-sent elles-mêmes; hé! pourquoy, puisque les hommes ont bien connu les herbes qui empoisonnent, ne connoistroient-ils pas celles qui ont la vertu de les guérir."

23 Waksman, *Conquest of Tuberculosis*, pp. 28–9.

24 Grimarest, *Vie de Molière*, p. 112.

25 *Ibid.*, p. 109. ". . . une fenêtre ouverte ou fermée un moment devant ou après le tems qu'il l'avoit ordonné, metoit Molière en convulsion; it étoit petit dans ces ocasions. Si on lui avoit dérangé un livre, c'en étoit assez pour qu'il ne

travaillât de quinze jours; il y avoit peu de domestiques qu'il ne trouvât en deffaut; et la vieille servante la Forest y étoit prise aussi souvent que les autres, quoiqu'elle dût être acoutumée à cette fatigante régularité que Molière exigeoit de tout le monde. Et même il étoit prévenue que c'étoit une vertu; de sorte que celui de ses amis qui étoit le plus régulier, et le plus arangé, étoit celui qu'il estimoit le plus."

26 Jurgens and Maxfield-Miller, *Cent Ans*, pp. 473–5.

27 Jean Mignot, who acted as Mondorge, was at Albi with the troupe of Gaston d'Orléans in 1657, where his paths and Molière's could have crossed. He jumped from troupe to troupe, and may have been out of a job in the season of 1671–72. Mongrédien and Robert, *Comédiens français*, p. 152.

28 Grimarest, *Vie de Molière*, p. 75. "Eh bien, je vais lui donner quatre pistoles pour moi, puisque vous le jugez à propos: mais en voilà vingt autres que je lui donnerai pour vous: je veux qu'il connoisse que c'est à vous qu'il a l'obligation du service que je lui rens. J'ai aussi un habit de Théâtre, dont je crois que je n'aurai plus de besoin, qu'on le lui donne. . . ."

29 A letter from Saint-Evremond to Anne Hervart of November 25, 1669 mentions the actors of the Palais-Royal: "Nous avons ici des Comédiens assez bons pour le comique, détestables pour la tragédie à la réserve d'une très bonne comédienne pour tout; ils ont joué *Tartuffe . . .*" By 1669 Marquise Du Parc had left the company, so the reference to the actress "very good in both" tragedy and comedy must be to Madeleine. Georges Mongrédien and Jacques Vanuxen, "Recueil des Textes et de documents du XVIIe siècle relatifs à Molière: Supplement," *XVIIe Siècle* 98–99 (1973), p. 132.

30 Jurgens and Maxfield-Miller, *Cent Ans*, p. 656.

31 Soulié, *Recherches*, pp. 243, 249.

32 The contracts suggest that she may have invested as much as 6,000 *livres* in the tannery. She was also responsible for the lease of the building in the faubourg St-Victor where the tannery was to be located. Unfortunately, no evidence survives as to the outcome of this venture.

33 Soulié, *Recherches*, pp. 249–52.

34 Toubel, later a doorkeeper at the theatre on the rue Mazarine, was related to a family of provincial actors that included Philippe Toubel, known as Alcidor. Jurgens and Maxfield-Miller, *Cent Ans*, p. 445n and Mongrédien and Robert, *Comédiens français*, pp. 194–5. Molière was godfather to Toubel's daughter on September 10, 1669.

35 Chardon, *M. de Modène*, p. 403. "Comment Molière, dont le premier enfant avait été tenu sur les fonts au nom du roi et de Henriette d'Angleterre, consentit-il à prendre pour parrrain de sa fille l'ancien amant de Madeleine, et à ressusciter aux yeux de tous et surtout aux yeux de sa femme ce lointain passé qu'il avait tout intérêt à faire oublier? Comment s'exposait-il, surtout au milieu de sa crise conjugale, à donner à Armande la preuve d'un pareil oubli de sens moral?"

36 Jurgens and Maxfield-Miller, *Cent Ans*, p. 655.

37 Molière, *Oeuvres complètes*, II, 656. ". . . vous avez entendu dire qu'il fallait

cajoler les mères pour obtenir les filles; mais ici, par malheur, tout cela devient inutile, et je me suis engagée à laisser le choix tout entier à l'inclination de ma fille."

38 *Ibid.* "Je ne recherche la princesse Ériphile que parce qu'elle est votre sang; je la trouve charmante par tout ce qu'elle tient de vous, et c'est vous que j'adore en elle."

39 *Ibid.*, pp. 656–7. "Mon Dieu! Prince, je ne donne point dans tous ces galimatias où donnent la plupart des femmes; je veux être mère, parce que je la suis, et ce serait en vain que je ne la voudrais pas être. Ce titre n'a rien qui me choque, puisque, de mon consentement, je me suis exposée à la recevoir. C'est une faible de notre sexe, dont, grâce au Ciel, je suis exempte; et je ne m'embarrasse point de ces grandes disputes d'âge, sur quoi nous voyons tant de folles."

40 Jurgens and Maxfield-Miller, *Cent Ans*, p. 504n. Recorded by Père Léonard in a note dated 1682.

41 Soulié, *Recherches*, pp. 243–5.

42 *Ibid.*, p. 246.

43 Jurgens and Maxfield-Miller, *Cent Ans*, p. 397.

44 *Ibid.*, p. 570.

45 At court the "two little Graces" were played by daughters of Du Croisy and La Thorillière, who were older than Esprit-Madeleine. *Livret de Psyché* in Molière, *Oeuvres complètes*, II, 802.

46 Soulié, *Recherches*, pp. 303–17.

47 Molière, *Oeuvres complètes*, II, 854. "Votre mère Venus est de l'humeur des belles, / Qui n'aiment point des grands enfants."

48 Grimarest, *Vie de Molière*, p. 118.

49 The lease is reprinted by Jurgens and Maxfield-Miller, *Cent Ans*, pp. 524–6.

50 Information about Molière's movable property is taken from the inventory made after his death, *ibid.*, pp. 554–84.

51 That lease had expired at Easter 1672. Molière and Armande seem to have taken interim lodging, since they are described in the new lease as living on the rue St-Honoré, parish St-Eustache. Their apartment on the rue St-Thomas-du-Louvre was in the parish St-Germain l'Auxerrois.

52 Grimarest, *Vie de Molière*, p. 110.

53 The anecdote reminds us of Boileau, who wanted Molière to leave the stage, but Boileau reacted very badly to Grimarest's book, in part, it is usually assumed, because he was not interviewed for it.

54 Grimarest, *Vie de Molière*, pp. 106–7. "Eh, bien, je vous conseille de prendre sa profession; la nôtre ne vous convient point; c'est la derniere ressource de ceux qui ne sauroient mieux faire, ou des Libertins, qui veulent se soustraire au travail. D'ailleurs, c'est enfoncer le poignard dans le coeur de vos parens, que de monter sur le Théâtre; vous en savez les raisons, je me suis toujours reproché d'avoir donné ce déplaisir à ma famille. Et je vous avoue que si c'étoit à recommencer, je ne choisirois jamais cette profession. Vous croyez qu'elle a ses agrémens; vous vous trompez. Il est vrai que nous sommes en

apparence recherchés des grands Seigneurs, mais ils nous assujettissent à leurs plaisirs; et c'ést la plus triste de toutes les situations, que d'être l'esclave de leur phantaisie. Le reste du monde nous regarde comme des gens perdus, et nous méprise. Ainsi, Monsieur, quittez un dessein si contraire à votre honneur et à votre repos. . . . Representez-vous la peine que nous avons. Incommodez, ou non, il faut être prêts à marcher au premier ordre, et à donner du plaisir quand nous sommes bien souvent acablés de chagrin; à souffrir la rusticité de la pluspart des gens avec qui nous avons à vivre, et à captiver les bonnes grâces d'un public, qui est en droit de nous gourmander pour l'argent qu'il nous donne."

55 Donneau de Visé, "Oraison funebre," pp. 35–6. ". . . il estoit tout comédien depuis les pieds jusques à la teste; il sembloit qu'il eust plusieurs voix, tout parloit en luy, et d'un pas, d'un sourire, d'un clin d'oeil et d'un remüement de teste il faisoit plus concevoir de choses que le plus grand parleur n'auroit pû dire d'un heure."

56 La Grange, *Registre*, I, 142. "Ce mesme jour aprez la comedie sur les 10 heures de soir Monsieur de Moliere mourust dans sa maison rue de Richelieu, ayant joué le roosle du dt. Malade Imaginaire fort incommode d'un rhume et fluction sur la poitrine qui luy causoit une grande toux de sorte que dans les grans effortz qu'il fist pour cracher il se rompit une veyne dans le corps et ne vescut pas demye heure ou trois quartz d'heures depuis la dt veyne rompue."

57 Grimarest, *Vie de Molière*, pp. 119–20. "Tant que ma vie a été mêlée également de douleur et de plaisir, je me suis cru heureux; mais aujourd'hui que je suis acablé de peines sans pouvoir compter sur aucuns momens de satisfaction et de douceur, je vois bien qu'il me faut quitter la partie; je ne puis plus tenir contre les douleurs et les déplaisirs, que ne me donnent pas un instant de relâche . . . qu'un homme souffre avant que de mourir! Cependant, je sens bien que je finis."

58 *Ibid.*, "Molière representa avec beaucoup de difficulté; et la moitié des Spectateurs s'aperçurent qu'en prononçant, *Juro*, dans la cérémonie du *Malade Imaginaire*, il lui prit une convulsion. Aïant remarqué lui-même que l'on s'en étoit aperçu, il se fit un effort, et cacha par un ris forcé ce qui venoit de lui arriver."

59 *Ibid.*, pp. 121–3.

60 Jurgens and Maxfield-Miller, *Cent Ans*, p. 551. ". . . vendredy dernier . . . sur les neuf heures du soir, ledict feu sieur Molière s'estant trouvé mal de la maladie dont il deceda environ une heure après, il voulut dans le moment, temoigner des marque de repentir de ses fautes et mourir bon chrestien; a l'effect de quoy . . . il demanda un prestre pour recevoir les sacremens, et envoya par plusieurs fois son valet et servante à Sainct-Eustache, sa paroisse, lesquels s'adresserent à Messieurs Lenfant et Lechat, deux prestres habitués en ladicte parish, qui refuserent plusieurs fois de venir."

61 Mongrédien, *Recueil*, II, 443.

62 Grimarest, *Vie de Molière*, p. 123.

63 Mongrédien, *Recueil*, II, 443.
64 *Ibid.*, 442–3.
65 *Ibid.*, 442.
66 *Ibid.*, 446–77.
67 *Ibid.*, 471. "Sous ce tombeau gisent Plaute et Térence, / Et cependant le seul Molière y git. / Il les faisait revivre en son esprit, / Par leur bel art réjouissant la France. / Ils sont partis! et j'ai peu d'espérance / De les revoir malgré tous nos efforts. / Pour un long temps, selon toute apparence, / Térence et Plaute, et Molière sont morts."
68 *Ibid.*, 469. "Puisqu'à Paris l'on dénie / La Terre après le Trépas / A ceux qui durant leur vie / Ont joué la comédie, / Pourquoi ne jette-t-on pas / Les Dévots à la voirie? / Ils sont dans le même cas."
69 *Ibid.*, I, 399–401.
70 *Ibid.*, II, 466. "Passant . . . si de ce poète fameux / La gentillesse te fut chère, / A cet esprit plein de lumière / Donne au moins un soupir ou deux, / Et dis, approchant de sa bière: / Adieu les ris . . ."

12 ENVOI

1 Chardon, *M. de Modène*, p. 450. "Je n'ay veu personne de chez Mademoiselle Molière, c'est pourquoy je ne vous puis rien dire; . . . . Je vous asseure que l'on ne parle pas non plus du pauvre Molière que sy il n'avoit jamais esté et que son théâtre qui a fait tant de bruit, il y a si peu de tems, est entièrement aboly. . . . Ainsy la veuve a esté trompée par ce qu'elle s'attendoit bien à jouer."
2 For a complete history of the survival of Molière's troupe, see Virginia Scott, "Saved by the Magic Wand of *Circé*," *Theatre Survey*, 28:2 (1987): 1–16.
3 Howarth, *French Theatre*, pp. 183, 363.
4 Soulié, *Recherches*, pp. 304–17.
5 Titon de Tillet, *Le Parnasse français*, quoted by Louis Moland, "Le Sépulture ecclésiastique donnée à Molière," *Le Moliériste*, 6 (June 1884): 72–3.
6 *Ibid.*, p. 74.
7 Grimarest, *Vie de Molière*, p. 173. "J'ai trouvé la matière . . . si délicate et si difficile à traiter, que j'avoue franchement que je n'ai osé l'entreprendre."
8 Georges Monval, "Les Tombeaux de Molière et de La Fontaine," *Le Moliériste*, 4 (April 1882): 5.
9 Paul Lacroix (La Bibliophile Jacob), "Quelques Notes sur le tombeau et sur le cercueil de Molière," *Le Moliériste* 6 (August 1884): 136.

Works consulted

Adam, Antoine. *Histoire de la littérature française au XVIIe siècle*. 5 vols. Paris: Domat, Montchrestian, 1948–56.

Alberge, Claude. *Le Voyage de Molière en Languedoc: 1647–1657*. Montpellier: Les Presses de Languedoc, 1988.

Allier, Raoul. *La Cabale des dévots: 1620–1666*. Geneva: Slatkine Reprints, 1970.

Anon. *La Fameuse Comédienne, ou Histoire de la Guerin auparavant femme et veuve de Molière*. Geneva: Slatkine Reprints, 1968.

Anon. "Corps de métiers." In *Dictionnaire du grand siècle*, ed. François Bluche. Paris: Fayard, 1990.

Ariès, Philippe. *L'Enfant et la vie familial sous l'ancien régime*. New edn. Paris: Éditions du Seuil, 1973.

Aulanier, Christiane. *Histoire du Palais et du Musée du Louvre*. 10 vols. Paris: Éditions des Musées Nationaux, s.d.

Barker, Nancy Nichols. *Brother to the Sun King*. Baltimore, MD: The Johns Hopkins University Press, 1989.

Barnard, H. C. *The French Tradition in Education*. Cambridge University Press, 1922.

Bernardin, N.-M. *Un Précurseur de Racine, Tristan L'Hermite, sieur de Soliers (1601–1655), sa famille, sa vie, ses oeuvres*. Paris: A. Picard et fils, 1895.

Bluche, François. *Louis XIV*. Paris: Hachette, 1986.

Bluche, François, ed. *Dictionnaire du grand siècle*. Paris: Fayard, 1990.

Boileau, Nicolas. *Correspondance entre Boileau Despréaux et Brossette avec Mémoires de Brossette sur Boileau*, ed. August Laverdet. Paris: J. Techner, 1858.

Oeuvres complètes, ed. Ch. Gidel. Paris: Garnier frères, 1870.

Oeuvres complètes, ed. Françoise Escal. Paris: Gallimard, 1966.

Bonvallet, Pierre. *Molière de tous les jours: Echos, potins et anecdotes*. Paris: Le Pré aux Clercs, 1985.

Bordonove, Georges. *Molière génial et familier*. Paris: Robert Laffont, 1967.

Boucher, François. *Le Pont-Neuf*. 2 vols. Paris: Chez Le Goupy, 1925.

Boursault. *Le Portrait du Peintre*. In *Oeuvres complètes de Molière*, ed. Georges Couton. Paris: Gallimard, 1971, I, 1050–67.

Brackenhoffer, Elie. *Voyage de Paris en Italie: 1644–1646*. Paris: Berger-Levrault, 1925.

Bray, René. *Molière homme du théâtre*. 2nd edn. Paris: Mercure de France, 1963.

Brockliss, L. W. B. *French Higher Education in the Seventeenth and Eighteenth Centuries*. Oxford: The Clarendon Press, 1987.

Brossette. *Mémoires de Brossette sur Boileau* in *Correspondance entre Boileau Despréaux et Brossette*, ed. August Laverdet. Paris: J. Techner, 1858.

Cairncross, John. *Molière, bourgeois et libertine*. Paris: Nizet, 1963.

Celler, Ludovic [Leclerc]. *Les Décors, les costumes et la mise en scène au XVIIᵉ siècle*. Paris: Liepmannsohn et Dufour, 1869.

Chancerel, Léon. "Antoine de Ratabon et la démolition du Théâtre du Petit-Bourbon," *Revue d'Histoire du Théâtre* 2 (1950), 195–7.

Chapelle, [Claude-Emmanuel Luillier]. *Oeuvres de Chapelle et de Bachaumont*. Paris: P. Jannet, 1854.

Chappuzeau, Samuel. *Le Théâtre François*. Paris: Éditions d'Aujourd'hui, s.d.

Chardon, Henri. *M. de Modène, ses deux femmes et Madeleine Béjart*. Paris: A. Picard, 1886.

Chevalley, Sylvie. "Le Registre d'Hubert," *Revue d'Histoire du Théâtre* 25 (1973), 1–195.

Molière en son temps. Geneva: Minkoff, 1973.

Chevallier, Pierre. *Louis XIII, roi cornelian*. Paris: Fayard, 1979.

Corneille, Pierre. *Oeuvres complètes*, ed. Georges Couton. 3 vols. Paris: Gallimard, 1980–7.

Cosnac, Daniel de. *Mémoires*. 2 vols. Paris: Jules Renouard, 1852.

Dainville, François de. *L'Education des Jésuites: XVIᵉ-XVIIᵉ siècles*. Paris: Les Éditions de Minuit, 1978.

Dandret, Patrick. *Le "Cas" d'Argan: Molière et la maladie imaginaire*. Paris: Klincksieck, 1993.

Dassoucy, Charles Coypeau. *Aventures burlesques*. Paris: Audinet, 1677.

Delattre, Pierre, S.J. *Les Établissements des Jésuites en France*. 5 vols. Enghien: Institut Supérieur de Théolgie, 1955.

Demeures, Jean. "Les quatre amis de *Psyché*," *Mercure de France*, June 15, 1928, pp. 331–5.

Donneau de Visé, Jean. "Nouvelles nouvelles (1663)." In *Oeuvres complètes de Molière*, ed. Georges Couton, I, 1015–1023. Paris: Gallimard, 1971.

"Zélinde, ou la véritable critique de l'École des femmes (1663)." In *Oeuvres complètes de Molière*, ed. Georges Couton. Paris: Gallimard, 1971, I, 1024–49.

"La Vengeance des marquis (1664)." In *Oeuvres complètes de Molière*, ed. Georges Couton, I, 1094–1107. Paris: Gallimard, 1971.

"Oraison funèbre de Molière," *Mercure galant*, June 14, 1673. In *Collection Moliéresque*. Geneva: Slatkine Reprints, 1969.

Duchêne, Roger. *Molière*. Paris: Fayard, 1998.

Dulait, Suzanne. *Inventaire raisonné des autographes de Molière*. Geneva: Librairie Droz, 1967.

Fernandez, Ramon. *La Vie de Molière*. Paris: Gallimard, 1929.

France, Anatole. *Vaux-le-Vicomte*. Etrépilly: Les Presses du Village, 1987.

Fréart de Chantelou, Paul. *Diary of the Cavaliere Bernini's Visit to France*, ed., with introduction and notes, Anthony Blunt. Princeton, NJ: Princeton University Press, 1985.

Garboli, Cesare. *Prefazione* to *La Fameuse Comédienne ou Histoire de la Guerin auparavant femme et veuve de Molière* (Milan: Adelphi, 1997), which has also appeared, translated and slightly truncated, along with the text itself in *Comédie-Française: Les Cahiers* 31 (1999), 8–63.

Giraud, Yves. "La Fameuse Comédienne: problèmes et pespectives d'une édition critique." *Biblio 17: Studien zur Französischen Literatur des 17. Jahrhunderts.* Paris-Seattle-Tubingen, 1994, pp. 191–213

Grimaldi, Nicolas. "Descartes." In *Dictionnaire du grand siècle*, ed. François Bluche. Paris: Fayard, 1990.

Grimarest, Jean. *La Vie de M. de Molière*, ed. Georges Mongrédien. Paris: Michel Brient, 1955.

Guichardnaud, Jacques. *Molière, une aventure théâtrale.* Paris: Gallimard, 1963.

Herzel, Roger. *The Original Casting of Molière's Plays.* Ann Arbor, MI: UMI Research Press, 1981.

Howarth, William D., ed. *French Theatre in the Neo-Classical Era, 1550–1789.* Cambridge University Press, 1997.

Isherwood, Robert M. *Farce and Fantasy: Popular Entertainment in Eighteenth-Century Paris.* New York and Oxford: Oxford University Press, 1986.

Jurgens, Madeleine. "L'Aventure de l'Illustre Théâtre." *Revue d'Histoire Littéraire de la France* 72 (1972): 976–1006.

"Qui était Boulenger de Chalusset." *Revue d'Histoire du Théâtre* 24 (1972): 428–440.

Jurgens, Madeleine and Maxfield-Miller, Elizabeth. *Cent ans de recherches sur Molière, sur sa famille et sur les comédiens de sa troupe.* Paris: S.E.V.P.E.N, 1963.

La Comédie Française à la Grange-des-Près. Collection Salmigondines. Montpellier: Imprimerie Centrale du Midi, 1993.

La Fontaine, Jean de. *Oeuvres complètes. II. Oeuvres diverses*, ed. Pierre Clarac. Paris: Gallimard, 1958.

La Grange, Charles Varlet *dit. Registre.* 2 vols. Facsimile edn., eds. Bert E. and Grace P. Young. Paris: E. Droz, 1947.

La Grange, Charles Varlet *dit*, and Vivot. *Préface* to *Les Oeuvres de Molière* (1682). In *Oeuvres complètes de Molière*, ed. Georges Couton. Paris: Gallimard, 1971, I, 996–1002.

Lacroix, Paul [La Bibliophile Jacob]. "Quelques Notes sur le tombeau et sur le cercueil de Molière," *Le Moliériste* 6 (1884): 136.

Lancaster, H. C. *A History of French Dramatic Literature in the Seventeenth Century.* 9 vols. Baltimore, MD: The Johns Hopkins University Press, 1929–42.

"Jean Baptiste Raisin, le petit Raisin," *Modern Philology* 38 (1941): 335–49.

Larroumet, Gustave. "Une Comédienne au XVIIᵉ siècle: Madeleine Béjart," *Revue des Deux Mondes*, May 1, 1885, pp.123–57.

Lawner, Lynne. *Lives of the Courtesans: Portraits of the Renaissance.* New York: Rizzoli, 1987.

Lazare, Félix. *Dictionnaire administrative et historique des rues de Paris.* Paris: Félix Lazare, 1844.

Le Boulanger de Chalussay. *Élomire hypocondre, ou les médecins vengés.* In *Oeuvres complètes de Molière*, ed. George Couton. Paris: Gallimard, 1971, II, 1231–86.

LeNoir, Alexandre. *Musée des monuments français*. 9 vols. Paris: Imprimerie Nationale, 1800–21.

Le Songe de reveur. In *Collection Moliéresque*. Geneva: Slatkine Reprints, 1969.

Lespinasse, René de. *Les Métiers et corporations de la ville de Paris. II. Orfèverie, sculpture, mercerie, ouvriers en métaux, bâtiment et ameublement*. Paris: Imprimerie Nationale, 1892.

Les Plaisirs de l'Île enchantée, Course de bague, collation ornée de machines, comédie mêlée de danse et de musique, Ballet du Palais d'Alcine, Feu d'artifice et autres fêtes galantes et magnifique, faites par le Roi à Versailles, le 7 mai 1664 et continuées plusieurs autres jours. In *Oeuvres complètes de Molière*, ed. Georges Couton. Paris: Gallimard, 1971, I, 749–829.

Livet, Charles. *Lexique de la langue de Molière comparé à celle des écrivains de son temps*. 3 vols. Paris: Imprimerie Nationale, 1895.

Loiseleur, Jules. *L'Université d'Orléans pendant sa période de décadence*. Orléans: H. Herluison, 1886.

Loret, Jean. *La Muze historique*. 4 vols., eds. J. Ravenal and V. de La Pelouze. Paris: Jamet, 1859–78.

Louis XIV. *Mémoires pour l'instruction du Dauphin*, ed. Pierre Goubert. Paris: Imprimerie Nationale, 1992.

Mackey, Agnes Ethel. *La Fontaine and His Friends*. London: Garnstone Press, 1972.

Mallet, Francine. *Molière*. Paris: Grasset, 1990.

Mélèse, Pierre. *Le Théâtre et le public à Paris sous Louis XIV*. Geneva: Slatkine Reprints, 1976.

Michaut, Gustave. *I. La Jeunesse de Molière. II. Les Débuts de Molière. III. Les Luttes de Molière*. Paris: Hachette, 1922–5.

Moland, Louis. "Le Sépulture ecclésiastique donnée à Molière," *Le Moliériste* 6 (1884): 72–3.

Molière. *Oeuvres complètes*, eds. E. Despois and P. Mesnard. 13 vols. Paris: Hachette, 1873–1900.

Molière. *Oeuvres complètes*, ed. Georges Couton. 2 vols. Paris: Gallimard, 1971.

Mongrédien, Georges. *Comédies et pamphlets sur Molière*. Paris: A.-G. Nizet, 1986.

La Vie privée de Molière. Paris: Hachette, 1950.

Recueil des textes et des documents du XVIIe siècle relatifs à Molière. 2 vols. Paris: Éditions du Centre Nationale de la Recherche Scientifique, 1965.

Daily Life in the French Theatre at the Time of Molière. Translated by Clair Eliane Engel. London: George Allen and Unwin, 1969.

La Querelle de L'École des femmes. Paris: Marcel Didier, 1971.

Mongrédien, Georges and Robert, Jean. *Les Comédiens français du XVIIe siècle: Dictionnaire biographique*. 3rd edn. Paris: Éditions de Centre Nationale de la Recherche Scientifique, 1981.

Mongrédien, Georges and Vanuxen, Jacques. "Recueil des Textes et de documents du XVIIe siècle relatifs à Molière: Supplement," *XVIIe Siècle* 98–99 (1973), 123–42.

Monval, Georges. "Les Tombeaux de Molière et de La Fontaine," *Le Moliériste* 4 (1882): 5.

Monval, Georges, ed. *Lettres au Mercure sur Molière, sa vie, ses oeuvres, et les comédiens de son temps*. Geneva: Slatkine Reprints, 1969.

Mousnier, Roland. *Recherches sur la stratification sociale à Paris aux XVIIe et XVIIIe siècles*. Paris: Éditions A. Pedone, 1976.

Paris. Capitale au temps de Richelieu et de Mazarin. Paris: Éditions A. Pedone, 1978.

Nuitter, Charles and Thoinan, Ernest. *Les Origines de l'opéra français*. Paris: Librairie Plon, 1886.

Palmer, John. *Molière*. New York: Benjamin Blom Reprints, 1970.

Parfaict, François and Claude. *L'Histoire du théâtre français*. 15 vols. Amsterdam: Le Mercier, 1735–49.

Pelous, Jean-Michel. *Amour précieux, amour galant; essai sur la représentation de l'amour dans la littérature et la société mondaine*. Paris: Librairie Klincksieck, 1980.

Perrault, Charles. *Les Hommes illustres qui ont paru en France*. Geneva: Slatkine Reprints, 1970.

Picard, Raymond. *La Carrière de Jean Racine*. Paris: Gallimard, 1961.

Pillorget, René. *Nouvelle Histoire de Paris: Paris sous les premiers Bourbons, 1594–1661*. Paris: Hachette, 1988.

Pradel, Abraham du. *Le Livre commode*, ed. Édouard Fournier. 2 vols. Paris: Paul Daffis, 1878.

Prunières, Henri. *La Vie illustre et libertine de Jean-Baptiste Lully*. Paris: Librairie Plon, 1929.

Pure, abbé Michel de. *Les Prétieuses, ou les Mystères des ruelles*. 4 vols. Paris: Various, 1656–8.

Racine, Louis. *Mémoires sur la vie et les ouvrages de Jean Racine*. In *Oeuvres complètes de Racine*, ed. Raymond Picard, Paris: Gallimard, 1950.

Racine, Jean. *Oeuvres complètes*, ed. Raymond Picard. 2 vols. Paris: Gallimard, 1950–2.

Ragan, Bryant T., Jr. "The Enlightenment Confronts Homosexuality." In *Homosexuality in Modern France*, eds. Jeffrey M. Merrick and Bryant T. Ragan. New York and Oxford: Oxford University Press, 1996, pp. 8–29.

Rothschild, James de, ed. *Les Continuateurs de Loret*. 3 vols. Paris: Margand et Fatou, 1881–2.

Rousset, Jean. "*Psyché*, ou le plaisir des larmes," *Nouvelle Revue Française*, April 1966, pp. 1058–66.

Sauval, Henri. *Histoire et recherches des antiquités de la Ville de Paris*. 3 vols. Edn. of 1724. Geneva: Minkoff Reprints, 1973.

Scarron, Paul. *Le Roman comique*, ed. Yves Giraud. Paris: GF-Flammarion, 1981.

Scherer, Jacques. *Théâtre du XVIIe siècle*. Paris: Gallimard, 1975.

Scott, Virginia. "Saved by the Magic Wand of *Circé*," *Theatre Survey* 28:2 (1987): 1–16.

The Commedia dell'arte in Paris. Charlottesville, VA: University Press of Virginia, 1990.

Scudéry, Georges (Madeleine). *Almahide*. 5 vols. Paris: A. Courbé, T. Jolly, L. Billaine, 1660–3.

Silvestre de Sacy, Jacques. *Le Quartier des Halles*. Paris: Le Temps, 1969.

Simon, Alfred. *Molière par lui-même*. Paris: Éditions du Seuil, 1967.
  Molière, une vie. Lyon: La Manufacture, 1988.
  Molière. Paris: Éditions du Seuil, 1996.
Smith, Winifred. *Italian Actors of the Renaissance*. New York: Coward-McCann, 1939.
Soulié, Eudore. *Recherches sur Molière et sur sa famille*. Paris: Librairie de L. Hachette et Cie., 1863.
Tallemant des Réaux, Gédéon. *Historiettes*, ed. Antoine Adam. 2 vols. Paris: Gallimard, 1961.
Taviani, Ferdinando. "La Fleur et le guerrier: les actrices de la *commedia dell'arte*." *Buffoneries* 15/16, pp. 61–93.
Vitu, Auguste. *Le Jeu de paume des Métayers, ou l'Illustre Théâtre (1585–1883)*. Paris: Lemerre, 1883.
Voisin, abbé de. *Défense du traité du prince de Conti*. Paris: J.-B. Coignard, 1671.
Waksman, Selman A. *The Conquest of Tuberculosis*. Berkeley, CA: University of California Press, 1966.
Wolf, John B. *Louis XIV*. New York: W. W. Norton and Co., 1968.
Young, Bert Edward. *Michel Baron, Acteur et Auteur Dramatique*. Paris: Albert Fontemoing, Editeur, 1905.
Young, Bert Edward, and Young, Grace Philputt, eds. *Les Registre de La Grange*. Paris: E. Droz, 1947.

Index